Lecture Notes in Computer Science   **11685**

More information about this series at http://www.springer.com/series/7409

Ida Lindgren · Marijn Janssen ·
Habin Lee · Andrea Polini ·
Manuel Pedro Rodríguez Bolívar ·
Hans Jochen Scholl · Efthimios Tambouris (Eds.)

Electronic Government

18th IFIP WG 8.5 International Conference, EGOV 2019
San Benedetto Del Tronto, Italy, September 2–4, 2019
Proceedings

 Springer

Editors
Ida Lindgren
Linköping University
Linköping, Sweden

Marijn Janssen
Delft University of Technology
Delft, The Netherlands

Habin Lee
Brunel University London
Uxbridge, UK

Andrea Polini
University of Camerino
Camerino, Italy

Manuel Pedro Rodríguez Bolívar
University of Granada
Granada, Spain

Hans Jochen Scholl
University of Washington
Seattle, WA, USA

Efthimios Tambouris
University of Macedonia
Thessaloniki, Greece

ISSN 0302-9743 ISSN 1611-3349 (electronic)
Lecture Notes in Computer Science
ISBN 978-3-030-27324-8 ISBN 978-3-030-27325-5 (eBook)
https://doi.org/10.1007/978-3-030-27325-5

LNCS Sublibrary: SL3 – Information Systems and Applications, incl. Internet/Web, and HCI

This Springer imprint is published by the registered company Springer Nature Switzerland AG
The registered company address is: Gewerbestrasse 11, 6330 Cham, Switzerland

Preface

The EGOV-CeDEM-ePart 2019 represents the second-year edition after the merger of the IFIP WG 8.5 Electronic Government (EGOV), the IFIP WG 8.5 IFIP Electronic Participation (ePart), and the Conference for E-Democracy and Open Government Conference (CeDEM). The merged conference is dedicated to the broader area of electronic government, open government, smart governance, e-democracy, policy informatics, and electronic participation. Scholars from around the world have attended this premier academic forum for a long time, which has given EGOV a worldwide reputation as one of the top two conferences in the research domains of electronic, open, and smart government, as well as electronic participation.

This year's conference was held during September 2–4, 2019, in San Benedetto Del Tronto, and hosted by the University of Camerino, Italy. The call for papers attracted completed research papers, work-in-progress papers on ongoing research (including doctoral papers), project and case descriptions, as well as workshop and panel proposals. The submissions were assessed through a double-blind peer-review process, with at least two reviewers per submission. The conference tracks present advances in the socio-technological domain of the public sphere, demonstrating cutting-edge concepts, methods, and styles of investigation by multiple disciplines. The papers were distributed over the following tracks:

- General E-Government and Open Government Track
- General E-Democracy and eParticipation Track
- Smart Cities (Government, Communities, and Regions) Track
- AI, Data Analytics, and Automated Decision Making Track
- Social Media Track
- Social Innovation Track
- Open Data: Social and Technical Aspects Track
- Digital Society
- Practitioners' Track

Among the full research paper submissions, 27 papers (empirical and conceptual) from the general E-Government and Open Government track, as well as the tracks on Smart Cities, AI, and Open Data were accepted for this year's Springer LNCS EGOV proceedings (vol. 11685), whereas another 13 papers of completed research papers from the General ePart Track and the Policy Modeling and Policy Informatics Track went into the LNCS ePart proceedings (vol. 11686). The papers included in this volume have been clustered under the following headings:

- E-Government Foundations
- E-Government Services and Open Government
- Open Data: Social and Technical Aspects
- AI, Data Analytics, and Automated Decision Making
- Smart Cities

As in the previous years and per the recommendation of the Paper Awards Committee under the leadership of Gabriela Viale Pereira, Danube University Krems, Austria, the IFIP EGOV-CeDEM-ePart 2019 Conference Organizing Committee again granted outstanding paper awards in three distinct categories:

- The most interdisciplinary and innovative research contribution
- The most compelling critical research reflection
- The most promising practical concept

The winners in each category were announced in the award ceremony at the conference dinner, which has always been a highlight of the conferences.

Many people make large events like this conference happen. We thank the members of the Program Committee and the additional reviewers for their great efforts in reviewing the submitted papers. We would like to express our gratitude to Andrea Polini, Barbara Re, and Flavio Corradini, and the team from University of Camerino for hosting the conference. The University of Camerino has a seven-decade long history, starting in 1336 when it was founded as Studium Generale. Today the university is ranked first among the small-scale Italian Universities (http://international. unicam.it/). University of Camerino is responsible for research and training in multiple areas and the local organization belongs to the Computer Science Division (http://computerscience.unicam.it). This is a vibrant and young research group that is part of the School of Science and Technology. The division has a research background in modeling, analysis, verification and deployment of distributed systems. They provide the following teaching programs: BSc in Informatics, MSc in Computer Science, and PhD in Computer Science.

September 2019

Ida Lindgren
Marijn Janssen
Habin Lee
Andrea Polini
Manuel Pedro Rodríguez Bolívar
Hans Jochen Scholl
Efthimios Tambouris

Organization

Conference Lead Organizer

Marijn Janssen   Delft University of Technology, The Netherlands

General E-Government and Open Government Track

Ida Lindgren (Lead)   Linköping University, Sweden
Hans Jochen Scholl   University of Washington, USA
Gabriela Viale Pereira   Danube University Krems, Austria

General E-Democracy and eParticipation Track

Panos Panagiotopoulos   Queen Mary University of London, UK
  (Lead)
Robert Krimmer   Tallinn University of Technology, Estonia
Peter Parycek   Fraunhofer Fokus, Germany,
                                and Danube-University Krems, Austria

Smart Cities (Government, Communities and Regions) Track

Manuel Pedro Rodríguez   University of Granada, Spain
  Bolívar (Lead)
Karin Axelsson   Linköping University, Sweden
Nuno Lopes   DTx: Digital Transformation Colab, Portugal

AI, Data Analytics and Automated Decision Making Track

Habin Lee (Lead)   Brunel University London, UK
Euripidis Loukis   University of Aegean, Greece
Tomasz Janowski   Gdansk University of Technology, Poland,
                                and Danube University Krems, Austria

Social Media Track

Noella Edelmann (Lead)   Danube University Krems, Austria
Sarah Hoffmann   University of Agder, Norway
Marius Rohde Johannessen   University of South-Eastern Norway, Norway

Social Innovation Track

Gianluca Misuraca (Lead)	European Commission's Joint Research Centre, Spain
Marijn Janssen	Delft University of Technology, The Netherlands
Csaba Csaki	Corvinus Business School, Hungary

Open Data: Social and Technical Aspects Track

Efthimios Tambouris (Lead)	University of Macedonia, Greece
Anneke Zuiderwijk	Delft University of Technology, The Netherlands
Ramon Gil-Garcia	University at Albany, USA

Digital Society

Thomas Lampoltshammer (Lead)	Danube University Krems, Austria
David Osimo	The Lisbon Council, Spain
Martijn Hartog	Delft University of Technology, The Netherlands

Practitioners' Track

Peter Reichstädter (Lead)	Austrian Parliament, Austria
Morten Meyerhoff Nielsen	United Nations University, Portugal
Francesco Mureddu	The Lisbon Council, Belgium
Francesco Molinari	Politecnico di Milano, Italy

Chair of Outstanding Papers Awards

Gabriela Viale Pereira	Danube University Krems, Austria

PhD Colloquium Chairs

Gabriela Viale Pereira (Lead)	Danube University Krems, Austria
J. Ramon Gil-Garcia	University at Albany, SUNY, USA
Ida Lindgren	Linköping University, Sweden
Anneke Zuiderwijk	Delft University of Technology, The Netherlands
Evangelos Kalampokis	University of Macedonia, Greece

Program Committee

Suha Alawadhi	Kuwait University, Kuwait
Laura Alcaide	University of Granada, Spain
Charalampos Alexopoulos	University of the Aegean, Greece
Karin Axelsson	Linköping University, Sweden
Peter Bellström	Karlstad University, Sweden

Lasse Berntzen	University of South-Eastern Norway, Norway
Radomir Bolgov	Saint Petersburg State University, Russia
Alessio Maria Braccini	Università degli Studi della Tuscia, Italy
Vasily Bunakov	STFC, UK
Jesus Cano	UNED, Spain
Walter Castelnovo	University of Insubria, Italy
Bojan Cestnik	Temida d.o.o., Jožef Stefan Institute, Slovenia
Yannis Charalabidis	National Technical University of Athens, Greece
Soon Chun	City University of New York, USA
Wichian Chutimaskul	King Mongkut's University of Technology Thonburi, Thailand
Meghan Cook	SUNY Albany CTG, USA
Ignacio Criado	Universidad Autónoma de Madrid, Spain
Peter Cruickshank	Edinburgh Napier University, UK
Jonathan Crusoe	Linköping University, Sweden
Csaba Csaki	Corvinus University, Corvinus Business School, Hungary
Frank Danielsen	University of Agder, Norway
Todd Davies	Stanford University, USA
Athanasios Deligiannis	International Hellenic University, Greece
Edna Dias Canedo	Universidade de Brasília, Brazil
Bettina Distel	Universität Münster, Germany
Noella Edelmann	Danube University Krems, Austria
Carl Erik Moe	University of Agder, Norway
Loukis Euripides	University of the Aegean, Greece
Francisco Falcone	Universidad Publica de Navarra, Spain
Montathar Faraon	Kristianstad University, Sweden
Sabrina Franceschini	Regione Emilia-Romagna, Italy
Luz Maria Garcia	Universidad de la Sierra Sur, Mexico
Miguel García	Zabala Innovation Consulting S.A., Spain
Francisco García Morán	European Commission, Luxembourg
Paul Gibson	Mines Telecom, France
J. Ramon Gil-Garcia	University at Albany, State University of New York, USA
Stevan Gostojic	University of Novi Sad, Serbia
Dimitris Gouscos	University of Athens, Greece
Malin Granath	Linköping University, Sweden
Christine Grosse	Mid Sweden University, Sweden
Sara Gustafsson	Linköping University, Sweden
Martijn Hartog	Delft University of Technology, The Netherlands
Helle Zinner Henriksen	Copenhagen Business School, Denmark
Sara Hofmann	University of Agder, Norway
Joris Hulstijn	Tilburg University, The Netherlands
Bettina Höchtl	Danube University Krems, Austria
Roumiana Ilieva	Technical University of Sofia, Bulgaria

Tomasz Janowski	Gdansk University of Technology, Poland, and Danube University Krems, Austria
Marijn Janssen	Delft University of Technology, The Netherlands
Marius Rohde Johannessen	University of South-Eastern Norway, Norway
Yury Kabanov	National Research University Higher School of Economics, Russia
Muneo Kaigo	University of Tsukuba, Japan
Evangelos Kalampokis	University of Macedonia, Greece
Eleni Kanellou	National Technical University of Athens, Greece
Evika Karamagioli	University of Paris 8, France
Divya Kirti Gupta	Indus Business Academy, India
Bram Klievink	Delft University of Technology, the Netherlands
Elena Korge	Taltech University, Estonia
Robert Krimmer	Tallinn University of Technology, Estonia
Toomas Kästik	Estonian Business School, Estonia
Thomas J. Lampoltshammer	Danube University Krems, Austria
Habin Lee	Brunel University, UK
Azi Lev-On	Ariel University, Israel
Katarina Lindblad Gidlund	Midsweden University, Sweden
Ida Lindgren	Linköping University, Sweden
Ralf Lindner	Fraunhofer, Germany
Helen Liu	The University of Hong Kong, SAR China
Euripidis Loukis	University of the Aegean, Greece
Rui Pedro Lourenço	INESC Coimbra, FEUC, Portugal
Luis Luna-Reyes	University at Albany, SUNY, USA
Bjorn Lundell	University of Skövde, Sweden
Truls Löfstedt	Linköping University, Sweden
Cristiano Maciel	Universidade Federal de Mato Grosso, Brazil
Christian Madsen	IT University of Copenhagen, Denmark
Agnes Mainka	HHU Düsseldorf, Germany
Keegan Mcbride	Tallinn University of Technology, Estonia
John McNutt	University of Delaware, USA
Ulf Melin	Linköping University, Sweden
Sehl Mellouli	Laval University, Canada
Tobias Mettler	University of Lausanne, Switzerland
Morten Meyerhoff Nielsen	Tallinn University of Technology, Estonia
Andras Micsik	SZTAKI, Hungary
Yuri Misnikov	University of Leeds, UK
Gianluca Misuraca	European Commission, JRC-IPTS, Spain
Francesco Molinari	Politecnico di Milano, Italy
Josémaría Moreno-Jiménez	Universidad de Zaragoza, Spain
Vadym Mozgovoy	UNIL, IDHEAP, Switzerland
Francesco Mureddu	Lisbon Council, Portugal
Karine Nahon	University of Washington, USA, and Interdisciplinary Center at Herzliya, Israel
Morten Nielsen	The Open University, UK

Maria Nikolova	New Bulgarian University, Bulgaria
Vanessa Nunes	UnB, CIC, Brazil
Adegboyega Ojo	Insight Centre for Data Analytics, National University of Ireland, Ireland
Michele Osella	Istituto Superiore Mario Boella, Italy
David Osimo	The Lisbon Council, Portugal
Kerley Pires	United Nations University, Portugal
Jenny Palm	Lund University, Sweden
Panos Panagiotopoulos	Queen Mary University of London, UK
Darcy Parks	Linköping University, Sweden
Peter Parycek	Danube University Krems, Austria
Luiz Paulo Silva	UNIRIO, Brazil
Manuel Pedro Rodríguez Bolívar	University of Granada, Spain
Vasilis Peristeras	International Hellenic University, Greece
Sofie Pilemalm	Linköping University, Sweden
Vigan Raca	Ss. Cyril and Methodius University in Skopje, Republic of North Macedonia
Peter Reichstaedter	The Austrian Parliament, Austria
Nicolau Reinhard	University of São Paulo, Brazil
Harald Rohracher	Linköping University, Sweden
Athanasia Routzouni	University of the Aegean, Greece
Boriana Rukanova	Delft University of Technology, Netherlands
Michael Räckers	WWU Münster, ERCIS, Germany
Mariana S. Gustafsson	Linköping University, Sweden
Michael Sachs	Danube University Krems, Austria
Rodrigo Sandoval Almazan	Universidad Autonoma del Estado de Mexico, Mexico
Günther Schefbeck	The Austrian Parliament, Austria
Hans J. Scholl	University of Washington, USA
Margit Scholl	TH Wildau, Germany
Hendrik Scholta	University of Münster, ERCIS, Germany
Harrie Scholtens	European Institute of Public Administration, The Netherlands
Johannes Scholz	Graz University of Technology, Austria
Judith Schossboeck	Danube University Krems, Austria
Erich Schweighofer	University of Vienna, Austria
Johanna Sefyrin	Linköping University, Sweden
Tobias Siebenlist	Heinrich Heine University Düsseldorf, Germany
Andrzej M. J. Skulimowski	AGH University of Science and Technology, Poland
Simon Smith Charles	University in Prague, Czech Republic
Mauricio Solar	Universidad Tecnica Federico Santa Maria, Chile
Maddalena Sorrentino	University of Milan, Italy
Witold Staniszkis	Rodan Systems, Poland
Leif Sundberg	Mid Sweden University, Sweden
Iryna Susha	Örebro University, Sweden
Jakob Svensson	Malmö University, Sweden

Øystein Sæbø	University of Agder, Norway
Fredrik Söderström	Linköping University, Sweden
Efthimios Tambouris	University of Macedonia, Greece
Ella Taylor-Smith	Napier University, UK
Luis Terán	University of Fribourg, Switzerland
Peter Teufl	IAIK, Graz University of Technology, Austria
Lörinc Thurnay	Danube University Krems, Austria
Jolien Ubacht	Delft University of Technology, The Netherlands
Nuno Vasco	DTx: Digital Transformation CoLAB, Portugal
Marco Velicogna	Consiglio Nazionale delle Ricerche (CNR), Italy
Natasa Veljkovic	Faculty of Electronic Engineering in Nis, Serbia
Gabriela Viale Pereira	Danube University Krems, Austria
Shefali Virkar	Danube University Krems, Austria
Wilfred Warioba	Commission for Human Rights and Good Governance, Tanzania
Elin Wihlborg	Linköping University, Sweden
Maria Wimmer	Universität Koblenz-Landau, Germany
Chien-Chih Yu	National ChengChi University, Taiwan
Pär-Ola Zander	Aalborg University, Denmark
Thomas Zefferer	A-SIT Plus GmbH, Austria
Saleem Zoughbi	International Adviser, Palestine
Anneke Zuiderwijk	Delft University of Technology, The Netherlands
Stefanos Gritzalis	University of the Aegean, Greece

Additional Reviewers

Eiri Elvestad	University of South-Eastern, Norway
Zoi Lachana	University of the Aegean, Greece
Michalis Avgerinos Loutsaris	University of the Aegean, Greece
Vasiliki Diamantopoulou	University of the Aegean, Greece
Thodoris Papadopoulos	Greece
Enrico Ferro	Istituto Superiore Mario Boella, Italy
Aggeliki Androutsopoulou	University of the Aegean, Greece
Zoi Lachana	University of the Aegean, Greece
Anna-Sophie Novak	Danube University Krems, Austria
Hong Joo Lee	Catholic University of Korea, South Korea
Truong Van Nguyen	Brunel University London, UK
Maria Karyda	University of the Aegean, Greece
Amal Marzouki	Université Laval, Canada
Vasiliki Diamantopoulou	University of the Aegean, Greece
Changwoo Suh	Brunel University London, UK
Amal Ben Rjab	Université Laval, Canada

Contents

Open Data: Social and Technical Aspects

AI, Data Analytics and Automated Decision Making

Smart Cities

E-Government Foundations

The Three Generations of Electronic Government: From Service Provision to Open Data and to Policy Analytics

Yannis Charalabidis, Euripidis Loukis, Charalampos Alexopoulos[✉],
and Zoi Lachana

Department of Information and Communication Systems Engineering,
University of the Aegean, Samos 83200, Greece
{yannisx, eloukis, alexop, zoi}@aegean.gr

Abstract. For long time research and practice in the area of Electronic Government (e-government) has been focusing on the use of information and communication technologies (ICT) for improving the efficiency government agencies' internal operations, as well as transactions with citizens and firms. However, the increased needs and expectations of citizens, and the proliferation of 'participatory democracy' ideas, gave rise to a new generation of ICT exploitation by government for increasing and enhancing citizens' participation. Furthermore, the increasing social problems and challenges that had to be addressed by government through appropriate public policies, such as the increasing inequalities and poverty, the aging society, the environmental degradation, and the rising number of 'unpredictable' events, such as the financial and economic crisis, give rise to the development of a new wave of e-government focusing on policy analytics for supporting the design of effective responses - public policies for these challenges. Therefore, evolutions in the needs of modern societies, in combination with technological evolutions, give rise to evolutions in e-government, and the emergence of new generations of it. This paper aims at the identification and better understanding of the main characteristics of the different e-Government generations, using an analytical framework based on two rounds of literature review. The results of the study provide insights on the main features of the three main e-government generations, regarding their main goals, obstacles, key methods and tools, and reveal the new emerging generation of e-Government 3.0 and its basic characteristics. Furthermore, within the first and to some extent the second e-Government generation there have been substantial advancements, which have created distinct sub-generations of them, revealed and analysed through extensive relevant growth/maturity stages research.

Keywords: Electronic government · (e-)government 1.0 · (e-)government 2.0 · (e-)government 3.0 · e-Government generations

I. Lindgren et al. (Eds.): EGOV 2019, LNCS 11685, pp. 3–17, 2019.
https://doi.org/10.1007/978-3-030-27325-5_1

1 Introduction

The objective of Electronic Government (e-Government) research and practice has been the exploitation of ICT in government, and the provision of ICT-based services to public servants, citizens and firms, aiming initially at efficiency and effectiveness improvements of government agencies' internal operations, as well as transactions with citizens and firms, and then at citizens' participation as well as transparency increase and enhancement. As the expectations and needs of citizens and societies in general are changing and growing, and also the capabilities offered by ICTs are evolving, we observe a shift in e-Government focus, leading to an evolution of e-Government. The evolution of e-Government is influenced on one hand by its wider external environment (such as economic, political and social), and on the other by its technological environment. In all these evolutions there is a common pattern: initially existing practices, processes and services are automated/supported through ICT, and then they are subjected of incremental ICT-based improvements or innovations that governments tend to adopt, by transforming the already existing practices, processes and services, or by adopting new ones [1].

These evolutions have generated several e-Government waves, which have been shaped by societies' problems and needs in combination them with technological developments. A first wave of e-government services was meant initially to exploit ICT in order to improve internal efficiency of government agencies, by automating or supporting their complex internal processes, and then to take advantage of the high penetration and use of the Internet in order to establish electronic transaction with citizens and firms through the web, by developing public e-services for them. This wave was aiming initially at the automation and support of public services, and then at the transformation of them, addressing issues of efficiency and effectiveness related to the public services provision. The proliferation of the 'participatory democracy' ideas in combination with the high penetration and use of the Internet gave rise to second wave of e-Government services for citizens and firms, which go beyond the support and enhancement of transaction with them, aiming at the support and enhancement of the relationship and communication of government with them. This second wave of e-Government attempts to utilize the power of the Internet, and later the social media, for establishing a more close and stronger interaction and collaboration with the society way. More participatory Internet-based services and capabilities were offered to citizens in order to be engaged and participate more in the policy making process. This wave is also associated with enhanced transparency and accountability through the development of services that open to the society important government data.

This succession of different waves/generations of e-government has changed perceptions about the content of e-government and has resulted in several definitions that have been formulated through years in order to describe e-government, as the notion is evolving, focusing on different characteristics of the emerging generations of it (e.g. [2–6]). Because of this, although there is an enormous frequency of use of the term "e-government", there is still not a clear and consistent understanding of the content of this concept among practitioners and academia. However, despite the fundamental importance of this evolution of the e-government domain for the society and the economy, limited systematic research of it has been conducted.

The current study aims to contribute to filling this research gap; its specific research objectives are:

(i)   to establish a common understanding of different e-government developments' categorization into specific e-government generations;
(ii) to provide integrated definitions for the different e-government generations and identify the main characteristics of them;
(iii) to understand internal evolutions within each of these e-government generations, and possibly identify sub-generations of them;
(iv) to develop an analysis framework for the above, setting up the analysis perspectives in the form of research questions towards the systematic investigation of e-government generations, which can be of wider usefulness for future research on this topic.

The rest of this paper is organized as follows. Section 2 provides background information on associated domains that illustrate similar evolution paths and should be considered in the analysis. Section 3 describes our methodological approach, while Sects. 4, 5 and 6 present the results of our research. Finally, Sect. 7 includes conclusions and suggestions for further research on this topic.

2   Background

With the ICT constituting key enablers for the evolution and even the disruption of most sectors [7], including the government one (through the development of e-government), completely new opportunities for the societies, the private and the public sector, are being created for exploiting ICT for addressing complex problems and challenges, and for facilitating economic growth. Technological advances have driven dramatic transformations and evolutions in many domains and have led to the emergence of new generations of them. In the domains of the electronic content publishing [8, 9], and also the industry [10, 11], where we can observe evolution paths which are most probably closely related to the e-government one, we observe the emergence of different generations of them: Web 1.0, Web 2.0 and Web 3.0, and also Industry "1.0", "2.0", "3.0" and occasionally "4.0".

2.1   The Evolution of the Web

In the area of electronic content publishing we can distinguish different generations of the web, driven by technological evolutions [8, 9]. In Web 1.0, applications were generally aimed at publishing mainly 'read-only' content, to be 'consumed' by users, but allowing limited interaction with it. Subsequently, Web 2.0 has been the term used to describe a new generation of the web, allowing more interaction with already published, development of 'user-generated' content, transforming passive content consumers to more active content 'prosumers' (producers and consumers), and also development of networks for content dissemination. The most recent generation, Web 3.0, is about a 'semantic' web of data, which through the semantic annotation of its data provided enhanced data search and link capabilities, allowing this web of data to interface better with itself, and also to feed data to other web applications being used by people around the internet. Web 3.0 technologies are the response to the ever-increasing amounts of data generated by the users and organizations, which have to be searched and exploited more efficiently. Furthermore, as no single platform will be able to handle such amounts of data, the necessity arises for the decentralization of the relevant services, which is reflected in the emergence of technologies like distributed computing or blockchain.

2.2   The Evolution of the Industry

Similarly, in industry we can distinguish some distinct generations of it, driven by technological evolutions [10, 11]. Industry 1.0 introduced the concept of mechanical mass production, by using water- and steam-powered machines, while Industry 2.0 utilized the power of electricity, and at the same time it developed new methods for increasing the efficiency and effectiveness of manufacturing facilities, through the improved allocation of various manufacturing resources. Industry 3.0, also known as the third industrial revolution, was based on the development of electronic hardware and software, which was used for improving planning of industrial operations, as well as extending automation of previously manual production tasks; also, these offered new services and capabilities based on optimizing warehouses management, which are completely beyond the realm of inventory control and shipping logistics. Recently Industry 4.0 has emerged, which refers to the advanced digitalization and use of the 'Internet of Things', big data and analytics technologies within factories, in order to generate new production-related information, which can be used for increasing further production efficiency (production process innovations), and also for the development of novel products and services (product and process innovations). Among the core characteristics of Industry 4.0 are: quicker decision-making, decentralization, and products/services customization and personalization, with the use of big data as an important factor driving industry 4.0.

3   Methodology

The main research objective of this study is the identification and better understanding of the different generations of e-Government. In order to define to the necessary elements/perspectives of each generation to be examined and analysed we developed an analysis framework, based on the method for the analysis and development of science base in a domain proposed in [12], which has been adapted to the needs of this study. Each identified analysis element/perspective was converted into a research question. The final analysis framework we constructed in this way is shown in Table 1, which presents the different analysis perspectives we used to investigate the major characteristics of each e-government generation, along with the corresponding research questions and their detailed explanations.

As a second step, we proceeded with the identification of the main literature that contains the available definitions for the different generations of e-government. From a preliminary search we found that previous e-government literature distinguished three

Table 1. Analysis framework: main perspectives, research questions, explanations

#	Main perspective	Research question	Explanations
1	Main Goal	What is every generation aiming to achieve?	The result/objective that each generation of eGovernment aims to achieve
2	Main Method	How can their goal(s) be achieved?	An established, prescribed, or logical, practice or systematic process of achieving the main goal with accuracy and efficiency based on a credible approach
3	Usual Application Level	Which is the targeted government level?	Related environment of offered services
4	Key Tools	Technological tools for accomplishing their goal(s)?	Main technological tools used for accomplishing/achieving the main goal
5	Key Obstacles/Risks	Are there any obstacles/risks?	Determining factors capable of preventing the main goal to be achieved. Could be a policy or the users' resistance to change
6	Key ICT Areas	Which technologies are being used?	Key enabling technologies allowing the deployment of the main method and the development of the key tool
7	Most Needed Discipline, beyond ICT	Which are the important scientific discipline(s) to be leveraged beyond ICT?	Identification of the most important scientific discipline(s), beyond ICT, for the achievement of the major goal of each generation

main generations of e-Government, referred to as "e-Government 1.0", "e-Government 2.0" and "e-Government 3.0", or even using the terms "Government 1.0", "Government 2.0", and "Government 3.0". So we searched the EGRL (V. 13.5, is renamed DGRL - Digital Government Reference Library) and Google Scholar using the above terms as keywords, as well as "eGovernment definition", in order to find publications enabling us to answer the above seven fundamental research questions of our analysis framework (see above Table 1). We found 17 papers in total, which however did not include sufficiently detailed information for providing all the necessary answers to the above seven research questions, but provided us more detailed keywords for conducting a second round of more extended literature search. In this second round, in addition to the previously used EGRL (V. 13.5), we extended out search to the Scopus library and Google Scholar. We found 126 papers, from which initially were examined their abstracts, in order to select the most appropriate ones for answering the above research questions. Finally, 35 papers were selected as more relevant to be thoroughly analysed.

As a last step, based on these papers we proceeded to the description of the above mentioned seven main perspectives of each e-government generation. The results are presented in the following Sect. 5, enabling a better in-depth understanding the characteristics of the different generations of e-government.

4   The Three Generations of e-Government

In Table 2 we can see the key findings concerning the abovementioned seven main perspectives/questions of the three e-government generations, as well as their supporting literature. A main similarity identified concerns the perspective/question 5 of 'key obstacles/risks': the same main obstacle has been identified for all three generations of e-government, which is emphasized in all relevant papers: public sector mentality, which does not favour risk taking and innovation. Public servants and politicians seem to be reluctant to be early adopters of new technological advancements in order to achieve the main goal of each generation.

Table 2. Generations of digital government

#		e-GOV 1.0	e-GOV 2.0	e-GOV 3.0
1	Main Goal	Better Services [13–16]	Openness & Collaboration [13, 17–21]	Societal problem-solving citizen well-being, optimization of resources [22, 23]
2	Main Method	Interoperability for Connected Governance [14, 24, 25]	Open & Collaborative Governance [17–21]	Smart Governance & data-intensive decision-policy making [22, 23, 26]
3	Usual Application Level	National [13, 25]	National & Local [17, 18]	Local to International [27]
4	Key Tool	Portal [16, 18, 28]	Social Media [13, 17–21]	Ubiquitous Sensors/Smart Devices/Apps/AI [29, 30]
5	Key Obstacles/Risk	Public Sector Mentality [20, 25, 31]	Public Sector Mentality [17, 27, 31]	Public Sector Mentality [27]
6	Key ICT Area	Organizational Infrastructures [15, 20]	Social Media & Open and Big Data [17, 19, 20, 25]	Artificial Intelligence & IoT [22, 23]
7	Most Needed Discipline, beyond ICT	Management [14, 25, 31, 32]	Social and Political Sciences [20, 21]	A wide variety of disciplines concerning the domains of government activity, such as economic, environmental, behavioural sciences [33]

With the only exception of this perspective/question 5 concerning the obstacles/ risks remarkable differences have been identified between the three generations in all the other examined perspective/questions. For perspective/question 1 about the main goal of each generation we can conclude there is a shift in the main goal/scope in e-government through the years. While e-Government 1.0 pursues the provision of better transactional services by the public sector for the businesses and the citizens [13–16], e-Government 2.0 offers capabilities towards increasing citizens' participation, as well as openness and accountability of governments [13, 17–21], and thus enhancing the quality of democracy. Finally, e-Government 3.0 comes as the logical response on one hand to the growing problems and challenges that modern societies and have to be managed through effective government policies, and on the other hand to the deluge of data produced from the second generation of e-government (mainly large quantities of textual data from various social media sources), as well from new technologies (sensors, Internet of Things (IoT), etc.); it is aiming to exploit these data for providing support to policy-making, societal problem solving, as well as citizens' well-being (e.g. for citizen-level decision support services i.e. find the quickest route to your destination by-passing high traffic areas) and data-intensive decision making (policy informatics) [22, 23].

In order to achieve these goals in e-Government 1.0 the most common methods and tools are interoperability between IS of government agencies, as well as towards central electronic 'one-stop shops' and national portals [14, 24, 25]. In e-Government 2.0 social media [13, 17–21] play an important role for the development of new governance models, characterised by more participation of and collaboration with the society (individual citizens, communities, stakeholder groups, firms, professional and business associations), with the most advanced governments to adopt this new way of communication with the citizens, as well as citizens' participation to governmental decisions [17–21]. Moreover, e-Government 2.0 emphasises the opening and release of government data by developing national and local open government data portals, in order to promote transparency [17, 18]. In e-Government 3.0 the increased use of sensors and smart devices producing big data [23], ranging from human text to sensor data, combined with advanced analytics and modelling, which increasingly make use of highly sophisticated AI techniques, and possibly ubiquitous services (i.e. cloud) [29, 30], allowing data-intensive and evidence-based decision and policy making [22, 23, 26].

The key ICT area of e-Government 1.0 is organizational ICT infrastructures [15, 20], while for e-Government 2.0 it is social media for citizens involvement, and open and big data [17, 19, 20, 25], while for e-Government 3.0 it is analytics, modelling, artificial intelligence and Internet of Things. Finally, in order for all the above to be achieved the most needed 'complementary' discipline, beyond ICT, is management for e-Government 1.0 [14, 15, 31, 32], social and political sciences for e-Government 2.0 [20, 21], and a wide variety of disciplines for e-Government 3.0, concerning the multiple domains of government activity, such as economic, environmental and behavioural sciences [33].

From studying in detail the above literature, it can be concluded that e-Government 1.0 focuses on the delivery of informational and transactional services, as well as on their production through government agencies' internal processes, being based on static ICTs and Web 1.0. On the contrary e-Government 2.0 focuses on the delivery of consultation, participation and open data services, and uses the concepts of Web 2.0 in combination with various social media management tools and technologies, as well as textual data analysis techniques; it aims at improving the openness and transparency of government, and at the same time collecting useful information and knowledge from the citizens about social problems and challenges, as well as ideas and proposals for managing them, applying crowdsourcing ideas in government, which lead to the development of the 'citizen-sourcing' [34–36]. The emerging new generation of e-Government 3.0 focuses on supporting and enhancing higher level policy-making functions of government, and for this purpose it exploits e-Government's 1.0 and e-Government's 2.0 technologies, and also some emerging innovative technologies, such as big data, analytics, AI and IoT [30, 33].

Taking into account the above literature we can provide the following definitions of these three e-Government generations:

– e-Government 1.0 refers to the utilization of ICTs and web-based technologies for improving or enhancing the efficiency and effectiveness of public service production and delivery to citizens and firms; therefore, it includes both government agencies' internal intra-organizational information systems (IS) for improving the efficiency of their internal operations and processes, and also Internet-based IS enabling electronic transactions of citizens and firms with government agencies.
– e-Government 2.0 refers to the use of the collaborative tools and approaches of Web 2.0, as well as to the opening of public information, in order to achieve more open, accountable and responsive government, and promote government transparency, and citizens' participation and collaboration.
– e-Government 3.0 refers to the use of new disruptive ICTs (such as big data, IoT, analytics, machine learning, AI), in combination with established ICTs (such as distributed technologies for data storage and service delivery), and taking advantage of the wisdom of crowd (crowd/citizen-sourcing and value co-creation), for supporting data-driven and evidence-based decision and policy making.

Furthermore, it is worth mentioning that in both the first two generations the reviewed relevant literature distinguishes two distinct stages: the first is oriented towards the support of existing practices, processes and services of government agencies, while the second is oriented towards the ICT-based transformation of them [1]. We expect something similar to happen with the third generation as well. In general ICT, though not immediately but after some time required for learning, seems to transform the way public administrations operate and interact with citizens and businesses, offering valuable new capabilities.

5 e-Government 3.0

Since e-Government 3.0 is the latest generation of e-Government, there is limited literature about it, so it is worth analysing further its main characteristics:

• It constitutes a major advancement of e-Government, strongly differentiated from the previous two generations, with respect to both objectives (to support higher government agencies' functions: high-level decision-making as well as policy-making), and technologies used (established ICTs, in combination with high sophisticated new disruptive ICTs, such as big data, IoT, analytics, machine learning, AI, blockchain, etc.).

- It is motivated and driven by both social factors (increasing intensity and complexity of social problems and challenges) and technological factors (the need to utilize the above disruptive ICT in order to exploit and extract value from the large amounts of data collected and possessed by government).
- One of its main directions is the exploitation of the IoT by government agencies. The use of a sensors on physical devices, vehicles, infrastructures allows the collection of large quantities of data that enable the prosion of valuable services to citizens, firms as well as public servants. A large-scale use of IoT enables in the context of modern cities addressing the big challenges created by their continuing growth, and improving citizens' quality of life, through the development of smart cities [30].
- The availability of vast amounts of data in government agencies enables the use of AI and machine learning for constructing useful models that support and enhance decision and policy making.
- Movement towards decentralization: the necessity to deal with vast amounts of data efficiently (once only principle) and securely (principle of trustworthiness and security) warrant the use of distributed technologies like blockchain, which are expected to be widely used for government services [37].

It also worth mentioning that the term "e-Government 3.0" has been first used by South Korea in order to describe its efforts mainly within its 'Open Government Partnership' [38]. It involves four main commitments: (i) to increase the availability of information about governmental activities; (ii) to support civic participation; (iii) to implement the highest standards of professional integrity throughout our administrations; and (iv) to increase access to new technologies for openness and accountability. So, we remark that the main elements of this South Korean definition of "e-Government 3.0" are actually the ones included in the existing definitions of "e-Government 2.0".

6   e-Government Generations' Elaboration: Sub-generations

If we elaborate further the identified three e-Government generations, we can distinguish distinct sub-generations in the first two of them. In particular, within e-Government 1.0 and 2.0 generations there have been substantial advancements, which have created distinct sub-generations of them that have been revealed and investigated through extensive relevant growth/maturity stages research. Most of this research has dealt with the first generation of e-Government 1.0, focusing on a part of it that concerns informational and transactional electronic services provision. Layne and Lee [39] developed a model of e-government growth, which focuses on these services, and consists of four stages: (i) the "catalogue" stage, in which static information is provided by government agencies to citizens and firms through the web; (ii) the "transaction" stage, in which citizens and firms are offered the capability to conduct their transactions with the government (e.g. applications, declarations, etc.) through the web; (iii) the "vertical integration" stage, which involves integration/interconnection of IS of government agencies of different levels (e.g. local, regional, national level) belonging to the same thematic domain (so that transactions conducted by citizens and firms at one of these levels are automatically propagated to and update all the other levels); (iv) the "horizontal integration" stage, which involves integration/interconnection of IS of government agencies that belong to different thematic domains (so that transactions conducted by citizens and firms with one government agency can update databases of government agencies from other thematic domains, and also use such databases in the processing of the above transactions), enabling the establishment of electronic one stop shops (regarded as the highest level of electronic transaction services). These four stages describe an interesting advancement that has taken place within the e-Government 1.0 generation with respect to the capabilities offered to the citizens and firms, and constitute four different distinct sub-generations of it. Subsequently, based on the above model many extensions/elaborations of it have been developed, which identify growth/maturity stages with respect to informational and transactional electronic services provision by government; comprehensive reviews/syntheses of them are provided in [40–43]. According to the most recent of them [43] these models share the following main growth/maturity stages: (a) publication of information on websites; (b) bi-directional communication with citizens via electronic channels; (c) offering transaction e-services online; (d) delivery of integrated e-government services, which involve multiple government agencies from the same or even from different thematic domains, in an 'electronic one-stop shop' mode; (e) some models include also an additional stage that concerns the above second generation of e-Government 2.0: e-democracy/e-participation related e-services. Furthermore, the same publication [43] distinguishes two additional stages of more advanced e-government transactional services, which go beyond the abovementioned electronic one-stop shop: the 'limited no-stop shop' and the 'no-stop shop' stages (in which the citizen has to perform only limited actions, or does not have to perform any action at all, respectively, in order to activate/receive government services). The maturity stages (a) to (d) (but not stage (e), as it concerns the second generation of e-Government 2.0, and not the first generation of Government 1.0), followed by the abovementioned two additional maturity stages identified in [43], constitute six distinct sub-generations of the first e-Government 1.0 generation, which are highly differentiated with respect to the capabilities offered to citizens and firms, and also the infrastructures and capacities that have to be developed by government agencies. However, it should be noted that there is a lack of similar maturity stages research concerning the other more 'basic' part of this e-Government 1.0 generation concerning the use of ICT for improving the efficiency of their internal operations and processes through internal intra-organizational IS of government agencies, though this is of critical importance for modern government and consume most of its ICT budget.

Much less similar research has been conducted for the second generation of e-Government 2.0, for identifying growth/maturity stages within this generation, and therefore corresponding sub-generations of it. In [17] has been developed an maturity model concerning the use of social media by government agencies for promoting public engagement and open government, which consists of five stages: (i) the "initial conditions stage", in which limited open government capabilities exist and social media is seldom used; (ii) the "data transparency" stage, in which social media are used for increasing transparency of government processes and performance by publishing relevant data online and sharing it with the public; (iii) the "open participation" stage, in which social media are used for promoting open participation of the public in government work and decision, aiming to enhance policy decisions and government services by utilizing the input of the public; (iv) the "open collaboration" stage, in which social media are used in order to foster open collaboration among government agencies, the public, and the private sector, for completing collaboratively complex tasks or projects that aim to co-create specific outputs; (v) the "ubiquitous engagement" stage, in which the main objective is to expand the scope and depth of social media use by citizens for all the above purposes, by making this easier and more universally accessible through mobile and ubiquitous computing devices and applications (so that the public can access government data and also participate and collaborate with government agencies using a wide variety of devices, such as smart phones, tablets, laptops, desktops, etc.). The first four of these maturity stages constitute distinct sub-generations of the second e-Government 2.0 generation with respect to purpose/objective of social media use.

Recently, a more focused maturity model has been developed concerning the use of social media by government agencies for 'citizen-sourcing', in order to collect useful public policy-related information, knowledge, proposals/ideas and opinions from citizens [44]; it can be viewed as an elaboration mainly of stages (iii) and (v) of the previously described model of [17]. It consists of five maturity stages of social media use for citizen-sourcing from a more technical perspective: (a) set-up and manual operation of social media accounts; (b) centrally managed automated operation of multiple social media accounts; (c) centrally managed and automated monitoring of external social media accounts; (d) centrally managed and automated monitoring of external social media accounts with quality filtering; (e) use of internal social media for the internal dissemination of the information, knowledge, proposals/ideas and opinions from citizens collected through the mechanisms defined in the previous stages, as well as for internal consultation on them; it should be noted that stages (b) to (e) include automated processing of content created in them by citizens for extracting the main issues as well as sentiment. We remark that while the stages of the previous maturity model described in [17] concern the purpose/objective of using social media by government agencies, the stages of the model maturity described in [44] have a more technical perspective, and concern mainly the kind of social media accounts to be used for citizen-sourcing, as well as the way of managing them and processing the content created in them by citizens. This indicates that for one e-Government generation we can have several divisions of it into sub-generations from various perspectives, such as the purpose/objective of ICT use perspective, the technical perspective, etc.

The above sub-generations we have identified for the first two generations of eGovernment 1.0 and 2.0 deepen our understanding about them, and indicate that they are not homogeneous and static; on the contrary, they are complex, heterogeneous and undergo important evolutions and advancements. Each of these sub-generations might require different organizational capacities and infrastructures from its previous ones, and have different risks, challenges and critical success factors.

7   Conclusion and Further Research

In this study, we analyse the three different generations of e-Government. In order for this to be achieved it was necessary to first develop an appropriate analysis framework: to properly identify the main analysis perspectives, i.e. their main characteristics of these generations to be examined. For these generation definitions were developed as a result of our research, and the main characteristics of them were identified, as well as their important differences in goals, orientations and means. It has been concluded that these three e-Government generations differ substantially in the targeted government function to be supported and enhanced using ICT: internal operations and transactions with citizens/firms for e-Government 1.0, communication and consultation with the society for e-Government 2.0, and decision/policy-making for e-Government 3.0. Furthermore, they differ in the specific ICT they use for supporting/enhancing their targeted government function, with each generation employing the most appropriate ICT for the function it targets: ICT infrastructures and interoperability, as well as web 1.0 for e-Government 1.0, web 2.0 and social media for e-Government 2.0, big data, IoT, analytics, machine learning and AI for e-Government 3.0.

Further research is required on one hand concerning the first two e-Government generations, in order to deepen our understanding of them, by introducing more analysis perspectives, such as the transformations they have driven, and their interplay with economic and social evolutions; also, it is necessary to analyse each of the identified sub-generations of them separately using the analysis framework developed in Sect. 3. On the other hand, concerning the emerging e-Government 3.0 generation much more research is required, in order to address the fundamental questions it poses: Which are the main new disruptive technologies that will influence its development and shape it? How we can use these new disruptive ICTs in the public sector, on one hand for policy and decision making, and on the other hand for other functions of government agencies? – What major transformations they can drive in government agencies' policy and decision making, and also operations and work practices, transaction and consultation with citizens and firms, and in general in governance models? – Are there evolutions and advancements that create sub-generations within the e-Government 3.0 generation.

References

1. Janowski, T.: Digital government evolution: from transformation to contextualization. Gov. Inf. Q. **32**, 221–236 (2015)
2. Okot-Uma, R.W.O., London, C.S.: Electronic Governance: Re-inventing Good Governance. Commonwealth Secretariat, London (2000)

3. Chen, Y.N., Chen, H.M., Huang, W., Ching, R.K.: E-government strategies in developed and developing countries: an implementation framework and case study. J. Global Inf. Manag. **14**(1), 23–46 (2006)
4. Maumbe, B.M., Owei, V., Alexander, H.: Questioning the pace and pathway of e-government development in Africa: a case study of South Africa's Cape Gateway project. Gov. Inf. Q. **25**(4), 757–777 (2008)
5. Di Maio, A.: Government 2.0: Gartner Definition. Industry Research (2009)
6. Baumgarten, J., Chui, M.: E-government 2.0. McKinsey Q. **4**(2), 26–31 (2009)
7. Christensen, C.M., Raynor, M., McDonald, R.: What is disruptive innovation. Harvard Bus. Rev. **93**(12), 44–53 (2015)
8. O'Reilly, T.: What is web 2.0: design patterns and business models for the next generation of software. Commun. Strat. **65**, 17–37 (2007)
9. Sharma, A.: Introducing The Concept Of Web 3.0 http://www.tweakandtrick.com/2012/05/web-30.html. Accessed 08 Dec 2017
10. Lasi, H., Fettke, P., Kemper, H.G., Feld, T., Hoffmann, M.: Industry 4.0. Bus. Inf. Syst. Eng. **6**, 239–242 (2014)
11. Lu, Y.: Industry 4.0: a survey on technologies, applications and open research issues. J. Ind. Inf. Integr. **6**, 1–10 (2017)
12. Charalabidis, Y., Gonçalves, R.J., Popplewell, K.: Towards a scientific foundation for interoperability. In: Charalabidis, Y. (ed.) Interoperability in Digital Public Services and Administration: Bridging E-Government and E-Business, pp. 355–373. IGI Global, Hershey (2011). Information Science Reference
13. Chun, S., Shulman, S., Sandoval, R., Hovy, E.: Government 2.0: making connections between citizens, data and government. Inf. Polity **15**(1,2), 1–9 (2010)
14. Pardo, T.A., Nam, T., Burke, G.B.: E-government interoperability: Interaction of policy, management, and technology dimensions. Soc. Sci. Comput. Rev. **30**(1), 7–23 (2012)
15. Ebrahim, Z., Irani, Z.: E-government adoption: architecture and barriers. Bus. Process Manag. J. **11**(5), 589–611 (2005)
16. Howard, M.: E-government across the globe: how will 'e' change government. Gov. Finan. Rev. (2001)
17. Lee, G., Kwak, Y.H.: An open government maturity model for social media-based public engagement. Gov. Inf. Q. **29**(4), 492–503 (2012)
18. Open Government Partnership, https://www.opengovpartnership.org/. Accessed 20 May 2019
19. Noveck, B.S.: Wiki Government: How Technology Can Make Government Better, Democracy Stronger, and Citizens More Powerful. Brookings Institution Press, Washington, DC (2009)
20. Charalabidis, Y., Koussouris, S.: Empowering Open and Collaborative Governance: Technologies and Methods for Online Citizen Engagement in Public Policy Making. Springer, Heidelberg (2012). https://doi.org/10.1007/978-3-642-27219-6
21. Wirtz, B. W., Daiser, P.: E-Government: Strategy Process Instruments. Textbook for the Digital Society, 2nd edn., Speyer (2017). http://www.uni-speyer.de/files/de/Lehrstuhle/Wirtz/WirtzDaiser_2017_EGovernment.pdf
22. Pereira, G., et al.: Scientific foundations training and entrepreneurship activities in the domain of ICT-enabled Governance. In: Proceedings of the 19th Annual International Conference on Digital Government Research: Governance in the Data Age, Delft, The Netherlands (2018)

23. Alexopoulos C., Lachana Z., Androutsopoulou A., Diamantopoulou V., Charalabidis Y., Loutsaris M.: How machine learning is changing e-Government. In: Proceedings of the 12th International Conference on Theory and Practice of Electronic Governance (ICEGOV2019). ACM Press, Melbourne (2019)
24. Casalino, N.: Learning to connect: a training model for public sector on advanced e-government services and inter-organizational cooperation. Int. J. Adv. Corp. Learn. (iJAC) 7(1), 24–31 (2014)
25. Casalino, N., Buonocore, F., Rossignoli, C., Ricciardi, F.: Transparency, openness and knowledge sharing for rebuilding and strengthening government institutions. In: Proceedings of the WBE 2013 Conference, IASTED-ACTA Press Zurich, Innsbruck, Austria (2013)
26. Janssen, M., Attard, J., Alexopoulos, C.: Introduction to the Minitrack on data-driven government: creating value from big and open linked data. In: Proceedings of the 52nd Hawaii International Conference on System Sciences (2019)
27. Kassen, M.: E-Government as a universal political value. In: Understanding Systems of e-Government, pp. 1–26. Rowman & Littlefield, New York (2015)
28. Vlahovic, N., Vracic, T.: An overview of e-government 3.0 implementation. In: Khosrow-Pour, M. (ed.) Encyclopedia of Information Science and Technology, 3rd edn, pp. 2700–2708. IGI Global, Hershey (2015). Information Science Reference
29. Scholl, H.J.: Five trends that matter: challenges to 21st century electronic government. Inf. Polity 17(3–4), 317–327 (2012)
30. Ojo, A., Millard, J.: Government 3.0–Next Generation Government Technology Infrastructure and Services: Roadmaps, Enabling Technologies & Challenges, vol. 32. Springer, Cham (2017). https://doi.org/10.1007/978-3-319-63743-3
31. Katsonis, M., Botros, A.: Digital government: a primer and professional perspectives. Aust. J. Public Adm. 74(1), 42–52 (2015)
32. Smelser, N.J., Baltes, P.B.: International Encyclopedia of the Social & Behavioral Sciences, vol. 11. Elsevier, Amsterdam (2001)
33. Nielsen, M.M.: Governance failure in light of Government 3.0: Foundations for building next generation eGovernment maturity models. In: Ojo, A., Millard, J. (eds.) Government 3.0–Next Generation Government Technology Infrastructure and Services, pp. 63–109. Springer, Cham (2017). https://doi.org/10.1007/978-3-319-63743-3_4
34. Charalabidis, Y., Loukis, E., Androutsopoulou, A., Karkaletsis, V., Triantafillou, A.: Passive crowdsourcing in government using social media. Transform. Gov. People Process Policy 8(2), 283–308 (2014)
35. Spiliotopoulou, L., Charalabidis, Y., Loukis, E., Diamantopoulou, V.: A framework for advanced social media exploitation in government for crowdsourcing. Transform. Gov. People Process Policy 8(4), 545–568 (2014)
36. Loukis, E.N.: Citizen-sourcing for public policy making: theoretical foundations, methods and evaluation. In: Gil-Garcia, J.R., Pardo, T.A., Luna-Reyes, L.F. (eds.) Policy Analytics, Modelling, and Informatics. PAIT, vol. 24, pp. 179–203. Springer, Cham (2018). https://doi.org/10.1007/978-3-319-61762-6_8
37. Ølnes, S., Ubacht, J., Janssen, M.: Blockchain in government. Benefits and implications of distributed ledger technology for information sharing. Gov. Inf. Q. 34(3), 355–364 (2017)
38. National Information Society Agency, Government 3.0: Dreaming New Korea (2013). http://www.gov30.kr
39. Layne, K., Lee, J.: Developing fully functional e-government: a four stage model. Gov. Inf. Q. 18(2), 122–136 (2001)
40. Lee, J.: 10 year retrospect on stage models of e-Government: a qualitative meta-synthesis. Gov. Inf. Q. 27(3), 220–230 (2010)

41. DeBrí, F., Bannister, F.: e-Government stage models: a contextual critique. In: Proceedings of 48th Hawaii International Conference on System Sciences (2015)
42. Almuftah, H., Weerakkody, V., Sivarajah, U.: Comparing and contrasting e-government maturity models: a qualitative-meta synthesis. In: Scholl, H.J., et al. (eds.) Electronic Government and Electronic Participation. IOS Press, Amsterdam (2016)
43. Scholta, H., Mertens, W., Kowalkiewicz, M., Becker, J.: From one-stop shop to no-stop shop: an e-government stage model. Gov. Inf. Q. **36**(1), 11–26 (2019)
44. Androutsopoulou, A., Charalabidis, Y., Loukis, E.: Policy informatics in the social media era: analyzing opinions for policy making. In: Edelmann, N., Parycek, P., Misuraca, G., Panagiotopoulos, P., Charalabidis, Y., Virkar, S. (eds.) ePart 2018. LNCS, vol. 11021, pp. 129–142. Springer, Cham (2018). https://doi.org/10.1007/978-3-319-98578-7_11

E-Government Research Domain: Comparing the International and Russian Research Agenda

Yury Kabanov[1,2(✉)], Andrei V. Chugunov[1],
and Boris Nizomutdinov[1]

[1] ITMO University, St. Petersburg, Russia
ykabanov@hse.ru, chugunov@corp.ifmo.ru,
boris-wels@yandex.ru
[2] National Research University Higher School of Economics,
St. Petersburg, Russia

Abstract. Positioning e-government as a discipline is a matter of continuous discussion, and it remains topical to estimate its conceptual integrity and explore the interconnection between the main research contexts, especially due to the emergence of new areas like e-participation. The analysis of the national research programs and their comparison to the global agenda is also becoming more salient. Addressing these two issues by means of a scientometrics approach, we explore the extended e-government domain on the global scale and in the Russian Federation. Findings suggest that the global e-government represents a coherent field, although further integration between research contexts is important. At the same time, the Russian e-government research is lagging behind, due to low internationalization and few stimuli for knowledge production.

Keywords: E-Government · E-Participation · E-Democracy · Scientometrics

1 Introduction

The shape of e-government as a discipline is a matter of continuous discussions. Scholars emphasize its fragmentation due to the diversified researchers' background [22, 25] or the overall discipline immaturity [24]. While further specialization has led to the emergence of the new, relatively independent areas, like e-participation [27], the field may benefit from this variety, as put by Scholl, if "developing into an integrative science with multi-, inter-, and transdisciplinary characteristics" [31, p. 35]. It calls for further analysis of the research domain, its conceptual structure, integrity and inter-disciplinarity, when taken along with e-participation and e-democracy areas.

At the same time, it is no less important to contrast the global research agenda with the national patterns of knowledge production, which are usually "under the radar" of the international academia, despite the growing interest in this subject [6, 7, 9]. Such analysis is helpful in formulating steps forward for national research, and to asses the e-government research domain in a more complex way.

I. Lindgren et al. (Eds.): EGOV 2019, LNCS 11685, pp. 18–30, 2019.
https://doi.org/10.1007/978-3-030-27325-5_2

The goal of this paper is hence twofold: first, to overview the extended e-government domain in order to reveal the major research contexts, their interconnections and dynamics. Secondly, to compare them to the national agenda of e-government studies, taking Russia as a case. The study employs a scientometrics analysis based on keyword co-occurrence. The structure of the paper is as follows. First, we overview the background literature on how scientometrics complements literature reviews in understanding e-government. Secondly, we present the methods and data we use. Empirical findings are described in the fourth and fifth sections, followed by a discussion of the results, limitations and possible steps forward.

2 Background

Systematic literature review is a demanding genre in e-government, aiming at assessing the maturity of the discipline [24], pointing out pitfalls [13, 36] and providing methodological coherence [22]. For e-participation, literature systematization [19, 20, 27, 32] became vital in establishing the field identity. As the research volume expands, more focused reviews emerge, introducing emerging topics [1, 12, 21], reviewing particular outlets [8, 11] or surveying scholars on their new topics of interest [29, 30]. Along with thematic and institutional angles, the geographical one is getting salience, where scholars evaluate local dynamics of knowledge production and discuss problems of internationalization [6, 7, 9, 10]. Despite their indisputable value, literature reviews are often criticized for their possible bias and errors in literature selection [26, 37], and here scientometrics tools seem a promising alternative, and their usage is now quite regular in e-government. There have been several attempts to run such analysis using various software, search queries and databases, mostly focusing on analyzing hotspots and emerging topics, and assessing the multidisciplinary and international nature of knowledge production.

The identification of trends depends on the timespan and technique employed. For instance, Cheng and Ding found 5 core themes in e-government research: (1) e-government development; (2) e-government evolution; (3) user research; (4) information storage and (5) standards and specification, with the emerging topic of performance evaluation [4]. The analysis by Jalali revealed that the trend in e-government is towards the analysis of openness, media, cloud services and participation [15]. For e-participation, the analysis by Qi et al. emphasized the increasing focus on democracy and social media [23].

A more nuanced analysis for both e-government and e-participation was presented by Alcaide–Muñoz et al. with *SciMAT* to build co-word networks and analyze the temporal dynamics [2, 26]. In the case of e-government they studied several sub-periods, identifying emerging, fading and established co-word clusters. The temporal evolution is justified by the set of concepts emerging (e.g. "social media" and "smart city") and fading (e.g. "administrative reform") overtime [2, p. 551]. In case of e-participation, they found several research foci, e.g. *techno-social, instrumental, contextual* and *technological* and consider that there is an "evolution of this field of knowledge to a more techno-social system" [26, p. 118].

The issues of collaboration between countries, institutions and authors are analyzed by co-citation or co-authorship analysis. Studies usually emphasize the low level of cooperation between authors and institutions, the gaps between developed and developing countries and the dominance of the US institutions in knowledge production [16]. While multidisciplinary dimensions seem evident, the interdisciplinary nature of the e-government domain (as described by Scholl) [31] is questionable, as suggested by Hwang and Murphy [14]. A similar conclusion is implied in Bohman's analysis of how various technologies are portrayed in e-participation research, when scholars seem to neglect "relevant theories of technology from adjacent fields such as information systems, sociology of technology, or evolutionary economics" [3, p. 88].

While much has been done, some challenges and research gaps remain. First, although several scholars have successfully identified the front edges of e-government studies, few attempts have been made to overview and visualize the domain in its integrity. Hence, rather than defining the emerging topics, we aim at mapping the whole area, using the tool which has a clear advantage in visualizing science maps (the *VOSviewer*). Secondly, previous results are usually fuzzy due to the various research queries: here we believe e-government, e-governance, e-participation, and e-democracy should be taken as the core topics in the integral sample. It helps to avoid overexpansion of the domain, e.g. by including all various forms of online participation [18], and to grasp the identity of the research area (i.e. authors using such words associate themselves with it). Thirdly, there is a problem in publication selection: conferences are usually ignored, whilst they have proved their significance [11, 30].

Fourthly, a clear research gap remains in terms of the multi-/interdisciplinary nature of e-government. It seems that standard tools are not very helpful (e.g. LNCS conference proceedings are usually related to Computer Science, while there can be issues from various disciplines). Rather, we suggest to look at the concepts used, how they can possibly relate to certain disciplinary dimensions, and then whether these concepts are shared by various disciplines or rather adhere to particular fields.

Finally, while previous literature suggests the importance of analyzing the national research agendas as well, still many cases remain under-explored. Although the recent article by Erzhenin [9] shed some light on some of the national e-government studies peculiarities (like their concentration on the Economics, Political Science and Law), this analysis employs a narrow definition of e-government and no network analysis is presented, so we hope to expand these findings both in scope and in methodology.

3   Research Design

Our scientometrics analysis is conducted using the *VOSviewer* software (http://www.vosviewer.com/), developed by van Eck and Waltman. Its key advantage is the interpretable visualization of bibliometric datasets [35], as science mapping "reflects the similarity of relatedness of the items as accurately as possible" [34, p. 5], giving more accurate results in normalization of co-occurrence [33], which is our main method. Co-occurrence helps to identify how often concepts are found together in various samples, thus helping to construct a conceptual map of the discipline.

For the analysis of the international and Russian research agenda we selected the *Web of Science (WoS)* database and *eLIBRARY* (https://elibrary.ru/) respectively. The analysis of the latter is challenging, as there is no automatic option to retrieve bibliographic data, so the information was gathered with a specifically developed parser.

In both databases we employed the query: *TS = ("e-governance" OR "egovernance" OR "electronic governance" OR "e-government" OR "electronic government" OR "egovernment" OR "e-participation" OR "electronic participation" OR "eparticipation" OR "e-democracy" OR "electronic democracy").* In the case of *WoS* we found 10,542 documents for 2000–2018 (most published in 2007–2018). Publications are almost equally distributed among journals and conference proceedings, and mostly in English. In *eLIBRARY,* 23,000 items were found, but some data (like publication year and citation) were missing due to technical reasons. Another limitation of *eLIBRARY* is that it indexes much more publications, but usually at the expense of quality. Also, some publications are indexed by both databases, though the overlap is tiny.

With the *VOSviewer* we conducted a co-occurrence keyword analysis for both international and Russian databases, which estimated the intensity of one term usage with another. A special thesaurus (442 terms) was compiled to translate Russian terms into English, to combine similar keywords (e.g. "electronic services" and "e-services") and to eliminate possible typos. For the final analysis we took only the keywords occurring at least 15 times in the sample, deliberately excluding the query terms: they obviously occur in most publications and skew the analysis. Thus the final selection of keywords comprises of 364 terms for the international database and 281 terms for the Russian one. The properties of *VOSviewer* were set for better representations of results: co-occurrence based on full counting method, with association strength normalization technique (attraction – "1", repulsion – "0") [35]. We set 15 terms (10 for *eLIBRARY*) as a minimum to form clusters, which are then analyzed by looking at the combinations of keywords of which they comprise. In the visualizations (Figs. 1 and 3) the label size depicts its total link strength, while the width of links portrays the strength between two terms. Only links with the minimum strength of 30 are shown.

4 Research Contexts in the International Agenda

As expected, the e-government represents a vast array of research contexts (Fig. 1). Based on the association strength between the keywords, five clusters were revealed. We refer them to as *Infrastructure* (green), *Adoption* (yellow), *Management* (blue), *Participation* (red) and *Development* (purple). Such labels were given in an attempt to cover the most widespread issues related to each of the clusters. Table 1 gives additional information, including the number of terms in each cluster and possible subtopics deduced from the keywords each cluster has. It should be noted that the list of such subtopics is not exclusive, and some clusters may overlap in addressing the same issue, and given mostly for a simplified reference to clusters.

Infrastructure cluster deals with how to create interoperable e-government information systems, set administrative workflows, provide usable and accessible services, thus also including public administration issues. It is rather disperse, falling into "hard" technical issues (like "interoperability" and "ontology"), administrative processes and questions of e-services' accommodation ("personalization", "usability"), including "m-government". Here it is more connected to the second cluster – *Adoption*. The latter is explicitly empirical, quantitative and casual, tying e-government to e-commerce and using several dominating adoption models (like TAM and IS success models). The concept of trust in various applications is also of high interest here.

The *Management* cluster seems to cover aspects of public sector's tackling of innovations, digital transformations and organizational change. This involves, among other things, coordination of the interaction between different stakeholders, strategic management, intraorganizational changes and impact.

The largest cluster in the domain is *Participation* – a binary star system of e-democracy and e-participation, with a scope broad enough to disperse throughout other research contexts. It is more prone to public management when it comes to openness (e.g. open government data), and gets closer to *Development* and *Adoption* in questions of equality and inclusion. Its core topics are those connected to governance, citizens involvement and control, social media, local governments, as well as smartness (smart city and government) and co-creation. The most dispersed cluster is *Development,* covering important issues of adaptation and use of new technologies, their impact on developing countries in general and quality of institutions.

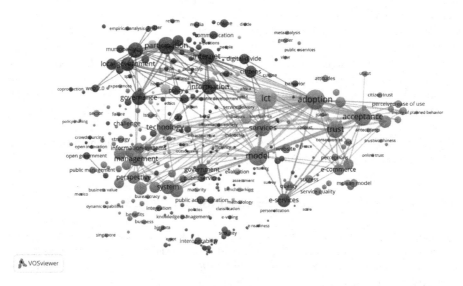

Fig. 1. Co-occurrence maps of keywords in the international agenda. Source: VOSviewer (Color figure online)

In general, we may agree with Scholl, that the e-government domain "has already established itself as a multi-discipline endeavor spanning the full spectrum of hard and soft as well as pure and applied sciences" [31, p. 32]. The international research agenda indeed seems to have "harder" (e.g. *Infrastructure*) and "softer" (e.g. *Participation*) contexts, where all clusters play their role in understanding the phenomena: how

Table 1. Clusters in E-government international research agenda

Cluster	Number of keywords	Indicative subtopics	Indicative keywords
Infrastructure (green)	86	E-Government architecture	ontology, semantic web, linked data, cloud computing
		Administrative workflow	standardization, information sharing
		Security	privacy, authentication, e-signature
		E-Services	personalization, usability, accessibility
		Process management	project management, business project
		Public administration	public services, government
Adoption (yellow)	56	Factors of adoption	structural equation modeling, meta-analysis
		Technology acceptance	perceived usefulness, ease of use
		IS success model	service quality, information quality
		Trust	consumer trust, online trust
Management (blue)	68	Interaction of actors	bureaucracy, stakeholders, collaboration
		Strategic management	innovations, implementation
		Intraorganizational	capabilities, leadership
		Impact	performance, public value
Participation (red)	106	Openness	open government, open data
		Equality	inclusion, digital divide
		Governance	policy, decision making
		Citizen involvement	deliberation, community
		Political communication	media, elections
		Social media	Facebook, twitter
		Public control	accountability, transparency
		Local & smart	municipality, smart city
Development (purple)	48	Adaptation and use	ethics, diffusion
		Developing countries	ICT4D, Africa,
		Productivity	sustainable development
		Institutional quality	Good governance
		Evaluation	Benchmarking, assessment

e-tools are created, implemented and adapted, successfully accepted and utilized, and what role they might play in fostering citizens' involvement and human development. Yet we need to point out several peculiarities of the domain. First, as keyword analysis suggests, the hard – soft balance is shifted to a certain extent towards the latter, where it comes to the issues of participation and democracy, or at least to the interim hard-soft disciplines, as far as *Management* and *Infrastructure* are concerned. It may be another indication of the trend that e-government is becoming more citizen-oriented [26], thus calling for the contribution from the Social Sciences field.

Secondly, though most concepts are linked to each other, the link strength between specific terms is rather weak. The clusters are mostly connected via more general anchor concepts like "ict", "internet", "services" but not on particular tools and applications where interdisciplinarity is of value. As an example, while "e-voting" is now more adjacent to *Infrastructure*, the research of this phenomenon can take advantage of "softer" insights as well. So does the concept of trust: while the need to study trust in e-participation was iterated a couple of years ago [28], there are few connections to *Participation*, in comparison to e-services.

Thirdly, though further research is needed, we may support earlier judgments that e-government is still a multi- rather than an interdisciplinary domain [14], and further integration is needed. This task is not an easy one, as the most internally cohesive clusters (that have strong internal links) – *Participation* and *Adoption* – appear to be rather independent from the others: the former is being institutionalized as e-participation area, the latter is keeping coherence due to the limited number of theoretical models (TAM, UTAUT, IS Success Model, etc.) and frequently used quantitative methods (surveys, structural equation modeling).

Another view on the same map is presented on Fig. 2, where we present the overlay visualization based on the impact of each concept in the domain. The size of the item

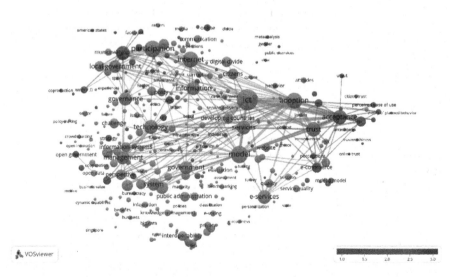

Fig. 2. Overlay visualization by the average normalized citation. Source: VOSviewer (Color figure online)

depicts the number of its occurrences in the sample, while the color represents its average normalized citation score: high (yellow), average (green) and low (blue). The map suggest that the issues covered in relatively more cited literature reside in *Participation* cluster (e.g. "social media", "government", "coproduction") and *Adoption* cluster (e.g. "technology acceptance model", "McLean model", "citizen trust"). Again it does not contradict earlier findings on emerging topics in e-government [2].

5 The Russian Research Agenda on E-Government

The analysis of the Russian research agenda was technically limited due to the reasons described in Sect. 3, so only the co-occurrence map is presented. Overall, 5 clusters were found, but the yellow and purple ones seem to be artifacts with PhD nomenclature terms. Others contain more meaningful and zoomed (Fig. 3), we refer them to as: *Public Services Provision* (deep blue), *ICT in Administration & Economy* (green), and *Internet & Politics* (red).

Even though the number of publications analyzed is much higher as in the previous section, there are fewer terms and clusters extracted, and keywords grouping is not the same. *Public Services Provision* resembles to a certain extent *Infrastructure* in its emphasis on public services ("e-services", "service state") and bureaucracy informatization ("e-document", "e-signature"). Some global hot topics ("open government", "transparency") are also addressed here. *ICT in Administration & Economy* has a topical overlap with *Management* in managerial ("transformation", "strategic planning") and performance ("effectiveness", "monitoring") issues, it also covers infrastructure ("optimization", "standardization") and recent trends towards digital economy

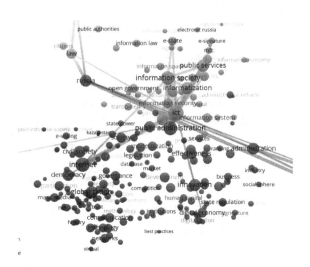

Fig. 3. Co-occurrence maps of keywords in the Russian Agenda. Source: VOSviewer (Color figure online)

("cloud computing", "blockchain"). *Internet & Politics* covers traditional topics of e-democracy ("e-voting") and e-participation ("public initiative"), but is largely focused on political communication.

Our findings echo Erzhenin [9] in that the domain mostly related to social sciences and economy: the balance between *hard* and *soft* sciences here is farther skewed towards the latter. Although some trendy concepts are used, the inclusion of new terms is quite reluctant (e.g. e-democracy is still much more frequently used to denote e-participation issues). At the same time, it is prominent for terms with little use outside the country. In other words, the Russian research agenda is lagging behind the international one in conceptual development, as well as the diversity of scope.

The most intuitive explanation for this is the low level of internationalization, which is indeed a usual suspect [6]. The first aspect of this problem is that few scholars from Russia participate in the international research. In the *Web of Science* sample from Sect. 4 only 123 documents are attributed to the representatives of Russian organizations, with just 96 in English. The majority of documents (71) are conference proceedings papers, and international collaboration is extremely low. This means that the national academic research is to a larger extent developing in isolation from global trends. Yet a more elaborate analysis should be conducted, for example, on the patterns of citation and co-citation in the Russian academia: what international literature "leaks out" to the national research, and to what extent the latter considers it.

The second aspect is the lack of stimuli for the academia to produce knowledge. The global trends in e-government research seem to affect the national agenda only to the extent they reflect the national e-government policy priorities. Thus, *Public Services Provision* relates to the first attempts of building e-government in Russia via e-services and informatization, while *Internet & Politics* (together with "open government") reflects the new period from 2012 onwards, with the attention to public involvement and the creation of e-participation tools [5]. The most recent development is the digital economy (green cluster), which became a national priority in 2018.[1]

Surely, keeping track of government policy is imperative. However, the absence of other stimuli seem to affect the disciplinary bias towards "softer" attempts to explain and justify policies, from the view of politics, economics management and law. The motivation to address e-government in a more holistic way is limited. Firstly, there is no clear impetus from the industry. The new public management, having become a basis for the Russian administrative reform [17], is still a common practice for government and enterprises. The dominance and reluctance of state corporate business produces a low level of demand for innovations in the country,[2] and the salience of globally recognized issues (like digital economy, smart cities, big data) is raised by the government itself, in order to wake the academia up. The similar situation persists in more participatory sectors: whereas government initiatives have fostered the interest towards e-participation and open government, low efficacy of such initiatives and non-competitive politics [5] hinder motivation from within.

---

[1] http://government.ru/rugovclassifier/614/events/.

[2] https://regnum.ru/news/2228216.html.

6 Discussion

Although scientometrics is not new to e-government studies, we hope to contribute to the existing literature of that kind in several respects. First of all, we took a holistic view on the research domain, visualized its general structure and highlight the concepts pertinent to various directions of the academic inquiry. The findings confirm the multidisciplinary nature of the domain, with a visible labor among various subfields in knowledge production, and overall balanced representation across *hard - soft* sciences. Most popular items were also distinguished, thus complementing and confirming earlier findings [2, 4, 15]. At the same time, it questions the interdisciplinarity in e-government research [14, 31], as the clusters are mostly connected via general concepts, though this issue needs further analysis. Our research calls for further collaboration on particular technologies and issues in e-government and e-participation. The presented map might be a guide for such loci of interdisciplinary cooperation.

Secondly, our study complements the research on national research programs [6, 7], by introducing the map of the Russian e-government research. Our findings reverberates the opinion [9] that it differs from the global agenda in scope and depth of inquiry. It is lagging behind the international conceptual and disciplinary development, being dominated. The low internationalization is evident, along with the lack of internal stimuli and demand from business and society to produce innovative and applied research. That raises the need of better cooperation among the Russian and international scholars, as well as collaboration with non-academic actors.

Surely, there are some limitations to this study, as it presents a continuous research project. The use of keyword co-occurrence needs to be complimented by the clustering of concepts from abstracts, and additional software is to be used for advanced network analysis. Some relevant papers might have been missing, not indexed in the *Web of Science*, or not containing the keywords for which we have searched. There are also some challenges in retrieving bibliometric data from the *eLIBRARY,* making it impossible to include other types of bibliometric analysis. We hope that these problems and limitations will be reduced in further research.

7 Conclusion

Though scientometrics should not substitute in-depth literature reviews [37], it seems a promising technique of academic and practical value. It allows to explore the conceptual integrity and institutionalization of the research field, and to reveal problems of the national research agenda. We believe this approach can enrich our knowledge of the field, at the same time facilitating its interdisciplinarity, integrity and identity.

As a work in progress, this paper has helped to find new directions of research. We plan to expand the scope by adding new data from alternative bibliometric databases, as well as by retrieving keywords from the abstracts, which help to include more important outlets and research contexts. This can be refined by using additional network analysis techniques to come to more rigorous findings. Also, one of our future research directions is the network analysis of publication sources (journals and conferences) to explore their significance and specialization in e-government research, as well as to reveal patterns of collaboration. It can improve our understanding of the domain from an institutional point of view. Also, since the number of scientometrics techniques and software tools is increasing, it might be an effective way to compare and cross-validate findings achieved. We believe such efforts would contribute to the discussion of the discipline state and perspectives.

Acknowledgement. The research was supported by the Russian Science Foundation, grant № 18-18-00360 'E-participation as Politics and Public Policy Dynamic Factor'.

References

1. Alarabiat, A., Soares, D.S., Estevez, E.: Electronic participation with a special reference to social media - a literature review. In: Tambouris, E., et al. (eds.) ePart 2016. LNCS, vol. 9821, pp. 41–52. Springer, Cham (2016). https://doi.org/10.1007/978-3-319-45074-2_4
2. Alcaide-Muñoz, L., Rodríguez-Bolívar, M.P., Cobo, M.J., Herrera-Viedma, E.: Analysing the scientific evolution of e-Government using a science mapping approach. Gov. Inf. Q. **34** (3), 545–555 (2017). https://doi.org/10.1016/j.giq.2017.05.002
3. Bohman, S.: Information technology in eParticipation research: a word frequency analysis. In: Tambouris, E., Macintosh, A., Bannister, F. (eds.) ePart 2014. LNCS, vol. 8654, pp. 78–89. Springer, Heidelberg (2014). https://doi.org/10.1007/978-3-662-44914-1_7
4. Cheng, S.Y., Ding, L.: Mapping of electronic government: the trend of research fronts. In: 2014 Seventh International Joint Conference on Computational Sciences and Optimization, pp. 509–513. IEEE (2014)
5. Chugunov, A.V., Kabanov, Y., Zenchenkova, K.: Russian e-petitions portal: exploring regional variance in use. In: Tambouris, E., Panagiotopoulos, P., Sæbø, Ø., Wimmer, M.A., Pardo, T.A., Charalabidis, Y., Soares, D.S., Janowski, T. (eds.) ePart 2016. LNCS, vol. 9821, pp. 109–122. Springer, Cham (2016). https://doi.org/10.1007/978-3-319-45074-2_9
6. Coelho, T.R., Przeybilovicz, E., Cunha, M.A., Echternacht, T.H.S.: Positioning Brazil in international eGov research: a proposal based from literature review. In: 2016 49th Hawaii International Conference on System Sciences (HICSS), pp. 2677–2686, IEEE (2016). https://doi.org/10.1109/hicss.2016.336
7. Dias, G.P.: A decade of Portuguese research in e-government: evolution, current standing, and ways forward. Electron. Gov. Int. J. **12**(3), 201–222 (2006)
8. Dwivedi, Y.K.: An analysis of e-Government research published in Transforming Government: People, Process and Policy (TGPPP). Transform. Gov. People Process Policy **3**(1), 7–15 (2009). https://doi.org/10.1108/17506160910940704
9. Erzhenin, R.V.: Electronic government: review of scientific publications and research. Public Adm. Issues **3**, 205–228 (2018). [in Russian]
10. Fonou Dombeu, J.V., Rannyai, N.: African e-government research landscape. Afr. J. Inf. Syst. **6**(3), 85–119 (2014)
11. Grönlund, Å.: State of the art in e-Gov research – a survey. In: Traunmüller, R. (ed.) EGOV 2004. LNCS, vol. 3183, pp. 178–185. Springer, Heidelberg (2004). https://doi.org/10.1007/978-3-540-30078-6_30
12. Hassan, L., Hamari, J.: Gamification of e-participation: a literature review. In: Proceedings of the 52nd Hawaii International Conference on System Sciences (2019). http://hdl.handle.net/10125/59744

13. Heeks, R., Bailur, S.: Analyzing e-government research: Perspectives, philosophies, theories, methods, and practice. Gov. Inf. Q. **24**(2), 243–265 (2007). https://doi.org/10.1016/j.giq.2006.06.005

14. Hwang, S., Murphy, P.: Mapping out e-government research literature: how interdisciplinary was it for the blooming decades? Electron. Gov. Int. J. **13**(3), 224–241 (2017). https://doi.org/10.1504/eg.2017.086684

15. Jafarjalali, S.M.: Visualizing e-government emerging and fading themes using SNA techniques. In: 2016 10th International Conference on e-Commerce in Developing Countries: with focus on e-Tourism (ECDC). IEEE (2016). https://doi.org/10.1109/ecdc.2016.7492983

16. Khan, G.F., Park, H.W.: The e-government research domain: a triple helix network analysis of collaboration at the regional, country, and institutional levels. Gov. Inf. Q. **30**(2), 182–193 (2013). https://doi.org/10.1016/j.giq.2012.09.003

17. Klimenko, A.V.: A decade of administrative reform: results and new challenges. Public Adm. Issues **1**, 8–51 (2014). [in Russian]

18. Lutz, C., Hoffmann, C.P., Meckel, M.: Beyond just politics: a systematic literature review of online participation. First Monday **19**(7), 1–36 (2014). https://doi.org/10.5210/fm.v19i7

19. Macintosh, A.: E-democracy and e-participation research in Europe. In: Chen, H., et al. (eds.) Digital Government Integrated Series in Information Systems, vol. 17, pp. 85–102. Springer, Boston (2008). https://doi.org/10.1007/978-0-387-71611-4_5

20. Medaglia, R.: eParticipation research: moving characterization forward (2006–2011). Gov. Inf. Q. **29**(3), 346–360 (2012). https://doi.org/10.1016/j.giq.2012.02.010

21. Meijer, A., Bolívar, M.P.R.: Governing the smart city: a review of the literature on smart urban governance. Int. Rev. Adm. Sci. **82**(2), 392–408 (2016). https://doi.org/10.1177/0020852314564308

22. Meijer, A., Bekkers, V.: A metatheory of e-government: creating some order in a fragmented research field. Gov. Inf. Q. **32**(3), 237–245 (2015). https://doi.org/10.1016/j.giq.2015.04.006

23. Qi, T., Wang, T., Ma, Y., Zhang, W., Zhu, Y.: A scientometric analysis of e-participation research. Int. J. Crowd Sci. **2**(2), 136–148 (2018). https://doi.org/10.1108/IJCS-08-2018-0015

24. Reece, B.: E-government literature review. J. E-gov. **3**(1), 69–110 (2006). https://doi.org/10.1300/J399v03n01_05

25. Ridley, G.: EGovernment: making sense of fragmentation and contradiction. In: E-gov pre-ECIS Workshop, 8th June 2008, Galway Ireland (2008). https://eprints.utas.edu.au/7062/

26. Rodríguez-Bolívar, M.P., Alcaide-Muñoz, L., Cobo, M.J.: Analyzing the scientific evolution and impact of e-Participation research in JCR journals using science mapping. Int. J. Inf. Manag. **40**, 111–119 (2018). https://doi.org/10.1016/j.ijinfomgt.2017.12.011

27. Sæbø, Ø., Rose, J., Flak, L.S.: The shape of eParticipation: characterizing an emerging research area. Gov. Inf. Q. **25**(3), 400–428 (2008). https://doi.org/10.1016/j.giq.2007.04.007

28. Scherer, S., Wimmer, M.A.: Trust in e-participation: literature review and emerging research needs. In: Proceedings of the 8th International Conference on Theory and Practice of Electronic Governance, ICEGOV, pp. 61–70, ACM (2014). https://doi.org/10.1145/2691195.2691237

29. Scholl, H.J.: Electronic government research: topical directions and preferences. In: Wimmer, Maria A., Janssen, M., Scholl, H.J. (eds.) EGOV 2013. LNCS, vol. 8074, pp. 1–13. Springer, Heidelberg (2013). https://doi.org/10.1007/978-3-642-40358-3_1

30. Scholl, H.J.J., Dwivedi, Y.K.: Forums for electronic government scholars: insights from a 2012/2013 study. Gov. Inf. Q. **31**(2), 229–242 (2014). https://doi.org/10.1016/j.giq.2013.10.008

31. Scholl, H.J.J.: Discipline or interdisciplinary study domain? Challenges and promises in electronic government research. In: Chen, H., et al. (eds.) Digital Government, Integrated Series in Information Systems, vol. 17, pp. 21–41. Springer, Boston (2008). https://doi.org/10.1007/978-0-387-71611-4_2

32. Susha, I., Grönlund, Å.: eParticipation research: systematizing the field. Gov. Inf. Q. **29**(3), 373–382 (2012). https://doi.org/10.1016/j.giq.2011.11.005

33. Van Eck, N.J.V., Waltman, L.: How to normalize cooccurrence data? An analysis of some well-known similarity measures. J. Am. Soc. Inform. Sci. Technol. **60**(8), 1635–1651 (2009). https://doi.org/10.1002/asi.21075

34. Van Eck, N.J., Waltman, L., Dekker, R., van den Berg, J.: A comparison of two techniques for bibliometric mapping: multidimensional scaling and VOS. J. Am. Soc. Inf. Soc. Tech. **61** (12), 2405–2416 (2010). https://doi.org/10.1002/asi.21421

35. Van Eck, N.J., Waltman, L.: Software survey: VOSviewer, a computer program for bibliometric mapping. Scientometrics **84**(2), 523–538 (2010). https://doi.org/10.1007/s11192-009-0146-3

36. Yildiz, M.: E-government research: reviewing the literature, limitations, and ways forward. Gov. Inf. Q. **24**(3), 646–665 (2007). https://doi.org/10.1016/j.giq.2007.01.00

37. Zupic, I., Čater, T.: Bibliometric methods in management and organization. Organ. Res. Meth. **18**(3), 429–472 (2015). https://doi.org/10.1177/1094428114562629

From Automatic Data Processing to Digitalization: What is Past is Prologue

Leif Sundberg$^{(\boxtimes)}$ [ID]

Mid Sweden University, Holmgatan 10, 851 70 Sundsvall, Sweden
leif.sundberg@miun.se

Abstract. Governments across the world are intensifying their use of digital technology. One way to generate an understanding of the effects of technology in the public sector is to study values. The purpose of this paper is to investigate how values in the Swedish national e-Government have developed over time. This research studies Swedish government documents between 1961 and 2018 during three periods of computerization: Automatic Data Processing, Information Technology, and Digitalization. A theoretical framework that consists of four value positions (i.e. professionalism, efficiency, service, and engagement) is utilized. The findings suggest that technological paradigms tend to generate value congruence in policy documents, followed by value divergence in evaluations. Currently, digitalization is perceived as the enabler of several values. While both IT and digitalization are referred to as tools or means, the development towards an information, knowledge, or data-driven society is also described as inevitable. The service ideal became dominant through the use of internet-based technology, while efficiency is often prioritized in large-scale projects. Engagement values are associated with a futuristic form of democracy in government documents, but rarely converted into practice. The role of professionalism is two-fold: it acts both as an enabler and as a constraint to the other values. The paper concludes with suggesting that the current development of adapting laws and regulations to enable digitalization might lead to an eroded bureaucracy, with uncertain value.

Keywords: e-Government · Digitalization · Values

1 Introduction

According to Heeks and Bailur [17], the term 'electronic government' was first mentioned in 1993; the abbreviation 'e-Government' gained prominence in 1997. This research field gained popularity at the end of the 1990s and has since steadily grown due to governments intensifying their use of digital technology. Another common term to describe practice and research in this area is 'digital government.' The digital aspect of digital government can be understood

Published by Springer Nature Switzerland AG 2019
I. Lindgren et al. (Eds.): EGOV 2019, LNCS 11685, pp. 31–42, 2019.
https://doi.org/10.1007/978-3-030-27325-5_3

as either the process of digitization (i.e. converting analog signals to digital) or digitalization, which refers to the macro-level changes associated with increased usage of digital technology [3]. In the public sector, digitalization can be linked to the idea of transformative government—a reformed sector that utilizes digital technology to enable certain values. Bannister and Connolly [2] argued that the ideals associated with transformative government can be expressed as public values, or modes of behavior that are considered "right." Bannister and Connolly [1] contended that governments, professionals, and scholars tend to focus on the latest technological developments before the older technologies have been fully exploited or understood. Fukumoto and Bozeman [15] argued that longitudinal and historical studies can improve theory and research on public values. Grönlund contended that eGovernment research must become "deeper", through an increased understanding of the relation between technology, organization and government values [16]. Stouby-Persson et al. [26] performed a study of how values developed over time in Denmark's e-Government strategies from 1994 and 2016. These authors called for additional studies on the stability of values in e-Government strategies over time in other national contexts.

Against this backdrop, the purpose of this paper is to investigate how values in Sweden's national e-Government have developed over time. The research is carried out through a content analysis of historical Swedish government documents.

The history of Swedish computing post World War II has been subject to a large number of publications in prior research (see e.g. [20,22,24]). This paper adds to this research by contributing with a public values perspective, and by adding material from the digitalization era.

The paper proceeds as follows. Section 2 provides a theoretical framework of e-Government values. Section 3 discusses materials and methods utilized in this study. The results are presented in Sect. 4, followed by a discussion in Sect. 5. Finally, conclusions are drawn in Sect. 6.

2   Theoretical Framework: e-Government Value Positions

Different paradigms in the public sector have replaced and advanced the roles of citizens, policymakers, and the government administration. Rose et al. [37], (see also [36]) presented a value classification based on these paradigms. This section continues with a more detailed outline of the respective positions, which are summarized in Table 1.

2.1   Professionalism

In traditional Weberian governments, rules, due process, and neutrality are the core values that should determine how the public sector acts. The bureaucracy is independent, robust, and consistent, governed by rule of law, where the public record is the basis of accountability. The role of e-Government, according to the professionalism ideal, is to provide a flexible and secure digital public record

Table 1. e-Government value positions

Position	Representative values
Professionalism	Durability, equity, legality and accountability
Efficiency	Value for money, productivity, and performance
Service	Public service, citizen centricity, service level and quality
Engagement	Democracy, deliberation, and participation

to support standardized administrative procedures; IT constitutes an information infrastructure that enacts the regulatory system. The public manager is a rational-legal authority limited by its sphere of competence within a hierarchical organization that builds on fixed areas of activities and division of labor [37] The bureaucratic organization is superior to other forms of organization: Weber compared the bureaucratic apparatus superiority with a machine's superior production ability over non-mechanical modes of production. Weber's view on the future of the bureaucracy was rather dystopic: he argued that we are destined to live in an 'iron cage' of rationalization where the individual has very little control [40].

2.2 Efficiency

In the 1980s, a new paradigm that is closely connected to the market economy emerged: new public management (NPM). According to NPM, Weberian bureaucracy failed to answer customer needs, which led to under-performance and poor legitimacy. The dominating core value of NPM is efficiency: The public administration is slim and efficient, minimizing waste of public resources. The citizen is seen as a customer whose demands can be satisfied by proper government supply. In NPM, the distinction between the public and private sectors is removed and accountability is achieved through obtaining results, which are measured in monetary terms. Furthermore, the ideal organizational structures are small competing units, inspired by private sector corporations [18]. IT is associated with automation, and is considered a tool for productivity that substitutes labor. The role of e-Government is to streamline, rationalize and transform the public administration around digital technologies [37].

2.3 Service

The main criticism of NPM is its emphasis on efficiency by copying features from the private sector. Moore [25] argued that, in the private sector, the individual can refrain from consuming a product whose value is perceived as limited, while in the public sector, the government uses its coercive power of taxation to produce services that may be mandatory for individuals. The challenge for the public manager is to identify what consequences will produce public value. IT is seen as a service enabler in relation to this ideal, increasing access and quality of services. Dunleavy et al. [9] used the term "digital-era governance" to describe this paradigm shift and identified three characteristic themes: reintegration (as opposed to fragmentation), needs-based holism (i.e. reorganization to create seamless, non-stop solutions) and digitization processes (e.g. electronic service delivery).

2.4 Engagement

The engagement ideal builds on the idea of actively engaging citizens through participatory processes. Based on liberal democratic ideas, civil society stakeholders are expected to act as co-creators in, for example, policy development. The role of IT and e-Government in this ideal is to support deliberative and communicative interaction between governments and citizens [37]. In this new paradigm, sometimes termed New Public Service, governance is based on democratic citizenship, community, and civil society. The primary role of the public servant in the engagement paradigm is to help citizens articulate and meet their shared interests rather than attempt to control or steer society [6].

2.5 Value Relationships

The value positions have some features in common, while others are fundamentally different. The end products of both Weberian bureaucracy and New public management is efficiency, while respective position's approach to ethics differ: Weber's bureaucracy is rule-based, while NPM is performance based: rule ethics versus consequence ethics. In one paradigm, the citizen is a client, in the other a customer. Value positions can be congruent or divergent; they can support or conflict with each other. Congruent value relations can be causal (i.e. one value will inevitably give rise to another value), a prerequisite (i.e. one value requires another value), a side effect (i.e. one value might cause another value), or synergistic (two or more values are entangled in a mutually dependent achievement). Divergent value relations can be competing (e.g. over resources), negating (i.e. one value may end another value), or transformative (i.e. one value will turn into another value) [37].

3 Materials and Methods

The unit of analysis in this paper was Swedish policy documents. The research took the following research steps:

1. Formulate and motivate purpose (Sect. 1).
2. Select and motivate sources of data (further elaborated on below).
3. Choose categories for coding the data (Sect. 2).
4. Interpret the material through content analysis.

The criterion used for inclusion is that the documents should reflect perceptions on values associated with digital technology (e.g. "Information Technology") in the public sector. The included documents are of three kinds: (a) results of comprehensive investigations on the use, or potential use, of digital technology (b) strategies from central government, and (c) evaluation reports from appointed agencies. The total number of documents studied is 22, which are referred to in the results section. The material is by no means a complete set of documents on Swedish computing history, but rather a sample of documents that reflects perceptions of values over time.

Since there is already an existing theory (see Sect. 2) about the phenomenon, directed content analysis was utilized [19], using an interpretative stance. In this type of analysis, existing theory is used to generate coding schemes for the included variables. The four value positions in Sect. 2 were used to create the coding categories and operational definitions. Content expressing values was highlighted and placed into one of the four categories (i.e. professionalism, efficiency, service, and engagement), together with an interpretation of their relation (i.e. congruence or divergence).

4 Results

This study identified three periods of computerization in the Swedish public sector following World War II: Automatic Data Processing (ADP), IT, and Digitalization. This section proceeds with the results from the content analysis presented in chronological order in 4.1–4.3.

4.1 Automatic Data Processing

In 1955, a committee was directed by the Department of Finance to investigate the potential use of electronic computational machines within public administration, particularly cost savings. The committee released two reports, describing how a computer worked (basically, the von Neumann architecture), together with potential areas of application (often in the form of keeping registries) and predictions about their future use. Although some concerns about questionable effects of computers in the United States are raised, the fast development of new and improved, transistor-based computers suggests a bright future: *The fast technical development is accompanied by an increased interest for the new machines. With increased knowledge, ADP is increasingly becoming a step towards increased rationalization.* ADP is described as a part of a structural transformation of society, which is characterized by increased automation. One section describes "online" use by establishing a remote connection to a computer. Although the current term 'interoperability' is not used in the report, ideas about how to interlink registers between systems started to take hold. To achieve this goal, additional investigations and standardization were deemed necessary [12,13]. One of the reports report concluded with a suggestion to create a new government entity to coordinate ADP. However, no new government entity was created.

Instead, the coordinating role was given to the The Swedish Agency for Public Management (APM), which, at the time, was responsible for rationalization matters.

The optimism of the 1960s was replaced in the 1970s by economic recession and worries about the potential harmful effects of computer technology. This decade was characterized by increased political control of technology. A 1972 report, points out that, *Through the coordination of several information systems, an increased amount of information can be processed. Due to this, ADP creates increased risks for privacy intrusions.* The responsible committee emphasizes both the concerns raised in the public debate and the benefits of using computers for rationalization purposes in the report [23]. The discussion and the political debate led to the Swedish Data Protection Law in 1973, one of the first of its kind in the world. This law essentially required government agencies to apply for a permit to create a register and allowed individuals to request a copy of the information about them found in the registers. The law was later replaced by the Data Protection Act in 1998, and the General Data Protection Regulation in 2018.

A 1976 report on the topic of ADP coordination includes a paragraph about the potential use of computers in political processes, stating: *One of the most spectacular forms of direct democratic participation that has been suggested is elections and voting processes aided by computer technology and telecommunications.* It is also recognized that ADP can upset the balance of power, not only within the public administration but also among individuals: Government agencies and individuals with access to ADP have significant advantages compared to those who do not. The committee also acknowledges the difficulties in assessing the effects of ADP in monetary terms since the impacts in the form of service improvements are often qualitative in nature. One recognized problem in the report is that the Swedish word for efficiency and effectiveness is the same (effektivitet), while the two terms have different meanings in English. The report concludes that cost savings should be the valid interpretation of the term [4]. A 1979 proposition from the central government emphasizes efficiency, but also recognize additional purposes with ADP, such as service improvements [27]. Computer technology changed during this time, shifting from large central computers to decentralized, networked desktop computers suitable for office use. In 1984, the National Audit Office (NAO) conducted an evaluation of investments in "small-scale ADP". They conclude that cost savings had not been achieved due to investments in technology not being accompanied by necessary organizational changes: initiatives are developed by enthusiasts rather than being based on benefit realization. However, the report also mentions improvements in quality and service [35]. During the 1980s, the APM released guides on how to develop and evaluate ADP investments in monetary terms. The APM had less influence on the computerization in the 1980s though, when decentralized evaluations became an important part of the long-term governance model (mentioned in [38]). Political control over computers was reduced during the 1980s, as computer investments should be decided on by each agency separately, in line with new management ideals.

4.2   Information Technology

In 1988, ADP and IT were considered synonyms by a minister, describing how the number of computerized work spaces in the public sector had tripled between 1983 and 1987 [28]. In 1994, a speech by the Swedish prime minister marked the starting point for when IT became the established term for computerized technology. Sweden should become a leading IT-nation no later than 2010. For the public sector, this goal meant adapting Internet-based technology to become a "24-hour government", a term that was used in parallel with a direct translation of "e-Government" [39]. Policies formulated by experts in collaboration with ministers express optimism regarding the potential values that can be achieved by IT, not only in the public sector, but in the whole society. Documents describe how the new technology, a convergence of several media such as computers, text, sound, television and radio technology, could give "wings to man's ability" in the "epoch shift" towards an "information-" or "knowledge society". Although IT is sometimes referred to as a tool or a means in these documents, the outcome in the form of a new society is described as inevitable [21,29]. The goal for the public sector in this society is to increase efficiency, service, and quality. Legality continued to serve as a constraint to these goals: *A range of legal obstacles prevent a rational use of IT. Moreover, current regulations do not offer enough protection to avoid misuse, and unwanted consequences of the new technology* [29]. An IT strategy from 2000 states, *Without a doubt, IT has improved the conditions for increased efficiency and quality...However, holistic indicators to follow up on these goals are missing...The websites of several agencies are offering good service at low cost* [30].

A series of investigations discuss the potential for the Internet to increase access to democratic spaces. A final report from the "democracy investigation" in 2001 summarizes the then-current initiatives as mostly part of a "service democracy," whereby information from politicians is supplied to civil society and not used as a tool for active engagement. Concerns are also raised about unequal access to and usage of technology depending on age, sex and income [5]. Subsequent government reports contain reservations concerning these digital divides since many policies build on the assumption that citizen demand, and use, government services.

After the millennium shift, which was characterized by a declining IT industry during the dotcom crisis, the effects of computerized technology in the public sector were questioned. In 2004, the NAO concludes that *...the [24-hour government] reform has had limited impact...Severe flaws prevent the implementation of electronic government, which have affected citizens, businesses and the government agencies* [34]. Due to a significant focus on cost savings, few advanced services targeted at smaller user groups were created. The use of email among government entities is described as a threat to the rule of law, and the work to remove legal obstacles to implement e-services is reported as slow. The report also criticized the lack of governance from the central government and parliament. A group of general directors known as the "e-Delegation" was formed in 2009 to enable coordination of e-Government issues. The e-Delegation was also tasked with exploring the possible development of e-democracy but eventually refrained from carrying out this investigation [10].

4.3 Digitalization

Like ADP and IT, digitalization and IT have existed in parallel. The European Union released a digital agenda for Europe in 2010. A Swedish digital agenda was released by the first expert group with the word 'digitalization' in its name in 2011: The Digitalization Council. They were replaced by a Digitalization commission in 2012. In the subsequent years, the service ideal received additional attention. A 2012 strategy titled "With the Citizen in the Center" contained three sub-goals for the Swedish e-Government: 1. An easier life for the citizen (through increased use of digital services), 2. An administration that supports innovation and participation (by enabling open data), and 3. increased quality and efficiency (through standardization, security and, increased digitalization) [31].

The title IT Minister was changed to Digitalization Minister in 2016. The material on digitalization contains several parallels to the IT movement in the 1990s: the goal to become a leading nation in technology and an increased optimism of what could be achieved with the new technology. The reports produced by the expert groups often describes digitalization as a highly transformative force, similar to how ADP was perceived in the 1960s and IT in the 1990s. A report from the Digitalization commission contends that digitalization is: *[T]he most transformative process since industrialization... Digitalization may enable the development of a democratic and sustainable welfare society that we can barely conceive today.* The report states that the public administration can achieve higher efficiency and create better welfare services through the use of digital technology. A rule-based bureaucracy is contrasted to individualization and flexibility, which are key-characteristics of the digital, data-driven society. Big data and machine learning are considered as potential remedies for the failure of earlier management ideals, however, privacy issues need to be subject to a "broad debate". In a scenario for the year 2030, digital technology is being used to enhance participation processes, as well as for digital voting [7]. A 2017 digitalization strategy states that the development of society is run and shaped by digitalization. While digitalization is not a means in itself, people need to be able to adapt to the change, which requires innovation and leadership. The public sector should strive to become *an innovative and collaborative public administration that is under the rule of law and is efficient, with well-developed quality, service, and accessibility, and that contributes to the work of the European Union* [32]. Further reports suggest that digital services should be the prioritized channel for governments ('digital first'). These reports include suggestions for regulations meant to improve the formalized governance of digitalization [14], legal investigations with the purpose of improving security when outsourcing, and allowing automatic decision-making by artificial intelligence [8].

In a series of evaluation reports, the National Financial Management Authority (NFMA) concludes that, many agencies are unaware of their IT costs, and generic tools for assessment are missing. NFMA also reveals that in large-scale projects internal efficiency tend to be the main goal, although citizen centricity is achieved by many agencies through user involvement in service design [11]. Similar findings are presented in a report on digital investments, where an expert group concludes that in large-scale projects, government agencies tend to prioritize efficiency [33].

5   Discussion

This section discusses the development of the value positions (i.e. professionalism, efficiency, service, and engagement) over time in the studied documents.

5.1   Professionalism

The computers in the public administration, which were installed in the 1960s, carried public records in large registers and constituted an infrastructure of which the main purpose was rationalization. It was soon realized that it was difficult to position and organize the use of computers within the bureaucratic system. The ability to connect computers to each other and coordinate the content of several registers had the potential to disrupt the structures of the public sector. Weberian bureaucracy favors hierarchical structures based on specialization and governed by the rule of law. Computerized technology, however, enables cross-organizational information flows through networks and integrated systems, which initially occurred through coordinating registries, later through networked desktop computers, and today, via Internet-based technology. The professionalism ideal has played two roles to this day: as both a constraint that negates other value positions and as a prerequisite that enables a secure and robust, yet flexible, public record. In the latest digitalization strategies, the work with adapting legal and organizational structures has intensified.

5.2   Efficiency

Throughout the entire period studied in this research, even before the establishment of the NPM ideals, efficiency plays a salient role in the computerization of the public sector. The purpose of investing in ADP was clear: to reduce the cost of the growing public sector. However, a recurring topic over time is how to assess these investments. In the 1970s, difficulties in assessing the effects of ADP implementations and concerns about cost overruns started taking hold. Moreover, the Swedish term effektivitet caused confusion since it can refer to both efficiency and effectiveness. The ideals of NPM during the IT and digitalization eras manifest themselves in continuous discussions about performance assessment, but also in the form of influence from private experts on the content of government policies. While the service ideal became dominant through the use of internet-based technology, reports suggest that efficiency remains prioritized in large-scale initiatives.

5.3   Service

Service improvements were initially regarded as competing interpretations, or at best, side effects of efficiency. When the ability to deliver services via Internet-based technology was established in the 2000s, service would eventually become a prominent value position in e-Government strategies. Through the notion of "digital first," all government entities should primarily choose the channel of digital technology. However, the increased use of digital technology also comes with a negative side-effect: digital divides. Thus, the service ideal builds on the idea that digitalization is developed based on citizen demands, but struggles with the fact that not everyone can (or want to) use digital services.

5.4   Engagement

Engagement values are expressed in conjunction with the rapid changes in structures that increased use of digital technology brings. The first trace of engagement in the material is found in the end of the 1970s, where a report describes the use of computers for engaging citizens as a futuristic form of democracy. During the IT era in the 1990s, possibilities for facilitating engagement processes over the Internet are mentioned in government reports. These investigations end with a report in 2001, which states that no major progress has occurred in the area. Engagement ideals return in documents on digitalization: as a potential outcome of the use of open government data, and in a future scenario for the year 2030 where increased engagement processes and digital voting have been implemented.

6   Conclusions

This paper aimed to investigate how values in Sweden's national e-Government have developed over time. The research was conducted via a content analysis of Swedish government documents on computerization produced between 1961 and 2018. Four value positions from prior research were utilized to analyze the material: professionalism, efficiency, service, and engagement. Drawing on a historical account of the Swedish context as a case study, the results of this research contribute to a growing body of research on value traditions associated with the implementation of technology in the public sector.

The name for computerized technology has shifted over time, from Automatic Data Processing to IT, and digitalization. These eras are initiated with value congruence in policies describing a future society enabled by technology. Previously, these expectations have led to disappointments due to fundamental challenges that remains unresolved, including assessment problems and digital divides. Currently, digitalization is perceived as an enabler of several values. While both IT and digitalization are referred to as tools or means, the development towards a new information- knowledge-, or data-driven society is also described as inevitable.

The service ideal became dominant through the use of internet-based technology, while efficiency is often prioritized in large-scale initiatives. Engagement values are associated with a futuristic form of democracy in government documents, but rarely converted into practice. Professionalism constrains the other values by acting as a barrier that prevents integration and interoperability, but also by enabling a secure public record that takes privacy issues into account. However, professionalism is also at stake, when laws and regulations are adapted to enable digitalization: when Weber's iron cage is replaced by a more fragile, digital construction, the current development might lead to an eroded bureaucracy, with uncertain value.

References

1. Bannister, F., Connolly, R.: Forward to the past: lessons for the future of e-government from the story so far. Inf. Polity **17**(3), 211–226 (2012)
2. Bannister, F., Connolly, R.: ICT, public values and transformative government: a framework and programme for research. Gov. Inf. Q. **31**(1), 119–128 (2014)
3. Brennen, S., Kreiss, D.: Digitization or digitalization. Culture Digitally (2014)
4. Datasamordningskommittén: SOU 1976:58: ADB och samordning. Finansdepartementet (1976)
5. Demokratiutredningen: SOU 2000:1: En uthållig demokrati! Politik för folkstyret på 2000-talet. Kulturdepartementet (2000)
6. Denhardt, R.B., Denhardt, J.V.: The new public service: serving rather than steering. Public Adm. Rev. **60**(6), 549–559 (2000)
7. Digitaliseringskommissionen: SOU 2016:89: För digitalisering i tiden. Näringsdepartementet (2016)
8. Digitaliseringsrättsutredningen: SOU 2018:25: Juridik som stöd för den förvaltningens digitalisering. Regeringskansliet (2018)
9. Dunleavy, P., Margetts, H., Bastow, S., Tinkler, J.: New public management is dead–long live digital-era governance. J. Public Adm. Res. Theor. **16**(3), 467–494 (2006)
10. E-delegationen: SOU 2015:66: En förvaltning som håller ihop. Näringsdepartementet (2015)
11. Ekonomistyrningsverket: Digitaliseringen av det offentliga Sverige - en uppföljning (2018)
12. Finansdepartementet: SOU1961:60: Den automatiska databehandlingens teknik (1961)
13. Finansdepartementet: SOU 1962:32: Automatisk databehandling (1962)
14. Finansdepartementet: SOU 2017:114: reboot - omstart för den digitala förvaltningen (2017)
15. Futumoto, E., Bozeman, B.: Public values theory: what is missing? Am. Rev. Public Adm. 1–14 (2018)
16. Grönlund, Å.: Ten years of e-government: the 'end of history' and new beginning. In: Wimmer, M.A., Chappelet, J.-L., Janssen, M., Scholl, H.J. (eds.) EGOV 2010. LNCS, vol. 6228, pp. 13–24. Springer, Heidelberg (2010). https://doi.org/10.1007/978-3-642-14799-9_2
17. Heeks, R., Bailur, S.: Analyzing e-government research: perspectives, philosophies, theories, methods, and practice. Gov. Inf. Q. **24**(2), 243–265 (2007)

18. Hood, C.: A public management for all seasons? Public Adm. **69**, 3–19 (1991)
19. Hsieh, H.F., Shannon, S.E.: Three approaches to qualitative content analysis. Qual. Health Res. **15**(9), 1277–1288 (2005)
20. Ilshammar, L., Bjurström, A., Grönlund, Å.: Public e-services in sweden - old wine in new bottles? Scand. J. Inf. Syst. **17**(2), 11–40 (2005)
21. IT-kommissionen: SOU 1994:118: Informationsteknologin: Vingar åt människans förmåga. Statsrådsberedningen (1994)
22. Johansson, M.: Smart, Fast and Beautiful : On Rhetoric of Technology and Computing Discourse in Sweden 1955–1995. No. 164 in Linköping Studies in Arts and Science (1997)
23. Justitiedepartementet: SOU 1972:47: Data och integritet (1972)
24. Lundin, P.: Computers in Swedish Society - Documenting Early Use and Trends. Springer, London (2012). https://doi.org/10.1007/978-1-4471-2933-2
25. Moore, M.H.: Creating Public Value - Strategic Management in Government. Harvard University Press, Cambridge (1995)
26. Persson, J.S., Reinwald, A., Skorve, E., Nielsen, P.A.: Value positions in e-government strategies: Something is (not) changing in the state of denmark. In: ECIS (2017)
27. Regeringen: Proposition 1978/79:121, om användningen av automatisk databehandling (ADB) i statsförvaltningen (1979)
28. Regeringen: Proposition 1987/88:95, om datapolitik för statsförvaltningen (1988)
29. Regeringen: Åtgärder för att bredda och utveckla användningen av informationsteknik (1996)
30. Regeringskansliet: Regeringens proposition 1999/2000:86 Ett informationssamhälle för alla. Näringsdepartementet (2000)
31. Regeringskansliet: Med medborgaren i centrum Regeringens strategi för en digitalt samverkande statsförvaltning. Näringsdepartementet (2012)
32. Regeringskansliet: För ett hållbart digitaliserat sverige - en digitaliseringsstrategi (2017)
33. Regeringskansliet: SOU 2018:72 Slutrapport. Expertgruppen för digitala investeringar (2018)
34. Riksrevisionen: Vem styr den elektroniska förvaltningen? (2004)
35. Riksrevisionsverket: Persondatorer och skrivautomater - användning i statsförvaltningen (1984)
36. Rose, J., Flak, L.S.: Øystein Sæbø: Stakeholder theory for the e-government context: framing a value-oriented normative core. Gov. Inf. Q. **35**(3), 362–374 (2018)
37. Rose, J., Persson, J.S., Heeager, L.T., Irani, Z.: Managing e-government: value positions and relationships. Inf. Syst. J. **25**(5), 531–571 (2015)
38. Statskontoret: Efterstudier - att utvärdera effekterna av AU/ADB (1987)
39. Statskontoret: Staten i omvandling (1996)
40. Weber, M.: Economy and Society (reprint of the original from 1922). Bedminster Press, New York (1968)

E-Government Services and Open Government

'It Is Always an Individual Assessment': A Case Study on Challenges of Automation of Income Support Services

Mariana S. Gustafsson$^{(\boxtimes)}$ ⓘ and Elin Wihlborg ⓘ

Department of Management and Engineering IEI, Linköping University,
581 83 Linköping, Sweden
`mariana.s.gustafsson@liu.se`

Abstract. Income support schemes are key policies in an inclusive welfare state. To make them legitimate they are strictly regulated. As such they provide good prerequisites for standardization and automation, in theory. The aim of this paper is to analyze a case of municipal administration of income support, where automatization is resisted despite managements' ambitions. We focus on the case workers' interpretations of changes conducive to automatization and discuss how different service logics may explain the tensions and resistance of the frontline case workers. Our findings suggest that digitalisation and automatization challenge the balance of two logics and raise concerns of accountability in exercise of public authority; and concerns of value in terms of support towards self-sustainability and social integration of the clients (We are humbly grateful to the research council FORTE, for the opportunity to carry this research, through financing of the project: "The computer says no!" – en studie om det offentligas legitimitet och medborgares tillit när e-förvaltningen växer fram. We are also grateful to our informants in the Income Support unit in the municipality who shared their perceptions and experiences in this research.).

Keywords: Automatization · Income support · Manufacturing logics ·
Service logics · e-services

1 Introduction

Social services are central in Scandinavian welfare systems, supporting the most vulnerable people to get an independent and reasonable standard of living as expressed in the social service legislation [1]. These extensive schemes, managed by local governments and municipalities, are based on a universalistic welfare model that rests upon principles of equality of living conditions, economic and social security and active participation in society. These schemes are thoroughly regulated and detailed regarding what to support, when, how and whom. As such the schemes are clear and provide good prerequisites for standardization and automation of case management, at least in theory. However, by virtue of the same legislation and the Administrative Procedure Act [2, 3], the case workers are guided to be accessible, transparent, supportive and guiding the client to be independent of the income support and empowered by the

© IFIP International Federation for Information Processing 2019
Published by Springer Nature Switzerland AG 2019
I. Lindgren et al. (Eds.): EGOV 2019, LNCS 11685, pp. 45–56, 2019.
https://doi.org/10.1007/978-3-030-27325-5_4

social workers - a dilemma of accommodating different logics is established that is enhanced by digitalization.

The effects of digitalisation, as is both claimed and demonstrated over time, for improved efficiency, impartiality and the rule of law in public administration (Heeks and Bailur 2007), public authorities are slowly introducing digital and automated processes in their service provision and administration [4, 5]. We argue hereby that social welfare is currently under digital transformation pressures, rife with tensions, where different logics that drive value production in social services clash with the logics of standardization and manufacturing that underlie imminent automation processes.

Scandinavian public welfare services are currently subject to advanced digitalization, in a context rife with diversified population needs and demands, governed by political goals of equal access to high quality services and constrained economic and personnel resources in municipal public administrations. The political ambition is to draw the benefits from technological developments to address the new demands from society [6]. In this context, frontline bureaucrats, as case workers, play a key role in the advanced use of digital systems in managing and administering e-services. Their discretion in case management, now mediated through technology, in relation to legal, organizational, and individual factors like competence, experiences and personal values can explain the outcomes of the welfare schemes [7].

The administrative organization of public services entails both principles of standardization of processes pursing management goals (NMP) and at the same time involving individualization of decisions based on clients' needs and life situations, pursuing professional ethics and social policy priorities. ICTs and automation are expected to enable and increase the manufacturing types of service production [8].

Aim

The aim of this paper is to analyze a case of municipal administration of income support, where automatization is disputed, by focusing on the case workers' interpretations of these changes and analyze how different logics may explain the concerns to change.

Research Questions

The research questions that will be pursed for this purpose are:

1. What automatization attempts can be discerned in the case of municipal administration of income support?
2. What concerns are raised in connection with automatization in this case?
3. What logics are at work and how they affect automatization in service provision of income support?

2   'Digital First' Principle in Public Administration in Sweden

In line with the European Digital Agenda, the Swedish national digital strategy is establishes the principle "digital first" [6, 9]. It implies that the contact with public authorities should primarily happen digitally. It involves submission of records in one instance, in order to streamline the case management and facilitate decision making. The clients however meet different prospects and challenges to meet the public authority, based on their municipality geographic configuration, demographic land-scape and the volume of administrative resources.

2.1   The Role of Municipalities in the Swedish Public Administration

The social services in Sweden are a crucial part of the welfare state and it is formed and managed at the cross-road of two main governance principles: universalism and local autonomy [10]. The income support defined in the Swedish Social Service Act [1] has is to be delivered impartially to all inhabitants, by all municipalities. National equality is key for the implementation by municipal administrations, which are to follow clear regulations and guides for application of the legislation in practice. On the other hand, the municipalities have constitutional autonomy [11], and act upon self-government powers [3].

2.2   Social Service and Income Support Schemes: Promise of Automatization

The income support scheme includes two key dimensions: a thoroughly regulated administration of records on living conditions and cost of the client and an individual coaching-support service for the client that aims towards employment and financial independence. The records including living expenses and income are collected in connection to the application to entitlement for Income support and are subsequently reported monthly. Municipalities have well developed digital registries to collect, store and administer such records. The individualized coaching services involve a systematic planning, in collaboration with other authorities - both local and national - of activities to support the client to become fit for work and gain financial independence [12].

Although implementing a heavily regulated scheme, the municipalities have large powers, due to the local autonomy, to choose and develop own case management systems. Although a certain systematics for registration of records is common for the municipalities there are no standardized processes of case management in practice. A few municipalities develop their own systems, but the usual practice is to buy IT-solutions on the market [13]. Such solutions, commonly built on a model developed for one municipality, are subsequently sold to other municipalities with the promise of adaptation to the municipality's needs and case management processes.

Models of automation has already started to be implemented in public adminis-tration in Sweden, with a few examples from national agencies [14]. A majority (55%) of the Swedish municipalities report offering e-services with either totally or partially automatized service management [15]. There is an abundance of studies focusing on the effects of digitalization in public sector but less on automatization of processes in social welfare services. There are some examples in human resources-processes, where software robots collect records from several different IT systems and register data rapidly and without bias [16]. In the Swedish municipalities we can find several recent examples. The most known model is from the social services in Trelleborg, that has been described as a success model for automation in social services: extra time and personnel resources could be allocated on coaching the clients towards reintegration on labor market [17, 18]. This model is currently disseminated in 14 municipalities with support from national agencies as Vinnova and SALAR [19].

In other municipalities, this model has been criticized. One of the most discussed cases is from Kungsbacka municipality, where 12 out of 16 social workers resigned in protest to the plans for automation of income support [20]. The protesting social workers acknowledged that digitalization may save time, but they questioned that a robot can make individual assessments of their clients' needs. Other critique involved the shift to a labor market perspective from social care, the fear for losing the professional identity under an administrative organizational change (from social care unit to a labor market unit in the municipal administration) and the lacking dialog between leadership and the social workers [20]. The two examples of automatization: in Trelleborg municipality and Kungsbacka municipality show that one single model of automation – when copied to other municipalities – got different response and support from the frontline case workers. Thus, it was important for us to follow closely similar implementation practices conducive to automatization changes and examine what tensions and logics guided the process.

3   Implementation Barriers for Digitalization in Public Administration

Research on innovation in public administration focusing e-government reforms has specifically and predominantly been concerned with barriers to adoption and advancement [21–23]. But there are also approaches focusing on flexibility and agility in implementation processes [24]. Building on these approaches we will also open for an analysis of logics and values embedded into public administration practices to search explanations of the case workers hesitations to innovate.

3.1   Barriers in Implementing Digital Innovations in Public Services

Digital government barriers are predominantly studied as technical challenges, disincentivizing actions, dysfunctional organizations and ambiguous institutional structures that constrain practice, lack of- or unclear policy [25]. Barriers have been systematized according to different models. However, compared to the attention given to technological, organizational and structural barriers, considerable less attention has been attributed to cultural barriers [26]. Cultural barriers in digital government, as studied by Margetts and Dunleavy [27], refer to a scaring image of technology in organizations, according to which minor mistakes in usage may lead to terrible consequences. Such perceptions pose hinders to implementation of technological change. In a more flexible and agile approach, Gong and Janssen [24] identify four keys for good implementation of digital government processes: separating the process from the service, pre-planned (not event-driven) integration and orchestration of implementation, embedding knowledge and resources into the process of change.

Framing in governance of innovation has shown to play a key part in successful innovation and of government strategies to address resistance to technological change.

Meijer [26] has found that connecting technological opportunities to the production of public value are crucial in this respect. In similar ways, Pors [28] found that digitalization fundamentally changed the modes of work of frontline bureaucracy and their interaction with citizens, from providing citizen service to providing citizen support. Through digitalization and co-production in a 'digital first' setting, citizens took over a part of the administrative tasks through digital systems which gave the frontline case workers new possibilities to guide and support the citizens, rather than solve their clients' cases. This research shows that implementation of digital innovations for services towards citizens in these practices opens for and requires new logics of service provision.

3.2   Logics of Digital Service Provision

Digitalization of public services transform the organization of public sector [8, 29, 30] and challenge the Weberian model of public service production. Cordella, Paletti [8] identify two different logics of value creation: manufacturing logic and service logic.

The *manufacturing logic,* following industrial production and market logics, is reflected in standardization of production processes to create value. The manufacturing logic involves essentially the standardization principle, according to which the organization focuses on improving organizational set-ups and streamlining of production processes and means in order to produce a desired value. Digitalization opens even further for new ways to organize and manage NPM based service production in public sector. Such effects, argue Cordella, Paletti [8] leads to a shift in logics of production in public organizations towards *service logic* of value creation, involving market and civil society actors in co-production of public services. The resources available for such a process complement the in-house resources of public administrations opening the value creation process to external resources, processes, interests and capabilities. The two logics of service production and value creation are summarized as follows, in Table 1.

Table 1. Logics of service production and value creation

	Manufacturing Logic of service production and value creation	Service Logic of service production and value creation
Planning	Centralized	Decentralized
Production cycle	Closed	Open
Production process	In-house, or inter-organizational	Co-production
Resources	Exclusively internal Reduction variation	Combining internal with external Openness for variation
Contribution	Is known, defined and measurable	Is not completely known, fuzzy and only partially measurable
ICT-use	For standardization, optimization and efficiency	For enabling co-production
Value is created based on	Impartiality, standardization, rule of law	Personal interaction, adoption to co-production needs and individual values

Adapted from [8]

Public values such as impartiality, fairness and equality are fundamental for all public services both logics of service production and guide the public administrations. However, within these core values there are different values underlying the two logics. The 'manufacturing logic' are more standardized and less flexible, a service logic emphasize values of individualization and flexibility. This model will guide our analysis of how and why the municipal case workers may address different assignments – controlling or coaching – in their daily working meeting with clients and the automated system.

4   Methods and Research Design for the Case Study

Being part of a larger project that focused on understanding of legitimate exercise of public authority in the context of automated case processing and decision making, this study was designed as a single case study of implementation practices in units that were introducing e-services and aiming at automatization. Material collection included elements of action research and abduction in terms of connection to the theory [31]. While working on the case we shared knowledge with the municipality. The research is based on *two planning meetings*, gathering researchers, unit management and municipality digitalisation strategist, where we participated and documented discussions focusing on organizational set up, the change management, implementation process, as well challenges. Observations under *two demonstration workshops* aiming to acquaint all the case workers with the function 'My Pages' (*'Mina sidor'*), and 'e-Application' (*'e-Ansökan'*). *Five semi-structured interviews* were carried with key personnel in the unit: the unit manager, the lead case worker (most experienced in the team), two case workers who were 'super-users' of the platform (most knowledgeable IT-users in the unit, who also have qualifications for testing new functions and e-services on their cases before the rest of the case workers start using them). In addition, we coordinated *two knowledge meetings* with the management and *one workshop* with the entire unit, focusing on validation and discussion of our research findings, their organizational implications and practical advice.

The model comparing the two service production logics has been used in the analysis to discern qualitatively the organizational set-up for the change that involves introduction of e-services, as well as to the underlying logics that explained the different experiences and interpretations of the different professionals in the public sector.

5   The Income Support in the Municipality

5.1   Organizational Set-Up Accommodating Both Manufacturing and Service Logics

The municipal organizational set-up for the Income support services is following a hierarchical structure where the manager of the unit is accountable to a chain of managers higher up in the administration of social services. The financial resources making up the budget are drawn from the municipal pool of publicly collected taxes.

Such an organization, follows centralized municipal planning and by law relies on a close production cycle, thus following a manufacturing logic. The case workers are the sole professionals with mandates to exercise public authority upon income support decisions. However, in the process re-habilitation and re-integration of the client in society, the case workers must collaborate with other authorities as described below. Such a collaboration between the authorities, involves a pooling of resources across organizations, thus making the production cycle open and employing co-production practices.

5.2   Integrating E-Services Challenges the Accommodation of the Two Logics

Case management of the income support in the municipality is administered through the internal IT-system, VIVA, where case workers register, follow up and handle all the cases and the pertaining records. When the client submits a paper-application for income support, a new case is opened and the records are manually introduced in VIVA. The records on income and expenses from the application, are currently manually registered in VIVA. Besides place of residence, family members' residence and their employment situation, the records include public social insurance allowances such as unemployment, sick leave and child benefits. The new records are usually incomplete, which always requires a cross-check through the registry system s of the different authorities (Tax Authority, Social Insurance Agency, Swedish Board of Student Finance, Public Employment Service and the Unemployment Insurance Funds). Record registration and their clarification makes up the part of the services that is mostly regulated, standardized and repetitive, is clearly following a manufacturing logic. This part of the service is expected to become more effective and time saving through e-services and automatization.

Following the national digitalization policies and the municipality action plan, the unit is currently introducing the e-services 'e-Application' (*e-Ansökan*) and 'My Pages' (*Mina sidor*) for the income support scheme. This initiative was initiated in 2017 and is still under implementation. It intends to partially digitalize the application process that is currently entirely made on paper. The plan is that the very first application will still be done on paper, while the subsequent ones, from the same client, will be done online through e-Application and My Pages. The e-Application service was integrated in VIVA by e-Lab during in 2018. The ambitions are that the e-services will increase the accessibility for the client and facilitate them to submit more and correct records.

Both management and part of the case workers expected the quality of the records to improve and the process to be more effective, streamlining it towards better decisions and more coaching towards employment and social re-integration. The main risks that were foreseen by the case workers were the clients who could abuse the service and the increase in the number of cases per case worker. Consequently, in terms of improving quality of records and their registration – part of the case workers' and the management - agree that ICTs and automatization can enable time saving and effective processes. In terms of coaching and support, steered by a service-logics, both by law and by professional ethics, the image becomes more complicated.

5.3   Individual Micro-Assessments the Basis of Targeted Interventions in Social Assistance and Service Logics as Its Core

Upon each application for income support, the case worker needs to get all relevant and correct records on income and expenses, where the latter ones always exceed the former one. Besides pursuing the calculations entitling the client for financial support, the case worker needs to make individual 'micro-assessments' on whether the expenses are eligible and legitimate to cover through the scheme. In such micro-assessments, the case worker has important discretionary power: how many jobs has the client applied for, participation in rehabilitation activities (ex. practical training, work training). Based on the principle of individually targeted interventions in social assistance, in every assessment, the case worker considers holistically the individual's records and his specific life situation: how do they act to improve their living, do they do what they must, what is reasonable to require from the person, how are their children affected by the decision?

These micro-assessments which underlie the authority decisions to provide income support, in combination with coaching are fundamental in steering the clients' actions towards financial independence. It implies guiding the clients in a desired direction, as a service logic to pursue rehabilitation, re-connect with family, follow doctors' prescriptions and finally apply for jobs. Value production involves meaningful communication with the client to calibrate the demands, to clarify the expectations and to plan for further activities that aim to return the client on the work market and financial independence. This part of the service production and value creation is thus guided by a service logic that builds on an interaction and communication with the individual client on the one side and case workers from other authorities on the other, in order to guide, advice and support toward self-sufficiency and independence.

The accommodation of manufacturing logics that underlies planning and organizational set-up, but also records registration in case work - with a service logic, that underlies coaching and support seems to be challenged by the prospects of automatization, as illustrated by the citation below:

> We talk a lot about saving time, specifically concerning applications. We spend a lot of time to process the application, to work with papers… to go through the manual records, bills and invoices. The entire process is very time consuming, but we would like to spend more time with the people, meet them more and spend more time on coaching them to go on and get an own maintenance. Everything that can save time for us is welcome. For example, if the records are matched automatically to the open cases and we skip filling these manually, could save 1 min per application. If you deal with 70 applications and save 1 h that can be used on coaching the client or receive one extra visit. (Case worker 1)

At the same time, concerns arise related to responsibility and legality of decisions making based on individual assessment and ambiguities arising from the delegation of exercise of authority to a non-human:

> It is difficult for me to imagine that I would not sit at the computer and press the button, because of individual assessments. But say a computer shall make the decision, who is to be accountable for that decision? It should always be a human behind the decision, legally speaking… I feel worried, because all the decisions that I am delegated to, I shall be in charge and knowledgeable of. Shall a computer make decisions that were delegated to me? And if the client would like to enquire on the decision, who is he to call if it was entirely made by a computer? (Case worker 2)

Importantly, for such a management to work and for individual micro-assessments to be possible, it needs personal interaction with the client to understand the individual's needs and capability, as well as channels of trust and constructive communication that will allow coaching towards financial independence. This is a logic of service provision, where the pursued public value is the independent and socially integrated individual. This logic is contrasting the manufacturing logic of standardization, that would not allow for individual coaching, empowerment and care. It indicates that the case workers are both striving to meet standardization of assessments and control data through automated systems, and to be service minded by coaching and service.

5.4   No Drastic Changes in Terms of Case Management Process and Time but Hope on Better Quality of Cases and Decisions

Although the automated system will imply introducing new routines in handling the cases, no drastic changes will occur in daily work, according to the interviewed case workers. The experiences of using the e-Application for 12 months, when the case workers had only seen a Beta-version of the system, are raising more questions rather than answers for the them. The following quotations illustrate the pursuit of manufacturing-oriented logic and values such as effectiveness in terms of time saving, legality and correctness of records. The case workers are concerned with ambiguities of the new technical changes in the system and their implication for the routines.

> It would be very good if it became more effective, that I saved time so that I can use that time to get them out to work or on motivating them... But I am doubtful that it will do that, because I will anyway need to make the calculations and the inspection just as usual: check that we have received the application, that it is complete, send requests for complementary information. I have difficulties seeing where I can save the time. But it can be that that I don't know too much yet. For example, what about the paper receipts that need to be attached to the application? We need to see the medicine that has been purchased and the doctor visits. Shall they scan these receipts, or shall they submit them on paper?' (Case worker 2)

A similar hesitation was raised by another case worker saying:

> We will do the same things that we are doing today..., but we won't need a paper-application to inspect. Instead everything will be done on the computer. So, I don't think we will work differently with the applications. Everything will be stored on the computer. It will surely take as much time as it takes today, no more – no less. (Case worker 1)

The manufacturing logics shows up when the case worker reflects upon the legality and correctness of the records that can be improved by the e-Application process.

5.5   An Algorithm Could Not Make the Job Entirely – Or?

If record management through the digital platforms - is somewhat positively seen by the interviewees, with potential to increase accuracy of data and facilitate correct decisions. The part involving meaningful communication, coaching and steering cannot be done by the automated processes, according to our interviewees. It proved difficult for the case workers to see how algorithms could make individual micro-assessments, with no meaningful communication with the client and no understanding of the client's broader life situation that goes beyond the individual records from the application. The interviewees emphasized that there are many circumstances that should be considered. The demands that a case worker posed one month, were not raised the month after due to ex. negative effects on children involved, or death of family member, as illustrated by the utterance below:

> We have the rules and the regulations... So to take an example with reimbursing the expenses for a bus card. The rule sets up 3 km as a minimum distance to the destination of the planned activity (f.ex. studies, work, work training). In such a case we also make individual assessments. For example, if we get a medical certificate that proves that the person cannot walk 3 km, then we can grant him the bus card anyway. So, things like that, I think I'm having trouble seeing how it would work. And this is the issue with most of our individual assessments. So, it's difficult for me to see how these can be automated, actually. (Case worker 2)

Again, the service-logic, the responsibility for pursuing the steering of individual towards independence is illustrated in the reflection below – a logic that defies automated decision making and standardization:

> You shall see to the human individual that he attains a reasonable standard of living. If the person cannot reach the workplace and cannot manage it in a good way because I denied him this bus card... I think it is my responsibility to offer this prerequisite so that he can manage his work. Otherwise, maybe if I just reject it, I think maybe that person may not be able to get to work, may not manage to do his job and even his mental health may get worse. This then may lead to that he loses his income support because he didn't show up at work. (Case worker 1).

At the same time, the case worker admitted that probably some unambiguous or non-complicated cases could be automatized, although the total exclusion of human contact seemed unreasonable. For example, such cases, that are scarce, would be when the client is not capable of returning to the labor market and no such demands are posed on him, his actual benefits, ex. partial sick leave benefits are fixed and his expenses are more or less the same every month. Consequently, correct and complete formal records is a pre-condition for making rightful assessments, but even when these are present, the more complicated cases involve almost always cooperating with other authorities. It is common that complications arise when the different authorities make different assessments in the same case. For example, when assessing the client's ability to work, the Employment agency can assess that the client as not able to work, while a doctor decides differently. The case worker's role, where the client finally turns to, is then to untangle the problem and such entanglements cannot be fixed automatically, it was explained.

6 Conclusions

The ambitions to make public administration more efficient by using different forms digital support systems and not at least new forms of automatization have clear implications on the legitimacy of exercise of public authority. Importantly, our case study shows that while Swedish social assistance services in Income support are managed in a legal and organizational set-up that accommodates manufacturing logics with service logics underlying social assistance regulations and professional ethics.

Digitalisation and automatization challenge this balance and raises concerns of accountability in exercise of public authority; and concerns of value in terms of support towards self-sustainability and social integration. This points to the need for further studies only.

Our case study has shown that the main hesitation among the professional street-level to towards implementation of automatization is based in their fear that it would bring encompassing manufacturing services logic. They are doubtful and hesitant since the automatization of the income-support builds on high degree of standardizations, hiding the large variation among the clients and thereby also reducing their discretion to coach and support the clients in different ways. Thus, we can see that there is a need to design and manage automatization of public administration in ways that it is seen as keeping and promoting a service logic giving space for values like individual adoption and flexibility.

References

1. SFS 2001:453, Socialtjänstlag [Social Services Act]
2. SFS 2017:900, Förvaltningslag [Administrative Procedure Act]
3. SFS 2017:725, Kommunallag [Local Government Act]
4. Heeks, R., Bailur, S.: Analyzing e-government research: perspectives, philosophies, theories, methods, and practice. Gov. Inf. Q. 24(2), 243–265 (2007)
5. Bannister, F.: In defence of bureaucracy: governance and public values in a digital age. In: Paulin, A.A., Anthopoulos, L.G., Reddick, C.G. (eds.) Beyond Bureaucracy. PAIT, vol. 25, pp. 27–47. Springer, Cham (2017). https://doi.org/10.1007/978-3-319-54142-6_3
6. European Commission: Communication from the Commission: A Digital Agenda for Europe (2010)
7. Busch, P.A., Henriksen, H.Z.: Digital discretion: a systematic literature review of ICT and street-level discretion. Inf. Polity Int. J. Gov. Democracy Inf. Age 23(1), 3–28 (2018)
8. Cordella, A., Paletti, A.: ICTs and value creation in public sector: manufacturing logic vs service logic. Inf. Polity Int. J. Gov. Democracy Inf. Age 23(2), 125–141 (2018)
9. Regeringskansliet, F.: ett hållbart digitaliserat Sverige –en digitaliseringsstrategi. Stockholm, Näringsdepartementet (2017)
10. Trydegard, G.B., Thorslund, M.: One Uniform Welfare State or a Multitude of Welfare Municipalities? The Evolution of Local Variation in Swedish Elder Care, p. 495. Blackwell Publishing Ltd., Great Britain (2010)
11. SFS 1974:152, Regeringsformen [Instrument of Government]
12. Socialstyrelsen, Handläggning och dokumentation inom socialtjänsten [Processing and documentation of cases in social services] (2015)
13. Jansson, G.: En legitim (elektronisk) förvaltning? Om IT-utveckling i kommunal förvaltning. Linköping Studies in Arts and Science. Linköping: Linköpings universitet, Institutionen för ekonomisk och industriell utveckling (2013)
14. Wihlborg, E., Larsson, H., Hedstrom, K.: "The Computer Says No!" -A Case Study on Automated Decision-Making in Public Authorities. In: HICSS. IEEE, Kauai (2016)
15. RIR 2016:14, Den offentliga förvaltningens digitalisering – En enklare, öppnare och effektivare förvaltning?, Riksrevisionen, Editor
16. Willcocks, L., Lacity, M.: Service Automation Robots and the Future of Work. SB Publishing, Ashford (2016)

17. Valcon, Process automation in Trelleborg municipality (2017)
18. Ranerup, A., Henriksen, H.Z.: Value positions in digitalization and automated decision-making in social work, in SWEG 2018, 31 January-1 February. Copenhagen Business School (2018)
19. Scaramuzzino, G.: Socialarbetare om automatisering i socialt arbete: En webbenkätun-dersökning [Social workers on automatisation of social work: a websurvey]. Lunds universitet, Socialhögskolan (2019)
20. Persson, E., Succémodellen i Trelleborg möter motstånd: "Man kopierar" [The Success model in Trelleborg meets resistance: "They copy"], in Arbetarvärlden [Newspaper article] (2018)
21. Savoldelli, A., Codagnone, C., Misuraca, G.: Understanding the e-government paradox: learning from literature and practice on barriers to adoption. Gov. Inf. Q. **31**, S63–S71 (2014)
22. Schwester, R.W.: Examining the barriers to e-government adoption. Electron. J. e-Gov. **7**(1), 113–122 (2009)
23. Mergel, I.: Open innovation in the public sector: drivers and barriers for the adoption of Challenge.gov. Public Manag. Rev. **20**(5), 726–745 (2018)
24. Gong, Y., Janssen, M.: From policy implementation to business process management: principles for creating flexibility and agility. Gov. Inf. Q. **29**(Supplement 1), S61–S71 (2012)
25. Gustafsson, M.S.: Reassembling local e-government: a study of actors' translations of digitalisation in public administration. In: Linköping Studies in Arts and Science, p. 132. Linköping University Electronic Press, Linköping (2017)
26. Meijer, A.: E-governance innovation: barriers and strategies. Gov. Inf. Q. **32**(2), 198–206 (2015)
27. Margetts, H., Dunleavy, P.: Cultural Barriers to E-government. National Audit Office, London (2002)
28. Pors, A.S.: Becoming digital - passages to service in the digitized bureaucracy. J. Organ. Ethnography **4**(2), 177–192 (2015)
29. Cordella, A., Tempini, N.: E-government and organizational change: reappraising the role of ICT and bureaucracy in public service delivery. Gov. Inf. Q. **32**(3), 279–286 (2015)
30. Margetts, H., Dunleavy, P.: The second wave of digital-era governance: a quasi-paradigm for government on the Web. Philos. Trans. R. Soc. A Math. Phys. Eng. Sci. **371**(1987), 20120382 (2013)
31. Alvesson, M., Sköldberg, K.: Reflexive Methodology: New Vistas for Qualitative Research. SAGE, Los Angeles (2009)

C2G Online Trust, Perceived Government Responsiveness and User Experience

A Pilot Survey in St. Petersburg, Russia

Yury Kabanov[1,2(✉)] and Lyudmila Vidiasova[1]

[1] ITMO University, St. Petersburg, Russia
bershadskaya.lyudmila@gmail.com
[2] National Research University Higher School of Economics,
St. Petersburg, Russia
ykabanov@hse.ru

Abstract. The paper presents the results of the pilot study of *C2G online trust*, that covers citizens' trust in communication with the government via e-government, e-participation and social media channels. Based on the survey carried out in St. Petersburg, we explore dimensions of *C2G trust* and test the impact of perceived government responsiveness, user experience and socio-demographic factors in shaping trust. Our findings suggest that both perceived responsiveness and user experience influence the level of trust, while age, gender and education are not significant when controlled to the frequency of Internet use. The research proposes to view *C2G trust* as a multidimensional phenomenon, as its dynamics may vary across the tools and sectors used. Implications for future research are given.

Keywords: Trust · Online trust · E-government · E-participation ·
Perceived government responsiveness · User experience

1 Introduction

Despite the growing volume of research, the question of how to make effective citizen-government (C2G) communication online remains open [39]. Among the numerous prerequisites for making e-government and e-participation meaningful, there is the multifaceted concept of trust [34], which, however, poses a challenge for its holistic evaluation and practical development. In this paper, we aim at contributing to the research on *C2G online trust*, i.e. a person's trust in communicating with public officials via e-government, e-participation or the social media. We present pilot results of the project exploring this phenomenon and factors that impact its dynamics, focusing on St. Petersburg, Russia. It is a new empirical case for online trust and ICT adoption studies, which are often centered on the US, Europe, Asia or the Middle East [40]. In this paper we explore the peculiarities of *C2G online trust* in a large Russian city, as well as test the impact of user experience, perceived government responsiveness and socio-demographic characteristics on trust. We analyze the data we obtained from the pilot opinion survey (600 respondents), carried out in St. Petersburg in 2018.

© IFIP International Federation for Information Processing 2019
Published by Springer Nature Switzerland AG 2019
I. Lindgren et al. (Eds.): EGOV 2019, LNCS 11685, pp. 57–68, 2019.
https://doi.org/10.1007/978-3-030-27325-5_5

The paper is structured as follows. Firstly, we briefly outline the state-of-the-art in online trust research in relation to e-government/e-participation. Secondly, we describe the methodology of research and overview the data. In the third part we present the findings, followed by discussion of the results, limitations and future steps.

2   C2G Online Trust: State of the Art

Due to the multifaceted nature of trust, it is important to outline, at least roughly, the key directions of its research in relation to e-government (e-participation). For this purpose we apply scientometrics approach: using *VOSviewer* software [38], we have created a keyword co-occurrence map (the intensity of keywords occurring together in a single item) from 823 articles, indexed in the Web of Science database, retrieved by the search query: *TS = (trust) AND TS = (e-government OR e-participation OR egovernment OR eparticipation)*. For the analysis we have selected 98 keywords that occur at least 10 times in the sample, excluding the query terms, as they may be found in practically all samples and skew the analysis. The minimum threshold for cluster formation is 5 terms (attraction – "2", repulsion – "0").

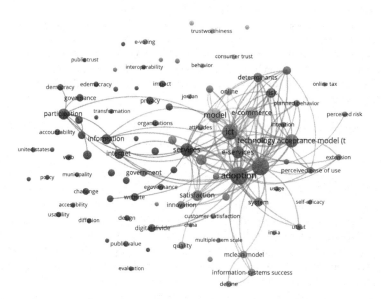

Fig. 1. Keyword co-occurrence map of trust in e-government/e-participation research. Source: *VOSviewer (*http://vosviewer.com) (Color figure online)

In the visualization (Fig. 1) the size of items depicts its occurrences, while the lines show the links strength between items. We may see that the research area is divided into several interconnected research contexts. Methodologically, the literature on trust in e-government (e-participation) seems to be dominated by several theoretical models. The first one (the green cluster) is the technology acceptance model [7] with its modifications and variables (perceived ease of use, risk and usefulness), with a topical focus on e-services and a close connection to e-commerce (the purple cluster). The yellow cluster focuses on the interaction between trust and user satisfaction issues, based mostly on the information systems success model that takes into account quality of systems and information [14, 30]. In this segment (the green, purple and yellow clusters) trust is mostly used as a dependent or moderating variable that impacts the intentions of ICT users, especially in relation to public and commercial services. On the contrary, the blue and red clusters are less internally coherent, with less occurring concepts and fewer strong connections. They seem to represent the research on how trust, e-tools use and government performance reinforce each other, and deals with such issues as transparency, responsiveness and accountability [21, 36]. It also touches such dimensions of C2G interaction as e-democracy, e-governance, e-voting, open government and social media. The visualization reveals further that trust is a multi-faceted concept, with different dimensions being considered by different research foci. Thus, while the red and blue clusters tend to analyze political and institutional trust, others deal with more personal facets (e.g. consumer and interpersonal trust).

Despite a lot of research, there are several challenges in the empirical study of trust, which are complicated by the multidisciplinary nature of the phenomenon [4]. The first problem occurs in defining and operationalizing the concept: what kind of trust actually matters for adoption and use of new technologies? Although trust in government and trust in the Internet (technology) are the usual suspects [8, 11, 40], there is no single answer if both are equally important [9, 18], or whether there is a reversed causal link between e-government use and trust formation [29]. Some scholars studied another important dimension of trust, i.e. trust in e-government, as well as trust in e-participation, which is explored less [33]. It is not necessarily a covariate of trust in government or technology [18], and can be viewed as a complex phenomenon on its own right, as proposed for e-government [28], or e-participation [31].

Exploring the predictors of trust in e-government or e-participation is the second challenging issue. So far various factors have proven their significance, like technology acceptance model variables [1, 24, 34], user satisfaction [20] quality of information and services [22], trust in technology or government [4] etc. Recently sociodemographic characteristics – age, gender, education level - have drawn the attention of the academia [3, 5]. While the research on trust determinants seems fruitful, the findings are usually based on opinion surveys and thus need to be verified in other contexts. Moreover, it is hard to combine all factors in a general fit-all-model.

Finally, the interpretation of results are usually affected by the difficulty to set a single causal link. As there is no single unified theory, depending on model specifications, trust, user satisfaction, ICT usage etc. are utilized as both dependent and independent variables [26]. And even more, it seems intuitive, because, as Scherer and Wimmer put it, trust is at the same time a condition and an outcome of e-participation, as well as enshrined into the very process of it [33].

In sum, despite a substantial progress, research gaps remain, and still work is needed in both new empirical research and theoretical conceptualization of trust in e-government and e-participation contexts.

3 Research Design

Dependent Variable. In our definition of trust we concentrate on trust in communication with the government online, i.e. whether a citizen considers interaction with public authorities on the Internet trustworthy. It is a certain reduction and simplification of the previous elaborate models [28, 34]. But on the other hand, we believe such communication trust is the essence that underpin successful e-projects, while other elements are either its predictors or outcomes. At the same time, by using the term – *C2G online trust* – we hope to synthesize previous studies on trust in e-government and e-participation. This is due to the fact that both have become complex, in many respects, intertwined systems of different tools. Moreover, new dimensions should count, like social media, which, is another domain of C2G interaction that may involve trust relations [2].

In this regards, *C2G online trust* needs to be taken as a related but conceptually distinct phenomenon from both trust in government and in technologies. Such an approach is based on previous studies of trust in e-government [18], as well as on the assumption that offline perceptions, attitudes and activities may have different dynamics than their online manifestations, for instance, in cases of political participation [17] and efficacy [32], close correlates of trust. At the same time, *C2G online trust* is not a single attitude and does not equate to online trust in general, since the latter, as found by Constante et al. [12] and Bart et al. [6], might have different dynamics across domains (e-commerce, e-health etc.) and particular websites. Hence, we might argue such trust is a multidimensional resultant of a person's encounter (or non-use) and attitudes to various e-government (e-participation, the social media) tools.

Thus, we measure the level of trust asking people whether they trust ICTs (the Internet, mobile technologies etc.) in the following situations: (1) getting e-services; (2) e-complaints submission; (3) e-petitions submission; (4) voting for e-petitions; (5) communication with the government via social media. The 4-point Likert scale was used to assess their level of trust to each: from "fully trust" to "don't trust".

Independent Variables. The pilot study is limited, making it impossible to test all promising hypotheses. We focus on three aspects, which also have visible practical applications: user experience, perceived government responsiveness, and socio-demographic characteristics.

User experience is usually analyzed in the context of user satisfaction or skillfulness [5, 19]. However, in this paper we mostly deal with the actual exposure to e-tools, with the goal to contribute to the literature on different perceptions of new technologies by users and non-users [27, 37]. Again, we take a multidimensional approach, following Distel that "nonadoption may not affect all available e-government services but only selected services" [15, p. 99]. Thus we ask citizens whether they have experience in using the selected e-tools in Russia: e-service portal (gosuslugi.ru), city e-complaint portal "Our Petersburg", federal e-petitions portal "Russian Public Initiative" and submitting e-complaints or appeals (via e-mails, special website forms etc.).

Perceived government responsiveness is another usual suspect that moderates trust and online interaction with the government [21, 23, 25, 35, 36]. Its meaning is close to the external political efficacy - the feeling citizens can actually influence the government [13], but unlike the latter, is related to more specific actions of decision-makers, the evaluation of the government as acting in accordance with public demands [16]. We ask citizens to what extent they agree that the development of the Internet makes public agencies more attentive to public complaints, more responsive to citizens and focused on citizens' problems.

The final set of variables are used to address the research gap with understanding *sociodemographic dimensions* of trust, in particular gender, age and education level, a promising but underexplored area that needs other empirical evidence [3–5]. The list of variables and its operationalization in the survey and the statistical analysis is presented in Table 1. In general, our hypotheses are that higher level of trust in G2C communication online is positively defined by the (1) citizens' experience of using the tools; (2) higher levels of perceived government responsiveness; (3) younger age; (4) higher level of education and (5) gender characteristics, when controlled by the level of the Internet use.

Table 1. Operationalization of the concepts

Concept	Variable	Question	Answers/Coding
Responsiveness	Perceived government responsiveness	Do you agree with the statement "As the Internet use increases, government bodies pay more attention to citizens' demands (become more responsive, attentive to citizens)"	4-Fully agree 3-Somewhat agree 2-Somewhat disagree 1-Fully disagree
C2G trust online	in e-services in e-complaints and appeals in e-petition submission in voting for e-petitions in G2C communication in the social media	Do you trust ICTs as a communication tool in the following cases (e-services acquisition, e-complaints submission..)?	4-Yes, fully trust 3-Somewhat yes 2-Somewhat no 1-No
User experience	of the federal e-service portal usage (gosuslugi.ru) of the regional Our Petersburg portal usage of the federal e-petition portal RPI usage of submitting e-complaints and appeals to public authorities	Do you have a personal experience in: submitting an e-complaint, usage of the federal e-service portal...	4-Yes, and it is a positive experience 3-Yes, and it is a negative experience 2-No, but I want to try 1-No, and I do not want to try
Sociodemographic variables	Internet use frequency	5-Almost always online; 4-Every day; 3-Several times a week; 2-Several times a month; 1-Never	
	Age	6 – 18–25 years old; 5 – 26–35; 4 – 36–45; 3 – 46–55; 2 – 56–65; 1 – over 65 years old	
	Gender	1 – male; 0 – female	
	Education	3 – University; 2 – College; 1 – High School	

Data and Methods. The data we use come from the public opinion survey held in November 2018 in St. Petersburg. The sample contains 600 responses from visitors, randomly asked questions (Table 1) at six multi-functional centers that provide state and municipal services for citizens. The sample calculated is representative on the size, age and gender, the sampling error does not exceed 4%. Respondents were profiled by the level of the Internet use, age, gender and occupation. Overall there are 43% of men and 57% of women in the sample. The majority of the respondents are employees/specialists (39%), workers/guards/drivers (20%) and students (10%). To test the hypothesis we use several statistical methods. First, we run the exploratory correlation analysis (Kendall's tau) to find associations between the variables. Secondly, we use factor analysis to study dimensions of trust and reduce them into a single scale variable, which is used as an independent variable in the linear regression.

4   Empirical Analysis

Exploratory Correlation Analysis. The survey confirms that *C2G online trust* is indeed a multidimensional phenomenon, as the level of trust varies across channels.

In the correlation analysis (Table 2): while all dimensions of *G2C online trust* correlate positively and significantly with each other, the strength of association differs. Trust in e-services has the strongest correlation with trust in e-complaints, and trust in communication via social media is related closer to submitting e-petitions, thus forming two profiles of more formal and informal (or managerial and political) communication with public institutions. Although nothing can be said about causation at this point, most of our independent variables correlate positively with trust levels. For instance, perceived government responsiveness seems a promising predictor of trust. It presents rather similar significance across the sectors. The situation is more complicated with the user experience. On the one hand, at large, users tend to trust more than non-users, and indeed, exposure to particular channels in some cases correlates more strongly with trust to specific forms of communication (e-services, e-complaints and appeals). At the same time, experience of the Russian Public Initiative portal does not correlate with trust in e-petitioning, maybe due to the low level of its usage and efficacy [10].

Socio-demographic characteristics correlate significantly as well. Younger, more educated people and frequent Internet-users trust all online channels more. The weakest association here is with social media mechanisms, i.e. distrust in this channel is more or less equal among different social groups. While gender proves to be important is some cases (male respondents trust more in submitting e-complaints), other correlations are not so significant. It is important to note that previous studies in Saudi Arabia have shown reverse results [5], which proves that the context does matter.

Regression Analysis. Preliminary correlation analysis helps to identify the most promising predictors for the regression model. Before running the linear regression analysis, a single independent variable – *C2G online trust* – was calculated out of the measured dimensions. This was done by the factor analysis (principal component method), to reveal a possible latent factor that drives all of the dimensions. Based on the predefined settings of extraction (eigenvalues over 1), only one component was

Table 2. Results of the correlation analysis

	Trust (e-services)	Trust (e-complaints & appeals)	Trust (e-petition submission)	Trust (e-petition voting)	Trust (social media)
Trust (e-services)		,734** (600)	,670** (600)	,581** (600)	,549** (600)
Trust (e-complaints & appeals)	,734** (600)		,812** (600)	,727** (600)	,519** (600)
Trust (e-petition submission)	,670** (600)	,812** (600)		,857** (600)	,551** (600)
Trust (e-petition voting)	,581** (600)	,727** (600)	,857** (600)		,527** (600)
Trust (social media)	,549** (600)	,519** (600)	,551** (600)	,527** (600)	
Perceived government responsiveness	,446** (600)	,382** (600)	,454** (600)	,429** (600)	,399** (600)
Experience of e-services (Gosuslugi.ru)	,430** (562)	,388** (562)	,369** (562)	,320** (562)	,324** (562)
Experience of the Our Petersburg portal	,162** (528)	,128** (528)	,132** (528)	,119** (528)	,088* (528)
Experience of the Russian Public Initiative portal	,122** (509)	,047 (509)	,071 (509)	,059 (509)	,032 (509)
Experience of e-complaints submission	,307** (505)	,374** (505)	,348** (505)	,276** (505)	,273** (505)
Gender	,096* (600)	,104** (600)	,079* (600)	,090* (600)	,055 (600)
Age	,327** (600)	,429** (600)	,378** (600)	,313** (600)	,223** (600)
Level of education	,385** (600)	,373** (600)	,348** (600)	,333** (600)	,263** (600)
Frequency of the internet use	,509** (593)	,575** (593)	,524** (593)	,467** (593)	,359** (593)

Note: **For Tables** 2, **4 and** 5: ** - correlation significance at 0,01 level; * - correlation significance at 0,01 level, number of cases is indicated in brackets

revealed that explains about 77% of the variance. The component matrix (Table 3) shows substantially high loadings of all variables on the factor, and the extracted factor correlates highly and significantly with all the variables (Table 4). Although some of the data inevitably disappear during the procedure, it seems nevertheless justified to use the factor as a single scale independent variable.

The regression analysis (OLS) was carried out to identify the model that best suits the data. All models presented are checked on the basic assumptions of the lack of multicollinearity, autocorrelation and heteroscedasticity. We compare models and variables based on the standardized beta-coefficients of predictors, as well as take into account the percentage of explained variance (adjusted R-square) and the level of standardized error. The selected models are presented in Table 5.

Table 3. Component matrix – C2G online trust

Trust in...				
E-services	E-complaints & appeals	E-petition submission	E-petition voting	Social media
,862	,921	,941	,899	,758

Table 4. Results of the correlation analysis (Kendall's tau)

	Trust (e-services)	Trust (e-complaints & appeals)	Trust (e-petition submission)	Trust (e-petition voting)	Trust (social media)
C2G online trust	,726** (600)	,803** (600)	,844** (600)	,792** (600)	,638** (600)

Table 5. Regression models (dependent variable – C2G online trust)

Predictors	Standardized beta - coefficients					
	Model 1	Model 2	Model 3	Model 4	Model 5	Model 6
Perceived responsiveness	,280**	,277**	,292**	,290**	,289**	,315**
Experience of e-services	,057	,034	-	-	-	,161**
Experience of the Our Petersburg portal	,008	-	-	-	-	,018
Experience of the RPI portal	−,074	-	-	-	-	−,080
Experience of e-complaints	,102**	,101**	116**	,111**	,121**	,164**
Gender	−,010	,000	-	-	-	,008
Age	,066	,061	,065	-	-	,280**
Education	,081	,069	,089	0,88	-	,179**
Internet use	,453**	,467**	,451**	,497**	,540**	-
Adj. R-square	**,581**	**,574**	**,563**	**,562**	**,557**	**,521**
Std. error	**,634**	**,631**	**,640**	**,640**	**,644**	**,684**

The first finding is that the level of perceived government responsiveness remains a significant predictor of *C2G online trust* throughout all models and when controlled for other variables. Thus we may confirm the hypothesis that more positive views of government responsiveness positively influence the trustworthiness of C2G communications on the Internet from the citizens' viewpoint.

In the case of the user experience the results are more modest. Only experience in submitting e-complaints is significant when controlled for other factors, and the coefficient is not very high. It may be explained statistically, due to a relatively higher loading of trust in e-complaints in the final variable (Table 3), which makes it more connected to this particular experience. Also, a strong correlation between different experiences makes it problematic to use them in one model. Current results suggest partial confirmation of the hypothesis with the need of further testing.

While gender is not significant in all the models, age and education level can be considered relevant predictors, only when they are not controlled for the Internet use frequency (Model 6) and lose their significance in other models. In other words, while a more frequent use of the Internet is indeed expected from younger or more educated people, the former influences the level of trust more strongly. Thus the hypotheses related to these factors are rather rejected.

Overall, the best model we have found for the data is Model 5, which includes perceived government responsiveness, user experience in e-complaints and the frequency of Internet use. It explains about 56% of the variance. While this is a good result, more research is to be done to build a more comprehensive model.

5 Discussion

This pilot study is a starting point of the project, but its results may already contribute to the existing research. First of all, it presents a new empirical case, so far underexplored in the studies of online trust. Though the survey was carried out in one city and cannot be extrapolated to the whole country, the findings may be used to compare, how different national (regional) contexts moderate predictors of trust to C2G online communications. Secondly, our findings confirm the necessity to consider *C2G online trust* as a broad multidimensional concept that broadens and synthesizes the phenomena of trust in e-government and e-participation [28, 34], involves new issues like new media [2], and is a resultant of trust in communication with the government via different channels. Thirdly, we have tested the importance of perceived government responsiveness, different dynamics of user experience, and sociodemographic characteristics, thus providing new empirical evidence to these areas of inquiry. Finally, our scientometrics analysis can also be of use for further research on trust is e-government or e-participation contexts.

Of course, there are several limitations as well. Due to the survey-based statistical analysis, the findings are context-dependent and need to be contrasted against similar studies (e.g. [5]). The number of questions asked in the pilot survey was also limited, hence some possibly important items were not included. Limitations of the statistical analysis should also be considered, as the use of the Likert-scale and dummy variables cause complications in interpretation and leads to simplification of the models.

Finally, as most papers in the area, there is a problem of establishing causalities. This research deals with it empirically, assuming that user experience and prior feedback from the government influence the level of trust at the moment of survey. At the same time, we admit the link can go the other direction, which makes it necessary to continue developing a suitable theoretical model.

6 Conclusion

The research reiterates the importance of studying trust in relation to online communication with the government, exploring its dimensions and predictors. Several perspectives of further research can be discerned. Firstly, it is important to consider other dimensions of online trust (e.g. in e-commerce, e-health, e-education), institutional and interpersonal trust, and how they may relate or shape citizens' perceptions towards the government. Secondly, the presented models can be expanded in terms of new independent variables – user satisfaction, perceptions of security, depositions to trust – and specification of the models to particular sectors of e-government, e-participation and the social media. Thirdly, a new theoretical underpinning is to be developed, for better conceptualization of the findings. Most of these steps are planned in the forthcoming survey of 2019.

Acknowledgements. The study was performed with financial support by the grant from the Russian Foundation for Basic Research (project №18-311-20001): "The research of cybersocial trust in the context of the use and refusal of information technology".

References

1. Abu-Shanab, E.: Antecedents of trust in e-government services: an empirical test in Jordan. Transform. Gov. People Process. Policy **8**(4), 480–499 (2014). https://doi.org/10.1108/TG-08-2013-0027
2. Alarabiat, A., Soares, D.S., Estevez, E.: Predicting citizens acceptance of government-led e-participation initiatives through social Media: a theoretical model. In: Proceedings of the Hawaii International Conference on System Sciences (2017). https://doi.org/10.24251/hicss.2017.345
3. Albesher, A., et al.: The effects of individual differences on trust in e-Government services: an empirical evaluation. In: Janssen, M., et al. (eds.) Electronic Government and Electronic Participation, pp. 120–129. IOS Press, Amsterdam (2014)
4. Alzahrani, L., Al-Karaghouli, W., Weerakkody, V.: Analysing the critical factors influencing trust in e-government adoption from citizens' perspective: a systematic review and a conceptual framework. Int. Bus. Rev. **26**(1), 164–175 (2017). https://doi.org/10.1016/j.ibusrev.2016.06.004
5. Alzahrani, L., Al-Karaghouli, W., Weerakkody, V.: Investigating the impact of citizens' trust toward the successful adoption of e-government: a multigroup analysis of gender, age, and internet experience. Inf. Syst. Manag. **35**(2), 124–146 (2018). https://doi.org/10.1080/10580530.2018.1440730
6. Bart, Y., Shankar, V., Sultan, F., Urban, G.L.: Are the drivers and role of online trust the same for all web sites and consumers? A large-scale exploratory empirical study. J. Mark. **69**(4), 133–152 (2005). https://doi.org/10.1509/jmkg.2005.69.4.133
7. Belanche, D., Casaló, L.V., Flavián, C.: Integrating trust and personal values into the Technology Acceptance Model: the case of e-government services adoption. Cuadernos de Economía y Dirección de la Empresa **15**(4), 192–204 (2012). https://doi.org/10.1016/j.cede.2012.04.004
8. Carter, L., Bélanger, F.: The utilization of e-government services: citizen trust, innovation and acceptance factors. Inf. Syst. J. **15**(1), 5–25 (2005). https://doi.org/10.1111/j.1365-2575.2005.00183.x
9. Carter, L., Weerakkody, V., Phillips, B., Dwivedi, Y.K.: Citizen adoption of e-government services: exploring citizen perceptions of online services in the United States and United Kingdom. Inf. Syst. Manag. **33**(2), 124–140 (2016). https://doi.org/10.1080/10580530.2016.1155948
10. Chugunov, A.V., Kabanov, Y., Zenchenkova, K.: Russian e-petitions portal: exploring regional variance in use. In: Tambouris, E., et al. (eds.) ePart 2016. LNCS, vol. 9821, pp. 109–122. Springer, Cham (2016). https://doi.org/10.1007/978-3-319-45074-2_9
11. Colesca, S.E.: Understanding trust in e-government. Eng. Econ. **63**(4), 1–9 (2009). http://www.inzeko.ktu.lt/index.php/EE/article/view/11637
12. Costante, E., Den Hartog, J., Petkovic, M.: On-line trust perception: what really matters. In: 2011 1st Workshop on Socio-Technical Aspects in Security and Trust (STAST), pp. 52–59. IEEE (2011). https://doi.org/10.1109/stast.2011.6059256
13. Craig, S.C., Niemi, R.G., Silver, G.E.: Political efficacy and trust: a report on the NES pilot study items. Polit. Behav. **12**(3), 289–314 (1990). https://doi.org/10.1007/BF00992337
14. Delone, W.H., McLean, E.R.: The DeLone and McLean model of information systems success: a ten-year update. J. Manag. Inf. Syst. **19**(4), 9–30 (2003). https://doi.org/10.1.1.88.3031
15. Distel, B.: Bringing light into the shadows: a qualitative interview study on citizens' non-adoption of e-Government. Electron. J. e-Gov. **16**(2), 98–105 (2018)

16. Esaiasson, P., Kölln, A.K., Turper, S.: External efficacy and perceived responsiveness—Similar but distinct concepts. Int. J. Public Opin. Res. **27**(3), 432–445 (2015). https://doi.org/10.1093/ijpor/edv003
17. Gibson, R., Cantijoch, M.: Conceptualizing and measuring participation in the age of the internet: is online political engagement really different to offline? J. Polit. **75**(3), 701–716 (2013). https://doi.org/10.1017/s0022381613000431
18. Horsburgh, S., Goldfinch, S., Gauld, R.: Is public trust in government associated with trust in e-government? Soc. Sci. Comput. Rev. **29**(2), 232–241 (2011). https://doi.org/10.1177/0894439310368130
19. Irani, Z., et al.: An analysis of methodologies utilised in e-government research: a user satisfaction perspective. J. Enterp. Inf. Manag. **25**(3), 298–313 (2012). https://doi.org/10.1108/17410391211224417
20. Kassim, E.S., Jailani, S.F.A.K., Hairuddin, H., Zamzuri, N.H.: Information system acceptance and user satisfaction: the mediating role of trust. Procedia Soc. Behav. Sci. **57**, 412–418 (2012)
21. Kim, S., Lee, J.: E-participation, transparency, and trust in local government. Public Adm. Rev. **72**(6), 819–828 (2012). https://doi.org/10.1111/j.1540-6210.2012.02593.x
22. Lee, A., Levy, Y.: The effect of information quality on trust in e-government systems' transformation. Transform. Gov. People Process. Policy **8**(1), 76–100 (2014). https://doi.org/10.1108/TG-10-2012-0011
23. Lee, J., Kim, S.: Active citizen e-participation in local governance: do individual social capital and e-participation management matter? In: 2014 47th Hawaii International Conference on System Sciences, pp. 2044–2053. IEEE (2014). https://doi.org/10.1109/hicss.2014.259
24. Liu, Y., Zhou, C.: A citizen trust model for e-government. In: 2010 IEEE International Conference on Software Engineering and Service Sciences, pp. 751–754. IEEE (2010). https://doi.org/10.1109/icsess.2010.5552260
25. Ma, L.: How does E-government usage affect citizen trust: the mediating effects of government transparency and responsiveness. J. Public Adm. **9**(6), 44–63 (2016)
26. Mahmood, M., Osmani, M., Sivarajah, U.: The role of trust in e-government adoption: a systematic literature review. In: Americas Conference on Information Systems, Savannah, pp. 1–16 (2014)
27. Mpinganjira, M.: Use of e-government services: the role of trust. Int. J. Emerg. Mark. **10**(4), 622–633 (2015). https://doi.org/10.1108/IJoEM-12-2013-0151
28. Papadopoulou, P., Nikolaidou, M., Martakos, D.: What is trust in e-government? A proposed typology. In: 2010 43rd Hawaii International Conference on System Sciences, pp. 1–10. IEEE (2010). https://doi.org/10.1109/hicss.2010.491
29. Porumbescu, G.A.: Placing the effect? Gleaning insights into the relationship between citizens' use of e-government and trust in government. Public Manag. Rev. **18**(10), 1504–1535 (2016). https://doi.org/10.1080/14719037.2015.1122827
30. Sambasivan, M., Patrick Wemyss, G., Che Rose, R.: User acceptance of a G2B system: a case of electronic procurement system in Malaysia. Internet Res. **20**(2), 169–187 (2010). https://doi.org/10.1108/10662241011032236
31. Santamaría-Philco, A., Wimmer, M.A.: Trust in e-participation: an empirical research on the influencing factors. In: Proceedings of the 19th Annual International Conference on Digital Government Research: Governance in the Data Age, no. 64. ACM (2018). https://doi.org/10.1145/3209281.3209286
32. Sasaki, F.: Online political efficacy (OPE) as a reliable survey measure of political empowerment when using the internet. Policy Internet **8**(2), 197–214 (2016). https://doi.org/10.1002/poi3.114

33. Scherer, S., Wimmer, M.A.: Trust in e-participation: literature review and emerging research needs. In: Proceedings of the 8th International Conference on Theory and Practice of Electronic Governance, ICEGOV, pp. 61–70. ACM (2014). https://doi.org/10.1145/2691195.2691237

34. Scherer, S., Wimmer, M.A.: Conceptualising trust in E-participation contexts. In: Tambouris, E., Macintosh, A., Dannister, F. (eds.) Electronic Participation, ePart 2014. LNCS, vol. 8654, pp. 64–77. Springer, Heidelberg (2014). https://doi.org/10.1007/978-3-662-44914-1_6

35. Song, C., Lee, J.: Citizens' use of social media in government, perceived transparency, and trust in government. Public Perform. Manag. Rev. **39**(2), 430–453 (2016). https://doi.org/10.1080/15309576.2015.1108798

36. Tolbert, C.J., Mossberger, K.: The effects of e-government on trust and confidence in government. Public Adm. Rev. **66**(3), 354–369 (2006). https://doi.org/10.1111/j.1540-6210.2006.00594.x

37. Van de Walle, S., Zeibote, Z., Stacenko, S., Muravska, T., Migchelbrink, K.: Explaining non-adoption of electronic government services by citizens: a study among non-users of public e-services in Latvia. Information Polity (Preprint), 1–11 (2018)

38. Van Eck, N., Waltman, L.: Software survey: VOSviewer, a computer program for bibliometric mapping. Scientometrics **84**(2), 523–538 (2009). https://doi.org/10.1007/s11192-009-0146-3

39. Vidiasova, L., Tensina, I.: E-participation social effectiveness: case of "Our Petersburg" portal. In: Chugunov, A., Misnikov, Y., Roshchin, E., Trutnev, D. (eds.) Electronic Governance and Open Society: Challenges in Eurasia, EGOSE 2018. CCIS, vol. 947, pp. 308–318. Springer, Cham (2018). https://doi.org/10.1007/978-3-030-13283-5_23

40. Zolotov, M.N., Oliveira, T., Casteleyn, S.: E-participation adoption models research in the last 17 years: a weight and meta-analytical review. Comput. Hum. Behav. **81**, 350–365 (2018). https://doi.org/10.1016/j.chb.2017.12.031

Setting Up Government 3.0 Solutions Based on Open Source Software: The Case of X-Road

Gregorio Robles[1,2]([envelope]), Jonas Gamalielsson[1], and Björn Lundell[1]

[1] Software Systems Research Group, University of Skövde, Skövde, Sweden
{gregorio.robles,jonas.gamalielsson,bjorn.lundell}@his.se
[2] GSyC/LibreSoft, Universidad Rey Juan Carlos, Madrid, Spain

Abstract. Government 3.0, which builds on openness and transparency, sharing, increased communication and collaboration, government reorganization through integration and interoperability, and use of new technologies, is an emerging concept in eGovernance. However, few systems that qualify as Government 3.0 have been described in detail so far. And there is a lack of research on how governments can put in place such systems. This study investigates and characterizes an innovative eGovernment project, based on Open Source Software (OSS), that could be considered as an example of a Government 3.0 project. Therefore, we report from a case study of X-Road, an originally Estonian eGovernment project for creating a data sharing infrastructure, which today is also used in other countries. We present the main characteristics of X-Road from the point of view of Government 3.0, how the X-Road project is organized, compare its organization to other OSS projects, identify who contributes to the project, and point out what challenges are perceived by their stakeholders. We conclude offering some reflections on how X-Road and other Government 3.0 projects can benefit from OSS.

Keywords: eGovernment · Government 3.0 · Open Source Software · Platform · Interoperability · Community

1 Introduction

Government 3.0 has been proposed recently as a concept to describe the next generation of services and solutions offered by governments [28]. Although there is no widely agreed definition of what Government 3.0 means and supposes, there is agreement that it is based on openness and transparency, sharing, increased communication and collaboration, government reorganization through integration and interoperability, and use of new technologies [29].

Although there are few examples of what could be considered a Government 3.0 solution, there is some previous research that has already offered and discussed one, the Finnish Suomi.fi platform [38]. In this paper, we report on an

© IFIP International Federation for Information Processing 2019
Published by Springer Nature Switzerland AG 2019
I. Lindgren et al. (Eds.): EGOV 2019, LNCS 11685, pp. 69–81, 2019.
https://doi.org/10.1007/978-3-030-27325-5_6

investigation of how Governments can set up Government 3.0 solutions through the analysis of the X-Road project. X-Road comprises a data exchange layer solution which empowers different organizations to exchange data and information over the Internet and ensures confidentiality, integrity and interoperability between data exchange parties. X-Road is a central part of the Estonian eGovernment services and has been so for more than 15 years [16,18]. It offers the main infrastructure for the Estonian e-Residency [20] and is being used, among others, in health-care [35] and e-voting [36]. The Finnish Suomi.fi initiative mentioned above is also backed by X-Road [38].

An important characteristic of X-Road is that it has been conceived to be widely adopted, mainly by other states. So, together with the Finnish government, Estonians merged efforts in the Nordic Institute for Interoperability Solutions (NIIS) to foster X-road and related technologies. X-Road is provided as Open Source Software (OSS)[1], first under the European Union Public License and more recently under the MIT open source license[2]. While the involvement of governments in OSS is not new, X-Road can be considered as a new scenario, given that the requirements for Government 3.0 solutions require a different approach by Governments. For these reasons, we find that X-Road constitutes an interesting, and somewhat unique, initiative which motivates investigations and detailed scrutiny.

In particular, the overarching research goal pursued in this study is to characterize how a Government 3.0 solution can be (and is being) implemented through the deployment of the X-Road OSS project.

The study investigates four specific research questions (RQs):

- RQ1: What are the main characteristics of X-Road?
- RQ2: How is the organizational structure of X-Road and how does it differ from other OSS projects?
- RQ3: Who are the contributors to X-Road and what are their roles?
- RQ4: What challenges do different stakeholders of the X-Road project perceive?

The structure of this paper is as follows: In Sect. 2 we offer related research. Next, in Sect. 3, we present the research approach used in this study. Section 4 reports on the results of answering the four research questions. Finally, Sect. 5 discusses our results and contributions, and concludes the paper.

2   Related Research

Governments have led many initiatives regarding OSS in the past. Among these, we can point out the creation of infrastructure to enable sharing among different public institutions [12] or a wide legislative effort to adopt and sometimes

---

[1] Software provided under the terms of an OSS license allows use, modification and redistribution.

[2] https://opensource.org/licenses/MIT – Accessed 2019-03-15.

embrace OSS [25]. Governments have had interest in the adoption and use of OSS solutions [22,33]. Notably, there are many papers on the advantages of adopting OSS in governments [14,21] and how OSS technologies can be used to restructure the Public Sector [11] and develop new eGovernment services [17]. Other actions related to OSS by governments are OSOR.eu (an OSS sharing system for e-government solutions in the EU [13]) or the many OSS observatories [5]. The use of OSS in the public sector is not without its challenges. ICT procurement still is a burden to the use of OSS and open standards [23], and not infrequently the adoption of OSS in the public sector comes after difficult negotiations and the fulfillment of special conditions [34].

The nature of OSS projects contributes to the formation of communities around them. Several scholars have studied their social structure. One of the models that has been widely used for describing the roles of OSS participants is the so called "onion" model [4]: the most contributing developers are in the center of the project (the "core" developers), *surrounded* by a new layer of occasional contributors. In an outer layer, we can find the *end users*. The further away from the center, the less contributions and influence a person has in the project. For large OSS projects, the outer layers outnumber in orders of magnitude the inner ones. Projects are then considered to have a surrounding community of users and developers, which has many positive effects on the project [31].

X-Road has been a matter of study, or at least referenced, in several works in the research literature. The functional structure and economic advantages of the X-Road project were early emphasized in an effort to modernize the national databases of Estonia [16]. Paide et al. recently studied the systematic exploitation of the X-Road for strengthening Public-Private partnership, and specifically, in light of the limited private sector interest in X-Road so far, how to "make a platform more acceptable for both public as well as private entities" [30]. X-Road fosters interoperability. The importance of interoperability in a eGovernment context has been highlighted since many years ago [10], showing it to be a crucial aspect of the services that many governments want to offer [19,27]. A recent report by Inera with a focus on national interoperability has analysed how existing solutions in Sweden relate to X-Road and elaborates on challenges and issues that need to be addressed prior to adoption of a national IT solution for data exchange in Sweden [15].

3   Research Approach

To pursue our research goal and address the RQs, we report from a case study on the X-Road project. Benbasat et al. consider that "[a] case study examines a phenomenon in its natural setting, employing multiple data collection methods to gather information from a few entities. The boundaries of the phenomenon are not clearly evident at the outset of the research and no experimental control or manipulation is used" [1]. Therefore, a mixed-methods approach has been used in this research [3], combining qualitative and quantitative data sources to offer a more complete perspective of the project, based on the analysis of publicly available sources and by means of interviewing relevant stakeholders of the X-Road project.

3.1 Analysis of Publicly Available Sources

Two different types of publicly available sources were analyzed.

– *Public documents:* We collected secondary data from the NIIS web news articles and blog posts that were written about X-Road. The number of collected secondary data was more than 100 items.
– *Publicly available Open Source project and related artifacts:* X-Road's source code can be obtained from an open collaborative platform[3] since mid-2015. We have analyzed the version control system where the history of the sources are stored with the help of a tool called Perceval [6], in order to obtain the individuals who have contributed code to the project.

3.2 Interviews

In order to gain first-hand insight from the project participants on the project, we performed a number of interviews. We decided to perform open interviews based on a set of questions prepared in advance, which were supplemented with additional questions as the interview progressed. According to Walsham, "[i]nterviews should be supplemented by other forms of field data in an interpretive study, and these may include press, media and other publications on the sectoral context of the organizations being studied. Internal documents, if made available, may include strategies, plans and evaluations. Direct observation or participant observation of action is a further data source" [37].

The goals of the interviews are (i) to validate our previous observations gathered from documents, web pages and videos, and (ii) to obtain additional, relevant information on X-Road and its organization in order to supplement already collected data, to thereby further enrich the analysis.

Therefore, we designed questions that helped to achieve these goals. In particular, the questions were related to the following areas: (i) participant's role, aim and experience, (ii) aims of the project, (iii) roles in the project, (iv) organizational structure of the project, and (v) perceived challenges of the project.

Given the nature of the interviews, not all questions that where prepared in advance were asked, as the natural flow of the conversation resulted in the interviewee addressing at once more than one question. Also, related to some questions, follow-up questions were asked in order to probe further as the interview session progressed.

We have performed purposeful sampling when inviting interviewees, based on the results of RQ2 and RQ3. So, we first classify the different groups of stakeholders in X-Road (RQ2: How is X-Road organized?), and then we identify for each of the groups interview candidates (RQ3: Who are the contributors to X-Road?). As a result, we have interviewed one stakeholder working at NIIS, another one being contractor of NIIS, and 4 among the rest of stakeholders (three former software engineers affiliated to companies offering services based on X-Read, and one end user). The rationale for this selection will become clear

---

[3] https://github.com/nordic-institute/X-Road – Accessed 2019-03-15.

when we present the results of RQ2 and RQ3, and is related to the fact that the source of the 'official' information on web and documents is NIIS (and its contractors), so the amount of new information and the additional insight we gain from interviewing them is lower than for the rest of the stakeholders.

The interviews were performed over *confcall* (Skype or Google Hangout). Interviews were recorded and transcribed in order to aid analysis.

4   Results

The results to the RQs are presented in the following four subsections.

4.1   Characterizing X-Road

Figure 1 presents an overview of the X-Road data exchange framework and its purpose. Instead of building a centralized, very big database with all data (a very complex, risky and costly alternative), Estonians chose for creating a framework to support and facilitate data exchange between databases over the Internet. X-Road serves as a data exchange bus between many databases that implements a set of common features to support and facilitate data exchange. All data exchange is secure, as all outgoing data from X-Road is digitally signed and encrypted, and all incoming data is authenticated and logged. The transversal nature of X-Road makes it possible to not only offer services from Governments, but invites as well participants from the private sector [30].

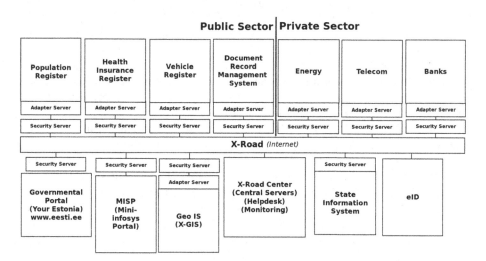

Fig. 1. X-Road data exchange framework   (Adapted- Original: World Bank - bit.ly/2WcIDB5)

The purpose of NIIS is to be "both a network and cooperation platform, and executioner of IT developments in members common interests. This is probably the first time in the world when a joint special purpose organization of two countries develops a OSS using agile software development methods." NIIS does not offer consultation services nor support for deploying independent X-Road instances. The X-Road website lists at this time five companies (three Finnish and two Estonian) who can be contacted on these matters.

As a result, we have observed that X-Road aims mainly to be an interoperability solution, that goes beyond just the public sector, and involves as well the private sector. To increase the adoption of such a solution, the X-Road project is released under a OSS license, so that use and reuse can be maximized. This way, the project addresses the problem of deployments being different in every country. This is because countries usually have a different usage context, as data and regulations are different from country to country.

4.2   Organizational Structure of X-Road

X-Road is a growing community[4]. It has been reported that X-Road in Estonia currently has 671 institutions and enterprises, 516 public sector institutions, 52,000 organizations are indirect users of X-Road services, 1620 interfaced information systems, 2706 services that can be used via X-Road, and 372 security servers installed by members[5]. X-Road is also implemented in Azerbaijan, Namibia and Faroe Islands[6].

The Department of State Information Systems of the Ministry of Transport and Communications in Estonia was initially governing the development of X-Road (known as "X-tee" in the Estonian context). A new governance regime was initiated in 2017 when the Estonian and Finnish governments established the Nordic Institute for Interoperability Solutions (NIIS) in a joint effort for further development of the X-Road project. The purpose of NIIS is to be "both a network and cooperation platform, and executioner of IT developments in members common interests"[7]. This may be the first time in history that a joint special purpose organization involving two countries governs an OSS project. Iceland became a partner of NIIS in September 2018.

Concerning NIIS, its highest body is "the General Meeting of its Members. The Members of NIIS are the Ministry of Finance on behalf of the Republic of Finland and the Ministry of Economic Affairs and Communication on behalf of the Republic of Estonia." and it "is managed and represented by the Management Board"[8]. The Management Board is elected for three years and may have one to three members. The members of NIIS have agreed that the Management Board shall comprise a single member who shall act as the Chief Executive Officer of the Institute. The CEO is in charge of the day-to-day management of the Institute. Further, NIIS has an advisory group which "is formed for the

---

[4] X-Road community portal: https://x-road.global/ – Accessed 2019-03-15.

[5] https://www.ria.ee/en/calendar/anniversary-x-tee-2018.html, Accessed 2019-03-15.

[6] http://e-estonia.com/solutions/interoperability-services/x-road, Accessed 19-03-15.

[7] https://www.niis.org/data-exchange-layer-x-road/, Accessed 2019-03-15.

[8] https://www.niis.org/organization-and-management/, Accessed 2019-03-15.

purpose of supporting the Chief Executive Officer and relaying information and instruction between the operative level and the General Meeting. For clarity, the Advisory Group is not a formal organ of the Institute and has no decision-making power on its own".

The technical requirements in X-Road stem from the NIIS members (currently Finland and Estonia), as NIIS is based on them. The technological decisions are taken by NIIS, as well. When it comes to strategic decisions, the CTO is the one responsible for them, although they are discussed internally at NIIS (and consulted with the Finish and Estonian governments).

All in all, from our analysis of the X-Road project we conceptualize three layers in the organization of X-Road. In the center, being in charge of the strategic decisions and of the funding of the project, we have NIIS with its member states. A second layer is formed by contractors, who develop the system and/or deploy it in the different contexts. Contractors depend financially from NIIS, although they can offer services to the private sector as well. Finally, a third layer is composed by users and external developers, usually affiliated to companies who offer services around X-Road, some of these being former contractors.

A first difference to other forms of organization found in OSS projects is that their members are usually individuals or organizations/companies – in the case of X-Road, only countries can be members, although partnership is offered to private companies. Iceland is partner at the moment, although NIIS hopes that it will become a member in the near future. The aim in the near future is to find new countries to join NIIS and participate.

A second difference lies in the fact that in OSS projects, a central group of developers (known as the *core*) is the one responsible for a large majority of the actions – in the case of contributions to the code, the share of the core group usually ranges from 80 to 90% [32]. In X-Road, the central role is played by NIIS. But its contribution to the code is very limited, as this is mainly done by contractors.

A third difference is who takes the decisions. In X-Road, although there is no strict control in place of the development as stated by one of the contractors, the final decision -be it technical or not- is taken by NIIS. In comparison, in other OSS projects these type of decisions are taken by the developers (e.g., in GNOME [8]) or by low-level committees (e.g., Apache [7]). One of the external consultants interviewed, deepened in this situation. He stated that his company had launched a proprietary product that reimplemented X-Road from scratch, based on their experience of designing and implementing X-Road for years. This could be seen as a *fork*, an independent branch of the software that evolves independently (i.e., the developer teams and those who take decisions differ) [31]. Forks are intrinsic to the OSS licensing model, so they are not illegal. However, they are seen usually negatively as they duplicate efforts and often produce unnecessary tensions. In the opinion of this interviewee, their *fork* -even if it has a proprietary license- is more *open* to participation and is making progress in building a community than the X-Road project.

All in all, we see that X-Road deviates from the classical onion model found in OSS projects. The economic, decisional and strategic power resides in the center (NIIS and its members), but in comparison to what we find in OSS projects, it is not the main driver of (development) activity of the project. The development activity is mainly performed by an outer layer, contractors who financially depend on NIIS. Other stakeholders (including users) are in the outer layers, and have few control and decision power, even concerning minor decisions.

4.3   X-Road Contributors and Their Roles

X-Road and associated components are hosted on an open collaborative platform[9] to allow for world wide contributions from individuals and organizations. In total, 32 individuals have contributed to X-Road core from 2014 (based on analysis of author identifiers) until December 2018 (whereof 26 authors have made more than a single contribution). The five most active contributing individuals are Ilkka Seppälä (Gofore Oy, 305 contributions), Jarkko Hyöty (Gofore Oy, 230 contributions), Toomas Mölder (Republic of Estonia Information System Authority, 108 contributions), Joni Laurila (Gofore Oy, 107 contributions), and Tatu Repo (Gofore Oy, 96 contributions). There are 11 different organizational affiliations for committers (based on assessment of author email domains). The five most active contributing organizations are Gofore Oy (923 contributions), Cybernetica (133 contributions), Republic of Estonia Information System Authority (122 contributions), NIIS (56 contributions), and Qautomate Oy (42 contributions).

We asked interviewees the different roles that exist in the X-Road community. This does not only allow to compare their point of view with the roles that we had identified previously, but we also hypothesized that it could offer insight into how they perceive the community. To our surprise, we obtained a variety of responses. Interestingly enough, the organization who leads X-Road and the end-user offered a simpler model of the community, with less roles. So, according to NIIS, there are three different types of roles:

1. NIIS members: currently Estonia and Finland (with operator organizations responsible of running X-Road at the national level)
2. NIIS partners: currently Iceland and other organizations exchanging data (public bodies, private companies)
3. Citizens: those using servers, anyone can be member of that community (informally).

For end users, the picture is similar, although the differentiation is between public bodies, the private sector and citizens. This is understandable as end-users are not that much aware of the organization and participation in the community, and simplify these matters. For them, the prominent aspects are that the technology works, that it is free and gratis (not necessarily in that order).

---

[9] https://github.com/nordic-institute/X-Road,   https://github.com/jointxroad   – Accessed 2019-03-15.

It is other developers and external consultants who offer a much diverse community, much more in line with the identification of roles that we had performed. They see X-Road as a project with more actors, a sign that they see more opportunities in the X-Road project.

4.4 Challenges

Several challenges have been identified from the analysis of the interview responses.

We find that the current onboarding process is complex based on the analysis of the responses. New developers who want to contribute have to face a steady learning curve. In addition, very few vendors have experience and knowledge on X-Road and its technologies.

According to NIIS, the private sector is involved, primarily in Estonia. Several companies provide services (development, support, deployment, consulting, maintenance). However, no source code contribution so far has been received from the private sector. External developers and consultants have pointed out other initiatives where companies have used X-Road in their business strategy in many countries, far beyond Estonia and Finland.

Even if there is interest in many countries, the pace at which Governments move forward is slower than other organizations. The interviewees note that there is a lot of political *wheel*, and that a lot of explanations and consultations are to be expected for any new member to join.

From the point of view of strategic challenges, the nature of NIIS makes the project heavily dependent on its member countries. It has to be said that at the moment, all interviewees see a strong political support and do not expect this to be affected by a change in government in the near future. All respondents perceive that the support is so strong that this is independent of the political party that will be in the government.

5   Discussion and Conclusions

X-Road is an important project to investigate, not only because of its technological innovation, but as well because of its organizational structure. The fact that the members of the project are countries is novel in OSS. This also influences the type of organization that drives the project, how the strategy is considered and decisions are taken.

From the public documents and information that we have analyzed, and based on our analysis of observations, experiences and insights we have obtained from the interviewees, we have reflected on the goals that the X-Road project pursues. Thus, we have identified following goals: (i) to set up an interoperability solution, ready for being used by the public and private sector (the X-Road framework), (ii) to offer an OSS software that implements the aforementioned solution (the X-Road project), and (iii) to create a community of stakeholders, from the public and private sector, but as well final users/citizens.

In comparison to other OSS organizations, we find that X-Road has a more rigid structure. In addition, although other organizations try to have a structure that is more flat, in X-Road we note that strategy and decisions are mostly top-down. This makes sense and is aligned with the (political) priorities, and can be seen by the project structure. However, it has as well its potential drawbacks, as the creation of a community is not promoted in such a way as other OSS projects do, including those that are driven by a single company or a consortium of companies [9]. We acknowledge that NIIS has taken various initiatives for online training in order to promote the broader X-Road community.

We have found that different experiences and views emerged from the interviews. So, while for NIIS, the organization in charge of its development and promotion, see X-Road as a project, the companies that are active in the project (as a subcontractor of NIIS or as external consultants) see X-Road as a more complex structure, with elements that make X-Road be conceived as a software ecosystem [26] (i.e., initiatives around X-Road beyond the *official* one exist). Further research should address the fact that Governments may want to create not only technology infrastructure, but how to offer opportunities for the private sector to embrace the effort. In this sense, we see *forking* as a less sensitive issue, if interoperability and a healthy ecosystem (probably with all software being OSS) is maintained.

It is noteworthy to see that one of these initiatives has resulted in a derivative project - with the intention to become a fork. The permissive license of X-Road allows for further creation of proprietary solutions from vendors. It is our understanding that the current organizational structure of the project would have benefited from a copyleft license, as this would imply that third party vendors (basically companies) have to distribute their enhancements under the same license. In this regard, based on the analysis and prior experience from implementation of specifications for data exchange in other domains [24], we conjecture that the LGPL license would have been a feasible alternative [2], and we consider that appropriate license choice for X-Road needs further investigations.

In this study we have conducted a single case study, with its particularities and peculiarities. Rich insights and experiences from those involved with X-Road and NIIS provide valuable findings which can be transferred to other similar contexts. However, we cannot claim that our results can be generalized to all contexts.

In conclusion, we have investigated the X-Road project, an OSS project that is led by an organization created by two countries. The nature of X-Road is of interest because of its organizational structure. By means of six interviews to several stakeholders holding different roles in X-Road we have gained some insight into the nature of the project.

References

1. Benbasat, I., Goldstein, D.K., Mead, M.: The case research strategy in studies of information systems. MIS Q. **11**, 369–386 (1987)
2. Colazo, J., Fang, Y.: Impact of license choice on open source software development activity. J. Am. Soc. Inf. Sci. Technol. **60**(5), 997–1011 (2009)
3. Creswell, J.W., Plano Clark, V.L., Gutmann, M.L., Hanson, W.E.: Advanced mixed methods research designs. In: Handbook of Mixed Methods in Social and Behavioral Research, vol. 209, p. 240 (2003)
4. Crowston, K., Howison, J.: The social structure of open source software development teams. First Monday **10**(2) (2005)
5. Davini, E., Faggioni, E., Tartari, D.: Open source software in public administration. A real example OSS for e-Government observatories. In: First International Conference on Open Source Systems, pp. 119–124 (2005)
6. Dueñas, S., Cosentino, V., Robles, G., Gonzalez-Barahona, J.M.: Perceval: software project data at your will. In: 40th ICSE Companion Proceedings, pp. 1–4 (2018)
7. Fielding, R.T.: Shared leadership in the Apache project. Commun. ACM **42**(4), 42–43 (1999)
8. German, D.M.: The evolution of the GNOME Project. In: Proceedings of the 2nd Workshop on Open Source Software Engineering, pp. 20–24 (2002)
9. Gonzalez-Barahona, J.M., Izquierdo-Cortazar, D., Maffulli, S., Robles, G.: Understanding how companies interact with free software communities. IEEE Softw. **30**(5), 38–45 (2013)
10. Guijarro, L.: Interoperability frameworks and enterprise architectures in e-government initiatives in Europe and the United States. Gov. Inf. Q. **24**(1), 89–101 (2007)
11. Hautamäki, A., Oksanen, K.: Digital platforms for restructuring the public sector. In: Smedlund, A., Lindblom, A., Mitronen, L. (eds.) Collaborative Value Co-creation in the Platform Economy. TSS, vol. 11, pp. 91–108. Springer, Singapore (2018). https://doi.org/10.1007/978-981-10-8956-5_5
12. Hollmann, V., Lee, H., Zo, H., Ciganek, A.P.: Examining success factors of open source software repositories: the case of OSOR.eu portal. Int. J. Bus. Inf. Syst. **14**(1), 1–20 (2013)
13. Hollmann, V., Zo, H.: OSOR.eu: an open source sharing system for e-Government solutions in the EU. In: Third International Conference on Convergence and Hybrid Information Technology, ICCIT 2008, vol. 2, pp. 992–996. IEEE (2008)
14. Huysmans, P., Ven, K., Verelst, J.: Reasons for the non-adoption of OpenOffice.org in a data-intensive public administration. First Monday **13**(10), 10 (2008)
15. Inera: En kunskaps PM om nationell interoperabilitet - Hur befintliga lösningar i Sverige idag förhåller sig till X-Road (2018). https://bit.ly/2FiayGQ
16. Kalja, A.: The X-Road project. A project to modernize Estonia's national databases. Baltic IT&T Rev. **24**, 47–48 (2002)
17. Kalja, A., Kindel, K., Kivi, R., Robal, T.: eGovernment services: how to develop them, how to manage them? In: Portland International Center for Management of Engineering and Technology, pp. 2795–2798. IEEE (2007)
18. Kalvet, T.: The Estonian information society developments since the 1990s. PRAXIS (2007)
19. Klievink, B., Zuiderwijk, A., Janssen, M.: Interconnecting governments, businesses and citizens – a comparison of two digital infrastructures. In: Janssen, M., Scholl, H.J., Wimmer, M.A., Bannister, F. (eds.) EGOV 2014. LNCS, vol. 8653, pp. 84–95. Springer, Heidelberg (2014). https://doi.org/10.1007/978-3-662-44426-9_7

20. Kotka, T., Vargas, C., Korjus, K.: Estonian e-residency: redefining the nation-state in the digital era. University of Oxford, Working Paper Series 3, 1–16 (2015)
21. Kovács, G.L., Drozdik, S., Succi, G., Zuliani, P.: Open source software for the public administration. In: Proceedings of the 6th International Workshop on Computer Science and Information Technologies (2004)
22. van Loon, A., Toshkov, D.: Adopting open source software in public administration: the importance of boundary spanners and political commitment. Gov. Inf. Q. **32**(2), 207–215 (2015)
23. Lundell, B.: e-Governance in public sector ICT procurement: what is shaping practice in Sweden? Eur. J. ePractice **12**(4), 66–78 (2011)
24. Lundell, B., van der Linden, F.: Open source software as open innovation: experiences from the medical domain. In: Eriksson Lundström, J., Wiberg, M., Hrastinski, S., Edenius, M., Ågerfalk, P. (eds.) Managing Open Innovation Technologies, pp. 3–16. Springer, Heidelberg (2013). https://doi.org/10.1007/978-3-642-31650-0_1
25. Maldonado, E.: The process of introducing FLOSS in the public administration: the case of Venezuela. J. Assoc. Inf. Syst. **11**(11), 756 (2010)
26. Messerschmitt, D.G., Szyperski, C., et al.: Software Ecosystem: Understanding an Indispensable Technology and Industry, vol. 1. MIT Press Books, Cambridge (2005)
27. Mondorf, A., Wimmer, M.A.: Requirements for an architecture framework for Pan-European E-Government services. In: Scholl, H.J., Glassey, O., Janssen, M., Klievink, B., Lindgren, I., Parycek, P., Tambouris, E., Wimmer, M.A., Janowski, T., Sá Soares, D. (eds.) EGOVIS 2016. LNCS, vol. 9820, pp. 135–150. Springer, Cham (2016). https://doi.org/10.1007/978-3-319-44421-5_11
28. Nam, T.: Government 3.0 in Korea: fad or fashion? In: Proceedings of the 7th International Conference on Theory and Practice of Electronic Governance, pp. 46–55. ACM (2013)
29. Nielsen, M.M.: Governance failure in light of Government 3.0: foundations for building next generation eGovernment maturity models. In: Ojo, A., Millard, J. (eds.) Government 3.0-Next Generation Government Technology Infrastructure and Services, vol. 32, pp. 63–109. Springer, Cham (2017). https://doi.org/10.1007/978-3-319-63743-3_4
30. Paide, K., Pappel, I., Vainsalu, H., Draheim, D.: On the systematic exploitation of the Estonian data exchange layer X-Road for strengthening public-private partnerships. In: Proceedings of the 11th International Conference on Theory and Practice of Electronic Governance, pp. 34–41. ACM (2018)
31. Robles, G., González-Barahona, J.M.: A comprehensive study of software forks: dates, reasons and outcomes. In: Hammouda, I., Lundell, B., Mikkonen, T., Scacchi, W. (eds.) OSS 2012. IAICT, vol. 378, pp. 1–14. Springer, Heidelberg (2012). https://doi.org/10.1007/978-3-642-33442-9_1
32. Robles, G., Gonzalez-Barahona, J.M., Herraiz, I.: Evolution of the core team of developers in libre software projects. In: MSR. IEEE (2009)
33. Rossi, B., Russo, B., Succi, G.: A study on the introduction of Open Source Software in the Public Administration. In: Damiani, E., Fitzgerald, B., Scacchi, W., Scotto, M., Succi, G. (eds.) OSS 2006. IIFIP, vol. 203, pp. 165–171. Springer, Boston, MA (2006). https://doi.org/10.1007/0-387-34226-5_16
34. Shaikh, M.: Negotiating open source software adoption in the UK public sector. Gov. Inf. Q. **33**(1), 115–132 (2016)
35. Tiik, M., Ross, P.: Patient opportunities in the Estonian electronic health record system. Stud. Health Technol. Inform. **156**, 171–7 (2010)

36. Tsahkna, A.G.: E-voting: lessons from Estonia. Euro. View **12**(1), 59–66 (2013)
37. Walsham, G.: Doing interpretive research. Eur. J. Inf. Syst. **15**(3), 320–330 (2006)
38. Yli-Huumo, J., Päivärinta, T., Rinne, J., Smolander, K.: Suomi.fi – towards government 3.0 with a national service platform. In: Parycek, P., Glassey, O., Janssen, M., Scholl, H.J., Tambouris, E., Kalampokis, E., Virkar, S. (eds.) EGOV 2018. LNCS, vol. 11020, pp. 3–14. Springer, Cham (2018). https://doi.org/10.1007/978-3-319-98690-6_1

An Intercountry Survey of Participatory Practices Used for Open Government Partnership National Action Plan Development

Athanasia Routzouni[1]([✉]) [iD], Athanasios P. Deligiannis[2] [iD],
Vassilios Peristeras[3] [iD], and Stefanos Gritzalis[1] [iD]

[1] University of the Aegean, 83200 Karlovassi, Samos, Greece
nroutzouni@aegean.gr
[2] International Hellenic University, 57001 Thessaloniki, Greece
[3] European Commission, DG Informatics | International Hellenic University,
57001 Thessaloniki, Greece

Abstract. This paper maps the participatory process applied during the development of open government commitments by twenty-nine Open Government Partnership countries. It investigates the role and perceived value of e-participation practices and their relationship to inclusive interaction with stakeholders. The insights of the paper on the perceived value of the tools and methods used and the main impediments to the open government commitment creation process may help governments more effectively design their public participation efforts and increase the level of civic engagement in policy making. Although the results of this analysis derive from activities related to open government reforms, they may also be applicable to introducing participatory public policy formulation approaches in a broader range of policy domains.

Keywords: Open government · Public policy co-creation · E-participation · Open Government Partnership

Track: General E-Government & Open Government

1 Introduction

This paper attempts to map participatory practices that are used by governments when designing public policy, specifically open government commitments. It analyzes public participation practices and tools that have been applied by twenty-nine governments that were active in the Open Government Partnership (OGP) during the development of National Action Plans (NAPs) with specific commitments on open government issues.

The presented practices have been applied to support an effective dialogue between government and civil society for policy formulation. Successful ones can be used as a tool to strengthen public accountability and transparency in government operations in an era characterized by an erosion of trust in government [1]. The analysis of the

---

A. Routzouni and A. P. Deligiannis—These authors contributed equally to the work.

© IFIP International Federation for Information Processing 2019
Published by Springer Nature Switzerland AG 2019
I. Lindgren et al. (Eds.): EGOV 2019, LNCS 11685, pp. 82–93, 2019.
https://doi.org/10.1007/978-3-030-27325-5_7

perceived value of the applied practices along with the identification of the main impediments to the process may also help governments more effectively design their relevant public participation processes and increase the level of public participation in policy making.

Although the results of this analysis derive from processes related to open government reforms, they may also be applicable to introducing participatory public policy formulation approaches in a broader range of policy domains.

1.1   The Concept of Participation in Public Policy Making

Embedding the principle of participation in public policy making is not a new concept. Arnstein [2] introduced in 1969 the "*ladder of citizen participation*" outlining different levels of citizen participation ranging from pretextual to truly meaningful. Medimorec [3] added a level, "codetermination", in which citizens co-decide, usually with politicians and administrators. The concept of participation evolved to Manzini's "*map of participation*" [4] which further describes the involvement of different actors in the design process along with their interaction. In light of research that points to a loss of social capital [5] combined with and a decline in trust of government [6], civic engagement is seen as a necessary prerequisite and central component of vital democracies.

The most common approaches to citizen engagement include: electoral approaches (running for office, volunteering at campaigns), legislative and administrative information exchange approaches (public hearings), civil society approaches (participation via volunteer organizations, social clubs, and other forms of association) and deliberative and consensus-based approaches (joint action across sectors of society, classes of people, or types of individuals) [7].

An open, participatory approach to government is suggested to restore legitimacy to government and improve trust in its operation by enhancing accountability [1, 8] and attenuate corruption [9]. By consulting with citizens, government can improve transparency, access and service quality [10].

Enabling meaningful civic participation is seen as a fundamental requirement of well-functioning democracies and should be a priority for governments [11]. The OECD recognizes three levels of participation: information provision, which although a one way flow from the government to a two-way interaction that enables citizens to provide feedback; and active citizen participation, in which citizen's engagement is requested for defining and shaping policies leaving the final decision under the responsibility of the government [12, 13].

An alternative citizen participation spectrum is offered by the International Association for Public Participation (IAP2) [14] with five levels: (1) Inform, which entails providing the public with the necessary information on a given issue; (2) Consult, describing efforts at getting simple feedback from the public; (3) Involve, which describes efforts to engage with the public in more interactive ways to more deeply address their concerns; (4) Collaborate, which entails a meaningful partnership with the public in each aspect of the decision making process utilizing co-creation methods; and (5) Empower, a stage that includes co-creation activities and puts the final decision-making in the hands of the public as well [15]. The IAP2 public participation spectrum [16] is used by OGP to classify the quality of public participation.

1.2   E-Participation in Public Policy Making

There is significant evidence that the use of Information and Communications Technology (ICT) can expand opportunities for civic engagement and increase opportunities for people to participate in decision-making processes and service delivery [17]. For these purposes e-participation can be defined as the *"process of engaging citizens through ICTs in policy, decision-making, and service design and delivery to make it participatory, inclusive, and deliberative"* [18].

According to OECD guidelines [11] e-participation is dependent on three main conditions: (i) a clear focus on policies, decisions and governance practices to align them with to people's needs; (ii) particular attention to the means of interaction – communication channels should be readily made available for people to offer their views and communicate among themselves as peers and with public authorities as partners; and (iii) clear focus on the characteristics of the interaction process between citizens and government to ensure the quality and legitimacy of e-participation efforts [19].

1.3   The Participation Principle in Formulating Open Government Public Policies

Open and participative governance has evolved into a central pillar in the effort to modernize public administration at a global level [20]. Formulating public policies on empowering citizens, enhancing transparency, promoting integrity and accountability are central to government efforts for administrative reforms. In parallel, many international, European and national initiatives assist governmental efforts to promote horizontal government policies on Open Government and Innovation [21].

Public policy formulation is part of the pre-decision phase of public policy making. This phase involves identifying a range of policy alternatives and specifying policy tools and solutions to address the challenges within the public policy agenda [22].

One of the most notable initiatives to support the global open government agenda is the Open Government Partnership (OGP), a multi-stakeholder platform launched in 2011, which in 2019 brings together 79 countries that have committed to making their governments more open and accountable [23]. Recognizing that the process of formulating open government policies involves a wide network of stakeholders and policymakers, OGP promotes effective collaboration between governments and civil society organizations in open government policy making [24].

Each OGP participating country delivers bi-annually a National Action Plan (NAP) [16] which is the product of a co-creation effort between the government and civil society to develop concrete, time-bound and measurable open government commitments. Engaging civil society, citizens, and other stakeholders is considered a core element throughout the developing, implementing, monitoring and reporting processes of the action planning cycle [25].

The action plan evaluation process is comprised of two activities; progress reports produced by country local researchers working for the Independent Reporting Mechanism of the OGP and self-assessment reports produced by the participating governments. OGP's Participation and Co-creation Standards set out requirements for engaging civil society, citizens, and other stakeholders throughout the OGP process.

These standards also guide the content to be included in Self-Assessment Reports and include feedback mechanisms, space for co-creation, and facilitating a multistakeholder forum [16].

OGP also uses the International Association for Public Participation's (IAP2) "Participation Spectrum" to define the levels of citizen participation in developing an open government action plan. As already mentioned, the spectrum's participation levels are: Inform, Consult, Involve, Collaborate and Empower—government and civil society make joint decisions [26].

2   Methodology

The methodology of the present study includes analysis of the responses to a survey questionnaire which collected information on practices and tools applied during the development of OGP National Action Plans. These responses have also been compared to the results of the assessment made by the OGP Independent Reporting Mechanism on the levels of participation during action plan creation, as well as indicators such as the IAP2 spectrum for each country.

2.1   Participants

The participants of this study were members of the official network of National Points of Contact (PoC) in OGP participating countries. In each participating government, the PoC is the person responsible for coordinating the government's activities in relation to OGP [27]. PoC's are working-level counterparts to a ministerial-level representative. They are direct advisors to the national representative of each country to OGP and are usually drawn from the civil service of each country. During the development of a National Action Plan, the PoC engages with civil society and other stakeholders and cooperates with Ministries and other government organizations involved in the agenda that emerges during the co-creation process. A PoC also engages with OGP Support Unit to receive information on the OGP Participation and Co-creation Standards and on international best practices that could be applicable to the national policy agenda.

Twenty-nine PoCs responded to the questionnaire which corresponds to 36.7% of the total OGP countries in 2018. The countries represented are: Argentina, Armenia, Brazil, Chile, Colombia, Finland, France, Germany, Greece, Israel, Italy, Jordan, Lithuania, Luxembourg, Malawi, Malta, Mongolia, Nigeria, Panama, Paraguay, Philippines, Republic of North Macedonia, Romania, Serbia, Sierra Leone, Slovakia, the Czech Republic, the Netherlands and Ukraine.

2.2   Research Sources and Procedures

Survey Questionnaire on the Co-creation of OGP National Action Plans
An original electronic survey questionnaire based on the OGP Participation and Co-creation Standards [16] and recent literature on co-creation methods and tools [28–31] was created to examine the co-creation approaches that OGP participating countries

have applied to develop open government National Action Plans. A pilot study was conducted to verify the validity of the structure and content of the questionnaire. Five officials from OGP, working for the Support Unit and the Independent Reporting Mechanism, examined the questionnaire. The comments provided were taken into consideration for the final version. The online questionnaire was subsequently distributed to the official network of the PoCs in all 79 OGP participating governments.

The questionnaire explored the latest NAP creation period (2016–2018) and aimed to collect information related to the following key factors of the co-creation process: who initiated the co-creation process within government; the profile of participating stakeholders and the level of their contribution; the process objectives in each government; the characteristics of the engagement approach; the co-creation methods and tools employed; the number of participants in the co-creation activities; the impediments to the process; and the perceived contribution of the co-creation process on improving the completion rate of the Action Plan reforms.

Use of E-participation Methods and Tools in the Co-creation Process
The questionnaire also aimed to identify ICT-supported methods or tools that were used in the co-creation process. Specifically: use of a virtual platform for stakeholder engagement; use of ICT-supported co-creation methods (including social network analysis, online public consultations); use of ICT-supported co-creation tools (including consultation platforms, social media accounts, mobile contribution application, web discussion forums, online surveys); and value of including face to face meetings versus virtual/distance approaches in the co-creation process.

Comparisons Between Questionnaire Responses and OGP Assessment Results
OGP evaluates country performance on their action plan creation process using both its Independent Reporting Mechanism (IRM) as well as other openly available indicators. OGP then publishes independent progress reports for each participating country via the IRM. For each National Action Plan, the report summarizes the assessment of the development process and the country's progress in fulfilling key open government principles. OGP also releases, in open formats, the data underlying these reports [32, 33]. OGP data include an assessment of how each country has implemented the OGP consultation guidelines and to what extent each government works together with the civil society to develop the National Action Plan. OGP has published co-creation process assessment data for eighteen out of the twenty-nine countries that filled-in the OGP Co-Creation Questionnaire. The responses have been compared to the following indicators derived from already available OGP assessment data: *Level of public influence* using IAP2 spectrum; *"Open participation" or "Invitation only"* approach during consultation; and *Consultation steps followed* via six indicators that represent the main steps to be followed during Action Plan development (Availability of timeline prior to the consultation; Adequate advance notice; Awareness raising activities; Online consultation; In person consultations with the national community; Online publication of a summary of the received comments).

3 Results

3.1 Analysis of the Survey Questionnaire Responses

According to the responses to the questionnaire, the surveyed PoCs indicate that in 55 percent of the cases the government itself initiated the Action Plan development process while in 7 countries (24%) the process has been initiated by the government together with the Civil Society. In the rest of the cases (6 countries, 21%), the process was started by a multi-stakeholder forum.

The top identified reasons for using co-creation methodologies are related to strengthening the role of the stakeholders in the process (Engage stakeholders 97%; Increase trust between stakeholders 83%; Identify stakeholder needs 72%; Create a sense of ownership with stakeholders 66%). Raising awareness and communication have also been important factors in the process (Raising the level of awareness on different topics 59%; Improving communication processes 56%). It is worth noting that only one country replied that the required OGP co-creation criteria have been a reason for using co-creation methodologies in the process.

A significant percentage of countries (41.4%) have involved more than 100 participants, while 37.9% have involved more between 31 and 100 participants and 17.2% involved smaller groups of 1–30 people. The participating PoCs (72%) stated that civil society had a high contribution during the co-creation phase (in a scale from *1. Very much* to *5. Not at all*, 1: 48%; 2: 24%; 3: 24%; 4: 3%, 5: 0%).

The majority of participating PoCs (69%) stated that the co-creation process improves the content of the action plan (in a scale from *1. Very much* to *5. Not at all*, 1: 55%; 2: 14%; 3: 17%; 4: 7%, 5: 7%). More than half of the participants (58%) agreed that the co-creation process also improves the level of completion of the National Action Plan reforms (in a scale from *1. Very much* to *5. Not at all*, 1: 24%; 2: 34%; 3: 28%; 4: 10%, 5: 3%).

In terms of involving specific stakeholder groups, all PoCs (100%) responded that they usually engage civil society organizations and government departments. PoCs also involve academics (72%), citizens (55%), as well as the private sector and subnational government representatives (both groups at 72%). Parliament (41%) and the OGP Support Unit (38%) were less frequently involved while political parties have been totally absent from the co-creation process in all 29 countries.

Less than half of the countries (38%) have used e-participation platforms to involve stakeholders in the co-creation process. Except for one country that used a financial award scheme for the most active participating civil society organization, no rewards were used for co-creation participants.

The most frequently used co-creation methods include: SWOT workshops (43%), strategic roadmaps (29%), Living Labs (29%), appraisal interviews (14%), Personas (14%) and social network analysis (14%). To support the co-creation methods, the following tools have been primarily used by the countries included in the survey: Social media (83%), Crowd-mapping (35%), Mobile contribution applications (26%), Mind maps/Collaboration maps (17%), Issue cards (13%) and Motivational matrices (13%).

The participating PoCs indicated that the main impediments in the co-creation process have been the limited resources (66%) and the lack of time (52%) on the part of stakeholders as well as the difficulty in engaging stakeholders (38%). Other impediments include discontinuities caused by government changes and the electoral cycle (28%), difficulties in achieving consensus (21%) and a lack of trust in the effectiveness of the co-creation process (17%).

The OGP PoCs have also been asked to assess the significance of key factors in the co-creation process. The existence of permanent structures and processes, specifically the existence of permanent government agencies responsible for co-creation as well as the existence of a permanent stakeholder forum have been highlighted as key factors for the effectiveness of the process as shown in Fig. 1.

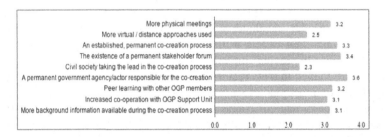

Fig. 1. Assessment of key factors in the co-creation process (Five-point Likert scale: 0 = not important, 4 = very important)

Almost a quarter of countries introduced ICT-supported methods in the OGP action plan co-creation process (24%). The main e-participation methods used are online public consultations and social network analysis. Less than half of the countries (38%) have used virtual platforms to engage with stakeholders but more countries have used e-participation tools (69%) in the co-creation process. The main e-participation tools used are social media (68%) and mobile contribution applications (21%). Some PoCs have also reported the use of web discussion forums (4%), online surveys (4%) and consultation platforms (4%).

PoCs report that use of a virtual engagement platforms does not make a significant contribution to NAP content quality. The countries that used a virtual platform, (38% of the total) reported 1: 55%; 2: 9%; 3: 18%; 4: 9%, 5: 9% while the rest reported 1: 56%; 2: 17%; 3: 17%; 4: 6%, 5: 6% (in a scale from *1. Very much to 5. Not at all*).

Adding face to face meetings during the co-creation process is reported by most PoCs (86%) as being of importance, more so than including virtual approaches in the co-creation process (55%).

3.2   Comparing Questionnaire Responses and OGP Assessment Results

Out of the 29 countries participating in this study, 18 participating countries have thus far been up assessed by OGP under the five levels of the IAP2 spectrum. They are classified in Table 1:

Comparing IAP2 levels with the use of e-participation tools reveals that of those countries belonging to lower IAP2 levels (Consult and Involve) half (50%) have used

Table 1. IAP2 Level of public influence in the co-creation process of OGP countries

IAP2 level	Countries
Inform	No countries
Consult	Jordan, Lithuania, Malawi, Malta, Netherlands, Serbia
Involve	Armenia, Czech Republic, Italy, Sierra Leone
Collaborate	Brazil, Chile, North Macedonia, Mongolia, Paraguay, Romania, Ukraine
Empower	Greece

e-participation tools while 75% of the countries in the upper IAP2 levels (Collaborate and Empower) have done the same.

OGP PoCs have been asked to indicate whether the co-creation process improves the content of the Action Plan[1]. Half of the countries (50%) belonging to the lower IAP2 levels (Consult and Involve) stated that the process improves the content of the Action Plan (in a scale from *1. Very much* to *5. Not at all*, 1: 40%; 2: 10%; 3: 30%; 4: 10%, 5: 0%). A higher percentage (75%) of the countries belonging to the upper IAP2 levels (Collaborate and Empower) agreed that co-creation improves the content of the Action Plan (1: 50%; 2: 25%; 3: 13%; 4: 0%, 5: 13%).

When asked if the co-creation process improves the level of completion of the included commitments, 40% of countries in the lower IAP2 levels (Consult and Involve) responded positively (1: 30%; 2: 10%; 3: 50%; 4: 10%, 5: 0%). More countries (63%) of the ones belonging to the upper IAP2 levels (Collaborate and Empower) have done the same (1: 13%; 2: 50%; 3: 13%; 4: 13%, 5: 13%).

PoCs have also been asked to assess the contribution of civil society organizations during the co-creation phase. Half of the countries (50%) belonging to the lower IAP2 levels (Consult and Involve) agreed that CSO's contributed highly (1: 30%; 2: 20%; 3: 50%; 4: 0%, 5: 0%). Most of the countries (88%) of the countries belonging to the upper IAP2 levels (Collaborate and Empower) agreed on the significant contribution of the CSO's in the process (1: 25%; 2: 63%; 3: 0%; 4: 13%, 5: 0%).

Regarding possible impediments to the co-creation process, half of the countries (50%) that are classified under the upper levels of public influence (Collaborate, Empower) have identified *"Difficulties in achieving consensus"* as an impediment to their process. On the other hand, no countries (0%) from the group of countries belonging to the lower IAP2 levels (Consult and Involve) recognized this impediment.

In terms of accessibility of the stakeholders to the consultation process, the 18 participating countries that have been assessed by OGP are classified under two relevant categories as follows: *Open Participation:* Armenia, Brazil, Chile, Greece, Italy, Lithuania, North Macedonia, Paraguay, Romania, Serbia, Sierra Leone and Ukraine, while *Invitation Only:* Czech Republic, Jordan, Malawi, Malta, Mongolia, Netherlands.

For countries that limited the process to invited stakeholders, the perceived contribution of the civil society organizations is lower compared to countries that applied

---

[1] All the results reported in this section of the paper are on a scale from 1: Very much to 5: Not at all, unless otherwise specified in the text.

open consultation procedures (responses for open participation are *1: 33%; 2: 50%; 3: 17%* and for invitation only 1: 17%; 2: 17%; 3: 50%; 4: 17%).

Out of the countries responding to the survey that have been classified by the OGP (18 countries) on their completion of the prescribed six consultation steps (timeline availability; advance notice; awareness raising; online consultation; in person consultations; summary of comments) most (67%) have followed all six.[2]

According to the OGP assessment, all countries have performed in-person consultations. (timeline availability: 78%; advance notice: 94%; awareness raising: 72%; online consultation: 83%; in-person consultations: 100%; summary of comments: 78%).

4   Discussion

According to the paper's key findings, a participatory, open, public policy design process is usually initiated by the government itself with a view to strengthen the role of the stakeholders in the process. Governments usually engage with stakeholders that represent civil society organizations, government departments and academic institutions while parliaments and political parties are less involved in the process. Most countries decide to design consultation procedures that are open and accessible, instead of limiting the process to invited stakeholders. They manage to reach the fourth highest level (*Collaborate*) in the IAP2 spectrum of public participation which points to a meaningful partnership with between stakeholders in the policy formulation and decision-making process.

Governments recognize the effective contribution of civil society organizations during the co-creation phase, especially in countries with a high IAP2 level of public participation. Some governments do introduce virtual platforms for stakeholders' engagement. However, it is not perceived as a practice that increases the effectiveness of the co-creation process or the quality of the process outputs.

Governments apply various co-creation approaches but the wide inclusion of e-participation practices is comparatively low. E-participation is enabled mainly through online public consultations and social network analysis. E-participation tools used mainly include consultation platforms, social media, mobile contribution applications, web discussion forums and online surveys. It is worth noting that e-participation tools are mostly used in co-creation processes in countries that have reached a significant IAP2 level.

Co-creation processes usually favor in-person meeting approaches such as SWOT workshops, strategic roadmaps and Living Labs. These processes might be assisted by ICT participation tools such as crowd-mapping, mind maps and issue cards but they usually require the participants to be present in the same physical setting.

Governments, especially in countries with a comparatively mature participatory process as indicated by their IAP2 level, consider that co-creation can highly improve

---

[2] The full classification is as follows: 1 step: Malta; 2 steps: Malawi; 3 steps: Jordan, Lithuania; 4 steps: Netherlands; 5 steps: Czech Republic; 6 steps: Armenia, Brazil, Chile, Greece, Italy, North Macedonia, Mongolia, Paraguay, Romania, Serbia, Sierra Leone, Ukraine.

the contents of the action plan and the level of commitment completion. Additionally, the existence of permanent structures and processes in the government along with the involvement of a permanent stakeholder forum are considered key factors for the effectiveness of co-creation processes.

Although virtual approaches are considered effective co-creation processes, governments give higher priority to face-to-face interaction with stakeholders to maximize the effectiveness of the process. In a similar vein, limited human resources and lack of time are considered key impediments to such processes – not lack of ICT tools.

Establishing central agencies that are responsible for citizen feedback and participatory process adoption and co-ordination can improve feedback quality, relevance and utility and significantly aid meaningful citizen participation. Participation efforts themselves could be submitted to stakeholders' review and examination and perhaps be co-created through citizen feedback. In some cases, meaningful engagement with citizens could suffer by the use if certain 'arm's length' ICT tools such as surveys, quick polls and others.

The key findings of the paper provide insights into the public participation practices used by governments when designing public policy in an open government setting. They point to a realization by government officials involved in supporting open government commitments and policies that citizen participation is understood not simply as an e-government or e-participation project but as an equal access and direct democracy issue. In such a scenario, meaningful participation and inclusive interaction with stakeholders is considered more important than the availability of ICT tools.

4.1 Limitations and Proposed Future Research

An analysis of the remaining OGP countries could address limitations arising from the fact that OGP had completed their assessment for a subset of the participating countries in this survey. This could improve conclusions based on comparing data obtained from survey responses and OGP assessment. By the end of 2019 OGP should officially publish all the evaluation reports for the relevant NAPs. These will provide further insights into the effectiveness of the Action Plan implementation in all twenty-nine countries. Future work could focus on further analyzing the data underlying these reports to identify possible associations between National Action Plan development practices and qualitative factors related to the completion and effectiveness of the Action Plan implementation. A follow-up study targeting the remaining OGP countries could also address the fact that of the twenty-nine countries that responded to the survey the representation of European states is comparatively high (52% of European OGP members, 32% of OGP countries in the Americas, 27% of Asia-Pacific countries and 14,3% of the African OGP countries responded).

References

1. Janssen, M., Charalabidis, Y., Zuiderwijk, A.: Benefits, adoption barriers and myths of open data and open government. Inf. Syst. Manag. **29**(4), 258–268 (2012)
2. Arnstein, S.R.: A ladder of citizen participation. J. Am. Inst. Plan. **35**(4), 216–224 (1969)

3. Medimorec, D., Parycek, P., Schossböck, J.: Vitalizing Democracy through E-participation and Open Government: An Austrian and Eastern European Perspective. Bertelsmann Stiftung, 14 (2011)
4. Manzini, E.: Design, When Everybody Designs: An Introduction to Design for Social Innovation. MIT Press, Cambridge (2015)
5. Putnam, R.D.: Tuning in, tuning out: the strange disappearance of social capital in America. PS Polit. Sci. Polit. **28**(4), 664–683 (1995)
6. Nye, J.S., Zelikow, P., King, D.C. (eds.): Why People Don't Trust Government. Harvard University Press, Cambridge (1997)
7. Cooper, T.L., Bryer, T.A., Meek, J.W.: Citizen-centered collaborative public management. Public Adm. Rev. **66**, 76–88 (2006)
8. Meijer, A.J., Curtin, D., Hillebrandt, M.: Open government: connecting vision and voice. Int. Rev. Admin. Sci. **78**(1), 10–29 (2012)
9. Bertot, J.C., Jaeger, P.T., Hansen, D.: The impact of polices on government social media usage: issues, challenges, and recommendations. Gov. Inf. Q. **29**(1), 30–40 (2012)
10. Hilgers, D., Ihl, C.: Citizensourcing: applying the concept of open innovation to the public sector. Int. J. Public Particip. **4**(1), 67–88 (2010)
11. Peña-López, I.: Citizens as Partners. OECD Handbook on Information, Consultation and Public Participation in Policy-Making. OECD, Paris (2001)
12. Macintosh, A.: Characterizing E-participation in policy-making. In: Proceedings of the Thirty-Seventh Annual Hawaii International Conference on System Sciences, HICSS-37, 5–8 January 2004
13. Ahmed, N.: An overview of e-participation models. UN Department of Economic and Social Affairs UNDESA (2006)
14. International Association for Public Participation. IAP2 spectrum of public participation (2007)
15. Wimmer, M.A.: Ontology for an e-participation virtual resource centre. In: Proceedings of the 1st International Conference on Theory and Practice of Electronic Governance, pp. 89–98. ACM (2007)
16. OGP Website: OGP Co-creation Standards. https://www.opengovpartnership.org/ogp-participation-co-creation-standards. Accessed 07 Mar 2019
17. United Nations: E-Government Survey 2016. UN, New York (2016)
18. United Nations: E-Government Survey 2012. UN, New York (2012)
19. Macintosh, A.: European e-participation Summary Report. European Commission - Information Society and Media DG, 30 (2009). http://europa.eu/information_society
20. Yu, H., Robinson, D.G.: The new ambiguity of open government. UCLA L. Rev. Discourse **59**, 178 (2011)
21. Piotrowski, S.J.: The "Open Government Reform" movement: the case of the open government partnership and US transparency policies. Am. Rev. Public Adm. **47**(2), 155–171 (2017)
22. Sidney, M.S.: Policy formulation: design and tools. In: Handbook of Public Policy Analysis, pp. 105–114. Routledge, London (2006)
23. OGP Website: About OGP. https://www.opengovpartnership.org/about/about-ogp. Accessed 15 Mar 2019
24. Frey, L.: Open government partnership four-year strategy 2015–2018 (2014). https://joinup.ec.europa.eu/document/open-government-partnership-four-years-strategy-2015-2018. Accessed 15 Mar 2019
25. OGP Website: OGP Articles of Governance. https://www.opengovpartnership.org/documents/current-articles-of-governance-pdf. Accessed 07 Mar 2019

26. OGP Website: OGP Participation and Co-Creation toolkit. https://www.opengovpartnership. org/sites/default/files/OGP_Participation-CoCreation-Toolkit_20180509.pdf. Accessed 07 Mar 2019

27. OGP Website: OGP Support Unit: Government Point of Contact Manual. https://www. opengovpartnership.org/sites/default/files/OGP_POC-Manual_2017_EN.pdf. Accessed 06 Mar 2019

28. De Koning, I.J.C., Crul, R.M, Wever, R.: Models of co-creation, Paper No. 31, TU Delft, The Netherlands (2016). http://www.ep.liu.se/ecp/125/022/ecp16125022.pdf

29. Spagnoli, F., van der Graaf, S., Brynskov, M.: The paradigm shift of living labs in service co-creation for smart cities: SynchroniCity validation. In: Lazazzara, A., Nacamulli, Raoul C.D., Rossignoli, C., Za, S. (eds.) Organizing for Digital Innovation. LNISO, vol. 27, pp. 135–147. Springer, Cham (2019). https://doi.org/10.1007/978-3-319-90500-6_11

30. Zolotov, M.N., Oliveira, T., Casteleyn, S.: E-participation adoption models research in the last 17 years: a weight and meta-analytical review. Comput. Hum. Behav. **81**, 350–365 (2018)

31. Porwol, L., Ojo, A., Breslin, J.G.: An ontology for next generation e-Participation initiatives. Gov. Inf. Q. **33**(3), 583–594 (2016)

32. OGP Website: IRM Frequently Asked Questions (n.d.). https://www.opengovpartnership. org/sites/default/files/ogp_irm_04FAQs.pdf. Accessed 17 Mar 2019

33. OGP Website: Explorer and IRM data (n.d.). https://www.opengovpartnership.org/about/ independent-reporting-mechanism/ogp-explorer-and-irm-data. View of the OGP Process Data-Set Accessed 07 Feb 2019

Designing Visualizations for Workplace Stress Management: Results of a Pilot Study at a Swiss Municipality

Stefan Stepanovic⬝, Vadym Mozgovoy⬝, and Tobias Mettler[(✉)]⬝

Swiss Graduate School of Public Administration,
University of Lausanne, Lausanne, Switzerland
{stefan.stepanovic,vadym.mozgovoy,
tobias.mettler}@unil.ch

Abstract. Job absenteeism and health problems are frequently caused by elevated exposure to work-related stress. The public sector is particularly affected by this development. Nevertheless, public sector organizations seem to have issues to reliably detect stress or to discuss about this topic in an objective and factual manner. Data visualizations have been found to be a powerful boundary object for sense-making and for unraveling issues that lie under the surface. Based on a pilot study at a medium-sized municipality in Switzerland, we thus developed, tested, and discussed various alternative visual representations for creating awareness about occupational stress. The results of this study showcase the hidden potential and perils of analyzing physiolytics data on aggregate level.

Keywords: Data visualization · Physiolytics · Stress management · Well-being

Preferred Conference Track: General e-government & open government track

1 Introduction

An increasing number of organizations are implementing wearable technologies such as biosensors, activity trackers or emotion trackers to monitor the physical and psychological well-being of their employees [1]. In private settings the development of these low-priced and ubiquitous systems (which in this article we will refer to as *physiolytics* [2]) has had great success and led to the formation of the "quantified-self" movement, which now slowly is arriving to the public sector as well. More and more public sector organizations are nowadays trying to seize the opportunity of collecting a broad range of biological, behavioral and other type of data. For example, prior research reports on the use of physiolytics, amongst others, in the areas of air traffic control [3], public transportation [4], firefighting [5], but also in regular office settings [6, 7]. The introduction of physiolytics devices in the workplace constitutes an upward trend: from a total of 485 million devices estimated to have been sold in 2018, more than 13 million were used in occupational health and safety programs [8].

© IFIP International Federation for Information Processing 2019
Published by Springer Nature Switzerland AG 2019
I. Lindgren et al. (Eds.): EGOV 2019, LNCS 11685, pp. 94–104, 2019.
https://doi.org/10.1007/978-3-030-27325-5_8

Given that work absenteeism and work-related diseases are on the rise in the public sector, distributing physiolytics devices among public servants could be a first measure to increase the personal consciousness of possible health and safety threats from elevated stress levels, sedentary behavior, or other unhealthy work habits. However, the organization as a whole might waste an important opportunity to systematically reflect, analyze, and thematize work-related health issues in the public administration if the collected sensor data is not exploited on an aggregated level. In this paper, we therefore set out to develop different data visualizations for composing a dashboard for stress management. Data visualizations have been found to be a powerful boundary object for sense-making, decision-making, or problem-solving [9]. For that matter, and against the backdrop of increasing health expenditures due to stress-related absenteeism in the public sector, we conducted a longitudinal pilot study at a medium-sized municipality in Switzerland in order to showcase how to purposefully use sensor data collected from physiolytics devices. In this paper, we want to deal with the question of how to visualize common physiolytics data as a means to creating awareness about work-related stress given that it frequently remains unnoticed or undiscussed in many public administrations.

2 Background

Physiolytics creates opportunities of rethinking and re-enacting health and well-being in the public administration, as it enables civil servants to have a data-driven approach to reflect and respond to health issues. Such systems track and record parameters like heart rate, body temperature or sleep, with the view to give a quick and easy access to information about one's health or performance. Characterized by their automaticity, autonomy and minimal costs in gathering large amounts of data, sensors constitute the key components of physiolytics [10–12]. However, just collecting large volumes of data is not sufficient for creating considerable value. For that to happen, sensor data needs to be transformed into a form (i.e. textual and visual representations) that is easily accessible and comprehensible [13].

Prior research shows that particularly data visualizations have a transformative effect: they drive individuals to reflect and eventually act in response to the represented data [14]. By translating sensor data into comprehensible visual representations, issues with health and well-being become more legible, accessible and foreseeable [15]. Therefore, they may help users to perform more punctuated health behavior changes because the action is based on informed insights of individual lifestyle issues rather than on subjective experiences [12]. To sum, visual representations are critical to our ability to process complex sensor data and to build better intuitions as to what aspects improve and what worsens health [16].

But how to do it? In the extant literature, we find a variety of meta-requirements that may guide the design of generic data visualizations [17, 18]:

- *Accurate*: Measures and quantities have to be accurate, so that users are ensured that they can exploit the health information that is displayed.

- *Easy-to-read*: A visual salience between metrics is desired. Still, superfluous features (e.g. flashy colors) or unnecessary components (e.g. side illustrations) should be avoided, as it may interfere with cognition.
- *Easy-to-understand*: Visualizations have to disseminate information to the general public. Users are not likely to be data scientists.
- *Clear and concise*: Too much information may hinder cognition.
- *Logical*: Visualizations have to be organized in a simple and logical way, so that users can promptly perceive the information displayed.
- *Meaningful to target audience*: The information provided has to resonate in the context of target audience.
- *Allow comparison*: Visualizations have to make it possible to easily compare quantities, relationships etc.
- *Convincing*: Visualizations should nudge users in exploiting the information.

Apart from the above mentioned meta-requirements, the literature has notably discussed the introduction of interactive visualizations [19], examined the insights they provide on use practices [15], or even conceptualized the creation of custom visualizations [20]. However, in most cases, there is a presupposition that data is accessible in their globality and that related visualizations can provide information without restriction. As most of the current literature on physiolytics is focused on medical professionals or on lifestyle consumers, the display of personal data (as well as its collection and manipulation) is primarily concerned with the perspective of a single individual. Little is known about the use of such data for organizational purposes, with the aim to build a big picture of the existing health and well-being status and to raise awareness and instigate individual or group action within an organization.

Privacy policies and data protection laws hinder organizations to establish a direct use of physiolytics to operate with sensitive and highly personal health-related data. In this context, it is important to differentiate two things: "medical information" that may reference health statuses and/or help to retrace medical conditions (e.g. continuous blood glucose monitoring or variation in one's heart rate) and non-invasive information such as step counting, minutes of activity or calories burned. Medical information is typically subject to confidentiality requirements regardless of how the employer obtains this information. On the other hand, non-sensitive health information does commonly not depend on constraints on disclosure [21]. Yet, evidence seems to indicate that the nature of tracked data may not be, in practice, the main source of concern for employees as regards their privacy. Prior research [22] has shown that metrics, such as air quality, noise, activity or mood have different degrees of privacy concerns for employees (e.g. air quality was projected to be less "problematical" than mood). Nonetheless, research indicates that privacy concerns were not primarily linked to the type of data collected but are rather linked to the level of anonymity that was provided respectively the concern of employees to lose their anonymity [23]. In sum, adding a new level of granularity in visualizations that ensures users that they will not be identified, could break down most barriers as regards to privacy concerns. Designing data visualizations in the workplace is therefore a matter of effectively erasing the individual, to focus on visualizations that apprehend group levels. We thus define some additional meta-requirements:

- *Non-identifiability of individual employee*: Employees have to feel that they are able to manage their level of intimacy and speech at work.
- *Transparency:* An employee should be able to identify what data are collected and how that may be used visually, in order to develop a form of user trust. This user trust builds upon the feeling that there is no manipulation in the data displayed and that sensor data visualizations are done for the common good in the workplace.
- *Community-oriented and participative design*: The design has therefore to be community-oriented and create potential for participation from users (e.g. possibility to include self-reporting data).
- *Rooted in the organizational context and culture*: Visualizations have to fit the general attitude towards sensors, with a capacity of adaption upon the interests, concerns or requests of employees (e.g. employees might prefer visualizations oriented on activity levels rather than stress levels). Same goes for an attention to the specificities of the workplace environment.

3   Methodology

Developing visual representations is a real-world problem that requires both, a technological and social viewpoint (i.e. practice-inspired research). On the one hand, we need to understand the possibilities and limitations of data management and responsiveness of physiolytics devices. On the other, we need to get a grasp on what is feasible, desired, and acceptable in an organizational context. In approaching this problem, we chose to apply *Action Design Research* (ADR) [24] to combine both a systematic thinking on designing an artifact (i.e. in our case a dashboard) with a human-centered lens regarding the emergent social dynamics which occurs when confronting users with unknown and/or highly sensitive solutions.

A particular characteristic of ADR is the preference of authenticity over controlled settings [24]. Accordingly, ADR is often conducted in field studies where the design of new artifacts is performed in a real-world setting, in a participatory manner together with dedicated users and/or pilot organizations [25]. In this sense, researchers and practitioners form what Sein and colleagues refer to as "*ADR team*" whose initial goal is to develop a mutual understanding of the scope, focus, and mode of inquiry before starting to build solutions. Contextual factors are supposed to play an important role in knowledge creation [26, 27].

In order to purposefully visualize physiolytics data for creating awareness about work stress in organizations, we chose to apply an *IT-dominant building, intervention, and evaluation logic*. This means that our initial focus was on developing different versions of visual representations and then improve selected design variants by continuously instantiating and repeatedly testing assumptions, expectations, and knowledge about and with users and their use environment. In this paper, we report on the findings from our *first design iteration*. Our pilot partner was a medium-sized municipality in Switzerland. Participation in our field study was voluntary for local administrators. We informed them before-hand about the specific goals of our project as well as about data privacy, security and functioning of physiolytics devices. We opted for a medical wearable (i.e. CE class IIa device) that is capable of accurately measuring a range of different parameters, amongst others heart rate, blood oxygenation, skin temperature, skin blood perfusion, respiration rate, heart rate variability, blood pulse wave and others (see Fig. 1).

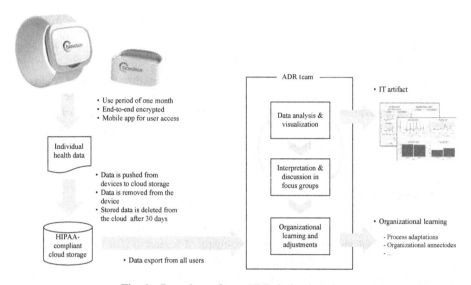

Fig. 1. Procedure of one ADR design iteration

A total of 20 local administrators (composing our ADR team) were equipped with the device during a one-month test period. We provided them with clear instructions on how to wear the device, how to access the stored personal data and how to secure the data to a HIPPA-compliant cloud storage. After this test period, we exported the collected, but anonymized data of all participants and developed multiple visual representations with the aim to capture some proxy for "stress" for the specific departments of the municipality and the organization as a whole.

To learn about both, the practical day-to-day issues with the medical wearables and the comprehensibility and accuracy of our developed data interpretations, we conducted a focus group session at the end of our design iteration. We opted for this format of inquiry as it offers a great flexibility and large amounts of rich data that can be used for artifact refinement [28]. Due to restrictions of length, in this paper we report only on the technical part of our research.

4 Results

4.1 Observing "Stress" on Organizational Level

In the course of our pilot study, we developed various visualizations to capture "stress" on organizational level. According to our theoretical findings, and in compliance with inputs from practitioners from our ADR team, the desirable properties were (1) non-identifiability of individual employee; (2) creation of "stress" measurement comparable over time; (3) reflection of local "stress" trend in the organization; (4) establishment of risk and safety intervals. Non-identifiability is achieved by aggregation of individual stress incidence on group level.

To develop stress measurement comparable over time, we created the Weighted Stress Incidence (WSI) indicator. It communicates the following information: how much of "stress" does an employee in organization experience per one hour of device use over a specific day on average. The amount of time each employee uses the device and the number of actual users is variable (not constant). Thus, the "Total Stress Count" is not directly comparable from one period to another. WSI incorporates those variables improving comparability over time compared to "Total Stress Count". Moreover, some employees wear devices during weekends when measurements may not reflect "work-related stress". WSI during weekends should be distinctive from WSI during working days on the dashboards.

A proper approximation of a stress trend in organization is achieved by displaying of polynomial trend function. A risk zone is defined above a 90th percentile of historical data. Safety zone is defined above a 90th percentile of historical data. This is again an arbitrary criterion for displaying risk and safety zones.

Figure 2 displays WSI at organizational level. Left side of the visualization takes into account measurement from both working days (white background) and weekends (purple background). The right side of the visualization considers only working days. The upper part displays daily WSI in a line plot. The bottom part illustrates monthly sums of WSI in a bar plot. Red polynomial trend shows that on middle of November, beginning of December, it was the most "stressful" period in the municipality overall while from middle of December onward it was in decline again. The majority of observations are in the safety zone. During the weekends employees typically get more "stress" then during working hours (note: we explicitly interdicted participants to wear the device during leisure time). From the focus group discussion, we know that there has been a special occasion which required some administrators to work over weekends which could explain the higher stress levels. Overall November and December are equivalent in terms of WSI at organizational level.

4.2 Observing "Stress" on Departmental Level

Given that stress is not distributed equally among all the employees, a highest order aggregation (organizational level) may degenerate quality of stress indicators when there are a lot of employees in the unit of aggregation. For example, when 100 employees are "stressed" and 100 are relaxed, an average employee feels fine when data is aggregated. Therefore, for getting a more precise picture we introduce an

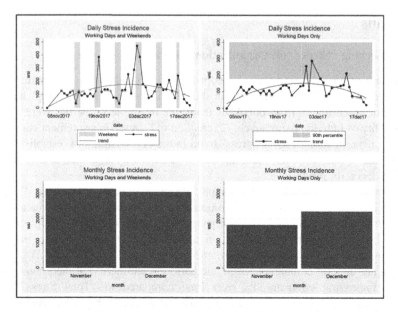

Fig. 2. Stress measurement on organizational with the Weighted Stress Incidence (WSI) (Color figure online)

additional visualization on a lower aggregation unit: organizational departments. This illustration relies on the same properties as the previous graph and additionally includes a display of outliers.

Figure 3 depicts the WSI on the departmental level. The left side incorporates working days only. It excludes outliers for better visibility of measurements shown on the same scale for each department. It shows that different departments have different stress-related patterns. For example, the City Chancellery has an upward stress trend, whereas the Construction Management department is close to the straight line. It also shows that the Tax Office experienced a lot of stress, particularly at the end of

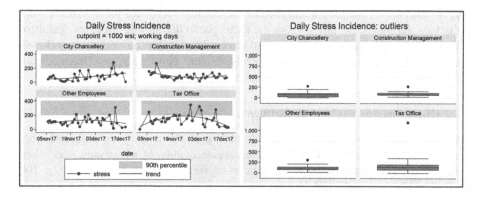

Fig. 3. Stress measurement on departmental level

November and in the first half of December, reaching a risk zone. Persistent and long-time stay in a risk zone may be a signal for management to launch a psychosocial intervention [29] in order to improve employees' well-being, reduce stress and improve work-related performance. Further, on the right side of Fig. 3, we see the outliers of a department. There is one observation that lies remotely from others in the Tax Office. However, one single measurement may be caused by a one-time event and it does not have a strong impact on the "stress" trend overall.

4.3   Reflecting on the Reliability of the Data for Measuring Organizational Stress

Correct inferences and proper responses to elevated stress can only be developed, when the data basis is reliable. Hence, we propose to take a closer look at the motion activity (MA), that is the average value of motion intensity per hour, and the frequency of use, that is the amount of time a user spends wearing a device per day.

Right side of Fig. 4 shows MA. When MA distribution is close to uniform having low variability over time (see the case of the City Chancellery), a dynamical change in WSI trend most likely happens to be due to emotional stress and other components. When MA is not uniform and fluctuates (see the case of the Tax Office) a change over time in WSI may be due to combination of MA, emotional stress and other conditions. The fact that MA is not always uniform across departments shows that we need to take it into account when interpreting stress-related indicators for users of physiolytics devices, because BPW is reactive to motion intensity.

Left side of the Fig. 4 shows that users were not always wearing our distributed devices uniformly during the pilot study. The frequency of use fluctuates. This gives us some indication about the reliability of measurement. First of all, stress measurement should be done per a fixed unit of time (like in case of the WSI) to provide comparability of measurements from one period to another. Moreover, if users spent only little time with the device per day, we may have obtained inaccurate or biased stress-related measurements. Therefore, it may be reasonable to exclude observations or only make cautious inferences about the stress level of a particular department. In the end,

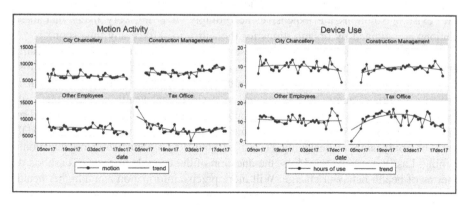

Fig. 4. Device use and motion activity during working days

the goal is always to make use this information to make some positive changes in the public administration. It could be highly counterproductive to act upon wrong assumptions.

5 Discussion

The goal of this paper was to show how sensor data collected from physiolytics devices could be purposefully visualized for creating awareness about work stress in the public administration. We did so because stress-related absenteeism is on the rise in the public sector and there is often no dialogue happening about this matter. Based on a pilot study in a medium-sized municipality in Switzerland, we wanted to showcase some early reflections on how to analyze and visualize "stress" on organizational and departmental level in order that occupational health and safety programs can respond more precisely to health and safety risks.

As with all design-oriented research, this work is iterative. There is still long way ahead of us and we especially need more in-depth testing together with the deployment of our solution to other branches of the public sector in order to get a more nuanced view. Particularly, we need to further evaluate the perceived utility and effectiveness in creating health awareness among employees and its influence on work absenteeism and other effects.

Another limitation of this work is also the interpretability of visualizations. The developed visualizations and indicators reflect a specific organizational and technical context. For instance, the developed indicator WSI is based on the BPW which is reactive to various stress-related conditions (and also bound to a specific physiolytics device). Improving separation between various components connected to stress, such as physical stress (intensive motion), emotional stress, hypertension, certainly will improve the quality and interpretability of stress-related indicators. It is still necessary to do a cross-validation of stress-identification procedure that serves for creation of any group-level metrics related to stress.

Furthermore, it is advantageous to consider alternative biological metrics having stronger links to stress, such as cortisol and galvanic skin response. For this, we would have to wait for new and affordable devices that are able to measure this (note: as for now, existing solutions are expensive; accordingly, it is not very likely that these solutions are adopted by organizations for the entire workforce any time soon).

As with any technology, continued use is key. In order to be able to accurately depict organizational stress levels, we also need to find ways to counter the usual loss in motivation (even by employees who initially supported the adoption). Also, it is necessary to reflect about how to set up an occupational health program that uses physiolytics devices in a meaningful way and how to guide change initiatives based on our proposed dashboard for stress management. This is particularly in the spirit of ADR which not only aims at designing IT artifacts but also systematizing organizational learning. Lastly, we have to address the question of the tangible impacts of dashboards in terms of health behavior change. Will more precise information and a higher health awareness really lead to noticeable effects? Answering these questions is of particular importance given that public organizations certainly expect a return on the investment (return on tax-money) of physiolytics devices and data analytics platform.

Acknowledgement. This research has been supported by the Swiss National Science Foundation (SNSF) grant no. 172740.

References

1. Tetrick, L.E., Winslow, C.J.: Workplace stress management interventions and health promotion. Annu. Rev. Organ. Psychol. Organ. Behav. **2**, 583–603 (2015)
2. Wilson, H.J.: Wearables in the workplace. Harvard Bus. Rev. **91**, 23–25 (2013)
3. Rodrigues, S., Paiva, J.S., Dias, D., Aleixo, M., Filipe, R., Cunha, J.P.S.: A wearable system for the stress monitoring of air traffic controllers during an air traffic control refresher training and the trier social stress test: a comparative study. Open Bioinform. J. **11**, 106–116 (2018)
4. Rodrigues, J.G.P., Kaiseler, M., Aguiar, A., Cunha, J.P.S., Barros, J.: A mobile sensing approach to stress detection and memory activation for public bus drivers. IEEE Trans. Intell. Transp. Syst. **16**, 3294–3303 (2015)
5. Lee, T.-G., Lee, S.-H.: Safe sensing network system and evaluation for emergency information services. Wireless Pers. Commun. **79**, 2425–2438 (2014)
6. Han, L., Zhang, Q., Chen, X., Zhan, Q., Yang, T., Zhao, Z.: Detecting work-related stress with a wearable device. Comput. Ind. **90**, 42–49 (2017)
7. Otenyo, E.E., Smith, E.A.: An overview of employee wellness programs (EWPs) in large U. S. cities: does geography matter? Public Pers. Manage. **46**, 3–24 (2017)
8. Giddens, L., Gonzalez, E., Leidner, D.: I track, therefore I Am: exploring the impact of wearable fitness devices on employee identity and well-being. In: Proceedings of the 22th Americas Conference on Information Systems, pp. 1–5 (2016)
9. Matheus, R., Janssen, M., Maheshwari, D.: Data science empowering the public: data-driven dashboards for transparent and accountable decision-making in smart cities. Gov. Inf. Q. (2019, forthcoming)
10. Lupton, D.: Beyond techno-utopia: critical approaches to digital health technologies. Societies **4**, 706–711 (2014)
11. Mettler, T., Wulf, J.: Physiolytics at the workplace: affordances and constraints of wearables use from an employee's perspective. Inf. Syst. J. **29**, 245–273 (2019)
12. Swan, M.: Sensor mania! The internet of things, wearable computing, objective metrics, and the quantified self 2.0. J. Sens. Actuator Netw. **1**, 217–253 (2012)
13. Oh, J., Lee, U.: Exploring UX issues in quantified self technologies. In: Proceedings of the 8th International Conference on Mobile Computing and Ubiquitous Networking, Hakodate, Japan, pp. 53–59 (2015)
14. Ruckenstein, M.: Visualized and interacted life: personal analytics and engagements with data doubles. Societies **4**, 68–84 (2014)
15. Pantzar, M., Ruckenstein, M.: The heart of everyday analytics: emotional, material and practical extensions in self-tracking market. Consum. Mark. Cult. **18**, 92–109 (2015)
16. Fox, P., Hendler, J.: Changing the equation on scientific data visualization. Science **331**, 705–708 (2011)
17. Marcengo, A., Rapp, A.: Visualization of human behavior data: the quantified self. In: Big Data: Concepts, Methodologies, Tools, and Applications, pp. 1582–1612. IGI Publishing, Hershey (2016)

18. Fawcett, T.: Mining the quantified self: personal knowledge discovery as a challenge for data science. Big Data **3**, 249–266 (2015)
19. Larsen, J.E., Cuttone, A., Jørgensen, S.L.: QS Spiral: visualizing periodic quantified self data. In: Proceedings of the 2013 CHI Workshop on Personal Informatics in the Wild: Hacking Habits for Health & Happiness, Paris, France, pp. 1–4 (2013)
20. Choe, E.K., Lee, N.B., Lee, B., Pratt, W., Kientz, J.A.: Understanding quantified-selfers' practices in collecting and exploring personal data. In: Proceedings of the 32nd Annual ACM Conference on Human Factors in Computing Systems, Toronto, Canada, pp. 1143–1152 (2014)
21. Moore, P., Piwek, L.: Regulating wellbeing in the brave new quantified workplace. Employee Relations **39**, 308–316 (2017)
22. Mathur, A., Van den Broeck, M., Vanderhulst, G., Mashhadi, A., Kawsar, F.: Tiny habits in the giant enterprise: understanding the dynamics of a quantified workplace. In: Proceedings of the 2015 ACM International Joint Conference on Pervasive and Ubiquitous Computing, Osaka, Japan, pp. 577–588 (2015)
23. Yassaee, M., Mettler, T.: Digital occupational health systems: what do employees think about it? Inf. Syst. Front. (2019, forthcoming)
24. Sein, M.K., Henfridsson, O., Purao, S., Rossi, M., Lindgren, R.: Action design research. MIS Q. **35**, 37–56 (2011)
25. Haj-Bolouri, A., Bernhardsson, L., Rossi, M.: PADRE: a method for participatory action design research. In: Proceedings of the 11th International Conference on Design Science Research in Information Systems and Technologies, St. John's, Canada, pp. 19–36 (2016)
26. Avgerou, C.: The significance of context in information systems and organizational change. Inf. Syst. J. **11**, 43–63 (2001)
27. Davison, R.M., Martinsons, M.G., Kock, N.: Principles of canonical action research. Inf. Syst. J. **14**, 65–86 (2004)
28. Tremblay, M.C., Hevner, A.R., Berndt, D.: Focus groups for artifact refinement and evaluation in design research. Commun. Assoc. Inf. Syst. **26**, 599–618 (2010)
29. Leka, S., Cox, T., Zwetsloot, G. (eds.): The European Framework for Psychosocial Risk Management. Institute of Work, Health and Organisations, Nottingham (2008)

Overwhelmed by Brute Force of Nature: First Response Management in the Wake of a Catastrophic Incident

Hans J. Scholl[(⊠)]

University of Washington, Seattle, USA
jscholl@uw.edu

Abstract. The four-day Cascadia Rising exercise of 2016, which simulated a magnitude 9+ rupture of the almost 700 miles long Cascadian subduction zone with up to 5 min of violent shaking followed by a 20 to 30 feet-high tsunami in the Northwestern United States, was one of the largest response exercises of a catastrophic incident ever conducted in the United States. It involved 23,000 professional responders in three states in the Pacific Northwest. In reality, the simulated catastrophe would likely carry a five-digit number of fatalities and send the entire region on a decades-long course of recovery to a "new" normal, in which nothing would be close to what it once had been. The study investigated the numerous managerial challenges that responders faced. Communication and coordination challenges were found the most prevalent among other challenges. The research also uncovered the lack of standardization of response structures, processes, and procedures as major inhibitors of a more effective response besides other inhibiting factors. While the "containment" and "effective mitigation" of a truly catastrophic incident is illusory, the study provides recommendations regarding preparation and problem mitigation in the management of the response.

Keywords: Emergency response management · Catastrophic incident ·
National Response Framework (NRF) ·
National Incident Management System (NIMS) ·
Incident Command System (ICS) · Coordination failure ·
Communication failure · Process standardization · Procedure standardization ·
Structure standardization · Infrastructure damage · Staffing problems ·
Humanitarian crisis

1 Introduction

1.1 Overview

The study of the now famous Cascadia Rising exercise of 2016 has produced a total of three reports, of which the one at hand is the third. The previous two reports covered the problems of situational awareness (SA) and the development of a common operating picture (COP) [40] as well as the assessment of the technology tools, which were used and needed [39] in order to arrive at an actionable SA/COP. As expounded in the first two reports, the potential gravity of impact and extraordinary peril from a

© IFIP International Federation for Information Processing 2019
Published by Springer Nature Switzerland AG 2019
I. Lindgren et al. (Eds.): EGOV 2019, LNCS 11685, pp. 105–124, 2019.
https://doi.org/10.1007/978-3-030-27325-5_9

megathrust in the Cascadian Subduction Zone (CSZ) to human lives and properties in the coastal zones of the Pacific Northwest of the United States was greatly unknown until the late 1980s [39, 40]. Only since then it gradually became better understood what extent of impacts had to be expected, and what challenges first responders might have to face. For addressing the latter, all levels of government in the three states of Idaho, Oregon, and Washington as well as FEMA region X jointly planned and conducted a four-day exercise, which simulated the response to a magnitude 9+ (M9+) earthquake and the resulting tsunami. This third report focuses on the particular managerial challenges, with which first responders were confronted. It complements and expands the findings of the other two reports.

1.2   Cascadia Rising 2016 Exercise Brief

The March 2011 megathrust and tsunami that ravaged the coastal areas of the Tōhoku region in Japan was the final push needed for policy makers and emergency managers to understand the gruesome reality of a pending catastrophic incident of this type and the high probability that something similar could happen in the Pacific Northwest at any point in time. Like the impacted Japanese region, the Northwestern coastline of the United States rises along a subduction zone. However, unlike all other subduction zones along the so-called Pacific Ring of Fire, the CSZ has not experienced a rupture in more than three centuries. As geological studies found out, M9+ CSZ ruptures recur with some regularity every 500 years [4, 49]; however, more recent studies suggest that the intervals between two consecutive megathrusts may be as short as 300 years on average [23]. The 2011 catastrophe in Japan suggested to emergency managers that response preparations for a M9+ CSZ rupture and tsunami had to be drastically revved up quickly, which led to the immediate launch of several projects culminating in the comprehensive Cascadia Rising 2016 exercise, which involved a total of 23,000 responders across three states in the Pacific Northwest during four days of exercise (June 7 to 11).

The exercise assumed violent shaking occurring for some five to six minutes, while the subduction zone ruptured from one end to the other in a zipper-like fashion. The initial shaking would be followed by an up to 40-feet high tsunami wrecking the coastal areas in the Pacific Northwest. The initial shaking would be followed by several heavy aftershocks, which would further damage already compromised structures. Total power outages along the West coast would ensue with numerous downed power feeder lines and destroyed substations, and power would not be fully restored in the impact areas for up to 18 months. Water mains would break stopping water supplies to households within a day. Sewage and wastewater lines would also break as well as gas and oil supply lines. Around 1,000 road and railroad bridges would collapse. The latter has the grim consequence that "islands" with no ingress nor egress would trap and almost hermetically insulate populations in the hundreds, or, even more so, in the several thousands with no power, no water, no sewage disposal capabilities, no fuel supplies, and no food supplies. Up to four hundred such "islands" could be forged by infrastructure destruction, which within a few days would result in a humanitarian crisis of much larger dimension than the initial impact of the megathrust and tsunami that might have already caused several ten thousand fatalities and an even higher number of injured victims. With power gone for extended periods of time, information and communication networks would become unavailable. Cell towers, which initially had remained operational after the various waves of shaking, would go silent after some 28 h, when the back-up batteries run down. The exercise was built on the basis of the results of the Homeland Infrastructure Threat and Risk Analysis Center (HITRAC) simulation study commissioned in 2011, which was compiled by Western Washington University's Resilience Institute into a detailed exercise scenario document [33].

1.3   Context and Paper Organization

As mentioned above, this paper is part of a study covering aspects of situational awareness, the common operating picture, the information and communication technologies used in the response, as well as the specific managerial challenges in response management after a catastrophic incident, the latter of which are the focus of this third paper. The study used to a large extent the theoretical frame and methodological instruments developed in an earlier study dedicated to a real-world disaster, which had occurred only a few years earlier [36, 37]. Interestingly, quite a number of responders that had been interviewed in the context of the real-world disaster were also involved in the CR16 exercise. Quite a few agreed to be interviewed again after the exercise. This circumstance gives the collected data a certain nuance and weight since these interviewees compared their real-world experiences from two years earlier to those from the exercise.

The paper organization is as follows: The next section presents the extant related literature succeeded by the methodology section and the research questions. Thereafter, the findings are presented for each research question, which then are discussed. Finally, future research avenues and concluding remarks are presented, which also detail the particular contributions of this research.

2   Literature Review

Managerial challenges in disaster response management have been studied, at least in part, for decades. Foci in these studies were the coordination challenges among and between organizational response units as well as between communities and professional responders [15, 34].

Central and indispensable for coordination of professional response activities and resource management as well as for collaboration with other internal and external response units is *actionable information*, which has been vetted, verified, and can be, and actually, is shared [5, 12, 36, 39, 40]. Besides actionable information, response units draw on pre-disaster planning (including interagency coordination) and rely on organizational structures and predefined practices, processes and procedures, for example, such as those defined by the US National Incident Management System (NIMS) and its core, the Incident Command System (ICS), as well as the National Response Framework (NRF), which together encompass "doctrines, concepts, principles, terminology, and organizational processes" for effective, scalable, and effective emergency response management [1, p. 3, 2]. While the emergency response system in the United States has been praised as one of the most comprehensive and probably most tested in the world of its kind [44], it has also drawn heavy criticism inside the United States from academic circles [14, 32, 48] at least during its early stages as an all-hazard response framework, while more recent assessments arrive at far more favorable conclusions regarding the system's effectiveness [6, 29, 47]. The latter is also supported by positive accounts, which practitioners provide [9, 13, 25], although other reports still point at incomplete implementations [27, 28] and inconsistent applications of the frameworks [16].

However, while NIMS/ICS and NRF have provided a common frame of reference and understanding, various managerial challenges remain, which engulf any response, and in particular, once scope, scale, and duration of on incident increase. What might work still passably well in emergency responses to smaller incidents such as those of up to DC-3 to DC-4 categories on the Fischer scale [18], however, once catastrophic incidents of DC-8 to DC-10 categories happen, the challenges of such a magnitude of incidents are much harder to meet in anticipation thereof, let alone when responders from multiple jurisdictions and levels of government have to coordinate among each other for effectively coping with the real thing. Besides the well-known (though unresolved) problem of breakdown of information sharing among responders [11] leading to incomplete situational awareness and a lack of a shared common operating picture, serious managerial challenges, for example, regarding coordination, collabo-ration, and resource management have been widely documented in recent literature [7, 8, 10, 21, 22, 24, 30, 31, 37, 42, 46].

As an example, in response to the DC-4/DC-5 2014 Oso/SR530 incident, serious and continued coordination and collaboration problems ensued for days and weeks between incident management teams (IMTs), the urban search and rescue teams (USARs), the County EOC and County leadership as well as the other 110+ agencies involved in the response [31, 36, 37]. In this particular incident a whole hillside had collapsed, and within a minute and a half debris of up to 21 feet high had completely covered a one-square mile area, killing 43 people, demolishing about fifty structures, and burying State Route 530 for a length of 1.5 miles [26, 31] When taking the Oso/SR530 incident response, which was rather limited in terms of scale and scope as a benchmark, then a catastrophic incident would present itself as a far graver and more complex challenge to responders from multiple jurisdictions and levels of government [3].

3   Methodology and Research Questions

3.1   Research Questions

Based on the review of the literature on the general subject as well as on the author's previous research on the particular subject matter of "managerial challenges" in response management, it is evident that coordination and communication challenges are prevalent along with a number of "other" managerial challenges not directly related to coordination/communication, which leads to the following two research questions:

Research Question #1 (RQ #1): How do coordination and collaboration challenges change or stay the same when responding to a catastrophic incident (as opposed to a non-catastrophic emergency response)?

Research Question #2 (RQ #2): How do other managerial challenges change or stay the same when responding to a catastrophic incident (as opposed to a non-catastrophic emergency response)?

3.2   Conceptual Framework, Instrument and Coding Scheme

This study has been conducted by employing the so-called "information perspective", which is a human actor and human action-centric approach to investigating managerial challenges of coordination procedures, processes, and structures as facilitators of human information needs, information behaviors, and information flows, which then lead to decision and actions. In disaster management, when looking at managerial challenges in terms of coordination and collaboration, the information perspective allows a detailed investigation of actions and interactions of responders as they are mediated via the existing and emerging information infrastructures and their various aforementioned elements [38, 41].

Based on the conceptual framework of resilient information infrastructures (RIIs) [41], a semi-structured interview protocol was devised upfront, which covered six topical areas of (1) management and organization, (2) technology, (3) governance, (4) information, (5) information infrastructure, and (6) resiliency/RIIs.

3.3   Data Selection and Analysis

Data Selection. The sample was purposive [35] and included seventeen responders from eight different groups: the (1) City Emergency Operations Centers, (2) County Emergency Operations Centers, (3) Washington State Emergency Management Division, (4) WA State Agencies, (5) Health Districts, (6) Regional Aviation, (7) Washington State National Guard, and (8) Federal Emergency Management Agency (FEMA), region X. Furthermore, twenty-three after-action reports (AARs) from all eight responder groups were collected and analyzed.

Data Extraction and Preparation. The interviews, which lasted between 33 to 107 min, were conducted between September 2016 and March 2017. Except for one interview, which was conducted via Skype video conferencing, all other interviews were performed in person. Notes were taken, and participant interaction was observed and recorded during the interviews. At minimum of two researchers transcribed and coded the audiotaped interviews. Also, response units' after-action reports and press interviews were collected, reviewed, and coded as appropriate.

Data Analysis. The conceptual RII framework mentioned above guided the design of the initial codebook, which contained six category codes (one for each topical area) and 141 sub-category codes. During data collection, in individual coding sessions, and in inter-coder sessions additional codes were introduced in a bottom-up fashion [19, 20, 43, 45] making the resulting codebook a hybrid of deductive and inductive analyses [17], which finally consisted of 176 sub-category codes in the six main categories.

Using a Web-based tool for qualitative and mixed-method data analyses (Dedoose main versions 7 and 8, dedoose.com), at least two researchers coded each transcript and document. Coded excerpts were compared showing high inter-coder reliability.

Code applications in the areas of "management and organization" (2,763), "information" (1,705), and "technology" (1,111) were the highest across the six main categories. For the purpose of the specific analysis on managerial challenges the code intersection represented by the sub-codes of "managerial structure," "address challenges of organizing," and "address challenges of improvising" was selected, which produced a total of 1,146 excerpts for all eight distinct responder groups. These excerpts, which could carry multiple codes, varied in length between one sentence/one paragraph and up to three paragraphs.

Separately per each responder team, the excerpts were conceptually analyzed in the subsequent phase of analysis. Recurring themes and main concepts were identified and named by means of short key phrases and keywords. These concepts/context clusters were transferred to the "canvas" of another Web-based tool (CMAP, version 6.03), a concept mapping tool. The concepts/context clusters were inspected and sorted into topical "bins" or "baskets," in which chronological, logical, and other relationships were identified. Relationship links between concepts/context clusters were established whenever evidence from the data supported that link.

Research Team and Processes. The research team consisted of the principal investigator (PI) and thirty-two research assistants (RAs). The PI and RAs worked individually and in small teams to transcribe, code, and conceptually/contextually analyze, and map the concepts. For the most part of the project, the research team met weekly in person or online and communicated via the research project site and the project listserv as well as via individual face-to-face and group meetings. Weekly meetings were streamed and recorded, which kept the whole research team in sync over extended periods of time.

4   Findings

Below the findings are presented in the order of the research questions.

4.1   Ad RQ #1 *(How Do Coordination and Collaboration Challenges Change or Stay the Same When Responding to a Catastrophic Incident (as Opposed to a Non-catastrophic Emergency Response)?)*

Physical Obstacles. As described in the exercise overview above, shortly after the megathrust electrical power would be immediately lost in wide geographical areas and not return for months and in some cases even for more than a year. In isolated areas here and there, and for some hours, or, for a couple of days at most, generator and backup battery-based communications and operations could be maintained on greatly degraded levels. However, the almost total loss of power would gravely impact all communication infrastructures. It would massively slow down all kinds of communications and significantly curtail information sharing capabilities, which would make coordination of response efforts and collaboration between response units exceedingly difficult. All responder groups emphasized that widespread loss of electrical power, and, with it, loss of most vital communication capabilities, would be the premier challenge in this particular response, which would require to be addressed in more realistic ways than in the initial CR16 exercise not only in future exercises but rather also in response plan development. Some responders remarked that in such situations the overall response would greatly slow down. Pre-established personal acquaintance and mutual trust between responders would become even more critical, since mainly trusted sources and recipients would be regarded premier channels of communication. Paper-based messages and T cards along with other non-electronic media would be the vehicles and primary means for organizing the response. Beyond the almost wiped-out communication infrastructure the transportation infrastructure would also be immensely degraded and bestrewn by barriers and impediments of all kinds (collapsed overpasses and bridges, blockages by landslides, fallen trees, tumbled-over buildings, downed powerlines, cracked-up road surfaces, fires, flooded areas, and spills of hazardous materials and fuels among others), so that even on-foot messengers or runners would find it difficult to deliver messages quickly. Physical obstacles would be met not only for message distribution and command coordination but also for movement coordination, for example, for moving people and resources in and out from the impact area. As one responder stated,

> "The whole issue of movement coordination in and out of the impacted area: So, you are on the one hand trying to bring in resources, be it personnel, be it equipment, be it commodities and at the same time you're wanting to evacuate parts of the population, etc., and you are having to do all of this with a tremendously impacted transportation infrastructure. So, the coordination of all this movement is a complex issue that has to be coordinated between the Federal and the State level. The complexity actually grows exponentially with a catastrophic incident." (quote #01)

While this particular responder focused on the State and Federal levels, movement coordination has also to be accomplished on local and County levels at the same time, all of which increases the order of complexity in response and responder coordination.

Interjurisdictional Coordination Challenges. As a recent study on a 2014 real, however, scale, scope, and duration-limited incident response had uncovered, when a relatively small part of the same impact area projected in CR16 was affected, challenges of coordination, communication, and collaboration abounded in this particular and far smaller response. Among those challenges jurisdictional bickering over who was in charge of what were prominent. As a reaction to these challenges, a Unified Command Structure was slowly formed, which could yet not completely overcome all effects of a certain unwillingness to collaborate on part of some responder groups. Also, besides those more subjective and interpersonal factors, the lack of standards, for example, in resource request procedures, and the difficulty of scaling up the response from daily routine to something more challenging gave responders considerable headaches. While the real response had to cope with an incident of DC-4 to DC-5 order of magnitude on the Fischer scale [18], the CR16 exercise addressed a simulated incident of DC-9 magnitude with a huge geographical scope (three states—Idaho, Oregon, Washington State, and the Canadian province of British Columbia), enormous scope (in terms of the disruption of critical infrastructures, overall damage, and loss of lives), and extended duration of disruption [18, p. 98] of several years before returning to a new normal.

Besides the physical obstacles presented before the response to this simulated DC-9 incident quickly proved much more complex than the response to the real incident two years earlier. While in some EOCs and ECCs at all levels the internal coordination worked reasonably well, the cross-jurisdictional coordination met numerous challenges. According to several interviewees and numerous after-action reports (AARs), the lack of pre-disaster plan integration across jurisdictions was experienced as painfully missing, when response actions and resource deployment needed instant vertical and horizontal coordination the most. The lack of plan integration between vertical and horizontal levels of government was immediately experienced, for example, in mass fatality management, transportation management, damage assessment, shelter management, and overall resource management. As the National Guard's CR16 AAR laconically concludes,

> "Planning partners must expend the capital and energy to pre-plan and synchronize their actions for this catastrophic event. State agencies, as organized by ESF, should develop linked plans under the Washington Emergency Management Catastrophic Incident Annex (CIA) and the Washington State CSZ Playbook, for the CSZ response." (quote #02)

However, such plan integration has to encompass also local and regional planning not only horizontally but also vertically, for example, between municipalities and counties as well as counties and State agencies, since the data also showed the lack of and need for this kind of integration. Furthermore, planning cycles across jurisdictions are not synchronized. Since jurisdictions of fairly diverse sizes and resources have to coordinate vertically and horizontally, this complex cross-jurisdictional plan coordination could become fairly challenging at least for smaller and less resourceful jurisdictions.

Lack of Standardized Operations, Processes, and Functions. While national frameworks such as NIMS/ICS and NRF provide an overall doctrine, a set of guiding principles, along with structural elements and their interplay, under the particular scenario of a M9+ CSZ rupture, the absence of more detailed standards on operational and other levels was experienced quickly. The adoption of NIMS/ICS by response units is voluntary, and its implementation leaves room for modifications and adjustments to local needs. As a consequence, responders from all groups reported about wide-spread confusion about roles (of positions) and tasks within the response framework, which led to a lot of friction in the collaboration between response units. Despite the usage of ICS forms, for example, ICS 213 (general message), ICS 201 (incident briefing), ICS 214 (activity log), or ICS 215 (operational planning worksheet) in many jurisdictions, the forms were modified or incompletely filled, and no standards existed for processes and procedures (such as message flows and distribution, message elements and composition, message and report frequency, situation report formats, orders for temporary flight restrictions, or resource tracking among others), or functions (such as incident-specific training, emergency support functions, and search and rescue), tactics, techniques, and accountability. As a result, responses were delayed and resources were allocated late. The lack of a regional standardized command and coordination structure, in which EOCs and ECCs at local and County levels, some of which had never fully activated before the exercise, had widely diverse organizational structures ranging from adherence to NIMS/ICS and NRF to other setups including some along the lines of the framework of Emergency Support Functions (ESFs), or a hybrid of NIMS/ICS and ESFs. This organizational variety and its resulting lack of detailed and specific standards for this particular type of incident led to a whole host of coordination issues such as confusion about roles, task assignments, lines of communication, interjurisdictional agreements, and relatively simple procedures such as shift turnovers, some of which occurred without a briefing and detailed handover to the next incident commander. In the latter case, a tremendous amount of rework and loss of operational and situational awareness was the result leading to further confusion and delays. As one AAR points out,

> "There was inadequate coordination between 1st and 2nd EOC shifts (with some notable exceptions). Several members from the first shift left without sufficiently briefing their successor, leading to significant confusion. This also meant that many of the processes and tools that had been developed in the first shift had to be 'relearned.'" (quote #03)

Liaisons. Under NIMS/ICS the deployment of liaison officers (LNOs) across and between governmental levels has become an important formal element to help with inter-organizational and inter-jurisdictional coordination. Required qualifications of LNOs increase with type (I to III) of response to the incident. For example, the State of Washington appointed an official LNO with FEMA Region X. Conversely, during CR16, FEMA deployed numerous support staff at local jurisdictions who essentially performed the roles of LNOs. Also, the Washington National Guard (WANG) had LNOs placed at numerous County and City EOCs. But, also inside jurisdictions liaisons would be used, for example, the Planning Section in a City EOC would have onsite support from the City IT department or other Emergency Support Functions (ESFs). State and counties deploy LNOs also to the various tribal organizations and the Native communities.

The role of a LNO is multifaceted and can be described as a combination of a representative and point-of-contact, an interpreter, a communicator, facilitator, matchmaker, and a subject matter expert who needs very good interpersonal and intercultural skills, excellent knowledge of both the home and the deployment jurisdictions, their structures, their important players as well as their processes, procedures, and plans. In many cases, LNOs in order to be effective need expert knowledge of technical resources, their tactical capabilities, and their availability. Ideally, LNOs would be cross-deployed so that practical coordination between any given response units would be smooth.

In many cases, LNOs played the role of observers only reporting back to their home unit in detail about the situation at hand at the hosting jurisdiction, which then gave that home unit a clearer picture of the overall situation, However, LNOs also played a major role in resource identification, requesting, and allocation. In many cases, it was the LNOs that made things happen when the official channels of communication or resource management were unavailable or not functional otherwise. In some cases, jurisdictions asked LNOs to help with operations and planning when their own staffing levels had gone low. In these cases, the original purpose of LNOs was compromised to some extent. Furthermore, several responder units were unable to fill LNO positions at the next-higher or neighboring governmental levels, for example, several counties had no LNOs at the State EOC, which considerably added to the communication and coordination challenges described above. However, in a real response to a DC-9 incident the latter two situations of repurposing a LNO or not even having a LNO deployed might well become a practical reality, which curtails coordination and communication. Said one County responder,

> "The one thing that we did learn was that we had some new people in the EOC from agencies that normally would show up, but that it was their first time to be in the EOC. So, they didn't really know where to be or what to do or what their role was, so one of the lessons learned is that we need to do a better job providing EOC liaison training establishing a base line of here are our expectations, here are the roles you perform." (quote #04)

Policy Coordination. While incident commanders at various levels of a response supervise and manage the execution of a given mission as detailed in an incident action plan, the overall policies, priorities, and objectives of a response are formulated by policy groups, that is, elected officials and other decision makers of a given jurisdiction who closely work with the incident commander(s) and the EOC/ECC in that jurisdiction. The coordination of policies of different jurisdictions is performed at the respective levels. If, for example, one municipality prefers transportation arterial clearance in mainly East-to-West direction, while the County and neighboring municipalities prefer arterial clearances in a predominantly North-to-South direction, then response teams in the various jurisdictions would likely pursue incompatible or mutually non-supportive objectives. Policy groups in these jurisdictions would be in need of a negotiated common objective, since those decisions would not be made at tactical and operational incident command level. Also, if an incident commander requests resources or actions, which involve long-term strategic capital investments or major structural changes for the jurisdiction, then the policy group would typically first authorize such requests and actions before execution. As one AAR confirms,

> "In some cases, an incident manager may possess the appropriate delegated authority for many or most decisions; however, given the long-term implications of certain decisions, they may either seek informal guidance, or in some cases a more formal policy decision from their agency administrator (e.g. elected official or governing body) prior to pursuing or implementing certain actions." (quote #05)

As the data show, internal and external policy coordination was missing in many cases leaving the incident management teams and their commanders in a state of inaction or undesired, since unauthorized, commitment. In part this was due to policy group members not participating in the exercise, which presented a missed opportunity for testing response procedures at a very critical junction. At State level, though, a Unified Command Group (UCG) was formed, which consisted of State, Federal, and military members, as well as a policy group of State Executives, which provided overall response directions and objectives. However, one needs to remember that the West Coast states are so-called home-rule jurisdictions, in which local authorities have the final say and cannot be overruled in their decision making by higher levels of government. Policy coordination, hence, requires some negotiation, although State and Federal agencies exert certain leverage over lower-level jurisdictions via resource allocation. Furthermore, the communication between the State EOC and the State Disaster Manager, on the one hand, and counties and major municipalities, on the other hand was seriously degraded, which led to an overall lack of policy coordination between the various levels of government. As a result, various missions were found in direct conflict with each other, and significant tensions and interpersonal communication problems were observed between responder units and individuals at and between different levels of government.

Comparison of the Two Responses. When taken findings from the aforementioned reports on the 2014 real landslide incident [31, 37, 39], it is obvious that the inner- and inter-jurisdictional coordination challenges, the LNO-related challenges, and the challenges regarding missing guidance from policy groups were similar in both cases, although they were far more serious during the simulation. With regard to physical obstacles, they were of significantly lesser degree in the real incident than in the simulated one. Although communication lines and cell towers were impacted by the landslide and were down for some days, electrical power was widely available, communications were reestablished quickly, and the site of impact was accessible on the ground from the East and the West as well as from the air. One of the characteristics of the early response to the 2014 incident was that the extent of the incident was initially greatly underestimated. After all, the Pacific Northwest is "landslide" country, and landslides abound every year. It took responders familiar with the "landslide" metaphor a significant amount of time to detect their own misconception and realize that the landslide at hand was an extraordinary one in terms of magnitude and extent of devastation. However, while electrical power and communications were available, the coordination of response efforts was relatively slow until the real extent of the incident was understood after some four to five days. In contrast, the CR16 exercise provided physical obstacles, which participants in terms of the assumable complete blackout were either outright ignored or greatly downplayed. Except for a couple of hours in some jurisdictions, electrical power and connectivity was assumed abundantly available, and operations continued as usual with no disruption as in daily routines, which made the exercise unrealistic from a fundamental perspective. However, both the real incident and the simulated one underscored the vulnerability and almost total dependency of response operations on modern energy and communication infrastructures. In terms of access to the site of impact and the respective multi-jurisdictional coordination problems the 2014 incident gave a sobering handsel of what to expect in a M9+ CSZ rupture incident. As one response unit leader put it,

> "I have heard in the exercise demands and witnessed this being said, 'Well, the major road arterials in the impacted area have to be open within three days.' Then I'm going, 'How long did it take us to open just one lane on the State Route 530 slide? Let alone two lanes?' That was one slide. That was only a mile and a half. One slide. It took months. And in a catastrophic incident, we are talking that times a thousand. So, we have to get real with our planning assumptions. Otherwise we are just kidding ourselves." (quote #06)

Summary of Findings (Ad RQ#1). It appears that in terms of inner- and interjurisdictional coordination challenges the 2014 landslide incident provided a micromodel of what would be experienced on a far larger scope, scale, and longer duration in a M9+ CSZ rupture incident. What did not coordinate well in the 2014 incident response, would not coordinate well in the catastrophic incident response. Moreover, what worked reasonably well after some time in terms of coordination in the real incident response might take far longer to work as well in the response to a catastrophe.

4.2   Ad RQ #2 (How Do Other Managerial Challenges Change or Stay the Same When Responding to a Catastrophic Incident (as Opposed to a Non-catastrophic Emergency Response)?)

Staffing. Without exception all responder groups reported of serious actual or antici-pated staffing problems after the real incident had occurred. During the exercise, quite a number of responders did not report to duty, and some carried out their task assign-ments in a daily-routine type of mode, or they were still occupied by their regular daily tasks during the exercise. However, in the real incident response, understaffing has to be expected as the norm, be it for reasons of victimization of staffers themselves, or physical obstacles in the path to the respective deployment site, or conflicts of interest between family care and reporting to duty, or, a combination of the aforementioned along with other contingencies. As a unit leader projected,

> "At best, we can assume that we are going to have a recall rate of 50% of our staff. At best. I'm saying, we're still optimistic if we get 50%. Because people want, the survival instinct come first and caring for your family and loved ones, and then reporting to duty. So that's going to be a big challenge on top of everything." (quote #07)

With understaffing experienced during the exercise and to be expected in the real response, essential expertise was and will be missing. Also, work hours were and would be extended, and the workload increased drastically leading to fatigue, wear-down, and mistakes, all of which limited the reasonable time of deployment or assignment. In some jurisdictions the loss of staff expertise was addressed by rotating staff through various positions so that backups became available, and expertise was hoped to be spread. However, the obvious and experienced downside of this approach was that expert knowledge was missing in a number of cases, when it was most needed, but unfortunately the expert had been deployed elsewhere. Among other staffing-related challenges were the reliance on volunteers who could disengage at any moment, trauma and stress handling for responders at shift end, as well as sheltering responders whose return to their own homes was impossible due to physical obstacles.

Planning. Many response units simply did not know about pre-existing plans, which could have been used in the response at least in part, and so they rather developed new and redundant plans from scratch under the duress of the simulated incident. However, while existing plans provide a starting point, they were generally not developed for coping with an incident of the M9+ CSZ order, nor were many of these plans up to date. In general, mass fatality plans, mass care and sheltering plans, and mass evac-uation plans as well as fuel and fuel distribution plans were missing. Also, many continuity-of-operations plans (COOPs) were found out of date or unsupported.

As mentioned before, plans were frequently not shared outside their own unit, and consequently they were not integrated with those of other response units inside their own jurisdiction nor with outside jurisdictions, nor were planning cycles synchronized among and between jurisdictions. Planning in some jurisdictions lacked even basic elements such as maintaining updated organizational charts, up-to-date contact information, current vendor lists, and lists of information access points.

Planning for paper-based response efforts was absent in most, if not all, jurisdictions. This deficit could have been found particularly disruptive during the exercise; however, as mentioned before, the total loss of power and of connectivity was greatly ignored for most portions of the exercise, which illustrates the need for way more realistic planning assumptions, also with regard to future exercises regarding a M9+ CSZ incident.

The CR16 exercise also revealed the lack of planning for currently mostly unprepared families and non-resilient communities, which would be badly affected by the thousands in the real incident. Due to this lack of preparedness a humanitarian crisis of proportions has to be anticipated, in which life-saving activities have to be given priority over fatality management.

In smaller incidents, before resources are committed and action is taken, a thorough assessment of the situation is performed. However, the tumultuous situation resulting from a M9+ CSZ incident may not allow for upholding this resource commitment paradigm calling for due and diligent upfront scrutiny and assessment of the situation. Yet, for reasons outlined above, local responders may simply not be in a position to perform the necessary assessments quickly enough. Responders from upper-level governmental agencies would therefore need to know about priorities, needs, and expectations of local jurisdictions, which could be communicated via sharing of local comprehensive emergency management plans, which could then be better reflected in higher-level response planning. While these plan synchronization and integration efforts are not only necessary, but rather indispensable, since they will provide a far better starting point in the real response, one State planner's sobering remark regarding the readiness for coping with an M9+ CSZ incident provides a chilling, but rather realistic perspective,

> "In the context of a catastrophic incident–I am removing 'ready' out of my vocabulary. It doesn't exist. We continue to prepare but all we're doing is we are mitigating the impact. We are lessening the impact. And we're hoping to be in a more advantageous position to respond and recover. That's all. So that we have to admit. Then we have to admit that the greatest good for the greatest number does not include everybody. And that is a bitter pill to swallow, but we have to admit that as well." (quote #08)

Resource Management. While resource management, and, in particular, resource request management, based on ICS structures and procedures appeared to have worked reasonably well between the State and FEMA, the same cannot be claimed for County and local jurisdictions. Despite the State's efforts to standardize the resource request forms and procedures after the 2014 landslide incident, for many jurisdictions the resource request and routing procedures were still unclear, and the same resources were requested multiple times for the lack of effective resource request tracking capabilities or for the lack of request acknowledgement and timely feedback from the target agency. Many resource requests were filled incompletely or incorrectly. Frequently, requests were not prioritized. Before requesting resources from elsewhere, jurisdictions were chartered with tracking their own resources first. However, many jurisdictions lacked tracking systems for their own resources. As in the 2014 landslide incident, some jurisdictions were also still unfamiliar with the FEMA resource reimbursement requirements. In many cases, it was also unclear who had the authority to approve resource requests. Bureaucratic hurdles slowed down speedy resource allocations, and verbal approvals by responders with the authority to approve such requests were not recognized by resource administrators. Lots of confusion and double work were the result.

During the CR16 exercise, Federal, military, and State responders implemented a push mechanism for the fast allocation of resources expected to be requested. As the Washington National Guard's AAR points out,

> "This 'push' concept does not comply with the principles of the NRF or NIMS and is foreign to most Emergency Managers and Incident Commanders. The traditional and universally accepted 'pull' methodology will cost lives in this scenario. A mindset shift is required in order to achieve the least time lost for life saving capabilities." (quote #09)

However, this led to further confusion about who at County and local levels had the authority to manage the staging, the assignment, and the re-directing of those pushed-down and unassigned resources, all of which took away part of the forward staging advantage and the potential shortening of resource allocation times. The push mechanism surfaced another problem, which was also observed in the 2014 landslide response, when responders at local and regional levels simply had no idea what to request in the absence of detail knowledge about advanced capabilities, in particular, maintained by the military and Federal agencies.

Comparison of the two Responses. In the 2014 landslide response, due to the limited area of impact and the mutual-aid agreements, staffing levels were high, although some responders had not worked in the assigned positions before. Furthermore, fatigue and wear-down was contained, and post-deployment trauma and stress was addressed via targeted treatment. Moreover, no responders were among the victims. However, in both cases, responders had to improvise and plan from scratch, since the extent of the respective incident in either case overwhelmed the responders initially. While in the landslide response except for the suboptimal fatality management the planning deficiencies were addressed quickly, in a M9+ CSZ incident the lack of integrated plans would be much more severely felt immediately and for some time thereafter. Resource management and resource request management was problematic, at least initially in the landslide response. In the catastrophic incident, resource management and resource request management would become a major issue. The practiced resource push mechanism designed for catastrophic incidents appears to require substantially more planning and pre-incident coordination between potentially involved jurisdictions in order to work effectively.

Summary of Findings (Ad RQ#2). Like in the findings to RQ#01 (coordination and collaboration), so in staffing, planning, and resource management quite many observations made during the real landslide response were observed again during the CR16 exercise. However, in the real M9+ CSZ incident response, the shortcomings in staffing, planning, and resource management would immediately have far more negative and far graver consequences than in the landslide incident response of 2014.

5   Discussion, Recommendations, and Concluding Remarks

Manifold Obstacles to Coordination and Collaboration. In the above mentioned previous investigations on situational awareness and the common operating picture (SA/COP) during the CR16 exercise [40], or rather the lack thereof in the early stages of the response, as well as on the uses of information and communication technologies (ICTs) in support of SA/COP [39], it became evident that the coordination of response activities and the collaboration between and among response units was critically dependent on both. SA/COP, it was found, heavily relied on the availability of ICTs; however, ICTs, equally heavily depended on the availability of electrical power and high-bandwidth network connectivity in order to arrive at full SA/COP as early as possible, which would still be days, if not weeks, in the best case. However, as this study uncovers, beyond SA/COP and ICTs as backbones of coordination and collaboration, other important issues exist, which would make effective coordination and collaboration between and among response units difficult to achieve. The devastation of other critical infrastructures, first and foremost, transportation, would severely stifle coordinated responses. A major obstacle was also found in the lack of integrated plans and synchronized planning for this particular type of incident. Neighboring jurisdictions and next higher-level jurisdictions need to establish and update such plans and maintain in sync their planning efforts. Another major obstacle was identified in the absence of standardization of structures, processes, procedures, and forms. Further, the policy decisions of hundreds of elected officials and appointed administrators in the affected region were identified in need of alignment, for which despite the NIMS/ICS concepts of Unified Command and Area Command currently no practical mechanisms exist.

Addressing Coordination Collaboration Obstacles. For this specific type of catastrophic incident and based on NIMS/ICS and NRF, it appears necessary for the likely M9+ CSZ incident impact areas in Alaska, Oregon, and Washington to develop and negotiate among governments of all levels a *"Regional Disaster Response Coordination Framework."* In the home-rule States of the Pacific Northwest such a framework cannot be imposed on jurisdictions, but rather it can only be jointly developed by all levels of government. It would need to define mechanisms for policy decision alignment between and among jurisdictions of the impact areas, plan integration, planning synchronization, and standardization of structures, processes, procedures, and forms, and the systematic and cross-jurisdictional use of liaisons. This undertaking would be in great need of a shared vision among jurisdictional partners, productive multiyear negotiations, and significant amounts of funding to successfully complete.

Need to Plan for and Practice Paper-Based Operations. While the CR16 exercise did not focus on practicing paper-based operations, it made clear that in the real M9+ CSZ incident operations and response management would be paper-based and messenger-based for extended periods of time. The pace of response would be dependent on the pace of communications. A mainly paper-based and messenger-based response would inevitably be slow. In order to speed up the response, equipping responders with much faster and more effective means of communications than paper and messengers would be paramount. Since power and connectivity would be only gradually restored, but sometimes even lost again, or, would remain available in a very degraded way, a mechanism for scaling up and scaling down such constrained operations would be needed. Planning for, providing for, and testing such scalable paper/ICT-based operations might present some unique challenges.

Planning for Backup Trained and Expert Staff. The lack of required staffing and staff qualification levels was already felt during the exercise, albeit in part for other reasons. However, in the real M9+ CSZ incident, staff levels were predicted to go below the 50% threshold in response units for all kinds of reasons. Planning for staffing backups is therefore an absolute necessity. The need for backup staffing might be even greater when considering the effects of fatigue and wear-down.

Resource Management Paradigm Shift. As described, Federal, military, and State responders concluded that a M9+ CSZ incident would require a paradigm shift in response resource management from "pull" to "push," which would allocate unrequested resources in presumed areas of need based on models and other assumptions. State and Federal planners have to make assumptions, use simulation models, and incorporate damage forecasts for planning so that resources can be committed to affected areas as quickly as possible.

The resource "push" method, however, would be in conflict with both the NIMS/ICS response doctrine as well as with the principle of home rule in the Pacific Northwest as the State and FEMA AARs remark. NIMS/ICS and NRF sanction a resource "pull" mechanism, which preserves the authority of resource requesting to the local authorities. As observed during the exercise, the implementation of a resource "push" regime is not without very practical problems. At the receiving end the pushing of resources led to confusion about responsibilities and accountability, and to questions about allocation authorities, along with quite a number of other problems. In practice, alignments in the command and decision structures would be required to make the resource "push" paradigm effective and legal from a governance standpoint. While the potential advantages of a "push" regime are undeniable, at least for the early phases of the response, the proposed *"Regional Disaster Response Coordination Framework"* appears to be the context, in which such temporary changes of command and decision structure and incident-specific changes of doctrine principle would have to find their negotiated place.

Extended Training/Re-training and Funding Needs. From this investigation it follows that improved levels of preparedness for the response to a M9+ CSZ incident can only be expected if the frequency of exercises is increased. Also, the types of exercises need adjustments, for example, functional exercises in scaling between paper-based and ICT-based operations. This needs to be accompanied by increased and intensified training efforts with regard to NIMS/ICS as well as the integrated plans in a to-be-developed incident-specific regional framework. It remains to be seen whether or not the tremendous amounts of funding, which these proposed efforts require for planning and ongoing training, can be made available. In any case, since responder units in the area are undergoing a massive staff turnover through retirement, additional training and exercises will be needed.

Exercise Specifics. Every response exercise has certain artificialities, which under-represent certain aspects of the real incident response. However, despite those artificialities, a fundamental and sobering insight from the CR16 exercise for responders was, for example, in the State of Washington, that current Statewide planning and preparedness levels were appropriate only for responding to non-catastrophic incidents and not for a M9+ CSZ incident response. Consequently, another large exercise is under planning to be conducted in 2022, this time also involving the State of Alaska.

Based on this research it is strongly recommended to integrate plans, synchronize planning, and test non-ICT-based operations prior to this exercise. It might also be desirable to have an impact area-wide schedule of smaller functional exercises after the 2022 exercise as part of a larger framework. In the 2022 exercise, it would be critical to have policy and decision makers more actively and practically involved than during CR16.

Conclusion and Outlook. It has been the object of this study to identify obstacles to coordination and collaboration of efforts in the response to a catastrophic incident and to provide recommendations for mitigating these obstacles. In so doing, the study contributes to both the academic understanding of the complexities of managing a catastrophic incident response and to the practical understanding of measures and choices available to response planners. Future investigations will follow up with assessing and evaluating the practical measures taken and the choices made by responders.

Acknowledgement. The following research assistants participated in the transcribing, coding, concept analyzing and mapping of the interviews: Ammi Bui, Hyung Jin Byoun, Sarah L. Carnes, Nuo Chen, Tiffany Chiu, Sukhman Dhillon, Sumedha Dubey, Ryan Dzakovic, Andy Herman, Yun Hsiao, Karyn Hubbell, Harsh Keswani, Manjiri Khakar, Priyanka Kshirsagar, Janani Kumar, Kung Jin Lee, Jeff Leonard, Chang Jay Liu, Christy (Hsin-yu) Lu, Ying Lu, Rachel Mahre, Grace Morris, Veslava Ovendale, Xiaoyu Qu, Jason Repko, Ed Slininger, Emily K. Smalligan, Sonal Srivastava, Rebecca Ta, Huong Thanh Thai, Xiaobin Tuo, Fan Yang, Qiaosi Wang, and several graduate assistants from Graduate Assistant Team. Special thanks to Sue Morgan who organized and orchestrated the online streaming and video recording of the weekly project sessions.

References

1. National Incident Management System. US Department of Homeland Security, pp. x/156. FEMA, Washington, DC (2008). https://www.fema.gov/pdf/emergency/nims/NIMS_core.pdf
2. National Response Framework. US Dept of Homeland Security, 3rd edn., pp. iv/52. FEMA, Washington, DC (2016). https://www.fema.gov/media-library-data/1466014682982-9bcf82 45ba4c60c120aa915abe74e15d/National_Response_Framework3rd.pdf
3. Abbasi, A., Kapucu, N.: Structural dynamics of organizations during the evolution of interorganizational networks in disaster response. J. Homel. Secur. Emerg. Manage. **9**, 1–19 (2012)
4. Atwater, B.F.: Summary of coastal geologic evidence for past great earthquakes at the Cascadia subduction zone. Earthq. Spectra **11**, 1–18 (1995)

5. Bharosa, N., Lee, J., Janssen, M.: Challenges and obstacles in sharing and coordinating information during multi-agency disaster response: propositions from field exercises. Inf. Syst. Front. **12**, 49–65 (2010)
6. Buck, D.A., Trainor, J.E., Aguirre, B.E.: A critical evaluation of the incident command system and NIMS. J. Homel. Secur. Emerg. Manage. **3**, 1–27 (2006)
7. Chen, R., Sharman, R., Rao, H.R., Upadhyaya, S.J., Cook-Cottone, C.P.: Coordination of emergency response: an examination of the roles of people, process, and information technology. In: Van De Walle, B., Turoff, M., Hiltz, S.R. (eds.) Information Systems for Emergency Management, vol. 16, pp. 150–174. Routledge, New York (2014)
8. Clarke, P.K., Campbell, L.: Coordination in theory, coordination in practice: the case of the Clusters. Disasters **42**, 655–673 (2018)
9. Cole, D.: The incident command system: a 25-year evaluation by California practitioners. National Fire Academy (2000)
10. Comfort, L.K.: Crisis management in hindsight: cognition, communication, coordination, and control. Public Adm. Rev. **67**, 189–197 (2007)
11. Davis, G.L., Robbin, A.: Network disaster response effectiveness: the case of ICTs and Hurricane Katrina. J. Homel. Secur. Emerg. Manage. **12**, 437–467 (2015)
12. Dawes, S.S., Birkland, T., Tayi, G.K., Schneider, C.A.: Information, Technology, and Coordination: Lessons from the World Trade Center Response. Center for Technology in Government (CTG), SUNY Albany (2004)
13. DeCapua, M.: Letter to the editor regarding incident command system (ICS). J. Homel. Secur. Emerg. Manage. **4**, 1 (2007)
14. Drabek, T.E., McEntire, D.A.: Emergent phenomena and multiorganizational coordination in disasters: lessons from the research literature. Int. J. Mass Emerg. Disasters **20**, 197–224 (2002)
15. Dynes, R.R., Aguirre, B.E.: Organizational adaptation to crises: mechanisms of coordination and structural change. Disasters **3**, 71–74 (1979)
16. Earle, C.R.: C2 agility for emergency management: examining the katrina and sandy responses. J. Homel. Secur. Emerg. Manage. **15**, 20170046 (2018)
17. Fereday, J., Muir-Cochrane, E.: Demonstrating rigor using thematic analysis: a hybrid approach of inductive and deductive coding and theme development. Int. J. Qual. Methods **5**, 1–11 (2006)
18. Fischer, H.W.: The sociology of disaster: definitions, research questions, & measurements continuation of the discussion in a post-September 11 environment. Int. J. Mass Emerg. Disasters **21**, 91–107 (2003)
19. Glaser, B.G.: The future of grounded theory. Qual. Health Res. **9**, 836–845 (1999)
20. Glaser, B.G., Strauss, A.L.: The Discovery of Grounded Theory; Strategies for Qualitative Research. Aldine Publication Co., Chicago (1967)
21. Groenendaal, J., Helsloot, I., Scholtens, A.: A critical examination of the assumptions regarding centralized coordination in large-scale emergency situations. J. Homel. Secur. Emerg. Manage. **10**, 113–135 (2013)
22. Guo, X., Kapucu, N.: Examining coordination in disaster response using simulation methods. J. Homel. Secur. Emerg. Manage. **12**, 891–914 (2015)
23. Seismological Society of America. https://www.seismosoc.org/annual-meeting/how-often-do-cascadias-megaquakes-occur/
24. Hambridge, N.B., Howitt, A.M., Giles, D.W.: Coordination in crises: implementation of the national incident management system by surface transportation agencies. Homel. Secur. Aff. **13**, 1–30 (2017)
25. Hansen, R.R.: Letter to the editor regarding incident command system (ICS). J. Homel. Secur. Emerg. Manage. **3**, 1–3 (2007)

26. Iverson, R.M., et al.: Landslide mobility and hazards: implications of the 2014 Oso disaster. Earth Planet. Sci. Lett. **412**, 197–208 (2015)
27. Jensen, J.: The current NIMS implementation behavior of United States counties. J. Homel. Secur. Emerg. Manage. **8**, 1–25 (2011)
28. Jensen, J., Waugh, W.L.: The United States' experience with the incident command system: what we think we know and what we need to know more about. J. Contingencies Crisis Manage. **22**, 5–17 (2014)
29. Jensen, J., Youngs, G.: Explaining implementation behaviour of the national incident management system (NIMS). Disasters **39**, 362–388 (2015)
30. Kapucu, N.: Interorganizational coordination in complex environments of disasters: the evolution of intergovernmental disaster response systems. J. Homel. Secur. Emerg. Manage. **6**, 1547–7355 (2009)
31. Lombardo, K., et al.: SR 530 landslide commission final report. In: Commission, S.L. (ed.), pp. v/49. SR 530 Landslide Commission, Olympia, WA (2014)
32. Neal, D.M., Phillips, B.D.: Effective emergency management: reconsidering the bureaucratic approach. Disasters **19**, 327–337 (1995)
33. Paci-Green, R., Boles, N., Black, T., Smith, K., Munkh-Erdene, E.: Cascadia Rising: Cascadia Subduction Zone (CSZ) Catastrophic Earthquake and Tsunami (Exercise Scenario Document) (2015)
34. Quarantelli, E.L.: Disaster crisis management - a summary of research findings. J. Manage. Stud. **25**, 373–385 (1988)
35. Ritchie, J., Lewis, J., Gillian, E.: Designing and selecting samples. In: Ritchie, J., Lewis, J. (eds.) Qualitative Research Practice: A Guide for Social Science Students and Researchers, pp. 77–108. Sage Publications, London (2003)
36. Scholl, H.J., Ballard, S., Carnes, S., Herman, A., Parker, N.: Informational challenges in early disaster response: the massive Oso/SR530 landslide 2014 as case in point. In: Sprague, R., Bui, T. (eds.) 50th Hawaii International Conference on System Sciences (HICSS-50), pp. 2498–2508. ScholarSpace, Waikoloa, Hawaii (2017)
37. Scholl, H.J., Carnes, S.L.: Managerial challenges in early disaster response: the case of the 2014 Oso/SR530 landslide disaster. In: Proceedings of the 14th ISCRAM Conference ISCRAM, pp. 961–972. Albi, France (2017)
38. Scholl, H.J., Chatfield, A.T.: The role of resilient information infrastructures: the case of radio fukushima during and after the 2011 eastern japan catastrophe. Int. J. Public Adm. Digital Age (IJPADA) **1**, 1–24 (2014)
39. Scholl, H.J., Hubbel, K., Leonard, J.: Communications and technology challenges to situational awareness: insights from the CR16 Exercise. In: Proceedings of the 1st ISCRAM Asia-Pacific Conference, pp. 1–15. ISCRAM, Wellington (2018)
40. Scholl, H.J., Hubbell, K., Leonard, J.G.: Information sharing and situational awareness: insights from the Cascadia rising exercise of June 2016. In: Proceedings of the 52nd Hawaii International Conference on System Sciences (HICSS-52), pp. 1–11, Maui (2019)
41. Scholl, H.J., Patin, B.J.: Resilient information infrastructures: criticality and role in responding to catastrophic incidents. Transform. Gov.: People, Process Policy **8**, 28–48 (2014)
42. Stambler, K.S., Barbera, J.A.: Engineering the incident command and multiagency coordination systems. J. Homel. Secur. Emerg. Manage. **8**, 1–27 (2011)
43. Strauss, A.L., Corbin, J.M.: Basics of Qualitative Research: Techniques and Procedures for Developing Grounded Theory. Sage Publications, Thousand Oaks (1998)
44. Tsai, J.-S., Chi, C.S.F.: Cultural influence on the implementation of incident command system for emergency management of natural disasters. J. Homel. Secur. Emerg. Manage. **9**, 1–22 (2012)

45. Urquhart, C., Lehmann, H., Myers, M.D.: Putting the 'theory' back into grounded theory: guidelines for grounded theory studies in information systems. Inf. Syst. **20**, 357–381 (2010)
46. Van de Walle, B., Turoff, M., Hiltz, S.R.: Coordination of emergency response: an examination of the roles of people, process, and information technology. In: Information Systems for Emergency Management, pp. 162–186. Routledge, Abingdon (2014)
47. Waugh, W.L.: Mechanisms for collaboration in emergency management: ICS, NIMS, and the problem with command and control. In: O'Leary, R., Bingham, L.B. (eds.) The Collaborative Public Manager: New Ideas For The Twenty-First Century, pp. 157–175. Georgetown University Press, Washington (2009)
48. Wenger, D., Quarantelli, E.L., Dynes, R.R.: Is the incident command system a plan for all seasons and emergency situations? Hazard Mon. **10**, 8–12 (1990)
49. West, D.O., McCrumb, D.R.: Coastline uplift in Oregon and Washington and the nature of Cascadia subduction-zone tectonics. Geology **16**, 169–172 (1988)

Creating Local Government Innovation

Lessons Learned from an Institutional Theory Perspective

Fredrik Söderström$^{(\boxtimes)}$ ⓘ and Ulf Melin ⓘ

Linköping University, SE-581 83 Linköping, Sweden
{fredrik.soderstrom, ulf.melin}@liu.se

Abstract. The public sector is facing an equation that cannot be solved by continuing doing business as usual. External demands of availability, quality and resilience of services, as well as internal demands of resource efficiency, are putting pressure on the public sector to seek for innovation. In this study, we focus on local government innovation where high expectations are set on better utilisation of employees' creativity and innovative capacity. Based on a qualitative case study of an innovation programme in a Swedish local government organisation, this study applies institutional theory as a theoretical lens to further investigate and analyse the relationship between formal and informal structures of local government innovation. The institutional structures related to norms and values, legitimacy and decoupling as well as digital artefacts as institutional carriers are discussed. Implications for practice show that formal structures, processes and digital artefacts to support local government innovation are important in this work. However, to achieve government innovation, equal attention should also be given to informal institutional structures of innovation. For research, this implies that government innovation studies can benefit from an institutional theory perspective to develop a better understanding of how informal structures affect related processes. We conclude by arguing that the needed change towards the innovative bureaucracy is a transformative innovation in itself that needs to be acknowledged.

Keywords: Local government innovation · Public sector innovation · Institutional theory · Public sector ICT · Digitalisation

1 Introduction

A general perception, in research as well as practice, is that public sector organisations face significant challenges in the present and future. These challenges are the result of increasing internal demands, e.g. increased efficiency, as well as external demands on quality, availability and resilience of services. Taking advantage of the internal intellectual capital in order to increase the innovative ability of public sector organisations is seen as a suitable means, or even a must, to aid in meeting current challenges [e.g. 1, 2]. By investigating a local government innovation initiative, this study aims at looking beyond current perspectives in research focusing on formal structures to support and facilitate government innovation. The focused local government innovation programme

© IFIP International Federation for Information Processing 2019
Published by Springer Nature Switzerland AG 2019
I. Lindgren et al. (Eds.): EGOV 2019, LNCS 11685, pp. 125–138, 2019.
https://doi.org/10.1007/978-3-030-27325-5_10

is the result of current internal and external demands or pressures put-on public-sector organisations in Sweden to increase their innovative ability. This ability is related to the creativity of co-workers, hence the aim is to facilitate internal innovation. In previous studies, innovations are described as new ways of structuring and arranging processes and activities in order to achieve significant improvement [e.g. 3]. An innovation always starts with an idea. The idea is the spark that ignites the process of innovation with the goal of implementing innovation into daily operations. However, an idea does not always become an innovation. The innovation process is associated with a significant amount of uncertainty and risk; hence this creates a need for structured and systematic process management [4], but at the same time, uncertainty and risk challenge the planning, control and coordination of innovation activities [5]. The innovation and operations must converge to be successful; the organisation needs to successfully manage "action knowledge and thinking knowledge" [6]. However, government innovation tends to be problematic, as confirmed by research and shown in this study.

Existing processes and structures are potentially challenged [7], and public organisations, as examples of bureaucracies, often have a "zero-error culture" [8]. Moreover, there are several contradictions regarding local government innovation. For example, municipalities have the mission to be politically driven tax-funded service providers. They are local bureaucracies, albeit with a positive connotation. One can, therefore, question whether local government innovation is in line with this mission and the public interest? What creates the acceptance and legitimacy for local government to spend resources on initiatives associated with significant risks, uncertainty and potential failure? In contrast to research and practice focusing on formal and rational ways of increasing government innovation, equal attention must be given to the social, behavioural and value-based prerequisites and capacity to innovate; i.e. the "actual patterns of behaviour and work routines" [9]. These informal structures are manifested in shared behaviour, culture, norms and values and have a potential impact in this area.

This study applies institutional theory[1] as a theoretical lens. As a point of departure, we see local government innovation as a collective behaviour that needs to be socially established [10], i.e. institutionalised, across the organisation. Institutional theory provides opportunities to better understand organisational irrationalities [11] as seen in this context as well as a way to relate formal and informal structures in local government innovation. Moreover, digital artefacts have an important role in facilitating government innovation. These artefacts can act as carriers of institutional ideas [12], i.e. government innovation as a desired collective behaviour, across organisational boundaries. This study addresses the following research questions: (RQ-1) What are the results and effects of a local government innovation programme? (RQ-2) What lessons can be learned from applying institutional theory on local government innovation? The paper structure is as follows: Section two covers related research in the areas of ideas and innovations, government innovation as well the institutional perspective. Section three presents the case study and the research approach followed by empirical findings from the case study presented in section four. The result of applying an institutional

---

[1] This should be considered being a new or neo-institutional perspective (see e.g. Scott, 2014).

perspective is discussed in section five, and the paper concludes with implications for research and practice as well as suggestions for further research in section six.

2 Related Research

2.1 Ideas and Innovations

There is some disagreement among researchers about the meaning of the concepts of ideas and innovations. However, there is a shared consensus that these two concepts are significantly different. Every innovation starts with an idea, but innovation also requires management and coordination to bring potential benefits [13]. Innovations depend on ideas but far from all ideas become innovations. The stage of idea generation can be seen as trivial while there are significant challenges during the realisation of ideas into innovations [13]. This study is based on the following definition: "Successful innovation is the creation and implementation of new processes, products, services and methods of delivery which result in significant improvements in outcomes efficiency, effectiveness or quality" [3]. The idea is the critical prerequisite, the spark, initiating the process of realising the idea into an innovation. Innovations are often described as processes [14], and one must also bear in mind that innovation processes do not always result in successful innovations [13]. Transferring an idea from the intellectual to conceptual level further on to the operational level is always related to significant risks. Systematic and structured innovation processes have a positive impact on realising ideas into innovations [4]. It is essential to identify and successfully manage different stages or phases in innovation work [15]. Innovations are categorised as incremental, radical or transformative [3]. While incremental innovations result in minor changes in existing activities, radical innovations lead to significant improvements while maintaining existing dynamics between actors (ibid.). Transformative innovations fundamentally change a sector's foundation and give rise to new organisational forms [3].

2.2 Government Innovation

Innovation has a critical strategic value for public management [16]. Government organisations face unprecedented challenges, and traditional established approaches will not be enough [1]. The processes supporting government innovation cannot be traditional top-down but instead must take advantage of all potential sources of innovation; internal as well as external to the organisation [1]. To be able to gain a positive result from innovation work, public organisations must be exposed, willing and responsive to innovation [17]. Like other organisational changes, there is a need for top-management support to create the legitimacy needed for innovation work across organisations [e.g. 7]. Government innovation addresses and challenges traditional structures and operations. It becomes essential to acknowledge the need for minimising the potential resistance to new and innovative ways of structuring work and performing activities [17]. Moreover, government innovation always occurs at the expense of regular activities [17]. Limited resources and strained operations in contemporary public sector organisations can, therefore, cause problems [17]. Government innovation differs from innovation work in the private sector. Public organisations are tax-financed and governed by laws and regulations; organisations must thereby fund the innovation work themselves instead of bringing in external venture capital [7]. The error margins in the public sector are also different from the private sector. Constant media coverage does not hesitate to make headlines of any failure [7].

Different approaches to tackle current and future societal challenges are put forth. For example, the concept of social innovation focuses on meeting social needs by developing and using new social processes [18]. Another strategy proposed specifically for government innovation is collaborative innovation [e.g. 1, 19, 20]. Collaborative innovation utilises diversity across the organisation while challenging existing organ- isational boundaries [1]. By opening up the innovation process and integrating different actors, the availability of resources and assets without bureaucratic boundaries become a crucial factor for this approach [19]. As a network-based approach, the origin of collaborative innovation is linked to historical research on governance networks and network governance [8]. Since the research field of government innovation is a rela- tively new subfield, researchers acknowledge a need for more studies [e.g. 8, 21]. Accordingly, this study is an answer to this call.

2.3 Institutions and Institutional Carriers

The institutional theory perspective emphasises the need for considering informal aspects of organising as well as formal and rational structures and activities [11]. The organisational context is thereby considered being of importance as having a significant influence on decisions and activities [22]. There is a need to acknowledge how different terms and variations in the organisational context affect organisational activities [23]. The focus is put on the tacit, implied or unspoken, for example, in the form of norms, values, beliefs and interpretations [23]. These are socially constructed meanings shared among individuals and transferred over time [9]. Institutions are systems of social control [24] or social structures that restrict and guide behaviour in social arrangements [9]. Studies apply the institutional perspective to analyse either the external, i.e. environment as an institution or the internal, i.e. organisation as an institution [25]. The concept of institutionalisation is a constructionist view addressing institutional ele- ments such as norms and values [25]. Organisational legitimacy is an essential factor that affects and is affected by institutional aspects such as norms and values [26]. Legitimacy is the appropriateness of action in line with existing definitions, beliefs, norms and values [26].

Decoupling is a critical aspect of institutionalisation and refers to the process of the organisation, avoiding integration of formal structures due to, for example, inconsis- tencies or anomalies [27]. Formal structures are changed only in a ceremonial manner letting organisational units perform their activities as usual [9]. Decoupling results in formal structures not being aligned or coupled with how work is being performed across the organisation. Institutions are also transferred across an organisation by different institutional carriers [9, 12, 28] such as values and expectations, activities and artefacts [9]. Studies have shown that for example, digital artefacts as carriers are important to consider when investigating the process of institutionalisation [e.g. 29, 30]. Although institutional theory has received considerable attention in e-government research, the application of this type of sociological perspective in government innovation research is still limited. However, this study is in line with previous research put forth by, for example [5].

3 Research Approach and Case Study

The presented research is the result of a study conducted at a municipality in 2017 and was initiated in late 2016 when the municipality contacted the authors. The municipality described a desire to evaluate the outcome of the idea and innovation programme, henceforth referred to as the innovation programme. In Sweden, municipalities are politically controlled local government entities governed by the local government act with responsibilities and services in areas such as preschool and education, health and social care, local business, environment and urban planning. The municipality has seven administrations operating the activities in committees' areas of interest and responsibility. The innovation programme was initiated before central guidance, and financial support was offered on a national level to promote this kind of development [e.g. 31–33]. At the time of this study, the municipality was seen as a forerunner in local government innovation. Although being a single case study, we argue that this case offers an opportunity for knowledge development regarding local government innovation. Conducing a qualitative interpretive case study [e.g. 34, 35] achieving generalisability across empirical settings is not sought. Instead, by applying an analytical perspective, we aim at developing a deeper understanding of local government innovation, which in turn can inform other settings focusing on this phenomenon [c.f. 36].

Mainly based on qualitative data, quantitative data was also used as a complementary source. During the first phase of the study, a web survey was designed and submitted to 40 respondents assigned to roles linked to the innovation programme. The online questionnaire consisted of 13 five-point Likert scale questions supplemented with six open-ended/free text questions. The web survey reached a response rate of 75%. The focus of this survey was to investigate the introduction of the programme, its outcome and current effects on a general organisational as well as operational level. The results were analysed using basic descriptive statistics and integrated into the overall qualitative case study. During the second phase of the study, ten semi-structured interviews [e.g. 37] were conducted face-to-face with respondents on different organisational levels across the organisation. Identified by referral sampling [38], all respondents had clear connections to the programme either as department managers, owners/coordinators of related processes or as assigned representatives to support the programme.

Distribution of respondents' roles[2]: manager (2), idea coach (2), IT strategist[3] (1), contact person (2), inspirer (3). The aim was to involve employees already involved in the programme to assess and evaluate the results and effects. The interviews were

---

[2] Please refer to Sect. 4.1 for a description of roles.

[3] A former employee involved in the development of the innovation programme.

guided by the preliminary result of the web survey and aimed at further investigating ideas and innovations as interpreted and translated among respondents as well as the level of operationalisation of the programme. In parallel with data collection activities, a hermeneutic literature review [39] was performed covering relevant areas of research. Institutional theory and previous research on innovations were used as a guide for further investigations and analysis [35]. A thematic approach was applied iteratively during data analysis allowing for constant focus shifts between empirical data and literature; i.e. a reflexive approach [40]. The analysis was performed on different levels such as individual, group and organisational. Digital artefacts were also handled as a level of analysis. During the case study, the researchers stayed in regular contact with the municipality. Emerging findings and tentative results were discussed in meetings and seminars in order to report work in progress as well as to validate results. The result and implications for practice were reported back in written form to the municipality in October 2017 and therefore also served as a process of validating the results.

4   Empirical Findings: The Innovation Programme

4.1   Formal Structure and Process

The innovation programme was established in 2015 with the objective to realise at least 100 ideas per year. The aim is to increase the ability to make use of employees' creativity and competence to handle current and future challenges. The programme should also support current initiatives in research and business development through increased cooperation between administrations. Employees are supported during assessment, development and realisation of their ideas. The programme should also facilitate administrations' prioritisation and implementation of proper development efforts. The programme consists of a formal structure and process, a central supporting function (the Idea Sluice)[4] and a web portal (the Idea Portal). There are defined roles assigned to the programme: (1) the carrier – an employee having an idea, (2) the coaches - central roles responsible for supporting the innovation process and (3) the counsels – which at the administrative level decides whether the idea is to be supported or not. On a general level, the municipality's innovation programme contains a formal innovation process consisting of four main phases as illustrated in Fig. 1 below. The first phase of *Assessment* (1) is performed by the carrier in cooperation with the coach with the aim of concretisation and quality assurance of the idea. The idea is then presented to the council deciding if the idea is to be supported or not. If supported, the second phase of *development, test and evaluation* (2) can be initiated. The result is presented to the council assessing and evaluating the result. If showing positive real-isability, the process can continue into the third phase of *expanded pilot testing* (3) and the fourth phase of *implementation* (4).

If the idea is dismissed by the council or administration, the carrier can always try to develop further and refine the idea and try to initiate another process cycle.

---

[4] The motive for using this term as a metaphor in this context is based on the purpose of the supporting function resembling a device for facilitating and controlling the flow of ideas within the organisation.

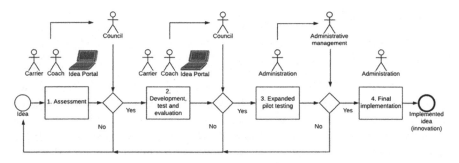

Fig. 1. The formal innovation process

The process is supported by a digital artefact, the Idea Portal, described in the next section. The programme also includes two additional roles not directly involved in the formal innovation process. The contact persons act as local contact points, and the aim of the inspirers is to support and facilitate the innovation programme at the local operational level.

4.2   The Digital Artefact: An Idea Web Portal

The digital artefact, the Idea Portal, is based on a traditional web interface and is accessible via the municipality's Intranet. The portal allows for basic functionality for submitting ideas and keeping information of ideas updated during the phases of the process, e.g. assigning different statuses with progress updates. The assigned status of an idea corresponds to the main phases of the process as previously described (see Fig. 1 above). Ideas can also be shown with a status of being cancelled, paused or redirected, i.e. passed on to a specific business area. The carrier can access their own ideas in a personalised view while all employees have access to the overall view of submitted ideas. The portal is mainly used by the coach and carrier during the first two phases, i.e. assessment (1) and development, test and evaluation (2). The Idea Portal is described as a positive incentive, for example, bringing visibility and transparency to the programme (Manager 2, 2017). *"I think it is important because it becomes a structure - otherwise it would have been totally invisible. [..] It [the portal] supports legitimacy and understanding."* (Inspirer 2, 2017). The part of the organisation affected by the idea and its current status becomes clear (Inspirer 1, 2017).

The Idea Portal has had a positive contribution; however, mostly focused on the initial phase of submitting ideas. This phase now has a much higher level of legitimacy, and the portal, together with assigned roles, has contributed to increased visibility (Contact Person 2, 2017). Instead of using a dedicated system, i.e. innovation management software, the portal is developed based on a traditional case management system (Coach 2, 2017). Respondents thus describe a need to further develop the portal, for example, regarding improved functionality for dialogue, interaction, cooperation as well as features for evaluating/rating ideas. Hence, the innovation process could potentially make better use of digital channels (Coach 2, 2017).

4.3   Results and Effects

The programme is described as having positive effects on a general level. According to one respondent: *"This is a municipality where you are serious about the idea work. You really want to take advantage of the employees' creativity."* (Inspirer 1, 2017). Respondents also emphasise that government innovation should not compete with regular business development activities but rather complement and handle ideas that cannot be handled by such systems (Coach 2, 2017; Inspirer 1, 2017). However, several challenges are put forth by respondents. The assigned roles work well, but the lack of establishment and top management support affect the programme (Manager 1, 2017; Coach 2, 2017; Inspirer 1, 2017). The central support function is described as an enabler, but limited resources are described as an impeding factor. The function is considered too understaffed (one manager and two coaches) to be able to support the potential amount of ideas (Coach 2, 2017). Although work so far has been positive, one respondent states that this initiative needs more allocated resources (Contact person 1, 2017). There is a perceived distance between assigned roles and areas covered by the programme. An example is a distance in time and space between the idea carrier, the support function and the decisions on the administrative management level (see phase 3 and 4 in Fig. 1 above).

With too much distance between regular operations and innovation process, the latter risks being perceived as too vague and unclear in turn resulting in a low degree of concern and commitment across the organisation. As a result of this challenge, some administrations have even actively decided not to support the innovation process at all since it is deemed to be redundant (Coach 1, 2017). Respondents, therefore, describe that a potential solution would be to move the central support function closer to local operations. Minimising this gap would facilitate a stronger connection between the innovation programme and regular development activities and in turn, promote a stable and sustainable approach, i.e. integrated with regular business development processes (Manager 2, 2017; Contact Person 2, 2017). In summary, the case study shows that the innovation process, its structure and supporting roles and artefact have had a positive contribution but this initiative has been created and introduced without enough support from regular operations (Manager 1, 2017).

5   Discussion

5.1   Norms and Values

The central concepts, i.e. the idea and the innovation, have not been problematised to any greater extent in the studied organisation during the introduction of the programme. The formal process and structure have been implemented and communicated across the organisation (see Sect. 4.1). Thus, the municipality has not taken any further notice of how these concepts are interpreted and institutionalised among employees. This motivates a discussion of normative or taken-for-granted assumptions [23] about the programme among respondents. In line with Tolbert and Zucker [41] we argue that the adoption of the programme can be determined by its level of institutionalisation. This social structure aims to guide employees towards being more creative in their workplace for the greater good of local operations as well as the organisation as a whole. To socially establish, i.e. institutionalise, the collective behaviour [10], the programme needs support from employees' norms and values and its perceived legitimacy. Norms and values are often discussed together without separating them. However, it is essential to acknowledge their differences. As conceptions of the desirable or the preferred, values must have standards for assessment and comparison of behaviours and structures [9]. The outcome of the assessment defines if a behaviour should be considered being of value or not.

We consider the official aim of the programme as such a standard, and it is notable that the organisation emphasises how employees' ideas can be used to support internal research and business development through increased cooperation across administrations. This approach can be justified in one sense since employees more easily can relate to ideas than innovations. However, we argue that it poses a significant risk. We find no traces of what is to be desirable or preferred regarding the ability to innovate. According to the programme, ideas are already there ready to be submitted via the Idea Portal for further development. To be able to manage innovations in a systematic and structured way [4], and to reach a higher level of success, the different stages of the innovation process should be handled [15]. We, therefore, argue that the municipality disregards a critical aspect of the innovation process; a work environment that promotes, values and utilises creativity. The working climate must promote creativity since government innovation occurs at the expense of regular activities [17]. Put shortly; the programme neither prescribes that the employee should be creative at the expense of daily work, nor does it say that the employee should take risks or even make any mistakes.

The municipality does not further elaborate on the tradition of government having a potential "zero-error culture" [8] hence being a bureaucracy. According to the programme, a network-based collaborative approach is desirable [8] resembling public sector collaborative innovation [e.g. 1]. Still, to accomplish this, collaboration must be facilitated, and deeply institutionalised organisational boundaries must be challenged and crossed [19]. So again, a non-valued behaviour becomes an assessment standard for other behaviours prescribed in the programme. Based on this discussion, we have identified a recurring pattern of focusing on idea-driven phases of the process as managed by the central support function. There is a lack of normative as well as value-based prescriptions, assessment standards and objectives to cover the later innovation-driven phases of the process.

5.2 Legitimacy and Decoupling

Legitimacy is "a generalised perception or assumption that the actions of an actor are desirable, proper, or appropriate within some socially constructed system of norms, values, beliefs, and definitions." [26]. The legitimacy of the programme is therefore closely interrelated to its norms and values. The programme consists of a complex, multi-faceted and dynamic set of processes. These processes affect and are affected by formal as well as informal structures. The programme can, on a general level, be seen as an example of an attempt to introduce structured and systematic innovation work [4]. The result of the programme is closely related to the level of internal legitimacy gained.

The municipality shows the ability and willingness to act and launches an ambitious programme as a response to internal and external pressures and demands. In line with national initiatives [e.g. 31–33], the aim is to develop and increase local government innovation. Gaining legitimacy by acting upon this pressure is also confirmed by respondents staying favourable of this work. However, respondents report that the programme lacks communicated and sustainable support from top management. Hence, the municipality needs to acknowledge the strategic value of government innovation [16] on the top management level.

While research describes this kind of support as critical for innovation initiatives [7], we also argue that this lack affects employees assigned to the central support function as well as the willingness among administrations to support the system. Respondents show apparent concerns about the support and sustainability of the municipality's innovation programme. We are in full agreement with researchers stating that "ideas are not innovations" [13]. Ideas are a critical part of innovations, but the innovation is so much more! As previously described, the municipality has neither clarified nor problematized these central terms or concepts but instead conflated the concept of ideas in the programme. We argue that this strategy causes fundamental problems and challenges. For example, the case study shows that there are varying interpretations of the aim and purpose of the programme, which in turn directly affect how the programme is perceived based on employees' norms and values. Thus, we argue that this has a direct effect on the programmes perceived legitimacy across the organisation.

As described, decoupling occurs when the integration of formal structures for some reason is avoided; hence, decoupling or coupling instead builds on the notion of the alignment of structures and activities in organisations [27]. We argue that this case shows clear signs of decoupling since a large number of administrations have not integrated the innovation programme into local operations. There can be several reasons for this outcome. For example, respondents report activities prescribed by the programme as conflicting with regular business development efforts [c.f. 27]. Another example is that the aim and purpose of the programme might be seen as ambiguous [27] by employees, especially among those with a lack of knowledge and experience in innovation work. Judging by the result of the case study, the formal structures of the programme works as intended, but in reality, the programme is buffered on the local administration level in turn effectively minimising any conflicts or disputes [27]. We, therefore, argue that the innovation programme, to a large extent, becomes an example of an organisation adopting the required structures but failing in operationalising them, i.e. to have them carried out in daily activities [9].

5.3   Institutional Carriers

Our findings indicate that carriers of institutional elements are important in local government innovation. This argument is in agreement with researchers stating that carriers are important when considering how institutions change in a way that is divergent or convergent [9]. Institutional carriers are not neutral; they affect the message they carry, as well as how this message will be received [9]. We, therefore, argue that these carriers become essential during the process of institutionalisation; what they are, the messages and inscriptions they convey and how actors interpret them. Institutions can, therefore, be transferred across social contexts such as organisations by institutional carriers of several types [28]. Examples of such carriers are relational and symbolic systems, as well as artefacts and activities [9]. The most notable example of a relational carrier, or role system, with defined patterns of interaction [9] in the innovation programme is the structure and process of the programme as a whole with clearly defined related roles on different levels in the organisation. For example, there are clear patterns of interaction in the programme regarding how ideas are assessed on an administrative level by the councils.

The symbolic system acting as a carrier in the programme is made up of the values, expectations and standards [9], in this case, regarding how the municipality will benefit from government innovation. However, the effectiveness and appropriateness of the symbolic system acting as an institutional carrier are also closely related, as previously described, to how the prescribed norms and values affect the organisation and the behaviour of employees, i.e. how these norms and values are institutionalised. The structured phases and tasks included in the formal process (see Fig. 1 above) are examples of activities as institutional carriers [9]. Moreover, the aim of the Idea Portal, acting as an artefact as a carrier [9], is to facilitate information and communication primarily during the first two phases of the innovation process.

Based on respondents' reports, the outcome of this artefact as a carrier of information between the Carrier and Coach during the phases of assessment (1) and development, test and evaluation (2) (see Fig. 1 above) seems to be positive. Respondents also report that the artefact brings transparency to the process for employees in assigned roles on central as well as administrative and individual levels. However, if the described carriers of the programme are considered in relation to how the institutional idea [12] of the entire process of government innovation as beneficial for the organisation are transferred, we have found that ideas are predominantly put in the foreground. Hence, there is a lack of how the carriers support the institutionalisation of the later phases of the innovation process; i.e. how the idea is further developed into an implemented innovation.

6 Concluding Remarks and Future Research

In this study, we focus on the results and effects of a local government innovation programme (RQ-1) and what lessons can be learned from applying institutional theory as a theoretical lens on local government innovation (RQ-2). Addressing the first research question, we conclude that the innovation programme, in the studied organisation, has been a limited success. The municipality has an established a formal structure and process supporting local government innovation. Findings show that the programme has had a positive impact on the opportunity for employees to submit ideas and receive support during initial development and evaluation. However, several shortcomings and challenges have also been identified regarding insufficient support, unclear responsibilities, lack of resources and distance in time and space all negatively affecting the programme (see Sect. 4.3). Addressing the second research question, themes were identified and discussed based on institutional theory. Findings from this analysis show limitation and fragmentation in informal systems and structures supporting the programme (see Sect. 5.1) as well as insufficient legitimacy and decoupling of the innovation programme from local operations (see Sect. 5.2). As a result of a limited process view, the Idea Portal, acting as an institutional carrier, fails to support operationalisation and institutionalisation of the innovation process as a whole (see Sect. 5.3).

As a general conclusion, we, therefore, argue that this study shows that formal and informal structures are equally important in the context of government innovation; government innovation needs to be operationalised as well as institutionalised. Although the innovation programme seems to be a coherent and adequate approach, this study reveals a recurring limited focus on the idea-driven phases of government innovation. This results in a significant lack of how the institutionalisation of the programme is supported; a lesson that goes beyond the studied case. Implications for research suggest a need for supplementing systematic and structured approaches on government innovation [4] with studies focusing on the institutionalisation of government innovation. In government innovation research, there seems to be a tendency to focus on how to encourage and support innovation from a management perspective [e.g. 1, 16, 17]. However, as Demircioglu [21] points out, there is a need for research on employees' attitudes and behaviour in relation to government innovation. In line with this call and based on this study, we put forth the importance of investigating how institutions, as structures of social control [e.g. 9, 24], guide or restrict government innovation. The institutional theory perspective brings a needed constructive potential to reveal the informal structures surrounding and affecting government innovation.

Implications for practice emphasise the importance of acknowledging government innovation as a fundamental government transformation or shift in paradigm across the public sector. In government innovation programmes there is a need to expand the perspective also to include conditions such as how to cultivate innovation culture in public sector organisations and the importance of not only focus on the outcomes regarding ideas and innovations. For example, the conditions for employees also need to facilitate and support creativity; thus, support can be in the form of facilitating creative environments as well as by increasing employees' margin of error. We argue that it becomes crucial to acknowledge local government innovation as a transformative innovation [3] in itself with a potential to fundamentally transform public sector organisations. One limitation in this study is the focus on one local government organisation, in a particular national setting. However, the patterns and results presented above can be linked to previous research and have an analytical generalisability. Although, there is room for expanding future research into new empirical settings and also to compare with other government organisations, on regional, and national level to contrast and to de- and re-contextualise empirical data and findings.

References

1. Eggers, W.D., Singh, S.K.: The Public Innovator's Playbook: Nurturing Bold Ideas in Government. Ash Institute, Harvard Kennedy School, Cambridge (2009)
2. OECD: Embracing Innovation in Government - Global Trends 2018 (2018)

3. Mulgan, G., Albury, D.: Innovation in the public sector. Strategy Unit, Cabinet Office, 1–40 (2003)

4. Anthony, S.D., Johnson, M.W., Sinfield, J.V., Altman, E.J.: The Innovator's Guide to Growth, pp. 353–379. Harvard Business Press, Boston (2008)

5. Van Assche, K., Beunen, R., Barba Lata, I., Duineveld, M.: Innovation in governance. In: Beunen, R., Van Assche, K., Duineveld, M. (eds.) Evolutionary Governance Theory, pp. 313–325. Springer, Cham (2015). https://doi.org/10.1007/978-3-319-12274-8_21

6. Frankelius, P.: Questioning two myths in innovation literature. J. High Technol. Manage. Res. **20**, 40–51 (2009)

7. Borins, S.: Encouraging innovation in the public sector. J. Intellect. Capital **2**, 310–319 (2001)

8. Sørensen, E., Torfing, J.: Enhancing collaborative innovation in the public sector. Adm. Soc. **43**, 842–868 (2011)

9. Scott, W.R.: Institutions and Organizations. Sage Publications Inc., Los Angeles (2014)

10. Hughes, E.C.: The ecological aspect of institutions. Am. Sociol. Rev. **1**, 180–189 (1936)

11. Avgerou, C.: IT and organizational change: an institutionalist perspective. Inf. Tech. & People **13**, 234–262 (2000)

12. Scott, W.R.: Institutional carriers: reviewing modes of transporting ideas over time and space and considering their consequences. Ind. Corp. Change **12**, 879–894 (2003)

13. Kastelle, T., Steen, J.: Ideas are not innovations. Prometheus **29**, 199–205 (2011)

14. Van de Ven, A.H., Polley, D., Garud, R.: The Innovation Journey. Oxford University Press, New York (2008)

15. West, M.A., Sacramento, C.A., Fay, D.: Creativity and innovation implementation in work groups: the paradoxical role of demands. In: Thompson, L.L., Choi, H.-S. (eds.) Creativity and Innovation in Organizational Teams, pp. 137–159 (2006)

16. Moore, M.H.: Break-through innovations and continuous improvement: two different models of innovative processes in the public sector. Public Money and Manage. **25**, 43–50 (2005)

17. Stewart-Weeks, M., Kastelle, T.: Innovation in the public sector. Aust. J. Pub. Adm. **74**, 63–72 (2015)

18. Grimm, R., Fox, C., Baines, S., Albertson, K.: Social innovation, an answer to contemporary societal challenges? Locating the concept in theory and practice. Innovation: Eur. J. Soc. Sci. Res. **26**, 436–455 (2013)

19. Bommert, B.: Collaborative innovation in the public sector. Int. Public. Manage. Rev. **11**, 15–33 (2010)

20. Nambisan, S.: Transforming Government Through Collaborative Innovation. IBM Center for the Business of Government, Washington DC (2008)

21. Demircioglu, M.A.: Reinventing the Wheel? Public Sector Innovation in the Age of Governance. Wiley Online Library, Chichester (2017)

22. Bowring, M.A.: De/constructing theory a look at the institutional theory that positivism built. J. Manage. Inq. **9**, 258–270 (2000)

23. Barley, S.R., Tolbert, P.S.: Institutionalization and structuration: studying the links between action and institution. Organ. Stud. **18**, 93–117 (1997)

24. Berger, P.L., Luckmann, T.: The social construction of reality - a treatise in the sociology of knowledge. In: Anchor Books, Random House Inc., New York (1967)

25. Zucker, L.G.: Institutional theories of organization. Ann. Rev. Sociol. **13**, 443–464 (1987)

26. Suchman, M.C.: Managing legitimacy: strategic and institutional approaches. Acad. Manage. Rev. **20**, 571–610 (1995)

27. Meyer, J.W., Rowan, B.: Institutionalized organizations: formal structure as myth and ceremony. Am. J. Sociol. **83**, 340–363 (1977)

28. Jepperson, R.L.: Institutions, institutional effects, and institutionalism. In: DiMaggio, P., Powell, W.W. (eds.) The New Institutionalism in Organizational Analysis, vol. 6, pp. 143–163. University of Chicago Press, Chicago (1991)
29. Melin, U., Axelsson, K., Löfstedt, T.: Understanding an integrated management system in a government agency – focusing institutional carriers. In: Parycek, P., Glassey, O., Janssen, M., Scholl, H.J., Tambouris, E., Kalampokis, E., Virkar, S. (eds.) EGOV 2018. LNCS, vol. 11020, pp. 15–28. Springer, Cham (2018). https://doi.org/10.1007/978-3-319-98690-6_2
30. Gosain, S.: Enterprise information systems as objects and carriers of institutional forces: the new iron cage? J. Assoc. Inf. Sys. **5**, 6 (2004)
31. Vinnova SKL: Överenskommelse: Stärkt innovationsförmåga i offentlig verksamhet 2015–2017. Vinnova SKL (2015)
32. Vinnova SKL: Reviderad sammanfattning av arbetsprogram - Stärkt innovationsförmåga i offentlig verksamhet 2015–2017. Vinnova SKL (2016)
33. Vinnova: Utlysning: Idéslussar i kommuner - Utvecklingsprojekt 2016. Vinnova (2016)
34. Myers, M.D.: Qualitative Research in Business & Management. SAGE Publications, London (2009)
35. Walsham, G.: Interpretive case studies in IS research: nature and method. Eur. J. Inf. Sys. **4**, 74–81 (1995)
36. Orlikowski, W.J., Baroudi, J.J.: Studying information technology in organizations: research approaches and assumptions. Inf. Sys. Res. **2**, 1–28 (1991)
37. Myers, M.D., Newman, M.: The qualitative interview in IS research: examining the craft. Inf. Organ. **17**, 2–26 (2007)
38. Biernacki, P., Waldorf, D.: Snowball sampling - problems and techniques of chain referral sampling. Sociol. Methods & Res. **10**, 141–163 (1981)
39. Boell, S.K., Cecez-Kecmanovic, D.: A hermeneutic approach for conducting literature reviews and literature searches. Commun. Assoc. Inf. Syst. **34**, 257–286 (2014)
40. Krippendorff, K.: Content Analysis: An Introduction to its Methodology. SAGE Publications, Thousand Oaks (2004)
41. Tolbert, P.S., Zucker, L.G.: Institutional sources of change in the formal structure of organizations: the diffusion of civil service reform, 1880–1935. Adm. Sci. Q. **28**, 22–39 (1983)

Channel Choice Complications

Exploring the Multiplex Nature of Citizens' Channel Choices

Christian Østergaard Madsen[1(✉)], Sara Hofmann[2],
and Willem Pieterson[3]

[1] IT University of Copenhagen, Copenhagen, Denmark
chrm@itu.dk
[2] University of Agder, Kristiansand, Norway
sara.hofmann@uia.no
[3] Center for eGovernment Studies, Enschede, The Netherlands
willem@pieterson.com

Abstract. In spite of massive investment and increased adoption of digital services, citizens continue to use traditional channels to interact with public organizations. The channel choice (CC) field of research tries to understand citizens' interactions with public authorities to make the interaction more efficient and increase citizen satisfaction. However, most studies have been conducted either as surveys of hypothetical services or in experimental settings, leading to a lack of empirical data from actual use contexts. Therefore, we present the results of a sequential mixed methods study which combines observations of citizen-caseworker interaction in a call center, contextual interviews with callers, and a survey classifying topics from 10,000 telephone calls. We contribute to the CC field and practice with rich empirical data from studies of actual channel choices. Specifically, the study explores the multiplex nature of real-life CC and demonstrate how telephone calls can be part of a process, which occurs across both traditional and digital channels. Moreover, we identify problems, which cause telephone calls related to digital services, and classify these in two groups: information related problems and action related problems.

Keywords: Channel choice · Mixed methods · Public services · e-Government · Multi-channel management · Channel behavior · Udbetaling Danmark

1 Introduction

To reduce costs, governments seek to migrate interaction with citizens from traditional channels to digital self-service channels. Early e-government studies assumed this process would happen automatically with the adoption of digital channels [1]. Recent studies, however, demonstrate that this is not always the case [2]. In Canada, the use of websites declined between 2008 and 2012 [3]. The continued use of traditional channels also occurs in settings where digital self-service channels are widely adopted,

I. Lindgren et al. (Eds.): EGOV 2019, LNCS 11685, pp. 139–151, 2019.
https://doi.org/10.1007/978-3-030-27325-5_11

for example in Denmark [4], a leader in e-government [5]. The question is why this happens. While many multi-channel management scholars [6, 7] have argued that electronic channels will not replace traditional ones [8], they do not explain why use of traditional channels remains so important. One possible explanation lies in the nature of existing research and theory on citizens' channel behaviors [9] and how these channel behaviors are incorporated in models of multi-channel service delivery [7]. First of all, most studies have focused on citizens' initial and singular choice of a single channel. Next, most studies have focused on discrete channel choices in clearly described situations. Lastly, most research is quantitative and revolves around building and testing hypothetical variance models based on surveys. This leads to two shortcomings of existing CC research:

1. By studying channel choices in isolation, studies ignore the possibility that channel choices can have a sequential or multiplex (see below) nature. For example, calling an organization after failing to find information online.
2. By asking to choose a single channel in hypothetical situations, studies ignore that channel choices and uses could happen in parallel. For example, a citizen could call while looking online to verify the correctness of the information.

To move the CC field further forwards, scholars have repeatedly called for new empirical studies from actual use settings, which directly explore citizens' use of multiple channels, reasons for the continued use of traditional channels, and the interactions between different channel types [10–13]. The objective of our research is to address these gaps in the extant CC literature. Herein, we present the results of a sequential mixed method study, employing observations, contextual interviews, and a survey of over 10,000 calls [14] to gain insights in CC in a real-life setting.

Aim of the Study and Research Questions
This purpose of this study is twofold. First, we aim to explore and measure the types of inquiries which are made by citizens who have adopted digital self-service channels, but still contact public authorities through traditional channels. Second, we seek to understand why these inquiries occur and explore the interplay between different channels, for example when channels are used sequentially or in parallel as one overall service interaction. In order words, we try to understand the multiplex nature of real-life channel choices. To achieve these goals, we present rich empirical examples of actual interaction between citizens and public authorities to put the identified topics into context. The research questions we seek to answer are:

1. To what extent are channel choices multiplex? (RQ1)
2. What causes this multiplexity, i.e. why do citizens that have adopted electronic service channels still choose traditional service channels? (RQ2)

The rest of this paper is organized as follows. The next section presents a brief outline of the literature on channel choice. Section three presents the research setting and method used. Section four discusses the findings. Section five presents concluding remarks, limitations and offers suggestions for future research.

2 Channel Choice Research

2.1 Channel Choice

Channel choice (CC) can be seen as the first step in what is called a process of channel behavior [15]. CC refers to *"an individual's specific decision to use a medium in a particular communication incident"* [15, p. 163] This is followed by the actual interaction (channel use) and an evaluation of that use. This evaluation can create experiences that might trigger future use. CC studies in the e-government literature seek to explain and understand citizens' choice of channels for interacting with government organizations and identify the factors that affect this choice and measure their influence.

Studies have typically considered CC as a multi-nominal selection where users at a singular point in time choose between several channels. For example, Pieterson [8] asked people to choose one channel in a number of hypothetical situations. Similarly, Reddick and Anthopoulos [3] asked people to indicate their channel preferences for a number of hypothetical situations (e.g. solving a problem). However, research shows that rather than being a one-time decision, CC is actually a more complex process in which channels are used sequentially or in parallel (cf. [2, 10, 17]). Regarding the latter, for example, Madsen and Kræmmergaard [17] found that digital and traditional channels often are used simultaneously, very often this entails people calling while looking at a website. Regarding the former, Pieterson [18] found that citizens typically use multiple channels in one service interaction and often have a first, preferred, channel and move to a second channel when their first choice fails to yield a result. These complex channel usage patterns require government organizations to consider cross-channel integration to ensure that the data and information citizens receive are consistent across all used channels. Scholars have called for further research on channel sequencing [7, 10] and suggest direct observations and more in-depth case studies to understand issues relevant to government channel integration [11].

Furthermore, research on citizens' CC has mainly focused on predefined factors such as channel, task, personal, and situational characteristics (cf. [8, 19]). For example, Ebbers et al. [19] test a model in which they relate task and channel factors, habits and personal characteristics to CC. While this yields valuable insights about the importance of these variables, it ignores other potential variables (see e.g. [9, 20] for overviews of possible channel choice determinants). This point of criticism is closely related to the majority of CC studies being quantitative in nature and relying on standardized surveys. In addition, many studies have been conducted in controlled and artificial settings, which may limit their explanatory power for actual use settings, cf. e.g. [19]. However, given the integrated nature of channel choices, as mentioned above, more exploratory insight into citizens' actual behaviors is needed [8, 19] as well as case studies and interviews with citizens on their actual channel choices [21]. Thus, instead of enquiring citizens about their preferences, CC research should rather focus on the process from the initial CC to continued channel use [22], such as through direct observations [3].

To sum up, the existing research on CC has helped us discover and understand the types of variables that impact singular channel choices and how these variables differ for different tasks, people and situations. However, these insights are inadequate to help us understand real-life CC behaviors, let alone providing prescriptive insights for governments' multi-channel strategies. Therefore, new theories and models are needed to capture the complex, multiplex, nature of real-life channel behaviors.

2.2   Channel Multiplexity

In communication theory, 'media multiplexity' was originally used to describe communication patterns of distributed scholars, with those with stronger ties using more means of communication [23]. More generally, the concept has been used to describe instances where communication relations are maintained by multiple media [24] and where media multiplexity is associated with a higher communication quality. This idea is similar to the notion of 'intermediality' [25] which refers to (a) communication through several discourses at once, (b) the combination of separate material vehicles of representation and (c) the interrelations among the media as institutions in society. This concept was born out of the observations that, as communication becomes more networked, media themselves become more fluid and interwoven. These ideas of multiplexity and intermediality contrast more traditional notions of media that try to isolate media and focus on the attributes of individual media [26] and see media choices as singular or "immediate incidents" [27]. The reality, of course, is more complicated. Research on technology use has shown that media are often used sequentially in what is considered one use case [26] and media are seen as compliments that can be used to satisfy certain communication needs [28].

We expect similar phenomena to happen in citizen-initiated contacts, where rather than perceiving and choosing channels as being discrete entities, citizens use a combination of channels sequentially or in parallel in what could be considered one service delivery contact. For example, a citizen might go online to a find the phone number of an organization and then call (sequential use) or a citizen could call an organization to confirm the validity of information shown online (parallel use). Thus, channel multiplexity refers to the interrelated (sequential and/or parallel) choice of channels within one overall service interaction and multiplexity appears as a fitting theoretical concept to help us understand real-life channel choices.

3   Research Setting

The study presented here was undertaken in 2017 in the Danish public authority Udbetaling Danmark (UDK) (Disbursement Denmark). UDK was established in 2012 by the Danish government to achieve economic savings in the administration of public benefits. The first author undertook the empirical studies in UDK's Parental leave division in the city of Vordingborg. The division is one of three, which administers parental leave. It consists of 50 caseworkers and two managers across two sections.

UDK follows the Danish e-government strategy whereby digital communication and digital self-service are mandatory for citizens and businesses. UDK's digital and channel strategies also seek to promote automation and digital self-service. The web portal borger.dk is the primary means of self-service for citizens, while written communication is handled via digital post, a national e-mail system. Citizens who need help can call UDK. Counter turn-ups are also possible, but rare due to the physical location of UDK's centers. Thus, the interaction primarily occurs online, centered around borger.dk and digital post, while the telephone call are supplementary.

The Parental Leave Scheme

While most citizens perceive parental leave as a single event, the leave itself consists of a variety of different schemes, such as pregnancy leave, maternity leave, paternity leave and parental leave. Each of these schemes have different underlying legal rules, duration, and payment amounts. For reasons of simplicity, we will refer to these using the joint term *parental leave*, although the majority of the leave is spent by mothers. When the individual leave schemes matter, we will refer to this specifically. Parental leave benefits are often the main source of income for the person on leave. This distinguished parental leave benefits from other types of public benefits, such as housing benefits, which supplement other sources of income. Therefore, parental leave may create more communication from citizens than other public services.

4   Method

Our study follows an inductive research strategy [29], informed by CC studies and 'media multiplexity'. Previous CC studies show, that people choose traditional channels when problems occur, while 'media multiplexity' explains that interaction often occur across multiple channels. We seek to explore the nature of problems in digital interaction, and their relationship to citizens' multiplex interaction with UDK.

We apply mixed methods, which is a research approach combining qualitative and quantitative techniques. According to Creswell: "(…) *this form of inquiry provides a more complete understanding of a research problem than either approach alone*" [30]. Mixed methods studies are conducted according to a pragmatic worldview, encouraging researchers to use the most suitable techniques for gaining insight into practice oriented, real-world problems [30]. We collected the data for our study through an exploratory sequential mixed method, as *"a three-phase procedure with the first phase as exploratory, the second as instrument development, and the third as administering the instrument to a sample of a population."* [30]. Madsen presents a detailed account of the instrument development [14].

Phase 1. Qualitative Data Collection

In March 2017, the first author co-listened to 50 calls made to the parental leave section, followed by brief contextual interviews with the callers [14]. By observing actual telephone conversations, we gained insight into channel choices as they occurred in a real-world setting. Moreover, this approach increased the validity of the findings and reduced retrospective sense making, where people's descriptions of their actions *(what they say)* and motivation are biased, and differ from their actual actions *(what they do)* [31, 32]. The co-listening occurred on a citizen line and an employer line. The callers were citizens, their representatives, employers, municipal caseworkers, and doctors. Upon answering the telephone, the caseworker asked callers for their permission for the first author to co-listen to the call and interview them. The caseworkers informed callers that the co-listening was voluntary, anonymous, and would not influence their cases in any way. One in ten callers declined to participate; non-participants were mostly doctors and other professionals who said they were too busy.

The first author documented observations and interviews, covering the event which initiated the call, the problems mentioned by the caller, the caseworkers' actions, previous communication with UDK and other authorities, next steps, and final comments by callers. The conversations and interviews were not recorded verbatim, although certain utterances were noted by the first author. Caseworkers and management served as highly knowledgeable informants, whose perspectives contributed to ensuring the validity of the first author's own interpretation of the qualitative data [32].

Phase 2. Instrument Development

In October 2017, the first author collaborated with UDK caseworkers and management to measure the frequency of the discovered topics. We developed a classification scheme to increase caseworkers' classification rates and the validity of the results. The caseworkers suggested additional topics and examples for the scheme and used their own terminology to describe each topic. Exercises and discussions further helped to create a joint understanding of the problems and categories. The caseworkers also helped to solve technical and practical issues surrounding call classification. The final classification scheme covers where in the parental leave process the caller is, and the main topic of the call. Due to limited space, we focus on the topics here.

Phase 3. Administration of Survey to Register Telephone Calls

The caseworkers registered 11,600 inbound calls from citizens during October and November 2017. Some calls did not lead to actual casework (wrong number etc.), therefore 10,106, or 95% of the completed calls were classified according to topic. The classification system requires the caseworkers to classify each call according to exactly one stage and one topic. However, a conversation may cover several topics and underlying problems. UDK administers maternity leave at three different locations, which receive calls on a rotation basis. According to caseworkers and management, there is no difference in calls received at the different locations. Thus, the collected data should be representative of all calls made to UDK on parental leave.

5   Findings

This section contains the results of our study. We begin answering our first RQ, on the multiplexity of citizens' CC, based on the observations. Then, we turn to our second RQ, why citizens supplement digital interaction with traditional channel use.

First, however, it is important to keep two aspects of the study in mind. The observations presented here occurred in a call-center. Thus, we only get insight into the service interactions where citizens call. We do not get insight into the majority of cases where citizens complete an interaction without calling. Second, digital self-service is mandatory in Denmark. In 2017, UDK's parental leave section received 768,000 visits to its website at borger.dk and 340,000 incoming telephone calls on the citizen lines. Thus, website visits still outnumber telephone calls by more than 2:1.

5.1   Citizens' Multiplex Channel Choice

Of the 50 calls observed in the call center, 32 were made by citizens, 17 by employers and one by a doctor. The majority of callers had previously contacted UDK for the same topic using one or two channels, pointing to the sequential nature of many interactions. Additionally, 14 of the 32 citizens who called had previously received digital post from UDK, either as letters concerning their parental leave or specifications of upcoming leave payments. Excluding contacts with their own company, 18 of the 50 callers had either called other organizations or visited their website for the same service interaction. We cannot make statistical generalizations from 50 observations. However, the majority of the interaction we have observed involves several channels, and roughly a third involve other organizations. These results are supported by the aggregated channel traffic to UDK. To explain these findings, we must study this interaction in more detail. Next, we present the results of the call classification, and then proceed to our observations of the calls and contextual interviews with callers.

5.2   Description and Examples of Call Topics

Table 1 presents the distribution of 10,100 calls received by UDK's parental leave section in October and November 2017 as classified by the caseworkers.

Table 1. Call topics to UDK's parental leave section

Topic	Share	Description
Planning	33%	Planning the overall leave, individual stages and transition between leave partners. Includes requests for guidance and specific information, requests for explanation or confirmation of rules applicability and financial impact
Status	25%	Concern the status of an ongoing case and case handling time, prompts for faster casework, and callers presenting new or correct information to UDK regarding their case
Monthly payment	13%	Concern the monthly payment of parental leave benefits. Questions concern when payments are made, the payment amount, and explanations and calculations behind payments
Illness	10%	The mother is ill during pregnancy or maternity leave. Often concern third party actors (doctors), and documentation regarding illness
Salary stop	6%	Salary stop concerns the specific process of switching from receiving a regular paycheck to receiving parental leave benefits. These calls often involve the callers' employer and documentation they have provided
Refund	4%	Concern instructions for how to refund benefits if too much money has been received, and special forms for this
Technical support	2%	Requests for technical support on the use of digital self-service applications for submitting and receiving information, including the use of digital post
Vacation	2%	Concern going on vacation while on parental leave, including requests for guidance, and how this will influence one's income
Other	5%	Calls not covered by any of the topics above

As shown in Table 1, three topics, planning, status and monthly payment, account for over 70% of all inbound calls. While the topics are presented as discreet units above, some calls revolved around several topics. In these cases, we asked the case-worker to classify the call according to the topic, which the call initially revolved around.

As we observed these interactions and interviewed callers, we gained insight into the various reasons which caused citizens to call. In many cases, the citizen had several problems, which needed to be solved. Contrary to previous studies, we found that the calls did not just revolve around accessing or understanding information. The caller may also need the caseworker to do something for them. This problem may generate additional channel traffic because such a request cannot be conducted by digital self-service applications. To demonstrate the complexity of such underlying problems and the multiplexity of the interaction, we present two observed calls.

Example 1. Planning the transition between leave partners (see Fig. 1)
A mother's maternity leave is ending, and the father is about to take over. She calls for an understanding of the rules for distributing the leave between parents and the options for extending her leave. She has received letters from UDK and visited borger. dk unsuccessfully. The caseworker informs her of the rules, how to extend her leave, and on the importance of not having any gaps between leave stages. Further, the caseworker says that extension will affect her employer, so the caller needs to inform her employer. The caller asks the caseworker to "spell it out to her" (explain in detail), and for the specific dates for the extended leave. Next, the caller inquires about the economic consequences of shifting from maternity to paternity leave on the household income. Finally, the caller says she wants to extend the leave, but needs to discuss this with the father and with her employer first.

Fig. 1. The sequence of interactions in example 1

Here, there are two underlying problems. The caller needs specific information instructions for how to extend her leave. Moreover, she needs to understand the consequences of these actions. Her need does not concern the rules in general, but rather how they apply to her specifically and what their economic consequences are for her family. We also see that the caseworker informs the caller of a problem, which the caller is unaware of – not having gaps in the leave. Finally, we see that the telephone call is at the middle of a series of interactions across several channels and with other actors besides UDK.

Example 2. Status of a case and discrepancy in information (see Fig. 2)
A mother calls because there is a discrepancy between the number of days left of her leave according to a letter from UDK, and information on borger.dk. She has

previously called her employer and UDK and been to borger.dk. She has trouble "navigating the parental leave rules". She is logged in to borger.dk while calling. She asks, which of the parents is entitled to the remaining leave. The caseworker informs her of several requirements which the father must meet to be entitled to leave. Next, the caller seeks to confirm that the size of the benefit depends on the employer and the father's collective agreement. She asks for this information in writing so she can forward it to her HR department. She has been unable to find it at borger.dk. The caseworker explains that she cannot reveal information concerning the father without his permission. Finally, they agree that the caseworker will send letters to both parents.

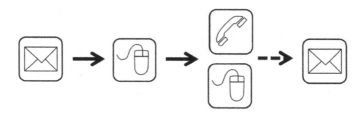

Fig. 2. The sequence of interactions in example 2

Again, the caller both needs information and to understand what it means to her, and what the economic consequences are. However, we also discover another problem, the information presented online does not correspond to the information received in a letter. Therefore, the caller first needs to know which information is correct, and then asks for evidence in the shape of a written letter, which she can forward to her employer. This is an example of an interaction which concern several actors: UDK, two parents, and at least one employer. Thus, the service interaction observed here is a long process occurring sequentially and simultaneously across three different channels: the website, the telephone and letters. Finally, we see that the call is initiated by an outbound letter and ends – for now – with another outbound letter.

5.3 Citizens' Supplementation of Digital Interaction with Traditional Channels

To answer why citizens who have already adopted digital channels still supplement an interaction through traditional channels, we returned to our observations and interviews. We analyzed these according to the underlying problems and needs which appeared during the callers' interaction with UDK or were mentioned in the contextual interviews. We identified five different types of problems and grouped these problems in two overall categories. The five identified problems are presented in Table 2.

Table 2. The types of problems which cause incoming calls

Category	Information related problems		Action related problems		
Problem type	Need for information	Need for explanation	Need for documentation	Need for negotiation	Need for revision
Examples	- Confirmation for submitted information - Guidelines for action - Status of case - Payments	- Of rules and consequences - For UDK decisions and received payments	Receipts - Case files, to self or third party	- Concerning interpretation of rules - For faster casework - For faster payment	- To registered or submitted information - To case and benefits received

Information related problems concern people's access to, and understanding of, information from the public authorities regarding public benefits. Information related problems are well-known known in the CC literature. They cover:

- **Need for information.** The caller knows what information they are seeking, but not necessarily where to access it. They may call simply because this is quick and convenient. The problems belonging to this group are well-suited for digitization, but at the time of the study, many of the requested features did not exist at the parental leave section of borger.dk.
- **Need for explanation.** The caller needs an explanation for the information, its application and consequences to their specific case, or to be certain their interpretation is correct. Offering explanations to people's specific cases is difficult online as it requires customization and decision-making, not merely presenting information.

Action related problems cover situations, where the caller needs the caseworker to perform an action for them. These are harder to digitalize because of their more complex nature and need for the caseworkers to exercise discretion. They cover:

- **Need for documentation.** The caller needs documentation about their case to be sent, either to themselves or a third party. Unlike the need for information, it is not necessarily the information itself which matters. Rather the documentation is needed as evidence to begin, or of a completed, administrative process.
- **Need for negotiation.** The caller seeks to persuade the caseworker to adopt their perspective or set act outside established procedures. An example could be to make an unscheduled payment or look at the caller's specific case, thereby speeding up processing times. This type of need appears to be very difficult to digitize as negotiation and persuasion requires a human partner.
- **Need for revision.** The caller needs UDK to make changes to their case or update specific information, either submitted by themselves or by a third party. Such actions can and have been digitized in a public context. It is, however, important to have control mechanisms in place.

6   Conclusions and Discussion

The goal of this paper was to explore the potentially multiplex nature of channel choices by citizens when interacting with governments. RQ1 focused on the extent to which channel choices are multiplex. While not being a quantitative, confirmatory study, our research does indicate a large proportion of channel interactions to be multiplex (i.e. the choice of multiple channels for what can be considered one interaction). This provides an important, possible, explanation for the observation that the overall number of channel interactions are increasing in many countries and citizens continue to use traditional channels after adopting digital service channels.

Our second research question (RQ2) focused on the causes of this multiplexity. Our analysis identified two main groups of causes. The first is *information related problems*, which result from people not being able to find the needed information and thus choosing a second channel or from citizens needing additional explanation or closure about the correctness and/or validity of the information. While these problems may stem from flaws in the design of a channel (e.g. the degree to which information is retrievable), they could also result from a lack of richness [16] of the channel to convey the required message. Surprisingly, there were few inquiries regarding access to and use of the digital channels. This indicates that citizens have the necessary digital skills, but lack knowledge of public services to use self-service application. The second group of causes are *action related problems*, which trigger some kind of transaction that might not be done in another original channel (e.g. the need for documentation, negotiation or revision of data).

Limitations and Future Studies
The study presented here is exploratory and provides the first insights into real-life channel choice behaviors and their often complex and multi-facetted nature. However, it has some limitations. While co-listening to calls and interviewing the callers, we did not explicitly ask for the problems that caused them to call UDK nor their channel choices. Rather, we deduced the problems from the cases the callers described. Furthermore, our study focused on welfare services in Denmark, which represents a mature research setting where social trust is high. Although this setting differs from other countries with non-mandatory e-government use and less social trust, we assume that our findings are valid for different cultural contexts as well.

More research on this topic is needed especially in three areas. The first is further explorations about the sequential and/or parallel nature of channel interactions to fully understand all combinations and their causes. The second is confirmatory research testing the extent to which these multiplex channel choices happen in real life. The third is research exploring ways to reduce multiplexity in order to improve channel efficiencies, for example through the design of channels, improved communication or channel marketing. Further, while we introduce the concept of channel multiplexity, this is by no means a fully fledged theory and more theoretical work is needed to fully understand the concept and embed it in the existing theories and extant CC research.

References

1. Layne, K., Lee, J.W.: Developing fully functional E-government: a four stage model. Gov. Inf. Q. **18**, 122–136 (2001)
2. Madsen, C.Ø., Kræmmergaard, P.: How to migrate citizens online and reduce traffic on traditional channels through multichannel management: a case study of cross-organizational collaboration surrounding a mandatory self-service application. In: IGI Global (ed.) Innovative Perspectives on Public Administration in the Digital Age, pp. 121–142 (2018)
3. Reddick, C., Anthopoulos, L.: Interactions with e-government, new digital media and traditional channel choices: citizen-initiated factors. Transform. Gov. People, Process Policy **8**, 398–419 (2014)
4. Statistics Denmark: ICT household survey 2016 (2016)
5. European Commission: Digital Economy and Society Index (DESI) 2018 Country Report Denmark (2018). https://doi.org/10.2118/140253-MS
6. Ebbers, W.E., Pieterson, W.J., Noordman, H.N.N.: Electronic government: rethinking channel management strategies. Gov. Inf. Q. **25**, 181–201 (2008)
7. Østergaard Madsen, C., Hofmann, S.: Multichannel management in the public sector: a literature review. Electron. J. e-Gov. **17**(1), 20–35 (2019)
8. Pieterson, W.: Citizens and service channels: channel choice and channel management implications. Int. J. Electron. Gov. Res. **6**, 37–53 (2010)
9. Madsen, C.Ø., Kræmmergaard, P.: Channel choice: a literature review. In: Tambouris, E., Janssen, M., Scholl, H.J., Wimmer, M.A., Tarabanis, K., Gascó, M., Klievink, B., Lindgren, I., Parycek, P. (eds.) EGOV 2015. LNCS, vol. 9248, pp. 3–18. Springer, Cham (2015). https://doi.org/10.1007/978-3-319-22479-4_1
10. Reddick, C., Turner, M.: Channel choice and public service delivery in Canada: comparing e-government to traditional service delivery. Gov. Inf. Q. **29**, 1–11 (2012)
11. Kernaghan, K.: Changing channels: managing channel integration and migration in public organizations. Can. Public Adm. **56**, 121–141 (2013)
12. Ganapati, S., Reddick, C.G.: The use of ICT for open government in U.S. municipalities: perceptions of chief administrative officers. Public Perform. Manage. Rev. **37**, 365–387 (2014)
13. Lindgren, I., Madsen, C.Ø., Hofmann, S., Melin, U.: Close encounters of the digital kind: a research agenda for the digitalization of public services. Gov. Inf. Q. (2019). https://doi.org/10.1016/j.giq.2019.03.002
14. Madsen, C.Ø.: Translating telephone calls to spreadsheets: generating knowledge on citizen multichannel behavior in collaboration with caseworkers. Electron. J. e-Gov. **16**, 106–118 (2018)
15. Pieterson, W., Teerling, M.: Citizen behavior in a multi-channel environment. In: Proceeding of 9th Annual International Digital Government Research, pp. 387–388
16. Trevino, L.K., Webster, J., Stein, E.W.: Making connections: complementary influences on communication media choices, attitudes, and use. Organ. Sci. **11**, 163–182 (2000)
17. Madsen, C.Ø., Kræmmergaard, P.: The efficiency of freedom. single parents' domestication of mandatory e-government. Gov. Inf. Q. **32**(4), 380–388 (2015)
18. Pieterson, W.: Channel Choice. Citizens' Channel Behavior and Public Service Channel Strategy (2009). https://www.utwente.nl/ctit/cfes/docs/proefschriften/2009-Channel_Choice_Final_web.PDF
19. Ebbers, W.E., Jansen, M.G.M., Pieterson, W.J., van de Wijngaert, L.A.L.: Facts and feelings: the role of rational and irrational factors in citizens' channel choices. Gov. Inf. Q. **33**, 506–515 (2016)

20. Pieterson, W., van Dijk, J.: Channel choice determinants; an exploration of the factors that determine the choice of a service channel in citizen initiated contacts. In: 8th Annual International Conference on Digital Government Research (dg.o 2007), pp. 173–182. Digital Government Research Center, Philadelphia, Pennsylvania (2007)
21. Schmidthuber, L., Hilgers, D.: Browse or brush? an exploration of citizen-government interaction in the municipal realm. In: Proceedings of the 50th Hawaii International Conference on System Science (HICSS-50), pp. 2418–2427 (2017)
22. Ebbers, W.E., Jansen, M.G.M.M., van Deursen, A.: Impact of the digital divide on e-government: expanding from channel choice to channel usage. Gov. Inf. Q. **33**, 685–692 (2016)
23. Haythornthwaite, C.: Social networks and internet connectivity effects. Inf. Commun. Soc. **8**, 125–147 (2005)
24. Ledbetter, A.M., Mazer, J.P.: Do online communication attitudes mitigate the association between Facebook use and relational interdependence? an extension of media multiplexity theory. New Media Soc. **16**(5), 806–822 (2014)
25. Jensen, K.B.: Intermediality. In: The International Encyclopedia of Communication Theory and Philosophy. Wiley, Chichester (2016)
26. Stephens, K.K., Sørnes, J.O., Rice, R.E., Browning, L.D., Sætre, A.S.: Discrete, sequential, and follow-up use of information and communication technology by experienced ICT users. Manage. Commun. Q. **22**(2), 197–231 (2008)
27. Saunders, C., Jones, J.W.: Temporal sequences in information acquisition for decision making: a focus on source and medium. Acad. Manag. Rev. **15**(1), 29–46 (2011)
28. Dutta-Bergman, M.J.: Complementarity in consumption of news types across traditional and new media. J. Broadcast. Electron. Media. **48**, 41–60 (2004)
29. Blaikie, N.: Approaches to Social Inquiry. Polity, Cambridge (2010)
30. Creswell, J.W.: Research Design. Qualitative, Quantitative, and Mixed Methods Approaches. SAGE, London (2014)
31. Blomberg, J., Giagomi, J., Mosher, A., Swenton-Wall, P.: Ethnographic field methods and their relation to design. In: Schuler, D., Namioka, A. (eds.) Participatory Design: Principles and Practices. CRC Press, New York (1993)
32. Eisenhardt, K., Graebner, M.: Theory building from cases: opportunities and challenges. Acad. Manage. Rev. **50**, 25–32 (2007)

Open Data: Social and Technical Aspects

Which Lobby Won the Vote? Visualizing Influence of Interest Groups in Swiss Parliament

Florian Evéquoz[1,2]([✉]) and Hugo Castanheiro[1]

[1] Institute Information Systems, HES-SO Valais-Wallis, Sierre, Switzerland
florian.evequoz@hes-so.ch
[2] Human-IST Institute, University of Fribourg, Fribourg, Switzerland
florian.evequoz@unifr.ch

Abstract. Members of national parliaments (MPs) often have ties to interest groups, or 'lobbies', which might try to influence policies. In order to quantify the influence of lobbies on parliamentary decisions, we design an online platform that allows users to explore votes results, focusing on how interest groups members voted, in order to identify which lobbies voted for or against a given measure and in which proportion. We apply this approach to the specific case of the Swiss Federal Parliament. To achieve this, we build a database that combines two sources of openly available data: (1) a register of politicians' interest ties, maintained by Lobbywatch.ch, an association dedicated to the monitoring of Swiss politicians' interest ties and (2) the individual votes results in the Swiss Federal Parliament, accessible through a web-service provided by the parliamentary service of the Swiss government. Our platform allows users to explore the following perspectives of the data: (1) general information about lobbies (e.g. size, domains), (2) individual votes results, with a drill-down by lobby that shows the distribution of votes in each interest group for each specific vote, and (3) overall (dis)agreement of individual MPs with their party and lobbies across all considered votes. We believe that such an exploration platform can be a powerful tool to help quantify the influence of lobbies in politics. Indeed, a qualitative evaluation of the prototype was conducted with 7 domain experts (5 journalists and 2 politicians). They were all able to complete successfully the submitted tasks. They rated its usability and usefulness as rather high (mean respectively 7.4/10 and 6.8/10). Moreover, most of them reported that such a platform has the potential to increase the accountability of politicians towards the people and consequentially to raise the trust of the population in their elected representatives.

Keywords: Lobby · Votes · Data visualization · Politics · Open data · User experience

© IFIP International Federation for Information Processing 2019
Published by Springer Nature Switzerland AG 2019
I. Lindgren et al. (Eds.): EGOV 2019, LNCS 11685, pp. 155–167, 2019.
https://doi.org/10.1007/978-3-030-27325-5_12

1   Introduction

Interest groups, or 'lobbies', are organized movements whose mission is to protect the interests of a group of people or corporations active in a particular field, generally by influencing public institutions and political representatives. In modern democracies, interest groups play in important role in bringing specific topics onto the public policy agenda and in shaping the opinion of the parliament and general public alike about issues that concerns them. Therefore, it is not surprising to observe a growing number of ties between members of parliaments (MPs) and interest groups [9,12]. Due to the raising influence of lobbies on the work of MPs and overall policy-making, several countries have legislated that MPs shall openly disclose their ties to lobbies. In addition to that effort, the media also plays a crucial role in bringing to light hidden interests of politicians that might not be documented in official registers [2].

Overall, the practical influence of lobbies can be witnessed in different stages along the policy-making process. While a lobby effect is certainly present already in early stages (like pre-parliamentary bureaucratic work, consultative procedures, parliamentary work in privately held commissions, etc.), it remains largely opaque and difficult to observe due to the confidential nature of the process in those stages. For long, common wisdom has considered that the greatest share of the influence of lobbies was carried out during those early moments and that, as such, it would stay mostly hidden to the public. However, recent work has shown that the trend towards the professionalization of politics has resulted in an increasing influence of lobbies on the parliamentary work itself, i.e. the work actually done in the parliament through votes and amendments of laws [20]. Now this stage is open to the scrutiny of the general public. Moreover, in many modern democracies, the individual votes of MPs can even be available publicly on web platforms or as open data.

How can the influence of interest groups on political decisions be assessed at the parliamentary level? Given the observations above, we formulate the postulate that the voting behavior of MPs in the parliament during the law-making process can be a valid proxy for the actual influence of lobbies on policy-making. To explore this hypothesis further, we introduce the design of an online platform that allows users to explore MP votes results, focusing on how interest groups members voted, in order to identify which lobbies voted for or against a given measure and in which proportion. We apply this approach to the specific case of the Swiss Federal Parliament. It should be noted that the implementation of our approach was made possible only by progresses in E-Government and Digital Government initiatives in Switzerland that have enabled the publication of votes and MPs' interest ties as open data [1].

The paper is organized as follows. We first present a state of the art of applications that aim at visualizing interest ties in politics, as well as previous research studying the impact of interest ties in policy-making at the parliamentary level. Then we introduce the platform that we developed ("Lobby & Votes") and a qualitative evaluation in the form of semi-directed interviews with 7 participants that we conducted to assess the usability and usefulness of this platform. We conclude by discussing the limitations of our approach and open perspectives for future research.

2   Related Work

Several visualizations have been developed in recent years to help in understanding the influence of lobbies on politics. Lobbyradar.org [14] is a website that shows the interest ties of German politicians in the form of a network of connected nodes. Colors are used to distinguish different types of nodes. Groups of interests, parties, companies and organizations are represented in green, while members of parliament are in blue and members of the government are in orange. Nodes representing individuals are linked to their interest ties. A search box allows users to find a particular politician or organization and see their connections. Overall, the visualization forms a dense network of connected nodes with details on-demand and serves as a global map of interest ties in German politics. In the same vein, Kdovpliva.si [21] presents the map of interest ties in Slovenia. The features are mostly the same as Lobbyradar.org, but it also offers additional details and perspectives on the map, in particular a network of contacts between businesses, their lobbyists, politicians and state institutions and a network of transactions between companies in which lobbyists are legal representatives. At the European Union level, [8] has created a social network of lobby organizations members and political representatives of the EU (commissioners, cabinet members and directors-general) that have met regularly in a certain period of time. This visualization allows the identification of ties between policy-makers and lobbyists. It was also published by the European edition of Politico [6]. In the USA, BrightPoint [4] has developed a visualization combining a chord diagram with a network that shows the amount of money received by individual US Congress members from the top 20 interest groups in the USA (Political Action Committees or PACs). In their visualization, colors map to political parties and size of the elements is proportional to the amount involved, which helps in identifying the largest interest ties. In Switzerland, the newspaper NZZ has developed a visualization showing all accredited guests to whom MPs have given access rights to Parliament [15]. In that visualization, individuals are shown as nodes organized in a circular layout in several strata. The links are hidden by default and revealed only when hovering or clicking on a node. Direct and indirect links of MPs and lobbyists with organizations and other MPs or lobbyists are made visible by interacting with the visualization. Martin Grandjean also published a series of static infographics based on networks that explore the interest ties of Swiss MPs through the lens of access rights (accredited guests) [11]. A more recent visualization by NZZ shows the aggregate number of mandates that party members in the federal parliaments have in all business branches. The visualization takes the form of a modified chord diagram and shows in which proportion parties are connected to interest groups and vice versa [3].

Most of the solutions above attempt to provide a view of ties between individual politicians and groups of interest at a broad level using different kinds of proxies: declared interests, mandates in business branches, meetings with lobby-ists, access rights, etc. However, none of them connects those ties to the actual policy-making process in order to evaluate their influence on the political deci-sions of individual MPs. This latter aspect was tackled by research in the field of Political Science that we shortly cover next.

Previous work in the field of Political Sciences has explored the dynamic of lobbies and their impact on votes in parliaments. A comprehensive state of the art of previous studies in the field was presented by [9]. In the following, we pick up only the specific research done in Switzerland that is relevant to our work. Pioneering research studying the voting behavior of MPs in relation to their interest ties have shown that MPs having ties with economic lobbies vote in a more cohesive fashion than MPs linked to public lobbies [13,19]. More recently, it was found that MPs affiliated with a large number of interest groups had a higher probability of voting against their constituents (i.e. the people who elected them in office in the first place): "the larger the number of sectional groups that support an MP, the higher the probability that the MP defects from her constituents" [10]. An econometric analysis based on the votes of politicians in the Swiss Parliament was conducted by [16]. They were interested in comparing loyalty to the political party versus loyalty to the interest groups with which MPs are affiliated. Their study identifies factors that influence the proximity of MPs to their political party typical voting behavior. Socio-demographic factors (gender, age, canton of origin) seem to play a role, but the authors also find evidence for a lobby effect: MPs with ties in banking, energy, insurance and transport tend to more often cast a vote that differs from the majority of their party colleagues. Their research therefore suggests that studying voting behavior of MPs with respect to their lobby affiliations can shed light on the role of lobbies in shaping public policies.

As we have seen, political science research has investigated the influence of lobby membership on votes at an aggregate level, i.e. for groups of politicians and considering all votes in a given time period. However, previous work in the visualization of interest ties did not explore systematically how interest ties impact the policy-making process through their influence on the votes of indi-vidual MPs. Our work presented in the next section attempts to fill this gap by relating MPs interest ties with their voting behavior through an online platform supported by data visualization.

3   'Lobbies & Votes' Platform

The platform developed in the context of this project takes the form of an online website that we called "Lobby & Votes". It allows the exploration of lobbies and votes in the Swiss Parliament along different perspectives and is supported by data visualizations and other navigation features. The platform introduces a novel perspective on the interweaving of interest ties, political parties and voting behavior of MPs. While our implementation does not have the ambition to go beyond the stage of a proof-of-concept realization, we believe its design can be influential and easily replicated in other countries.

Table 1. Some interest groups of Swiss Parliament members, French and English (excerpt).

Lobby name (French)	Lobby name (English)
Pharmaceutique	Pharmaceutical
Caisses maladie	Health insurance
Médecine	Medicine
Hôpitaux	Hospitals
Patients	Patients
Santé publique	Public health
Techniques médicales	Medical techniques
Musique	Music
Cantons/Régions	Cantons/Regions
Villes	Cities
Handicap	Handicap
Banques	Banks
Commerce de matiéres premiéres	Trade in raw materials
Immobilier et propriétaires fonciers	Real estate and landowners
Economie en général	Economy in general
Immigration	Immigration

3.1 Data and Infrastructure

The database we built for the website combines two sources of openly available data: (1) a register of Swiss federal MPs' interest ties, maintained by Lobbywatch.ch, an association dedicated to the monitoring of Swiss politicians' interest ties [2], and (2) the individual votes results in the Swiss Federal Parliament, made available through a web-service provided by the parliamentary service of the Swiss government itself [1].

The interest ties database was provided by the Lobbywatch association in an SQL format. Since then, this data was also made available through a JSON interface directly from their website. The Lobbywatch dataset is maintained by volunteer journalists and used as a high-quality source of information by the Swiss media. It has to be noted that this dataset differs from the one used in the research by [16], released later by the same authors [17]. Reasons for this choice are twofold. First, the Lobbywatch dataset is published as open data and readily available through a JSON interface. Second, the dataset by [17] only covers the politicians active in the 49th legislature and not the current one. The Lobbywatch dataset contains all 200 MPs from the vote dataset and a total of 137 different interest groups (e.g. Pharma, Patients, Pro-Nuclear, Pro-Environment, see also Table 1) that are distributed in 14 general domains or "branches" (e.g. Health, Energy). A total of 5040 interest ties connecting politicians with interest groups are documented in the database.

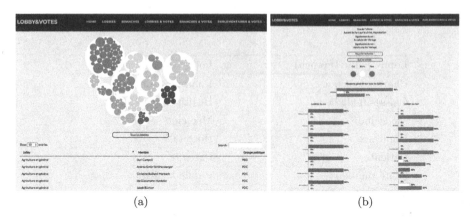

(a)   (b)

Fig. 1. (a) 'Lobbies' page presenting a visualization of all lobbies depicted as circles. Their color and position relate to the lobby branch (e.g. lobbies in Finance or Energy, etc.) and their size corresponds to the number of members in the lobby. A detailed list of lobby members is available as a sortable and searchable table underneath the visualization. (b) Detailed vote results drilled-down by lobbies. The affair title 'Accord de Paris sur le climat' is displayed along with meaning of 'Yes' and 'No' votes. The first chart on top shows the overall vote results. Green means 'Yes', red means 'No', white is 'Other vote'. Below the first chart, the left column contains detailed results for the 'Lobbies who voted Yes' ('Lobbies du oui') while the right column shows the 'Lobbies who voted No' ('Lobbies du non') sorted by decreasing score. (Color figure online)

We downloaded the vote data directly from the web-service of the Swiss Parliament in a JSON format. The vote data covers the first 14 months of the current (50th) legislature, from November 31, 2015 to March 7, 2017 in the National Council. The National Council is the lower house of the bicameral Federal Assembly of Switzerland. It comprises 200 seats apportioned to the Swiss Cantons populations. The votes of the higher house (Council of States) are not published as open data and could therefore not be integrated in our database. Our vote dataset comprises all 1536 votes of the National Council over the period considered.

The two datasets presented above were converted and merged into an SQL database. The server-side application was created in node.js and visualization templates have been implemented using the declarative languages Vega and Vega-Lite [18].

3.2   Platform Design

The prototype platform that we propose allows users to explore the following perspectives of the data: (1) general information about lobbies (e.g. size, domains), (2) individual votes results, with a drill-down by lobby that shows the distribution of votes in each interest group for each specific vote, and (3) overall (dis)agreement of individual MPs with their party and lobbies across all considered votes. In the remainder of this section, we discuss these three perspectives.

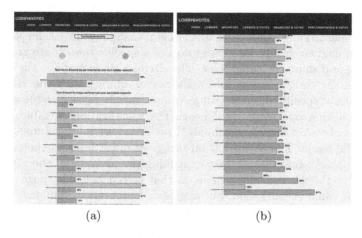

(a)

(b)

Fig. 2. (Dis)agreement of MPs with their respective lobbies. Turquoise bars represent the proportion of votes in agreement with the majority of the lobbies. Orange bars represent proportion of votes in disagreement. (a) The first chart on top shows the overall rate of (dis)agreement over all MPs and all lobbies. Below it, each chart represents the detailed (dis)agreement rate of each individual MP with their lobbies, sorted in decreasing order of agreement. (b) Detailed (dis)agreement continued: a view at the MPs that disagree the most with their lobbies. Christa Markwalder, who disagrees the most with her lobbies, was the president of the Parliament during the period and therefore abstained from most votes, which explains her score. (Color figure online)

(a)

Show 10 entries — Search:

Titre de l'affaire	Signification du oui	Signification du non	Lobbies	Majorité du lobby	Vote du parlementaire
Blocage et restitution des avoirs illicites de personnes politiquement exposées à l'étranger. Loi	Antrag der Mehrheit (gemäss SR)	Antrag der Minderheit Stamm (Festhalten)	Santé	Yes	No
Blocage et restitution des avoirs illicites de personnes politiquement exposées à l'étranger. Loi	Antrag der Mehrheit (gemäss SR)	Antrag der Minderheit Stamm (Festhalten)	Banques	No	No
Blocage et restitution des avoirs illicites de personnes politiquement exposées à l'étranger. Loi	Antrag der Mehrheit (gemäss SR)	Antrag der Minderheit Stamm (Festhalten)	Conseil en relations publiques	No	No
Blocage et restitution des avoirs illicites de personnes politiquement exposées à l'étranger. Loi	Antrag der Mehrheit (gemäss SR)	Antrag der Minderheit Stamm (Festhalten)	Economie en général	Yes	No
Blocage et restitution des avoirs illicites de personnes politiquement exposées à l'étranger. Loi	Antrag der Mehrheit (gemäss SR)	Antrag der Minderheit Stamm (Festhalten)	Politique en général	No	No
Blocage et restitution des avoirs illicites de personnes politiquement exposées à l'étranger. Loi	Antrag der Mehrheit (gemäss SR)	Antrag der Minderheit Stamm (Festhalten)	Politique en général	Yes	No
Blocage et restitution des avoirs illicites de personnes politiquement exposées à l'étranger. Loi	Antrag der Mehrheit (gemäss SR)	Antrag der Minderheit Stamm (Festhalten)	Relations commerciales	Yes	No
Blocage et restitution des avoirs illicites de personnes politiquement exposées à l'étranger. Loi	Antrag der Mehrheit (gemäss SR)	Antrag der Minderheit Stamm (Festhalten)	Industrie du gaz et du pétrole	No	No
Blocage et restitution des avoirs illicites de personnes politiquement exposées à l'étranger. Loi	Antrag der Mehrheit (gemäss SR)	Antrag der Minderheit Stamm (Festhalten)	Cabinets/Fiduciaires	Yes	No
Blocage et restitution des avoirs illicites de personnes politiquement exposées à l'étranger. Loi	Antrag der Mehrheit (gemäss SR)	Antrag der Minderheit Stamm (Festhalten)	Sport populaire	Yes	No

Showing 1 to 10 of 20,002 entries — Previous 1 2 3 4 5 … 2001 Next

(b)

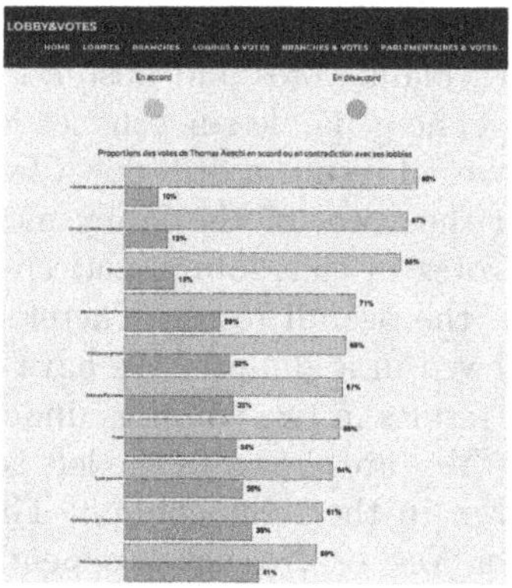

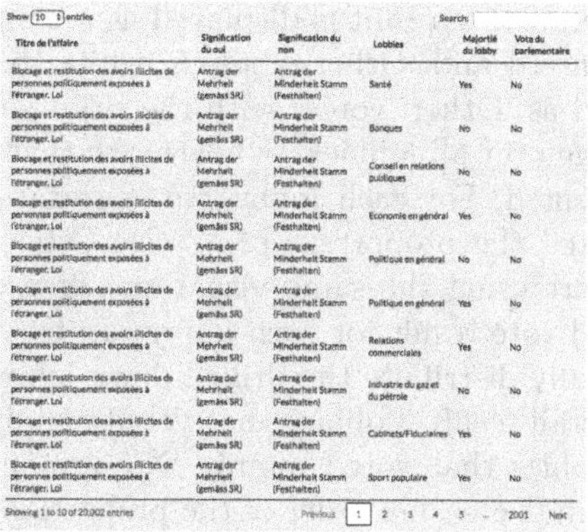

Fig. 3. Detailed agreement of a selected MP (Thomas Aeschi) with the lobbies he belongs to, presented (a) as summary charts per lobby and (b) as a detailed list of all votes per relevant lobbies. For example, the first chart on top in (a) shows that this MP followed the majority of the votes of the interest group "Oil and gas industry" in 90% of his votes. (Color figure online)

General Information About Lobbies. The 'Lobbies' page depicted in Fig. 1a shows a visualization of all lobbies in a circle-packing layout. Each colored circle is a specific interest group. Interest groups of a specific branch are grouped in a white circle and share the same color. The size of a circle maps to the number of members in the corresponding lobby. Users can interact with the visualization to see details of specific interest groups (name, members, size) by hovering over circles or clicking on them. Underneath the visualization, a table shows the detailed membership list of all lobbies. Users can sort it by columns or search for a specific name. The menu bar on top gives quick links to the other pages of the website. An information text explaining the meaning of the visualization is also given, though it is not visible on that screenshot. The page 'Branches' contains the same visualization, but aggregated by branch/domain.

This overview visualization allows user to understand some general trends, such as the respective size of lobbies and branches, the amount of interest groups in a given branch and the size of each interest group. Details are available on-demand.

Individual Vote Results. The pages 'Lobbies & Votes' and 'Branches & Votes' detail the result of each parliamentary vote and puts them into perspective with the interest ties of voters. In the page 'Lobbies and Votes', the full list of votes is initially presented in a searchable, sortable and filterable table. Upon selection of a specific vote, the individual vote results are shown. Figure 1b depicts the page after a vote has been selected. Under the vote title and general information, the overall vote result is displayed as a bar chart with 'Yes' votes in green, 'No' votes in red and 'Other' votes in white (both blank votes and abstentions are counted as 'Other' votes) with the title 'Moyenne générale sur tous les lobbies' 'Average over all lobbies'. Underneath that overall result, a drill-down by lobby is presented. For each lobby, we aggregated the votes of the lobby members, computed the proportion of Yes-No-Other votes in that lobby, and created a bar chart using the same visual encoding as the overall result. Therefore, the detailed vote result for each lobby can be viewed in a glimpse. We have chosen to visually distribute the drilled-down lobby results in two columns underneath the overall result. Lobbies that voted mainly 'Yes' are shown in the left column, and lobbies that voted mainly 'No' are shown in the right column. They are sorted in decreasing order of the proportion of 'Yes' or 'No' votes, depending on the column. Finally, the display of results can be limited to only one lobby by selecting it in the interface. Also, the individual results of the vote showing how each MP voted is displayed in a table underneath the dashboard. This allows users to quickly spot the decision of specific lobby members for a given vote.

Overall (Dis)agreement of Individual MPs with Their Party and Lobbies. The last perspective explored in our platform is the overall agreement level of individual MPs with their party and lobbies across all considered votes. Political parties are known to take position on certain topics and give voting instructions to their representatives in the parliament. These instructions will be followed with more or less discipline by individual MPs across the political spectrum. Interest groups are suspected to exhibit a similar behavior, though it remains largely hidden. In order to explore it, we computed the agreement of MPs with their interest groups and parties, taking inspiration from the work of [16].

We first computed the agreement between each MP and their respective lobbies by counting the proportion of votes in which that MP casted the same vote as the majority of members of the same lobby. This gives the proportion of votes in which the MP "agreed" or "disagreed" with that lobby. Then, to compute the overall agreement between each individual MP and all interest groups they belong to, we summed individual measures computed in the previous step across all relevant interest groups. A further aggregation step allows us to compute the overall agreement of all MPs with all the lobbies they belong to. Additionally, we computed the same measures for the political parties instead of the lobbies.

The results of those metrics are displayed on two pages of the platform. The first one shows the (dis)agreement of MPs with their party and the second one the (dis)agreement with their lobbies. This latter axis is certainly the most interesting and the most decisive in the analysis of the influence of lobbies in Swiss Federal politics. The visualization dashboards presented in those pages helps in assessing whether a MP is more influenced by her party or lobbies, and which lobbies in particular.

Figure 2 shows the visualization dashboards that depict the (dis)agreement of MPs with their respective lobbies. Turquoise bars represent the proportion of votes in agreement with the majority of the lobbies. Orange bars represent proportion of votes in disagreement. As in other pages, a detailed table is provided below those aggregated statistics, which allow users to search for specific votes. A drill-down by MP to explore the loyalty of their votes with regards to their respective lobbies is shown in Fig. 3. As explained above, although not depicted here, similar visualizations are provided for the political parties as well, therefore allowing users to inspect in detail the influence of both political party and interest group affiliations on the votes of individual MPs.

4   Evaluation and Potential Impact

We evaluated the platform qualitatively with 7 persons (2 female, 5 male). As we envisioned that this platform would particularly appeal to journalists but also to politicians themselves and the general public, we contacted 2 editors-in-chief of Swiss newspapers, 3 journalists specializing in Swiss politics, 1 member of the Federal Parliament and 1 person from the general public. We met them individually. The evaluation was conducted in the form of a small controlled use of the platform followed by semi-directed interviews. We first introduced the context of the project and we let them familiarize with the platform for 10 min. Then we asked them to perform three lookup tasks: (1) find a lobby in which there is only one member and name that member; (2) in the vote on the repeal of the anti-racism law, find the proportion of yes and no in the Anti-EU lobby; (3) find a vote for which Bastien Girod disagrees with the majority of his party. Next, we asked them to rate on a 10-point Likert scale their perception of the usability and usefulness the platform. Finally, we conducted a semi-directed interview about the potential impact of the platform by prompting them with the following questions: (1) Does the publication of this information make the Parliament more transparent? Why? (2) Does such a platform increase the accountability of the elected representatives towards the people. Why? (3) Does such a platform improve citizens' trust in their elected representatives? Why? Following a semi-directed approach, we encouraged people to elaborate their points of view and asked follow-up questions. Interviews were recorded.

All the participants succeeded in the 3 lookup tasks. They rated the usability of the platform as good (mean $= 7.4/10$) and the perceived usefulness as rather good (mean $= 6.8/10$). One editor-in-chief rated $4/10$ the usefulness of the platform, arguing that the information it contains is too complex for the general public to understand and explore effectively and is only useful to specialists. Without his mark, the mean interest would have been $7.3/10$.

The analysis of the data collected during the semi-directed interviews sheds light on the potential impact of the platform. According to all participants, this platform can make the parliament more transparent, because "it shows whether MPs defend the interest of their party or lobbies and everybody can see it". However, the politician we interviewed noted that lobby affiliation was not sufficiently detailed on the platform (i.e. he did not understand why he was affiliated to one specific lobby) and that this information should be more complete for a better transparency. A journalist noted that official registers are incomplete anyway and that this platform bridges the gap. Four participants think that the platform can increase the accountability of MPs because "it facilitates the explanation of voting behavior of representatives" and "because MPs will feel more surveilled", but only "if there is a good media coverage of it". Three participants think that it will not increase their accountability because "the information is already public" though not aggregated, or because the majority of "citizens are interested in personal values defended by politicians" rather than their behavior when elected, and finally because "some information is missing" like "the coherence of votes on a specific topic", which would facilitate the analysis of the results. Five people think that this platform will impact citizens' trust in their elected representatives, but not necessarily or immediately improve it: "they will understand who votes what and who is influenced by whom"; "anybody can understand who they really defend". Two political journalists think that such a platform will rather not impact the trust of citizen as "people trust speeches more than acts" and "the interest ties are already known".

Participants also provided useful comments and recommendations for the evolution of the platform. Overall, the pages displaying the proportion of votes in (dis)agreement with the majority of parties or lobbies were the most praised by our participants. They advised us to also take into account the canton represented by each MP as this can also have a strong influence on votes (i.e. MPs defending their regions and voters' interests). A link to the institutional Parliament's website which shows the vote result as a dashboard would also ease exploring the details of a particular vote. They also commented on the interaction and wished that charts were interactive, pictures of MPs were provided, or that the readability were better in some parts of the platform (text size too small and wording sometimes unclear).

5   Limitations and Perspectives

Our approach has limitations in several aspects. First, the influence of lobbies during pre-parliamentary work, consultative procedures and privately-held parliamentary commission remains opaque to an analysis of parliamentary votes such as ours. One might argue that the vote is a too late stage in the parliamentary process and that the negotiation has been done before parliamentary work, therefore effectively hiding the influence of lobbies. However, previous research has shown that parliamentary work has actually strengthened in Switzerland in recent years. In particular, the number of amendments to government proposals issued by the Swiss parliament has been on the rise [9]. This suggests that lobbies might still be very active during that phase of the law-making process and that the vote might be a valid proxy for the influence of lobbies on that process.

Moreover, in our approach, all lobbies are represented in votes results. Therefore, even if an interest group does not have any preference in the matter of a given vote, it will nonetheless appear in the results page, which creates unnecessary noise in the presentation of the results. On a more general note, with the high number of votes and the lack of a proper classification of vote issues and relevance to lobbies, it can be difficult to identify the role of a specific lobby in influencing a vote. Furthermore, the visualization of lobbies votes does not take into account the size of the lobbies and only represents the relative proportion of voters. A lobby with 3 members will appear as equally important as a larger 80-persons lobby. Finally, another limitation of our platform is that the votes of the second House of the Swiss Parliament (the Council of States) is not available as open data. The voting behavior of important MP in that House can therefore not be explored.

The platform could be improved in several ways, some of which were suggested by our study participants and stated in the previous section. Also, an analysis of the composition of lobbies (e.g. measuring the diversity of cantons and political parties represented in the lobby) and its impact on cohesiveness of lobby votes would help shed light on interest groups practices.

Perspectives for further research are manifolds. For example, it could be relevant to identify trends that go beyond a vote per vote analysis, e.g. which lobbies have the most influence in general, even more influence than political parties, on which topics. Developing metrics to measure it, as done by [16], could be a step in that direction. Although, doing this requires a more detailed vote dataset, informed of the topics of votes in such a way that it can be automatically connected to the interest of lobbies. One could try to identify automatically this connection and track evidence of vote instructions by specific lobbies, e.g. exhibited by a cohesive vote behavior of the MPs affiliated with them. Another approach would be to manually label the votes topics and connect them to lobbies (i.e. identify which vote decision is in the interest of which lobby). This could be done using crowd-sourced approaches based on services designed with a gamification approach [7].

6   Conclusion

Interest groups, or 'lobbies' are thought to play a key role in shaping public policies in modern democracies. However, identifying their actual influence in legislative work remains difficult. We proposed an approach that combines votes of the members of parliament and their affiliation with interest groups as a way to systematically explore the influence of lobbies in the law-making process and the loyalty of lobby members. We introduced a prototype platform that enables this exploration and applied it to the use case of 14 months of legislative work in the Swiss Federal Parliament. The initial reception of the platform prototype among a group of 7 people including a politician, journalists and members of the general public was good. We believe our platform introduces a novel perspective on the interweaving of interest ties, political parties and voting behavior of MPs. Furthermore, we think that our general approach and the design of our platform can inspire similar realizations in other countries, which could bring more transparency and accountability in politics.

Acknowledgements. This work was supported by HES-SO Valais-Wallis. An extensive discussion of the technical aspects as well as detailed results are available (in French) in [5]. The platform can be accessed online at the following URL: http://www.evequoz.name/lobbyandvotes/.

References

1. Swiss Parliament. https://www.parlament.ch/en
2. Lobbywatch.ch (2018). https://lobbywatch.ch/
3. Ruh, B., Rittmeyer, B.: Für wen lobbyiert das im Herbst 2015 neu gewählte Parlament? Eine Datenanalyse (2016). https://www.nzz.ch/schweiz/aktuelle-themen/lobbying-im-bundeshaus-interessenvertreter-von-links-bis-rechts-ld.7112
4. BrightPoint Inc.: Political influence, August 2015. http://www.brightpointinc.com/political_influence/
5. Castanheiro, H.: Visualiser l'influence des lobbies dans la politique suisse. Bachelor thesis, HES-SO Valais-Wallis, Sierre (2017)
6. Cerulus, L.: Lobbyists in Brussels - the social network, October 2015. https://www.politico.eu/interactive/lobbyists-brussels-social-network-meetings-commission-strategy/
7. Dargan, T., Evequoz, F.: Designing engaging e-government services by combining user-centered design and gamification: a use-case. In: Proceedings of the 15th European Conference on eGovernment 2015: ECEG 2015, pp. 70–78. Academic Conferences Limited (2015)

8. FASResearch: FASresearch NetExplorerJS: EC Meetings (2015). http://www. lobbyingnet.eu/
9. Gava, R., Varone, F., Mach, A., Eichenberger, S., Christe, J., Chao-Blanco, C.: Interests groups in Parliament: exploring MPs' interest affiliations (2000–2011). Swiss Polit. Sci. Rev. **23**(1), 77–94 (2017). https://doi.org/10.1111/spsr.12224. http://doi.wiley.com/10.1111/spsr.12224
10. Giger, N., Klüver, H.: Voting against your constituents? How lobbying affects representation. Am. J. Polit. Sci. **60**(1), 190–205 (2016). https://doi.org/10.1111/ajps. 12183. https://onlinelibrary.wiley.com/doi/abs/10.1111/ajps.12183
11. Grandjean, M.: Zones d'ombre : Cartographier les réseaux d'influence et groupes d'intérêts au Parlement (2013). http://www.martingrandjean.ch/cartographier-reseaux-influence-interets-parlement/
12. Haederli, A., Brönnimann, C., von Wyl, H., Evéquoz, F.: Les parlementaires fédéraux n'ont jamais été autant liés à des lobbys (2017). http://webspecial. lematindimanche.ch/longform/lobbys-au-parlement/
13. Lüthi, R., Meyer, L., Hirter, H.: Fraktionsdisziplin und die Vertretung von Partikulärinteressen im Nationalrat. In: Das Parlament - 'Oberste Gewalt des Bundes'? Festschrift der Bundesversammlung zur 700-Jahr-Feier der Eidgenossenschaft, pp. 53–71. Parlamentardienste, Berne (1991)
14. Netzpolitik: Open Lobbyradar (2015). https://www.lobbyradar.org/
15. Nicolussi, R., Pietsch, C., Matzat, L., Gassner, P., Wiederkehr, B., Grunwald, S.: Das Netz der Zutrittsberechtigten in Bundesbern (2014). https://storytelling.nzz. ch/2014/badge-basar/
16. Puddu, S., Peclat, M.: Dangerous Liaisons: interests groups and politicians' votes. A Swiss perspective. IRENE Working Paper 15–09, IRENE Institute of Economic Research, University of Neuchâtel, Neuchâtel (2015)
17. Péclat, M., Puddu, S.: Swiss politicians' ties: a comprehensive dataset. Swiss Polit. Sci. Rev. **23**(2), 175–190 (2017). https://doi.org/10.1111/spsr.12249. https://onlinelibrary.wiley.com/doi/abs/10.1111/spsr.12249
18. Satyanarayan, A., Russell, R., Hoffswell, J., Heer, J.: Reactive Vega: a streaming dataflow architecture for declarative interactive visualization. IEEE Trans. Vis. Comput. Graph. **22**(1), 659–668 (2016). https://doi.org/10.1109/TVCG.2015. 2467091
19. Schwarz, D., Bächtiger, A., Lutz, G.: Switzerland: agenda-setting power of government in a separation-of-powers framework. In: Rasch, B.E., Tsebelis, G. (eds.) The Role of Government in Legislative Agenda-Setting, pp. 127–143. Routledge Chapman & Hall, London (2011)
20. Sciarini, P., Fischer, M., Traber, D.: Political Decision-Making in Switzerland - The Consensus Model Under Pressure. Palgrave MacMillan (2015). http://www. palgrave.com/us/book/9781137508591
21. Slovenija, T.I.: Omrežja lobistov v sloveniji 2011–2014 (2015). http://www. kdovpliva.si/

Orchestrated Co-creation of High-Quality Open Data Within Large Groups

Giuseppe Ferretti[1], Delfina Malandrino[2], Maria Angela Pellegrino[2(✉)],
Andrea Petta[2], Gianluigi Renzi[1], Vittorio Scarano[2], and Luigi Serra[2]

[1] Consiglio Regionale della Campania, Napoli, Italy
{ferretti.giu,renzi.gia}@consiglio.regione.campania.it
[2] Dipartimento di Informatica, University of Salerno, Fisciano, Italy
{dmalandrino,mapellegrino,vitsca}@unisa.it,
andrpet@gmail.com, luigser@gmail.com

Abstract. According to Open Government Data, governments should co-operate with citizens in order to co-create Open Data (OD). When large groups are involved, there is the need to orchestrate the work by clearly defining and distributing roles. Our Regional Administration - the Council of the Campania Region in Italy - claimed a motivating use case which inspired the proposed roles involved in the OD production process. We consider *validator*, *creator*, and *filler* as roles. To each role tasks and responsibilities are attached. Roles and related activities are integrated into SPOD (a Social Platform for Open Data) to guide users in producing high-quality OD by proactive quality assurance techniques.

Keywords: Open Data · Open Government · Orchestration · Roles · Large groups · Co-creation · Quality assurance

1 Introduction

Open Data (OD) refer to *"data which are open for free access, use and modification to be shared for any purpose"* [15]. In the last years, the e-government communities manifest great interest in OD. Therefore, many initiatives and platforms have been developed in order to publish open data sets in several different fields such as mobility, security (e.g. crime rates), economy (e.g. statistics on business creations) [23]. This interest in OD is due to the interpretation of Open Data as an essential tool for the dissemination of the Open Government principles [20,23]. There is rich evidence stating that Open Government Data (OGD) has the potential to drive innovation [7,20], not only because it allows an increasing level of transparency but also because it helps empower citizens and communities [20]. However, simply providing OGD does not automatically result in significant value for society [20]: the potential benefits of OGD [20,29] will not be realized unless data are actually used. In truth, many data sets are available, but often repositories contain OD that users do not need and data sets that citizens need are not available (or not published) by Public Administrations (PAs) [36]. By involving citizens, not only heterogeneous skills can be exploited, but also effective needs can be considered during the OD creation.

Thus, our research question is *how to support PAs and citizens (without any upper limit on the group size) in working together to publish high-quality OD.*

By focusing on small groups (7–8 persons), they can exploit peer-to-peer methodologies without losing the overall picture of the rest of the group. We already had experience in managing small groups by an *agile* approach. In fact, SPOD (Social Platform for Open Data) supports an agile iterative, evolutionary, test-driven and collaborative methodology for the production of OD [13]. However, in environments in which the group size increases and there is a high diversity of partners and contributors, an *orchestrator* is needed in order to ensure valuable inputs and mitigate concerns from network actors [10]. The orchestration is a well-known strategy applied to large groups [17]. It ensures the creation and extraction of value, without the introduction of hard hierarchical authority [17]. Therefore, the participants do not work as equals but they can clearly define and distribute roles in such an *agile* way. If in the past the agile approach was considered suitable only for small groups, in the last years there is an increasing interest in exploit it also in large group management [18]. Moreover, McBride et al. [25] cite both the agile approach and the occurrence of different (motivated) stakeholders among the key factors of a co-creation process. Each stakeholder should play a specific role. Each role implies tasks and responsibilities. They must be distributed taking into account individual skills and the overall needs.

However, there is also a dark side of the orchestration: it is easy to produce data of low-level quality while working into a large group without a well-defined guide. In fact, it is easy to duplicate data or leave them incomplete when several different people are involved. The problem is raised by the difficulty to keep an overall vision of the whole data set. Also, data accuracy can be compromised if clear guidelines to produce data are not established in advance. *Completeness* and *accuracy* are two of the quality pillars [4]. Data quality issues are quoted among the principal barriers of complete exploitation of OD [7,20,34]. Data will cost too much to be transformed into a standard format [2]. For instance, poor data quality costs the US economy around \$3.1 trillion a year [9]. Moreover, according to a survey conducted by TMMData and the Digital Analytics Association, nearly 40% of data professionals spend more than 20 h per week accessing, blending, and preparing data rather than performing analysis. The situation becomes even more complex when the published data involved individuals' information. In that case, there is the need to ponder how to protect individual privacy to be compliant with the General Data Protection Regulation (GDPR or Regulation (EU) 2016/679) [1].

Our proposal is to scaffold PAs and citizens in working together by orchestrating the co-creation of OD in an agile way. Our approach is integrated into SPOD which already supports the agile co-creation of OD leading PAs and citizens in working together. The main *contribution* of this work is the introduction of *roles* into the OD creation process. Roles keep responsibilities and tasks clearly divided. Moreover, they lead to work orchestration. SPOD will guide participants in easily identify tasks and responsibilities attached to played roles. Roles will be distributed according to the skills of group members and baring in mind the final goal, i.e. produce high-quality data. In order to satisfy quality requirements, one of the role (the *creator* of the data set under definition) can attach constraints and rules to each column in order to avoid trivial syntactic errors.

This paper is structured as follows: in Sect. 2 related work is reported; in Sect. 3 we present the motivational use case which inspires the proposed roles and their responsibilities; in Sect. 4 we detail the implemented approach and how it is embedded into SPOD; then the article concludes with the future directions and some considerations.

2   Related Work

Orchestration. Network-orchestration activities include ensuring *knowledge mobility*, *network stability*, and *innovation appropriability*, as well as coordination [30]. According to the context, these activities can be emphasized to different extents (e.g. highlighting knowledge mobility over appropriability) and can be carried out in quite different ways (e.g. by simply facilitating different activities). Multiple members may participate in these activities. Acknowledging the orchestrator roles is therefore relevant. In literature, several different types of orchestrators have been proposed. Roijakkers et al. [31] divided users into *orchestrators* and *non-players*: an orchestrator typically is an actor that has relatively strong individual incentives within networks and ecosystems that he/she aims to influence, while non-player orchestrator influences and supports the network without being an active competitor in the end market. Furthermore, the existing literature provides examples where roles and tasks are defined according to specific scenarios [19,21,27]. According to our motivating use case (which will be presented in Sect. 3), we define the *validator* role who is the legal manager of the data set content since he/she validates manually each row and adds to the data set only those semantically correct; the *creator* role who is the manager of data set constraints and defines the form to guide the data set filling; the *filler* role is in charge of populating the data set. The filler can be qualified as (i) *advanced* if he/she can both populate the data set and have an overall vision of the whole data set; (ii) *plain* if he/she can only suggest a new row to the validator without consulting the rest of the data set.

Co-creation by an Agile Approach. OD platforms can simplify the interaction among citizens and organizations giving them the opportunity to collaborate with government organizations. These platforms can be seen as collaborative environments which enable participation in collective decision-making efforts [32]. The subjects involved in this activity (e.g. citizens and PAs) work on open data set through a platform (SPOD in our case) splitting tasks by roles, respecting rules, and exploiting the community [32]. Once established the final goal (co-create high-quality open data), the operative approach must be chosen. In the last years, there is an increasing interest in dropping down the classical waterfall-like approach and adopting a more agile process [34]. Toots et al. [34,35] propose a framework for data-driven public service co-production. They observed that, in traditional waterfall-like models, public administrators are steering and controlling the whole process with citizen input being occasionally, but not necessarily, sought. Agile development focuses on being able to adapt quickly to changes by following an *agile* approach. Similarly, Mergel [26] points out that in traditional waterfall project management approach each phase sequentially follows the previous step. In contrast, an agile approach focuses on shorter development phases and continuous collaboration with final users in each phase. By the agile development it is possible to incrementally create, test, and improve products [26]. Every (intermediate) result can be immediately tested. By applying the agile methodology to the OD co-production, each data set can be iteratively and incrementally discussed and improved during the definition phase and it can be used in a practical use case to test on the way the fitness-of-use [13] (e.g. users can test the data set by creating visualisations).

The Agile methodology for software is iterative, incremental, and evolutionary [5]. Madi et al. [22] extracted a list of values out of the agile manifesto: *Collaboration, Communication, Working software, Flexibility, Customer-centric, Incremental, Iterative, Feedback, Speed, Simplicity, Self-organizing, and Learning.* All these values are taken into account in developing the SPOD features.

Data Quality Control. By a reactive quality control, users try to improve the quality of already published data sets and make them compliant with specific needs. Once the data set is provided, it is possible to perform data quality assessment which *"is the identification of erroneous data items"* [24]. It can be performed by data profiling techniques in order to collect statistics and information about data [28]. There are several works which analyse data set content and infer metadata and data types, from actual values [3,11,33]. SPOD is provided of a type inference mechanism: first we infer the data type for each value based on its content and, consequently, we attach a data type to each column [16]. Besides basic data types - like dates, numbers, and text - we infer also types related to personal information - such as Social Security Numbers (SSN), company codes, IBAN, gender, ZIP code and so on. The recognized data types are principally inspired by the personal data defined in the GDPR. *Personal data is "any information relating to an identified or identifiable natural person ('data subject'); an identifiable natural person is one who can be identified, directly or indirectly, in particular by reference to an identifier such as a name, an identification number, location data, ..."* [1]. By the type inference, we report both quality issues - accuracy, completeness - and privacy concerns - i.e. breaches of personal data in a textual description or due to the structure of the data set [16].

On the other side, guiding the OD creation by *proactive* quality assurance could reduce the subsequent effort in quality control. Our goal is to guide OD creation by a set of rules and constraints on values to avoid trivial syntactical errors. Since this approach does not prevent semantic mistakes, the *validator* role is in charge of verifying the correctness of data and deciding which rows should be dropped down and which ones become part of the data set under construction. According to the European Data Portal [14] (EDP) (at time of writing), 29,26% are three-stars, and only 1,17% are four-stars data sets - referring to the *five stars rating system* [6]. A large number of three-star data sets on OD portals triggers the need to reduce their data quality issues. Therefore, we decided to focus on plain textual data without an attached schema.

3   Motivating Use Case

The need to distinguish among several roles and the identification of the proposed profiles are motivated by a concrete use case claimed by the Public Administration, the Council of the Campania Region in Italy, that we will name Motivating PA (MPA). Our MPA has established a Special Regional Committee since 2015 - named "Land of Fires" - which takes care of precise monitoring of the uncontrolled phenomenon of the occurrence of garbage scattered over a vast territory (90 municipalities between the province of Naples and Caserta). This monitoring takes place with the involvement of qualified stakeholders dedicated to the collection of both structured and non-structured data. These data concern not only the structural characteristics of the territory and its municipal resources dedicated to the problem of the rubbish fires but also the assessments and the indications of the operators about the usefulness (or not) of the legislative disposal that qualifies and encourages (also with money) the municipalities in this zone. The first objective of this commission was to verify the effectiveness of the application of the Regional Law (n. 20/2013) and several checks were carried out through the direct contact with 90 municipalities involved. Now, the ICT department of the MPA has been involved to streamline the process via automated tools. Several experiences were matured with questionnaires reported by using EU tools (EUsurvey). From the analysis of recovered data, the legislator will obtain valid tools to identify and implement more precise and timely intervention rules for the elimination of this dangerous phenomenon.

Nevertheless, the focus of MPA is now on the direct process of reporting these data as open data for citizens. The low-quality of collected data and the wide set of contributors must be tackled. In fact, actual tools only allow a simple "collect-and-send" data process. It is insufficient to support a complex mechanism of data collection, joint analysis and discussion, and publication as open data. For instance, previous experiences of required data collection were further elaborated through several successive meetings with other competent bodies and institutions in the field, with national government authorities, a list of chosen delegates from the major Municipalities involved and a series of public hearings held at the MPA site, where the (preliminary) results were presented and discussed.

The Special Regional Committee is now considering to extend the activities to a much wider audience of municipalities, involving all the towns of Campania. According to the plan to cover more than 500 towns, previous approaches are no longer sustainable. Thus, it is necessary to design a supportive environment that will guide the community in collecting, assembling, evaluating data for publication. Furthermore, automated tools for quality checking are needed. Because of the large number of participants, the orchestration is more suitable than peer working in order to clearly separate roles and tasks. There should be the supervisor role - which can be declined as *validator* if he/she has to inspect data or as *creator* if he/she has to define constraints and rules on data. Moreover, there is the necessity to involve a big number of stakeholders who play the role of *filler*.

In conclusion, the introduction of roles and orchestration into a social platform (SPOD) is due to the necessity to coordinate a huge number of users leading them in creating high-quality OD. The research described here has been conducted in strict cooperation with the MPA officials and their ICT department. In the conclusions, we will report on the current state of the project.

4   Our Orchestrated Open Data Co-creation

Based on the motivational use case, we define the following orchestrator roles:

- *validator:* he/she is a super partes verifier. He/She is in charge of inspecting the content of the data set and discarding all rows conceivably semantically incorrect. Moreover, he/she is the legal manager of the data set;
- *creator:* this role corresponds to the expert in the field and/or who is able to opportunely model the data set under the definition. He/She is in charge of defining the structure of the data set and its columns specifying their data types and, if necessary, constraints on them;
- *advanced filler* who is in charge of filling in the data set and has the privilege of having an overall vision of the whole data set;
- *plain filler* who can only fill in the data set but cannot have a look of the other rows of the data set.

Each role is attached to a set of tasks. Starting from a data set, the *creator* has to define a form in order to bind a data type to each column and/or force some constraints on them. The starting point could be an empty or a partially filled in data set. The minimum data set to be used as a starting point has to expose the column header. By asking for the form creation, the creator is guided in filling in the form which can refer to all the columns or a subset of them. For each column the *creator* can choose among basic data types - such as *text, number, date* -, geo-coordinates, files - specifying between images and documents -, drop-down lists - also called *select* options. A select option can be manually populated by the creator. Otherwise, the tool offers some built-in select options, such as the list of all Italian regions, provinces or municipalities. Based on the data type, the form will guide the creator in specifying extra parameters, if necessary. For example, if the creator asks for a numeric value, he/she can also bind minimum and maximum values. It is also possible to specify constraints on values in order to automatically validate the syntax of values inserted by the filler, e.g. by selecting *email* the data set will prevent the insertion of syntactically wrong emails.

Besides data types and constraints, the creator can also specify extra information, such as placeholders or tooltips, labels or descriptions, ask for mandatory fields or define a default value, which will help fillers in interpreting more easily which information should be inserted into the data set and in which format.

By correctly and deeply defining the form it is possible to minimize syntactical errors in the data set filling. Obviously, it does not prevent semantic errors. For example, by restricting the data type of a column to date the user will not be able to specify incorrect dates but there is no validation about its correctness.

The *filler* is in charge of filling in the form to populate the data set. The tool will force him/her to insert only syntactical valid inputs and prevent trivial errors which could compromise the overall data set quality. The distinction of *advanced* and *plain* filler is only on the visibility of the whole data set under construction. This distinction is due to security requirements: based on the situation there could be the need to involve a huge number of *filler* users. Since also unreliable people might be involved by accident, there is the need to avoid the suggestion of rows which can deliberately change the overall statistics of the data set. Therefore, we provide the opportunity to give access to the data set in reading mode only to reliable people - by providing them the *advanced* filler role - and preventing the access to others by the *plain* filler role. Therefore, the plain filler can only add rows to the data set without having the possibility to consult the already provided data. The advanced filler has the right to read - not modify - the whole data set under the definition.

To address also the semantic correctness of the data set, data suggested by the filler are not automatically added to the final data set. They are left in a *grey zone* until the validator check them.

The *validator* is the legal manager of the data set. Therefore, he/she has the power to decide which rows should be included into the final version of the data set, but he/she takes the responsibility of all the information which are included and also of those discarded. The validator has to manually inspect proposed data to filter out the wrong ones. Approved data will be moved from the *grey zone* to the actual data set under construction. By the validation step, also semantic errors are reduced. Syntactic and semantic checks assures high-quality OD.

In Fig. 1 the whole workflow is summarized: the creator defines the form starting from an empty or already partially filled data set; the filler proposes new candidate rows by filling in the form; the validator inspects the candidates rows and takes responsibility of the data effectively added to the data set under definition. Users are not forced by SPOD to follow these steps in this particular order. The creator can create the form at any time. The filler can start producing rows also before the form definition. The filler is not locked by the validator verification step. Therefore, users can choose the best operative approach according to their needs. In our *agile* approach, SPOD offers a set of tools (e.g. chat, co-creation rooms, form) which can be incrementally and iteratively exploited by users in any order and to any extent.

In Fig. 2 an example of form is reported. This is the layout of the form on the creator side. When the creator opens the form template, a box is created

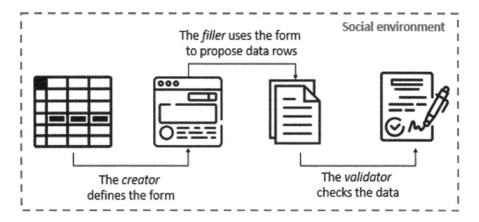

Fig. 1. Workflow of the orchestrated OD co-production process. Roles are reported in italic.

for each column. In this use case, the data set represents a citizen profile where the name, birthplace and birthdate, marital status and children number are reported. The creator decides to model the *name* as a string. By clicking on the plus icon on the right, the section delimited by a dotted line is opened. These options will provide extra information to fillers during the data set populating step. The *Date of birth* is modelled as a date while the *Birthplace* is modelled as a Province. The latter represents an example of auto-filled select: the creator has to simply decide the type of the column as Province, while the filler will have access to all the available provinces. The *Marital status* column is a select filled by the creator. By choosing this type, the creator has to specify which are the valid options. The *Children number* is modelled as a number and it is possible to specify the minimum and maximum value.

The described process has been included into SPOD where citizens, PAs, associations, and every kind of stakeholder can create or join online communities of interests, discussing around OD and their visualizations [8,12]. SPOD supports Data-Driven Discussions where citizens are engaged in participating in discussions of interest by using OD. It enables collaboration among users as a key aspect to ensure the creation of value form OD. Despite classical features of a social network - such as the wall with all the news, the possibility to share content, comment posts, chat - our platform is fully interoperable with existing OD portals. It implies that users can (i) directly access data sets available on the associated open data portal; (ii) create reusable visualizations; (iii) share, use and reuse data sets and visualizations within the discussions in a seamless way. About privacy concern, our platform allows every public administration or organization to have its own instances for local communities. In this way, stakeholders and partners can take advantage in terms of effectiveness since a dedicated platform avoid misleading mixing of topics and helps in focusing on specific discussions. The platform provides the possibility to create visualization

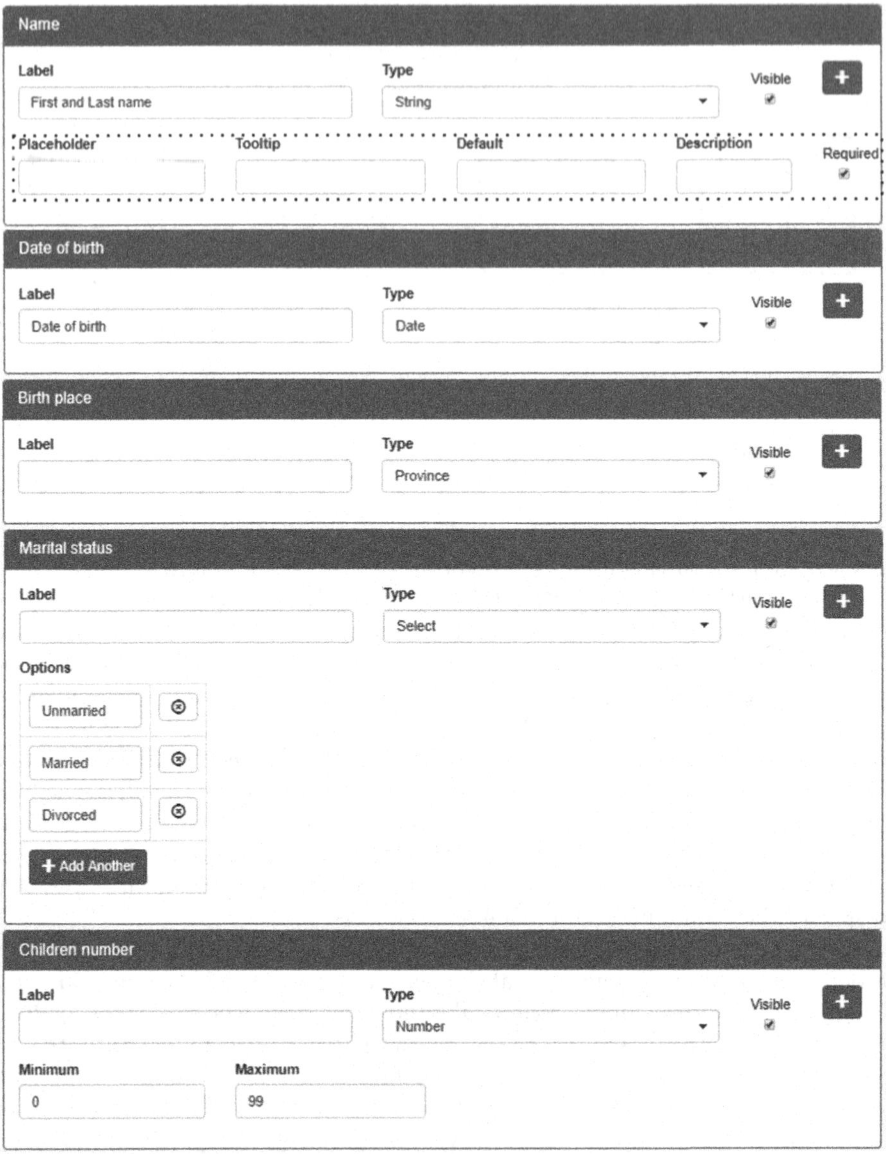

Fig. 2. Example of a form: for each column of the data set a box is provided. For each column, it is possible to specify the type, extra constraints, if necessary, and all the information which will guide the filler in the data set population step.

upon OD data sets; share and comment data sets and visualizations; conduct data-driven discuss in *agora*; create rooms of co-creation in order to create OD and share knowledge. Each participant can create a co-creation room to which other users can join. In these rooms, PAs and citizens - and different stakeholders in general - can work together to create shared data sets. The focus is on 3-star data set - according to the 5-star rating defined by Tim Berners Lee [6]. Upon a data set, users who play the role of *creator* can define the form as described before. Once confirmed the form, all the users who play the role of *filler* will be guided in filling in data set by the advised template. The form prevents the insertion of syntactical wrong data. Therefore, it represents a proactive quality assurance approach. Moreover, during the data set definition, every user can ask for a reactive *quality check* [16]. It is a set of tools to guarantee quality and avoid privacy issues. For each column, the quality check module infers the column data type by its actual content. Not only basic data types - such as string, date, number - are inferred but also types which try to catch the semantic value of the column content - such as region, province, municipality, name, surname, phone, email, SSN, IBAN and so on. Besides the type inference, the quality check module identifies typos and computes quality statistics considering the uniformity of column content and the completeness of values. About privacy issues, the same module detects if personal information is leaked into descriptive values and if the structure of the data set exposes a combination of information which could allow the unique identification of an individual. SPOD is online available on free at https://github.com/routetopa/spod. It can also be accessed by a mobile application. The latter can be particularly useful for *plain fillers* which can populate a data set in a practical and comfortable way simply accessing by their mobile and proposing new candidate rows. From a technological point of view, SPOD is released with an open source license. All the source code, as well as documentation, is published on GitHub at https://github.com/routetopa/spod.

5   Conclusions

Splitting the OD co-creation process into several different roles helps in detecting responsibilities for each role. According to personal skills, roles can be distributed. By the synergy of heterogeneous skills and profiles, high-quality data can be provided. In this paper, we have discussed how SPOD guides *creators* in defining a form to attach a schema (data types and rules) to data sets under the definition. This form prevents syntactic errors. Those semantic still need to be checked manually by the *validator*. The considered roles and the proposed approach are the results of cooperation with our Regional Administration MPA. We have now a working prototype that is actually being tested. We are, then, planning an evaluation phase on the field to verify if our solution completely satisfies the needs of the motivating use case, first with the previously contacted Municipalities (around 100) and then with the whole set of Municipalities in Campania. One of the future steps is to combine the proactive quality guide of the form with the reactive type inference module to help creators in defining a more complete data set profile in case of partially populated data set. The workflow will be that (1) the Creator defines a form starting from an already populated data set, (2) the *type inference* process is applied to infer the data types of each column, (3) the form is populated by the inferred data types, (4) the

Creator can either adopt them or relax the suggested rules and constraints, (5) finally, the form is published and can be used by the Filler.

References

1. General data protection regulation (GDPR) (2016). https://eur-lex.europa.eu/eli/reg/2016/679/oj
2. Open data goldbook for data manager and data holders (2016). European Data Portal. https://www.europeandataportal.eu/sites/default/files/goldbook.pdf. Accessed 1 Jan 2019
3. Alur, N., Joseph, R., Mehta, H., Nielsen, J.T., Vasconcelos, D.: IBM WebSphere information analyzer and data quality assessment (2007). http://www.redbooks.ibm.com/redbooks/pdfs/sg247508.pdf
4. Ballou, D.P., Pazer, H.L.: Modeling data and process quality in multi-input, multi-output information systems. Manag. Sci. **31**(2), 150–162 (1985)
5. Beck, K., et al.: Agile manifesto (2001). https://agilemanifesto.org
6. Berners-Lee, T.: Linked data - design issues (2006). http://www.w3.org/DesignIssues/LinkedData.html. Accessed 03 May 2018
7. Chan, C.M.L.: From open data to open innovation strategies: Creating e-services using open government data. In: 46th Hawaii International Conference on System Sciences, pp. 1890–1899 (2013)
8. Cordasco, G., et al.: Engaging citizens with a social platform for open data. In: Proceedings of the 18th Annual International Conference on Digital Government Research, pp. 242–249 (2017)
9. Big Data, I., Analytics Hub: infographics and animations: the four V's of big data (2017). https://www.ibmbigdatahub.com/infographic/four-vs-big-data
10. Dhanaraj, C., Parkhe, A.: Orchestrating innovation networks. Acad. Manag. Rev. **31**(3), 659–669 (2006)
11. Döhmen, T., Mühleisen, H., Boncz, P.: Multi-hypothesis CSV parsing. In: Proceedings of the 29th International Conference on Scientific and Statistical Database Management, p. 16. ACM (2017)
12. Donato, R.D., et al.: DatalEt-Ecosystem Provider (DEEP): scalable architecture for reusable, portable and user-friendly visualizations of open data. In: 2017 Conference for E-Democracy and Open Government, pp. 92–101 (2017)
13. Donato, R.D., et al.: Agile production of high quality open data. In: Proceedings of the 19th Annual International Conference on Digital Government Research, pp. 84:1–84:10 (2018)
14. European Commission: Open data portal (2017). https://www.europeandataportal.eu/data/it/dataset
15. European Data Portal: Protecting data and opening data (2019). https://www.europeandataportal.eu/en/highlights/protecting-data-and-opening-data
16. Ferretti, G., Malandrino, D., Pellegrino, M.A., Pirozzi, D., Renzi, G., Scarano, V.: A non-prescriptive environment to scaffold high quality and privacy-aware production of open data with AI. In: 20th Annual International Conference on Digital Government Research (2019)
17. Gausdal, A.H., Nilsen, E.R.: Orchestrating innovative SME networks. The case of "healthinnovation". J. Knowl. Econ. **2**(4), 586–600 (2011)
18. Gerster, D., Dremel, C., Brenner, W., Kelker, P.: How enterprises adopt agile structures: a multiple-case study. In: HICSS 2019 Proceedings (2019)

19. Hurmelinna-Laukkanen, P., Nätti, S.: Orchestrator types, roles and capabilities - a framework for innovation networks. Ind. Mark. Manag. **74**, 65–78 (2018)
20. Janssen, M., Charalabidis, Y., Zuiderwijk, A.: Benefits, adoption barriers and myths of open data and open government. Inf. Syst. Manag. **29**(4), 258–268 (2012)
21. Klimas, P., Czakon, W.: Innovative Networks in Knowledge-Intensive Industries - How to Make Them Work? An Empirical Investigation into the Polish Aviation Valley, pp. 133–157 (2014)
22. Madi, T., Dahalin, Z., Baharom, F.: Content analysis on agile values: a perception from software practitioners. In: Malaysian Conference in Software Engineering, pp. 423–428 (2011)
23. Martin, S., Foulonneau, M., Turki, S., Ihadjadene, M.: Open data: barriers, risks and opportunities. In: Proceedings of the European Conference on E-Government, vol. 58, pp. 301–309 (2013)
24. Maydanchik, A.: Data Quality Assessment. Technics Publications, LLC, Bradley Beach (2007)
25. McBride, K., Aavik, G., Toots, M., Kalvet, T., Krimmer, R.: How does open government data driven co-creation occur? six factors and a 'perfect storm'; insights from Chicago's food inspection forecasting model. Gov. Inf. Q. **36**(1), 88–97 (2019)
26. Mergel, I.: Agile innovation management in government: a research agenda. Gov. Inf. Q. **33**, 516–523 (2016)
27. Nambisan, S., Mohanbir, S.: Orchestration processes in network-centric innovation: evidence from the field. Acad. Manag. Perspect. **25**(3), 40–57 (2011)
28. Naumann, F.: Data profiling revisited. ACM SIGMOD Rec. **42**(4), 40–49 (2014)
29. OECD: Rebooting public service delivery - how can open government data help drive innovation? (2016)
30. Pikkarainen, M., Ervasti, M., Hurmelinna-Laukkanen, P., Nätti, S.: Orchestration roles to facilitate networked innovation in a healthcare ecosystem. Technol. Innov. Manag. Rev. **7**, 30–43 (2017)
31. Roijakkers, N., Leten, B., Vanhaverbeke, W., Clerix, A., Van Helleputte, J.: Orchestrating innovation ecosystems IMEC. In: Proceedings of the 35th DRUID Conference (2013)
32. Ruijer, E., Grimmelikhuijsen, S., Meijer, A.: Open data for democracy: developing a theoretical framework for open data use. Gov. Inf. Q. **34**(1), 45–52 (2017)
33. The Open Knowledge Foundation Ltd.: Library messytables link (2013). https://messytables.readthedocs.io/en/latest
34. Toots, M., McBride, K., Kalvet, T., Krimmer, R.: Open data as enabler of public service co-creation: exploring the drivers and barriers, pp. 102–112 (2017)
35. Toots, M., et al.: A framework for data-driven public service co-production. In: Electronic Government, pp. 264–275 (2017)
36. Zuiderwijk, A., Janssen, M.: The negative effects of open government data - investigating the dark side of open data. In: 15th Annual International Conference on Digital Government Research, pp. 147–152 (2014)

Towards Interoperable Open Statistical Data

Evangelos Kalampokis$^{(\boxtimes)}$ ⓘ, Areti Karamanou ⓘ,
and Konstantinos Tarabanis ⓘ

University of Macedonia, Thessaloniki, Greece
{ekal,akarm,kat}@uom.edu.gr

Abstract. An important part of Open Data is of statistical nature and describes economic and social indicators monitoring population size, inflation, trade, and employment. Combining and analysing Open Data from multiple datasets and sources enable the performance of advanced data analytics scenarios that could result in valuable services and data products. However, it is still difficult to discover and combine open statistical data that reside in different data portals. Although Linked Open Statistical Data (LOSD) provide standards and approaches to facilitate combining statistics on the Web, various interoperability challenges still exist. In this paper, we define interoperability conflicts that hamper combining and analysing LOSD from different portals. Towards this end, we start from a thorough literature review on databases and data warehouses interoperability conflicts. Based on this review, we define interoperability conflicts that may appear in LOSD. We defined two types of schema-level conflicts namely, naming conflicts and structural conflicts. Naming conflicts include homonyms and synonyms and result from the different URIs used in the data cubes. Structural conflicts result from different practices of modelling the structure of data cubes.

Keywords: Open Data · Linked statistical data · Interoperability

1 Introduction

During the last years, an increasing number of governments, public authorities, and companies have opened up their data providing a vast amount of Open Data through numerous portals [18]. Today, more than 2600 Open Data portals operate around the globe providing access to Open Data[1]. Open Data promise to offer many benefits to the society including transparency, accountability and economic growth by stimulating the creation of added value data-driven services and products [16].

---

[1] https://www.opendatasoft.com/a-comprehensive-list-of-all-open-data-portals-around-the-world/.

© IFIP International Federation for Information Processing 2019
Published by Springer Nature Switzerland AG 2019
I. Lindgren et al. (Eds.): EGOV 2019, LNCS 11685, pp. 180–191, 2019.
https://doi.org/10.1007/978-3-030-27325-5_14

An important part of Open Data is of statistical nature and describe economic and social indicators monitoring the population size, inflation, trade, and employment [10]. Statistical data are often described in a multidimensional manner. This means that a measure is described based on a number of dimensions, e.g., unemployment rate (measure) for different countries and years (dimensions) [15]. This type of data can be conceptualized as a cube, where the location of a cell is specified by the values of the dimensions, while the value of a cell specifies the measure. We onwards refer to these data as "data cubes" or just "cubes".

Integrating data from different sources will unleash the full potential of Open Data [26,27,33,35]. This will enable, for example, performing combined analytics on top of data published by different national statistics offices [17]. Linked data has been introduced as a promising paradigm towards this direction, since it facilitates data integration on the Web. In data cubes, linked data has the potential to realize the vision of performing data analytics on top of previously isolated cubes across the Web [19]. An important step towards this direction is the RDF data cube (QB) vocabulary [11], which enables modelling Linked Open Statistical Data (LOSD) in a standardised manner.

Today, many Open Data portals use standard vocabularies, such as QB, to publish LOSD. These include the portals of the Scottish Government, the UK Department for Communities and Local Government (DCLG), the Italian National Institute of Statistics (ISTAT), the Flemish Government, and the Irish Central Statistics Office. However, the flexibility of these vocabularies allows portals to use different practices when applying a vocabulary. As a result, the produced data become non-interoperable and thus isolated in data portals.

The issue of data interoperability is not new but has been raised in the past in the context of traditional databases and data warehouses. In particular, scientific literature (e.g., [8,20,28]) has already investigated and defined the different types of *interoperability conflicts* that result from creating different relational models or from having inconsistent data.

The aim of this paper is to define interoperability conflicts that hamper combining and analysing LOSD from different data portals. To this end, we first identify interoperability conflicts of databases and data warehouses using a thorough literature review and, subsequently, map those conflicts to LOSD interoperability conflicts.

The rest of the paper is organized as follows: Sect. 2 presents the approach of this research, Sect. 3 presents the background knowledge required to understand this research, Sect. 4 provides a review of the interoperability conflicts of traditional databases and data warehouses, while Sect. 5 presents the interoperability conflicts of LOSD. Finally, Sect. 6 summarizes the results and identifies open research issues.

2   Research Approach

The research approach of this paper includes the following steps:

- Step 1: Understand interoperability conflicts in databases and data warehouses. Towards this end, we conduct a systematic literature review on interoperability conflicts of database and data warehouses based on the state-of-the-art analysis method proposed by Webster and Watson [37]. According to this method, we initially perform a systematic search to accumulate a set of relevant scientific papers. Then, we perform a concept-centric analysis on the papers to extract a list of interoperability conflicts and their definitions.
- Step 2: Define LOSD interoperability conflicts based on the results of Step 1.

3   Background

This section briefly presents the background knowledge required to understand the contents of this paper. In particular, we describe (1) the Data Cube model, that is used to describe multidimensional data, (2) the main concepts of Linked Statistical Data, and (3) an overview of the official data portals that host LOSD.

3.1   The Data Cube Model

The data cube model was introduced to cover the needs of the Online Analytical Processing (OLAP) and data warehouse systems. A data cube has been defined in various ways. However, according to all definitions a data cube comprises: [3,6,12,35] (1) measures, which represent numerical values (e.g., unemployment), and (2) dimensions, which provide contextual information for the measures (e.g., geospatial or temporal dimension). In addition, each dimension has a set of distinct values e.g., a temporal dimension may have values like 2000, 2001 etc. Finally, the dimensions may be hierarchically organized into levels representing different granularities. For instance, the geospatial dimension may have levels like country, region, city etc.

An example of a data cube has one measure (i.e. unemployment) and three dimensions (i.e. year, countries, age group). The distinct values of the dimension "year" are 1999, 2000, and 2001, of the dimension "countries" are GR, EN, and FR, and of dimension age group are 00–24, 25–49, and 50+. All the dimensions have one hierarchical level, however there could be more e.g., the geospatial dimension may have both countries and regions.

3.2   Linked Statistical Data

Linked data are based on the Semantic Web philosophy and technologies and are mainly about publishing structured data in RDF using URIs rather than focusing on the ontological level or inferencing.

The QB vocabulary [11] is a *W3C* standard for publishing statistical data on the Web using the linked data principles. The core class of the vocabulary is the *qb:DataSet* that represents a data cube, which comprises a set of dimensions (*qb:DimensionProperty*), measures (*qb:MeasureProperty*), and attributes (*qb:AttributeProperty*). Attributes are used to represent structural metadata such as the unit of measurement. Finally a data cube has multiple *qb:Observation* that describe the cells of the data cube.

It is a common practice to re-use predefined code lists to populate the dimension values. For example, the values of a geospatial dimension can be populated by a code list defining the geographical or administrative divisions of a country. The code lists can be specified using either the QB vocabulary or the W3C standard Simple Knowledge Organization System (SKOS) [24] vocabulary. The values of the code list may also include hierarchical relations which can be expressed using the SKOS vocabulary (e.g., using the *skos:narrower* property), the QB vocabulary (e.g., using the *qb:parentChildProperty*) or the XKOS[2] vocabulary (e.g., using the *xkos:isPartOf* property).

Finally, the UK Government Linked Data Working Group[3] has developed a set of common concepts (e.g., dimensions, measures, attributes, and code lists) that can be reused. The definitions of these concepts are based on the SDMX guidelines[4]. For example, dimensions like *sdmx:timePeriod*, *sdmx:refArea*, and *sdmx:sex*, and measures like *sdmx:obsValue* have been proposed. Although these resources are not part of the QB vocabulary, they are currently widely used.

3.3 Portals with Linked Statistical Data

Today, a large volume of Linked Statistical Data is provided on the Web through dedicated data portals. For example, the Scottish Government provides official data on "Neighborhood Statistics" as Linked Statistical Data. In particular, they provide access to 238 data cubes categorized to 18 themes such as housing and transport. In addition, the UK's Department for Communities and Local Government (DCLG) provides statistical data that describe various indicators including local government finance and housing and homelessness. In particular, they provide access to 167 data cubes categorized to 14 themes (e.g., homelessness, societal well-being). The environmental department of the Flemish government also provides nine data cubes that describe environmental data as Linked Statistical Data, while the portal site of the Official Statistics in Japan (e-Stat) provides 78 data cubes from seven sources of statistics such as a population census, an economic census, and a labor force survey [1]. Finally, the Italian National Institute of Statistics (ISTAT) and the Irish Central Statistics Office have published as Linked Statistical Data the Italian Census 2011 (8 cubes) and the Irish Census 2011 (682 cubes) respectively.

A large volume of Linked Statistical Data has also been published by third parties activities (unofficial). For example, a linked data transformation of Eurostat's data[5], which was created in the course of a research project, includes more

---

[2] http://rdf-vocabulary.ddialliance.org/xkos.

[3] https://github.com/UKGovLD/publishing-statistical-data.

[4] https://sdmx.org/.

[5] http://eurostat.linked-statistics.org/.

than 5,000 cubes. Moreover, few statistical datasets from the European Central Bank, World Bank, UNESCO and other international organizations have been also transformed using the QB vocabulary in a third party activity [7].

4 A Systematic Literature Review on Interoperability Conflicts of Databases and Data-Warehouses

Based on the method described in Sect. 2 and after limiting out irrelevant papers, we resulted in 18 papers. We analysed these papers following a concept-centric approach i.e., we synthesized the literature by grouping and studying the main identified interoperability conflicts. After excluding conflicts that are not applicable to Linked Statistical Data, we resulted in two types of conflicts namely schema conflicts and data conflicts [4,20,28]. Schema conflicts are further classified into naming and structural conflicts. Data conflicts are further classified into scaling, precision, representation, and data value conflicts. Table 1 presents the scientific papers that are related to each type of conflict.

Table 1. Concept-centric analysis of the literature

	Schema conflicts			Data conflicts			
	Naming	Structural		Scaling	Precision	Representation	Data value
		Schematic discrep.	Isomorph.				
Tseng [35]	✓	-	-	✓	-	-	✓
Kim [20]	✓	✓	✓	✓	✓	✓	✓
Berger [4]	✓	✓	✓	✓	✓	-	✓
Ram [28]	✓	-	✓	✓	✓	✓	✓
Reddy [29]	✓	✓	-	✓	✓	-	-
Batini [2]	✓	✓	-	-	-	-	-
Sheth [31]	✓	✓	✓	✓	✓	✓	✓
Channah [8]	✓	-	-	-	✓	-	-
Doan [14]	✓	✓	-	-	-	-	✓
Bruckner [5]	✓	-	-	-	-	-	-
Spaccapietra [32]	✓	✓	-	✓	-	-	-
Lee [21]	-	✓	✓	✓	✓	✓	-
Lee [22]	✓	✓	✓	✓	✓	✓	-
Sboui [30]	✓	-	-	✓	-	-	-
Mangisengi [23]	✓	-	-	-	-	-	-
Diamantini [13]	✓	-	✓	✓	-	-	✓
Neumayr [25]	-	-	-	✓	-	-	-
Torlone [34]	✓	-	-	✓	-	-	✓

Based on the Entity Relationship (ER) model [9], entities, relations and attributes are the main *components* that can be used to model data. Schema-level conflicts result from using the components of data in different ways. Data-level conflicts result from incompatible or inconsistent data.

In the rest of the section we describe the above type of conflicts. To this end, we need to define the similarity relationship between two terms. In particular, two terms are "semantically similar" if they refer to the same concept, while they are "semantically unrelated" if they refer to different concepts. In order to support the description of the conflicts, we use the example presented in Fig. 1. The example presents two datasets (both schema and data) that describe a company's sales. The schema of dataset 1 contains three entities: "product", "sales" and "date", while the schema of dataset 2 contains two entities: "product" and "sales". Accordingly, dataset 1 includes three tables, while dataset 2 includes two tables.

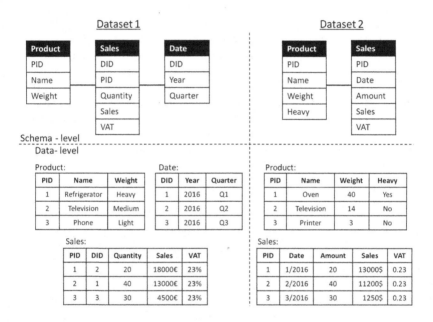

Fig. 1. Example of two database schema and data

4.1   Schema-Level Conflicts

Schema-level conflicts are classified into naming and structural conflicts.

Naming conflicts. Various names are used for the components of a dataset's schema [29] resulting in a proliferation of names as well as possible conflicts among them. There are two types of schema-level conflicts [2,8,14,20,29,31]:

- **Homonyms.** This type of conflict results from two semantically unrelated components that have the same name. In our example, a homonym conflict results from the fact that "Weight" of entity "Product" refers to *total weight* in dataset 1 and in *net weight* in dataset 2.

– **Synonyms.** This type of conflict results from two semantically similar components that have different names. For example the attribute "Quantity" of entity "Sales" in dataset 1 and the attribute "Amount" of the same entity in dataset 2 have different names although they refer to the same term. Multiple languages can also cause synonym problems, e.g., *week* (English) and *woche* (German) refer to the same concept using different language [5].

Structural conflicts. This type of conflict occurs when two semantically similar components use different modeling approaches [2]. In particular, there are two types of structural conflicts [20–22, 29, 31, 32]:

– **Schematic discrepancies.** This type of conflict occurs when the logical structure of a set of attributes and their values belonging to an entity class in one schema are organized to form a different structure in another schema [28, 31]. For example, in dataset 1, "date" is an entity while in dataset 2 an attribute of the "Sales" entity. A specific case of this conflict is defined in [31], where the value of an attribute in one case corresponds to an attribute in another case. For example, in dataset 1, the attribute "weight" of the entity "Product" has the value "heavy" in the first record of the table that corresponds to an attribute of the second dataset's "Product" entity.
– **Schema Isomorphism.** This type of conflict occurs when two semantically similar entities have different number of attributes [20, 21, 28, 31], e.g., in dataset 2 the "Product" entity has one extra attribute (i.e. "Heavy") related to the same entity at dataset 1.

4.2   Data-Level Conflicts

Data-level conflicts are classified into data scaling, data precision, data representation, and data value conflicts.

Data scaling conflicts. They result from data that are stored in semantically similar attributes and use different units of measure [20, 22, 29–31]. For instance, "sales" in dataset 1 are measured in euros and in dataset 2 in dollars.

Data precision conflicts. They result from data stored in semantically similar attributes and use different precisions [20, 21, 29, 31]. For example, the "weight" attribute of the Product entity (dataset 1) includes values like "heavy", "medium", and "light" while in dataset 2 the "weight" of the Product is measured in kilograms. Moreover, different levels of accuracy may be used e.g., weight can be measured up in milligrams or in grams.

Data representation conflicts. In some cases, although data stored in semantically similar attributes have the same unit of measure and precision, they have different formats [20–22, 28, 31] resulting in data representation conflicts. For example, attribute "VAT" of Sales (dataset 1) is a percentage (e.g., 23%) while in dataset 2 it is a decimal value (e.g., 0.23). Although different formats are used, both values are equivalent. Another example could be the date attributes that may use different formats, e.g., "dd/mm/yy" vs "mm/dd/yyyy".

Data value conflicts. They result from data have measurements with conflicting values [14,28,31,34,35]. For example, the Television sales for Q1 2016 in dataset 1 are 13000€ while in dataset 2 $11200 (the values are conflicting even after converting euros to dollars). Such conflicts occur due to wrong or obsolete data or when different statistical methods are employed [20].

5   Interoperability Conflicts of Linked Open Statistical Data

In this section we define the conflicts of the literature of traditional databases and data warehouses in the context of LOSD. We define only schema-level conflicts as data-level conflicts depend on the specific values of the data cubes.

5.1   Naming Conflicts

One of the principles of linked data is to name things using URIs. In the case of LOSD, naming conflicts may result from the URIs used for the dimensions, measures, measure units, dimension levels, and dimension values of the data cubes. A common practice in linked data is to reuse standardized vocabularies and create new vocabularies only when required [36]. Naming conflicts mainly occur because some linked data portals reuse standardized vocabularies, while other create their own vocabularies. For example, the SDMX vocabulary is commonly used by most linked data portals but not by all of them. The two types of naming conflicts in LOSD are *Homonyms* and *Synonyms*.

Homonym conflicts result from using the same URI to represent semantically unrelated elements (e.g., the measure property) of data cubes. In particular, LOSD publishers may use the same URI for semantically different measure properties. For example, *sdmx-measure:obsValue* is often used to represent semantically unrelated measures (e.g., unemployment, poverty etc.).

Synonym conflicts result from using different URIs for semantically similar elements. In particular, synonym conflicts in LOSD result from:

- Using different URIs for semantically similar measure properties. For example, some data portals define a new measure property to measure unemployment (e.g., *test:unemployment*), which is *rdfs:subPropertyOf sdmx:obsValue*. Other portals, however, define a new measure property that is not related to the *sdmx:obsValue*.
- Using different URIs for semantically similar dimension properties. For example, a common practice for the common dimensions (e.g., temporal, geospatial, gender, and age) is to re-use the dimension defined by SDMX (e.g., *sdmx:refArea* for the geospatial dimension). However, other practices may define a new dimension property (e.g., *eg:geo*) instead of re-using SDMX.
- Using different URIs for semantically similar hierarchical data (i.e., relations between data, and levels of hierarchies). For example, some data portals may use the *dcterms:isPartOf* and *dcterms:hasPart* to represent hierarchical relations while others may define new URIs.

- Using different URIs for the code lists (i.e, the code list for the unit of measure, the temporal dimension, and of the gender dimension). For example, two alternative practice could be to use the QUDT vocabulary or the DBpedia vocabulary for the unit of the measure.

5.2 Structural Conflicts

Structural conflicts are directly related to the structure of the data cubes. The two types of structural conflicts in LOSD include *Schema isomorphism* and *Schematic discrepancies*.

Schema isomorphism conflicts result from defining different number of components (i.e. dimension, measure, attribute) in semantically similar data cubes. In particular, schema isomorphism conflicts result from:

- Using different practices to model the measure and its parameters in semantically similar data cubes. For example, some data portals may define just the measure of the data cube, while others may define both the measure and the measure type (*qb:measureType*).
- Defining different number of measures in semantically similar data cubes. For example, different practices could be to define a single or multiple measures per data cube.
- Using different practices to model the unit of measure and its parameters in semantically similar data cubes. For example, some data portals may define only the unit of the measure while other may define also the unit multiplier, which is used to indicate the magnitude in the units of measurements (e.g., hundreds, thousands, tens of thousands etc.).
- Defining different number of units per measure in semantically similar data cubes. For example, data portals may publish several data cubes with a single or one data cube with multiple units per measure.
- Using different practices to define hierarchical levels. For example, some data portals may define one data cube to measure all hierarchical levels, while others may define one cube per hierarchical level.

Schematic discrepancies conflicts result from using different logical constructs to represent the same set of data cube components (e.g., when different practices are used to define more than one measure in a data cube). In particular, schematic discrepancies result from:

- Modelling semantically similar data cubes with multiple measures in different ways. For example, one practice is to define multiple *qb:MeasureProperty* components in the *qb:DataStructureDefinition* of the data cube (one for each measure), an instance of a single measure component in each observation, and an extra *qb:measureType* dimension that denotes the measure used in the observation. An alternative practice is to define multiple *qb:MeasureProperty* components in the *qb:DataStructureDefinition* of the data cube and also an instance of each defined measure component in each observation.

- Defining the unit of the measure in different levels of semantically similar data cubes. For example, a data portal practice defines the unit of measure in the *qb:Observation* level, while another practice defines the unit of measure in the *qb:MeasureProperty* level.
- Defining the single value dimensions (i.e., dimensions with the same value) of semantically similar data cubes in a different way. For example, a practice could be to define the single value dimension in the *qb:Dataset* level, and an alternative to define the dimension in the *qb:Slice* level.
- Defining aggregated values in a different way. For example, a practice could be to use a hierarchy and define total values on the top of the hierarchy, while another practice to define a unique total URI that could be used in every case (e.g., *sdmx:total*).
- Defining the values of the temporal dimension of semantically similar data cubes in a different way. For example, some data portals define the value of the temporal dimension along with its data type, i.e., *"2011"^^xsd:date* while others define only the value of the temporal dimension (e.g., 2011).
- Using different ways to associate dimensions with potential values. For example, some data portals use the *qb:codeList* property, while others define the *rdfs:range* of the *qb:DimensionProperty* as a *skos:Concept*.

6   Conclusion and Future Work

Interoperability among data cubes is crucial to unleash the full potential of linked statistical data. For example, it will enable performing combined analytics and visualizations on data published by different national statistics offices and other organisations. Currently, all official portals that publish linked statistical data are using the QB vocabulary, however they adopt different practices thus hampering the interoperability among their data.

In this paper we define the interoperability conflicts that hamper combining and analysing LOSD from different data portals. Our study was based on a thorough literature review on databases and data warehouses interoperability conflicts. We defined two types of schema-level conflicts namely, naming conflicts and structural conflicts. Naming conflicts include homonyms and synonyms and are mostly result from the URIs that are used in the data cubes. Structural conflicts result from different practices of modelling the structure of data cubes.

This work used a top-down approach to identify interoperability conflicts of LOSD. In the future, we plan to follow a bottom-up approach and study data cubes of LOSD data portals in order to understand the different practices they use to publish LOSD and, hence, result in interpretability conflicts.

Acknowledgments. This research is co-financed by Greece and the European Union (European Social Fund- ESF) through the Operational Program "Human Resources Development, Education and Lifelong Learning 2014–2020" in the context of the project "Integrating open statistical data using semantic technologies" (MIS 5007306).

References

1. Asano, Y., Takeyoshi, Y., Matsuda, J., Nishimura, S.: Publication of statistical linked open data in Japan. In: Proceedings of the 4th International Workshop on Semantic Statistics Co-Located with 15th International Semantic Web Conference (ISWC 2016). CEUR Workshop Proceedings (2016)
2. Batini, C., Lenzerini, M., Navathe, S.B.: A comparative analysis of methodologies for database schema integration. ACM Comput. Surv. **18**(4), 323–364 (1986)
3. Berger, S., Schrefl, M.: From federated databases to a federated data warehouse system. In: Proceedings of the 41st Annual Hawaii International Conference on System Sciences, pp. 394–394. IEEE (2008)
4. Berger, S., Schrefl, M.: FedDW global schema architect: UML-based design tool for the integration of data mart schemas. In: Song, I.Y., Golfarelli, M. (eds.) DOLAP, Maui, Hawaii, USA, pp. 33–40. ACM, November 2012
5. Bruckner, R.M., Ling, T.W., Mangisengi, O., et al.: A framework for a multidimensional OLAP model using topic maps. In: Proceedings of the 2nd International Conference on Web Information Systems Engineering 2001, vol. 2, pp. 109–118. IEEE (2001)
6. Cabibbo, L., Torlone, R.: A logical approach to multidimensional databases. In: Schek, H.-J., Alonso, G., Saltor, F., Ramos, I. (eds.) EDBT 1998. LNCS, vol. 1377, pp. 183–197. Springer, Heidelberg (1998). https://doi.org/10.1007/BFb0100985
7. Capadisli, S., Auer, S., Ngonga Ngomo, A.C.: Linked SDMX data. Semant. Web **6**(2), 105–112 (2015)
8. Channah, N., Aris, O.: A classification of semantic conflicts in heterogeneous database systems. J. Organ. Comput. **5**(2), 167–193 (1995)
9. Chen, P.P.S.: The entity-relationship model—toward a unified view of data. ACM Trans. Database Syst. (TODS) **1**(1), 9–36 (1976)
10. Cyganiak, R., Hausenblas, M., McCuirc, E.: Official statistics and the practice of data fidelity, pp. 135–151 (2011). https://doi.org/10.1007/978-1-4614-1767-5_7
11. Cyganiak, R., Reynolds, D.: The RDF data cube vocabulary: W3C recommendation, January 2014
12. Datta, A., Thomas, H.: The cube data model: a conceptual model and algebra for on-line analytical processing in data warehouses. Decis. Support. Syst. **27**(3), 289–301 (1999)
13. Diamantini, C., Potena, D., Storti, E.: Data mart reconciliation in virtual innovation factories. In: Iliadis, L., Papazoglou, M., Pohl, K. (eds.) CAiSE 2014. LNBIP, vol. 178, pp. 274–285. Springer, Cham (2014). https://doi.org/10.1007/978-3-319-07869-4_26
14. Doan, A., Halevy, A.Y.: Semantic integration research in the database community: a brief survey. AI Mag. **26**(1), 83–94 (2005)
15. Gnanadesikan, R.: Methods for Statistical data Analysis of Multivariate Observations, vol. 321. Wiley, Hoboken (2011)
16. Janssen, M., Charalabidis, Y., Zuiderwijk, A.: Benefits, adoption barriers and myths of open data and open government. Inf. Syst. Manag. **29**(4), 258–268 (2012). https://doi.org/10.1080/10580530.2012.716740
17. Kalampokis, E., Tambouris, E., Tarabanis, K.: Linked open cube analytics systems: potential and challenges. IEEE Intell. Syst. **31**(5), 89–92 (2016)
18. Kalampokis, E., Tambouris, E., Tarabanis, K.: A classification scheme for open government data: towards linking decentralised data. Int. J. Web Eng. Technol. **6**(3), 266–285 (2011)

19. Kalampokis, E., Tambouris, E., Tarabanis, K.: Linked open government data analytics. In: Wimmer, M.A., Janssen, M., Scholl, H.J. (eds.) EGOV 2013. LNCS, vol. 8074, pp. 99–110. Springer, Heidelberg (2013). https://doi.org/10.1007/978-3-642-40358-3_9
20. Kim, W., Seo, J.: Classifying schematic and data heterogeneity in multidatabase systems. Computer **24**(12), 12–18 (1991). https://doi.org/10.1109/2.116884
21. Lee, C., Chen, C.J., Lu, H.: An aspect of query optimization in multidatabase systems. SIGMOD Rec. **24**(3), 28–33 (1995). https://doi.org/10.1145/211990.212011
22. Lee, K.H., Kim, M.H., Lee, K.C., Kim, B.S., Lee, M.Y.: Conflict classification and resolution in heterogeneous information integration based on XML schema. In: Proceedings. 2002 IEEE Region 10 Conference on Computers, Communications, Control and Power Engineering, TENCON 2002, vol. 1, pp. 93–96. IEEE (2002)
23. Mangisengi, O., Huber, J., Hawel, C., Essmayr, W.: A framework for supporting interoperability of data warehouse islands using XML. Data Warehous. Knowl. Discov. **2114**, 328–338 (2001). https://doi.org/10.1007/3-540-44801-2_32
24. Miles, A., Bechhofer, S.: SKOS simple knowledge organization system reference: W3C recommendation, August 2009
25. Neumayr, B., Schrefl, M., Thalheim, B.: Hetero-homogeneous hierarchies in data warehouses. In: Song, I.Y., Golfarelli, M. (eds.) Proceedings 7th Asia-Pacific Conference on Conceptual Modelling, Brisbane, Australia, January 2010
26. Pedersen, T., Pedersen, D., Riis, K.: On-demand multidimensional data integration: toward a semantic foundation for cloud intelligence. J. Supercomput. **65**(1), 217–257 (2013). https://doi.org/10.1007/s11227-011-0712-3
27. Perez, J., Berlanga, R., Aramburu, M., Pedersen, T.: Integrating data warehouses with web data: a survey. IEEE Trans. Knowl. Data Eng. **20**(7), 940–955 (2008). https://doi.org/10.1109/TKDE.2007.190746
28. Ram, S., Park, J.: Semantic conflict resolution ontology (SCROL): an ontology for detecting and resolving data and schema-level semantic conflicts. IEEE Trans. Knowl. Data Eng. **16**(2), 189–202 (2004)
29. Reddy, M., Prasad, B.E., Reddy, P., Gupta, A.: A methodology for integration of heterogeneous databases. IEEE Trans. Knowl. Data Eng. **6**(6), 920–933 (1994)
30. Sboui, T., Bédard, Y., Brodeur, J., Badard, T.: A conceptual framework to support semantic interoperability of geospatial datacubes. In: Hainaut, J.L., et al. (eds.) ER 2007. LNCS, vol. 4802, pp. 378–387. Springer, Heidelberg (2007). https://doi.org/10.1007/978-3-540-76292-8_44
31. Sheth, A.P., Kashyap, V.: So far (schematically) yet so near (semantically). In: Proceedings of the IFIP WG2: Conference on Semantics of Interoperable Database Systems, Lorne, Victoria, Australia, pp. 283–312, November 1992
32. Spaccapietra, S., Parent, C., Dupont, Y.: Model independent assertions for integration of heterogeneous schemas. VLDB J. **1**(1), 81–126 (1992)
33. Torlone, R.: Two approaches to the integration of heterogeneous data warehouses. Distrib. Parallel Databases **23**, 69–97 (2008)
34. Torlone, R.: Interoperability in data warehouses. In: Liu, L., Özsu, M.T. (eds.) Encyclopedia of Database Systems, pp. 1560–1564. Springer, Boston (2009). https://doi.org/10.1007/978-0-387-39940-9
35. Tseng, F.S., Chen, C.W.: Integrating heterogeneous data warehouses using XML technologies. J. Inf. Sci. **31**(3), 209–229 (2005). https://doi.org/10.1177/0165551505052467
36. W3C: Best practices for publishing linked data. W3C Working Group Note (2014)
37. Webster, J., Watson, R.T.: Analyzing the past to prepare for the future: writing a literature review. Manag. Inf. Syst. Q. **26**(2), 3 (2002)

Linked Data in the European Data Portal: A Comprehensive Platform for Applying DCAT-AP

Fabian Kirstein[1,2(✉)], Benjamin Dittwald[1], Simon Dutkowski[1],
Yury Glikman[1], Sonja Schimmler[1,2], and Manfred Hauswirth[1,2,3]

[1] Fraunhofer FOKUS, Berlin, Germany
{fabian.kirstein,benjamin.dittwald,simon.dutkowski,yury.glikman,
sonja.schimmler,manfred.hauswirth}@fokus.fraunhofer.de
[2] Weizenbaum Institute for the Networked Society, Berlin, Germany
[3] Open Distributed Systems, TU Berlin, Berlin, Germany

Abstract. The European Data Portal (EDP) is a central access point for metadata of Open Data published by public authorities in Europe and acquires data from more than 70 national data providers. The platform is a starting point in adopting the Linked Data specification DCAT-AP, aiming to increase interoperability and accessibility of Open Data. In this paper, we present the design of the central data management components of the platform, responsible for metadata storage, data harvesting and quality assessment. The core component is based on CKAN, which is extended by the support for native Linked Data replication to a triplestore to ensure legacy compatibility and the support for DCAT-AP. Regular data harvesting and the creation of detailed quality reports are performed by custom components adressing the requirements of DCAT-AP. The EDP is well on track to become the core platform for European Open Data and fostered the acceptance of DCAT-AP. Our platform is available here: https://www.europeandataportal.eu.

Keywords: Open Data · Linked Data · CKAN · DCAT-AP · Data and information quality

Track: Open Data: Social and Technical Aspects

1 Introduction

Open Data is a driver for transparency and innovation. Freely available machine-readable data can help to foster participation and may create novel business models [21]. Typical Open Data is weather data, geographical data, traffic data, statistics, publications, protocols, laws and ordinances. The publication of Open Data is mainly conducted by public administrations and organisations, but a growing number of private companies have begun to initiate Open Data projects

© The Author(s) 2019
I. Lindgren et al. (Eds.): EGOV 2019, LNCS 11685, pp. 192–204, 2019.
https://doi.org/10.1007/978-3-030-27325-5_15

as well. If data is available as Open Data, it can be used, processed, refined and distributed by everyone at any time without mandatory registration, without restrictions and free of charge. The most typical channel of distribution of Open Data is through a Web portal. As of today, more than 2,600 portals exist [11].

In order to encourage reuse and application of Open Data, a common standard for storing and managing metadata is advisable. Especially, standardized access via an Application Programming Interface (API) is indispensable. Since 2013, a specification for describing public sector datasets in Europe, called DCAT Application profile for data portals in Europe (DCAT-AP) is developed by order of the European Commission (EC). The profile is based on Linked Data principles and the Resource Description Framework (RDF) vocabulary Data Catalogue Vocabulary (DCAT). It is designed to increase interoperability and allows the user to search for Open Data across multiple portals. The standard is constantly refined and currently published in version 1.2 [5].

1.1   The European Data Portal (EDP)

In November 2015, the EC launched the European Data Portal (EDP), which makes all metadata of Open Data published by public authorities of the European Union (EU) available in one portal [7]. As of February 2019, the EDP lists close to 900.000 datasets, in total consisting of about 60 million RDF triples, harvested from 77 data providers.[1] The EDP is Europe's Linked Data-enabled one-stop-shop for open public sector information. It is not limited to a metadata registry, but forms an entire ecosystem for fostering the manifestation, reuse and quality improvement of Open Data. The platform pioneered in adopting the DCAT-AP specification and represents its first reference implementation. The core metadata properties are available in all 24 official languages of the EU. Where translations are not provided by the original data provider, a machine-translation service is employed.

The design and implementation of the EDP posed some extensive challenges: (i) The user interface and API, on the one hand, had to be compliant with already established non-Linked Data standards of Open Data publishing in order to meet the expectations of Open Data users. The metadata, on the other hand, had to be stored in a native RDF data model, complying with the new DCAT-AP specifications. Hence, Linked Open Data (LOD) had been required, which enables the access to the metadata via a SPARQL endpoint. Therefore, a **metadata registry**, bridging these two concepts satisfactorily had been required for the EDP. (ii) Metadata from all European national Open Data portals had to be retrieved, harmonized and made available. Updates in the source metadata had to be reflected on the EDP without delay. Existing Open Data fetching tools did not fit the diversity and volume of the data providers for the EDP. Therefore, a suitable **harvesting** mechanism needed to be developed for the EDP. (iii) The completeness and compliance of metadata are key factors for a successful Open

---

[1] https://www.europeandataportal.eu/data/#/catalogues.

Data platform. Such metrics are rarely accessible or even reviewed. Therefore, a central aspect of the EDP had been the provision of **metadata quality** reports.

In this paper, we present the concept, the implementation, and our lessons learned from the EDP infrastructure with the key challenge to comply to the DCAT-AP specification. The paper is focused on the central components, forming the so-called EDP data segment:[2] the *Metadata Registry*, the *Harvester* and the *Metadata Quality Assurance*. After an overview of related work and established Open Data standards (Sect. 2), the high-level design is described (Sect. 3). In Sect. 4, solution statements for each central component (i.e., service) are given. The application of DCAT-AP, namely the linked data management, is then highlighted in Sect. 5. Finally, the impact of the presented work is evaluated (Sect. 6) and directions for future research are presented (Sect. 7).

2   Related Work

DCAT is a widely adopted and popular standard for describing datasets and establishing interoperability between data catalogues. DCAT-AP is a Linked Data extension of DCAT which adds metadata fields and mandatory ranges for specific properties [5]. These ranges are mostly provided as a Simple Knowledge Organization System (SKOS) controlled vocabulary, provided by the EC Publications Office. For instance, properties like language, spatial information or MIME type can be harmonised by applying the provided vocabulary [15]. The popularity of DCAT-AP is increasing and country-specific extensions have been published. E.g., the German IT Planning Council established DCAT-AP.de as the official exchange standard for open governmental data in Germany [8].

A lot of work has been invested in developing tools for making Open Data and Linked Data publicly available and easily accessible. The Open Source solution Comprehensive Knowledge Archive Network (CKAN) is a basic web application for building data catalogues, particularly for Open Data. It is the de-facto standard in the public sector, but is also applied by private companies. CKAN provides many features for mapping the process of publishing data catalogues. A comprehensive range of plug-ins is available. The CKAN API is extensively documented and provides a comprehensive way to retrieve the metadata of the data catalogue [4].

There exist several hybrid approaches, where the Linked Data interface is an additional layer on top of traditional data structures. An official plug-in for extending CKAN with a DCAT-AP interface is available.[3] However, it only maps the existing data structures to an RDF serialisation and does not provide native Linked Data capabilities. A proprietary and closed source alternative to CKAN is OpenDataSoft, which is also used by a variety of institutions for implementing Open Data platforms [13]. It focuses on interaction and visualization through automated API generation and has only limited support for DCAT-AP. An

---

[2] The entire EDP includes further tools, which are out of scope, e.g., a content management system, tools for visualisation and preview, a proxy-server and a load balancer.

[3] https://github.com/ckan/ckanext-dcat.

interoperability mode for mapping the default schema to DCAT-AP is available on demand [12]. The open access repository software DSpace follows a more elaborate approach [16]. A converter is available, which dynamically translates relational metadata into native RDF metadata. The converter stores the generated triples into a triplestore, and hence, offers the metadata via a SPARQL endpoint [6]. A very similar approach is followed by Wikidata, a community-driven knowledge base by the Wikimedia Foundation. Wikidata implements a custom data structure for storing statements about identifiable items, very similar to the concept of RDF. This data is periodically converted to native RDF and stored in a triplestore, whose endpoint is publicly accessible [17].

As an alternative to the above mentioned hybrid approaches, systems can be built upon native Linked Data. The W3C recommendation for Linked Data Platforms (LDPs) defines a low-level specification for managing Linked Data resources on the web. It is based on HTTP methods and defines guidelines for representation formats, collision detection and vocabulary reuse [18]. Several implementations of LDP exist, like OpenLink Virtuoso or Apache Marmotta [20]. The latter builds upon a straightforward native application of RDF with pluggable triplestores and targets organisations that want to publish Linked Data [1]. Virtuoso is a full-fledged and mature database management solution, supporting and combining multiple paradigms for storing data in a unique system. Foremost, it can be used as a highly scalable and versatile triplestore [14]. Klímek et al. [9] present a first system, which is entirely built upon native DCAT-AP and is used in the Czech National Open Data Catalog[4]. An interactive pipeline process is applied for harvesting DCAT-AP from official institutions and storing the metadata in both, a triplestore and an Apache Solr [2] search index.

In order to provide a practical and flexible solution, we also follow a hybrid approach, where all metadata is represented in both formats.

3   High-Level Design

The central objective of the design of the EDP is to address the requirements of the DCAT-AP-compliant metadata storage, the data acquisition and the quality assurance in a practical and scalable way. The general design follows a service-oriented approach, with a strict separation of concerns. This ensures high scalability, since every service can run independently on a separate machine. In addition, the services are designed statelessly, whenever possible, hence, allowing for a replication on multiple machines, if necessary. Figure 1 illustrates the interactions and deployment of the internal and external components. All services communicate via RESTful APIs with each other. The distributed architecture requires a central authentication service for securing restricted operations of the platform (e.g., for creating new datasets). The authentication service of the EC (EU Login[5]) is integrated for that purpose. It implements the single sign-on protocol Central Authentication Service (CAS).

---

[4] https://data.gov.cz.
[5] https://webgate.ec.europa.eu/cas.

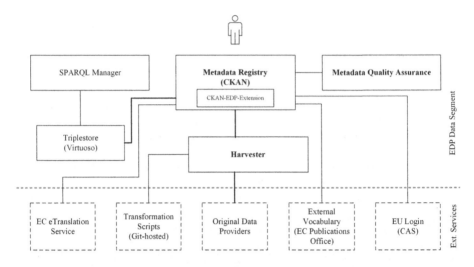

Fig. 1. Overview of the components of the EDP data segment

To enable backward compatibility within the existing European Open Data ecosystem, CKAN was used as a basis. This way, we ensure the provisioning of mature elementary features and the compliance with established methodologies and interfaces. Additional and modified functionalities of CKAN are implemented based on its rich extension interfaces, resulting in the *CKAN EDP extension*.

The central service of the EDP data segment is our **Metadata Registry**, which includes some features that concern the storage and management of metadata. Here, native DCAT-AP is integrated with a proven replication approach (see Sect. 2), where all metadata is additionally stored in a triplestore. As an appropriate solution for the diverse Open Data acquisition and transformation tasks, our **Harvester** was implemented as a second service of the EDP data segment. Based on custom transformation scripts, it is responsible for fetching the metadata and for converting it into the target data formats. As a third service of the EDP data segment, our **Metadata Quality Assurance (MQA)** service is continuously retrieving the metadata from the registry and is validating it against the target schema DCAT-AP. The validation results are summarized and accessible to the data provider.

4   Service Design

In the following, the three central services of the EDP data segment, which were overviewed in the last section, are discussed along with our approaches for solving the challenges we faced.

4.1 Metadata Registry

The Metadata Registry acts as the central data management unit for the EDP and the primary access point for users of the metadata. It adopts its core technology stack from the underlying CKAN, which is implemented in Python and which uses PostgreSQL as storage and Apache Solr for search. Figure 2 shows the main search page served by the Metadata Registry.

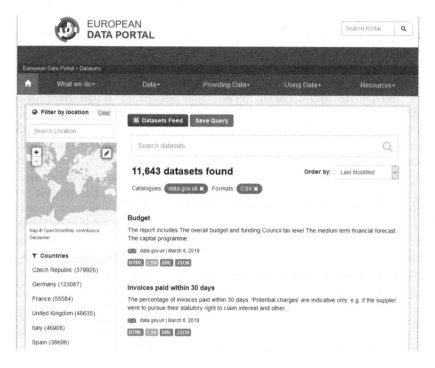

Fig. 2. Main search page for datasets

The CKAN EDP extension[6] introduces multiple features into the core system, where the most significant one is the management of DCAT-AP (see Sect. 5). Significant modifications concern the default data structure of CKAN, the CKAN Data Schema (CDS), which is extended. This includes support for textual metadata and other meta information in multiple languages. The underlying schema of the search server Solr is adjusted accordingly. Especially, language-aware analysers are introduced, e.g., for stemming. The actual translations are provided by the eTranslation service of the EC. In order to avoid any blocking functionality, the Metadata Registry accumulates certain literal metadata fields to batches and sends them to the eTranslation service. The Metadata Registry is then asynchronously updated with the machine-translated texts retrieved.

---

[6] https://gitlab.com/european-data-portal/ckanext-edp.

4.2   Harvester

The Harvester is a standalone service for acquiring metadata from the various source portals, and for transforming it into the DCAT-AP-compliant data structure of the EDP. It is designed to fit the specific needs of the EDP to deal with a wide diversity of source data formats and high update rates. Existing solutions for harvesting, especially the CKAN Harvest[7] extension could not cope well with these requirements. Especially, the development and management of custom adapters were too complex.

The Harvester currently supports 12 different input protocols and serialisation formats, most prominently, CKAN-API, SPARQL, RSS and OpenDataSoft-API, and the DCAT-AP-compliant data structure of the EDP as output format. A harvester represents a link between two repositories, where one acts as source and one as target. Each harvester is defined by transformation rules, which define how the source serialisation is converted into the target one. These rules are defined with simple scripting languages. Currently, we support eXtensible Stylesheet Language Transformations (XSLT) for XML serialisation and JavaScript for JSON serialisation. The scripts are managed by the system and are dynamically loaded.[8] This enables an agile reaction on changes in the payload of a data source. Listing 1 shows an excerpt of a transformation script. For configuring harvesters, a user-friendly web frontend is available. A harvester has a schedule, which can be configured individually (e.g., daily, weekly etc.). In order to avoid unnecessary update operations, a hash value for each source dataset is calculated and stored in the Metadata Registry. An update is only triggered, when the source data, and therefore the hash has changed.

```
if (input.organization) {
        output.publisher = {};
        output.publisher.type = "http://xmlns.com/foaf/0.1/Organization";
        output.publisher.name = input.organization.title;
}
```

Listing 1. Excerpt of a JavaScript transformation script

4.3   Metadata Quality Assurance (MQA)

The MQA[9] is a service, which periodically executes quality checks of the metadata stored in the Metadata Registry. Existing tools for Open Data quality assessment typically work on a less granular level and are updated infrequently, for example the Open Data Monitor.[10]

The validation is conducted on two levels: (i) First, the formal correctness of the metadata is checked. This is done by validating each set of metadata against a self-defined JSON Schema. This schema includes the constraints and

---

[7] https://github.com/ckan/ckanext-harvest/.

[8] https://gitlab.com/european-data-portal/transformation-scripts.

[9] https://www.europeandataportal.eu/mqa.

[10] https://opendatamonitor.eu.

specifications of DCAT-AP. It was chosen to perform the validation against the extended CKAN-API due to the maturity of JSON-based validation. Validation tools for RDF, like SHACL [19], had not been advanced enough at the time of development. The check provides a detailed report of schema validations, e.g., missing mandatory properties or wrong data types. (ii) Second, the actual content of specific metadata properties, which are shown in Table 1, is checked. The results are aggregated and visualised as illustrated in Fig. 3.

Table 1. Validation characteristics of the MQA

Feature	Description
Accessible Distributions	A HTTP GET request is performed on all distributions in order to determine their accessibility
Error Status Codes	If a distribution is not accessible, the HTTP error code is logged and reported
Ratio Machine-Readable Datasets	The ratio of machine-readable and non-machine-readable distributions is calculated. The determination is based on a list published by the Open Data Monitor[a]
Most Used Formats	The most used data formats are presented
Ratio Known to Unknown Licences	The ratio of known and unknown licenses is calculated. Therefore, the used licences are validated against a comprehensive list of Open Data licences[b]
Most Used Licences	The most used licences are presented

[a]https://github.com/opendatamonitor/odm.restapi/blob/master/odmapi/def_formatLists.py
[b]https://www.europeandataportal.eu/en/content/show-license

In addition, the MQA computes a list of datasets that are similar to a certain dataset based on their metadata. The feature uses a locality-sensitive hashing (LSH) algorithm [10] and the result is presented in the Metadata Registry. The MQA performs a full validation of the entire data pool of the EDP once every month. The entire process is resource-intense due to many external dependencies, e.g., resolving the URLs is time consuming.

5   Linked Data Management

The support of the DCAT-AP specification is a core feature of the EDP and handled by the Metadata Repository. The majority of the data providers do not serve DCAT-AP-compliant metadata or even Linked Data. In addition, the underlying CKAN of the Metadata Registry does not support native Linked Data (see Sect. 2). Therefore, a triplestore is introduced as additional database and

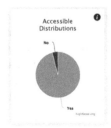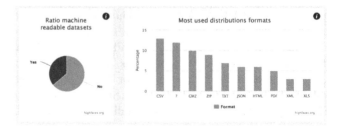

Fig. 3. MQA quality report

replication layer. Virtuoso is used here, due to its maturity and LDP-compliance. Hence, the source metadata needs to be represented in both formats, DCAT-AP and CKAN-JSON. Both serialisations have to be idem-potent, i.e., bi-directional conversion is possible without any losses. Therefore, a virtual data format for creating and managing the metadata is required. The CDS is extended in order to match the DCAT-AP data schema. All DCAT-AP properties and structures are mapped to the CDS correspondents and additional properties are added. Figure 4 shows an exemplary mapping for the property `contactPoint`.[11] The use of the extended CDS as the common data structure ensures compatibility with established practices.

```
- <dcat:contactPoint>
  - <vcard:Organization>
      <vcard:organization-name>Bundesanstalt für Geowissenschaften und Rohstoffe</vcard:organization-name>
      <vcard:hasEmail rdf:resource="mailto:geologie.daten@bgr.de"/>
    </vcard:Organization>
  </dcat:contactPoint>

                          "contact_point": [
                             {
                               "type": "http://www.w3.org/2006/vcard/ns#Organization",
                               "resource": "http://www.organization.resource",
                               "email": "mailto:geologie.daten@bgr.de",
                               "name": "Bundesanstalt für Geowissenschaften und Rohstoffe"
                             }
                          ]
```

Fig. 4. Mapping of DCAT-AP to CDS and vice versa

The Metadata Registry is exposing a compliant interface for both, the API and the Web frontend. When a new dataset is created, it is converted to native RDF and stored in the triplestore. The Python library rdflib is applied for that purpose. For each property, detailed creation rules are provided, ensuring the creation of rich DCAT-AP, following best practices for Linked Data. The creation of persistent URIs follows established practices [3]. For instance, the URI scheme

---

[11] Full mapping of all properties: https://gitlab.com/european-data-portal/ckanext-edp/wikis/schema.

`http://europeandataportal.eu/set/data/[name]` is used for datasets. The Linked Data representations of the entire registry can be accessed via a SPARQL endpoint. The integrated SPARQL Manager allows for the interactive creation and management of arbitrary queries. To release the full potential of the underlying LOD, the Metadata Registry supports content negation, allowing clients to retrieve every dataset in different RDF serialisation formats, by adding a trailing format indicator, e.g., .rdf or .ttl. Finally, the Metadata Registry is resolving properties (described with URIs of known vocabularies) to human-readable representations within the frontend. Mostly, the controlled vocabulary from the EC Publications Office is used here.

6 Evaluation

The EDP is employed in production, and is publicly accessible since November 2015. As of February 2019, it offers close to 900.000 datasets, from 35 countries in Europe and beyond, provided by 77 data providers. In total, about 60 million RDF triples are accessible. Its use and acceptance is constantly monitored since its launch. The web analytics tool Matomo[12] is integrated in all services for that purpose. Since its launch, the EDP had more than 870.000 unique visitors. Detailed statistics are aggregated on a quarterly basis. As an example, Table 2 shows an extraction of the data for Q2 to Q4 2018. Overall, the statistics show a productive adoption and stable service of the EDP. The numbers for the Page Views Data Segment are an indicator for the use of the components and services, which have been described in Sect. 4. The numbers for the SPARQL Manager are an indicator for the use of the native Linked Data, which has been described in Sect. 5.

Table 2. Extract of the use statistics of the EDP

	Q2 2018	Q3 2018	Q4 2018
Page Views	341.891	296.899	300.260
Page Views Data Segment	*257.183*	*227.221*	*220.204*
SPARQL Manager	*2.954*	*2.620*	*2.635*
Total Visits	114.570	102.454	99.772
Unique Visitors	105.989	94.852	91.736
Daily Average	1.259	1.114	1.084
Returning Visitors	19%	19%	20%

The acceptance of DCAT-AP has increased significantly since the release of the EDP. In 2015, only one data provider served DCAT-AP, whereas now, as of February 2019, 13 providers follow the specification. The transparent communication, the accessible reports of the MQA and the high visibility of the EDP

---

[12] Formerly Piwik.

helped fostering the awareness of the specification. However, the vast diversity of employed data structures, formats and vocabularies used by the different data providers impede a homogeneous presentation of the available data in the EDP. This has an impact on the usability and lowers the much higher potential of Open Data. Furthermore, the underlying platform CKAN is a great choice for building regional and national Open Data portals, but does not easily perform smoothly with the amount of data hosted by the EDP. It was necessary to restrict the update frequency to ensure stability and availability.

7   Conclusion and Outlook

In this paper, we have presented the design and implementation of the European Data Portal with focus on the EDP data segment and the adoption of the DCAT-AP Linked Data specification. With the EDP, we provide a comprehensive platform for acquiring, presenting and validating Open Data from all over the EU. It has established itself as a well-known one-stop-shop for Open Data and an advocate for the Linked Open Data movement. The presented approach successfully combines two concepts of representing and serving Open Data: the established data structure and API of CKAN and Linked Data via SPARQL. Currently, more and more national and regional data providers adopt the DCAT-AP standard, which the EDP already supports. In parallel, the importance of native and simple LOD increases. As a consequence, the replication of the metadata in two distinct data storages, which is complex, should be adapted. In addition, a transition from restricted, flat data structures to Linked Open Data is on-going. Furthermore, it can be expected that the overall amount of Open Data in Europe will increase. Thus, a stronger focus on high-performance solutions and support for faster harvesting updates will be necessary. Therefore, we currently adapt the presented architecture to accommodate these future requirements. A revised and improved version of the EDP is under active development, considering the learnings from the first EDP version described in this paper.

Acknowledgments. This work has been funded by the European Commission, Directorate-General Communications Networks, Content and Technology under service contract for SMART 2014/1072 "Deployment of an EU Open Data core platform: implementation of the pan-European Open Data portal and related services" and by the Federal Ministry of Education and Research of Germany (BMBF) under grant no. 16DII111 ("Deutsches Internet-Institut"). We would like to thank the European Commission for granting us access to the usage statistics. We would also like to thank the entire consortium of the European Data Portal for making this work possible.

References

1. Apache Software Foundation: Apache Marmotta. http://marmotta.apache.org/
2. Apache Software Foundation: Apache Solr. http://lucene.apache.org/solr/

3. Archer, P., Goedertier, S., Loutas, N.: D7.1.3 - Study on persistent URIs, with identification of best practices and recommendations on the topic forthe MSs and the EC, December 2012. https://joinup.ec.europa.eu/sites/default/files/document/2013-02/D7.1.3%20-%20Study%20on%20persistent%20URIs.pdf

4. CKAN Association: CKAN. https://ckan.org/

5. Dragan, A.: DCAT Application Profile for data portals in Europe, November 2018. https://joinup.ec.europa.eu/sites/default/files/distribution/access_url/2018-11/014bde52-eb3c-4060-8c3c-fcd0dfc07a8a/DCAT_AP_1.2.pdf

6. DuraSpace Wiki: Linked (Open) Data. https://wiki.duraspace.org/display/DSDOC6x/Linked+%28Open%29+Data. Accessed 11 Mar 2019

7. European Data Portal: The European Data Portal: Opening up Europe's public-data. https://www.europeandataportal.eu/sites/default/files/edp_factsheet_what_is_edp_project_online.pdf. Accessed 11 Mar 2019

8.]init[AG und SID Sachsen: DCAT-AP.de Spezifikation. https://www.dcat-ap.de/def/dcatde/1.0.1/spec/specification.pdf. Accessed 11 Mar 2019

9. Klímek, J., Skoda, P.: LinkedPipes DCAT-AP viewer: a native DCAT-AP DataCatalog. In: International Semantic Web Conference (2018). https://pdfs.semanticscholar.org/28ab/7bcdc1b5db660ac280e426556e96d599daed.pdf

10. Oliver, J., Cheng, C., Chen, Y.: TLSH - a locality sensitive hash. In: 2013 Fourth Cybercrime and Trustworthy Computing Workshop. pp. 7–13, November 2013. https://doi.org/10.1109/CTC.2013.9

11. OpenDataSoft: A Comprehensive List of 2600+ Open Data Portals around the World. https://www.opendatasoft.com/a-comprehensive-list-of-all-open-data-portals-around-the-world/. Accessed 11 Mar 2019

12. OpenDataSoft: Interoperability Metadata. https://help.opendatasoft.com/platform/en/publishing_data/06_configuring_metadata/interoperability_metadata.html. Accessed 11 Mar 2019

13. OpenDataSoft: Open Data Solution. https://www.opendatasoft.com/solutions/open-data/. Accessed 11 Mar 2019

14. OpenLink Software: About OpenLink Virtuoso. https://virtuoso.openlinksw.com/. Accessed 11 Mar 2019

15. Publications Office of the EU: Authority tables. https://publications.europa.eu/en/web/eu-vocabularies/authority-tables. Accessed 11 Mar 2019

16. Smith, M., et al.: DSpace: An Open Source Dynamic Digital Repository, January 2003. https://doi.org/10.1045/january2003-smith

17. Vrandečić, D., Krötzsch, M.: Wikidata: a free collaborative knowledgebase. Commun. ACM **57**(10), 78–85 (2014). https://doi.org/10.1145/2629489

18. W3C: Linked Data Platform 1.0. https://www.w3.org/TR/ldp/

19. W3C: Shapes Constraint Language (SHACL). https://www.w3.org/TR/shacl/

20. W3C Wiki: LDP Implementations. https://www.w3.org/wiki/LDP_Implementations. Accessed 11 Mar 2019

21. Zaki, M., Feldmann, N., Neely, A., Hartmann, P.M.: Capturing value from big data - a taxonomy of data-driven business models used by start-up firms. Int. J. Oper. Prod. Manag. **36**(10), 1382–1406 (2016). https://doi.org/10.1108/IJOPM-02-2014-0098

Optimising e-Government Data Centre Operations to Minimise Energy Consumption: A Simulation-Based Analytical Approach

Changwoo Suh[1], Mohammed Bahja[2,3], Youngseok Choi[1,2],
Truong Nguyen[1], and Habin Lee[1(✉)]

[1] Brunel University London, London UB8 3PH, UK
{Changwoo.Suh,Truong.Nguyen,Habin.Lee}@brunel.ac.uk
[2] LK Knowledge Engineering Ltd., London EC1V 2NX, UK
{Mohammed.Bahja,Youngseok.Choi}@lkknowledgeco.uk
[3] University of Birmingham, Birmingham B15 2TT, UK

Abstract. The energy consumption of data centres is increasing over and over. However, there are few decision support systems introduced for data centre practitioners to use it for their daily operations, including simulating their new server installation and forecasting power consumption for the target periods. We propose a simulation model based on CloudSim, which is widely used for data centre research. Our simulation model will be tested with datasets, including IT work-loads, cooling performance, and power consumption of servers and cooling devices. In the final stage, we provide a decision support system to monitor, forecast, and optimise the power consumption of a data centre easily on the web.

Keywords: Data centre · Optimisation · Simulation · Decision support system · GreenDC

1 Introduction

In recent years, the use of the information and communications technologies (ICT), comprising communication devices and applications, data centres (DCs), internet infrastructure, mobile devices, computer and network hardware and software and so on, has increased rapidly. Internet service providers such as Amazon, Google, Microsoft, etc., representing the most significant stakeholders in the IT sector, constructed a large number of geographically distributed internet data centres (IDC) to satisfy the growing demand and providing reliable low latency services to customers. These IDCs contain vast numbers of servers, large-scale storage units, networking equipment, infrastructure, etc., to distribute power and provide cooling. The number of IDCs owned by the leading IT companies is drastically increasing every year. As a result, the number of servers needed has reached an astonishing number. EPA (Environmental Protection Agency) reports that IDCs in the US use 61 billion kWh in 2006 (1.5% of US energy consumption), 91 billion kWh in 2013. Natural Resource Defence Council expects

© IFIP International Federation for Information Processing 2019
Published by Springer Nature Switzerland AG 2019
I. Lindgren et al. (Eds.): EGOV 2019, LNCS 11685, pp. 205–214, 2019.
https://doi.org/10.1007/978-3-030-27325-5_16

energy consumption of IDC will be increased up to 140 billion kWh annually by 2020 [1]. Due to the huge amount of energy implied and the related cost, IDC can make a significant contribution to the energy efficiency by reducing energy consumption and power management of IT ecosystems. It is why most researchers focus on reducing the power consumption of IDCs. Those efforts include designing innovative architecture of DCs to minimise loss of cool airs, heats from IT devices, protecting from outside heats and so on. Also, computer scientists developed energy efficient workload reallocation algorithms to distribute the peaked workloads of servers to minimise energy consumption and heat generation.

However, efforts to reduce energy consumption via efficient DC operations are still scarce. The two significant energy consumptions in DCs are IT devices and cooling devices, which consumers around 90% of total energy consumption in DCs. Specifically, many scholars reported that the power consumption of cooling devices are about 40% (e.g., [2]). It is believed that the energy consumption by two types of the device has a trade-off relationship as keeping lower temperatures in a DC will increase the energy consumption of cooling devices while decreases that of IT devices due to increased computing efficiency and vice versa. However, the literature has mixed results on the shape of the trade-off relationship via scientific experiments. Understanding the trade-off relationship will help DC managers to decide the optimal temperature of their DCs as the increase of the temperature has a significant impact on the total energy consumption of cooling devices and the DCs. In other words, DC managers are yet to find answers to such questions as what are the optimal temperature of the DCs to minimize energy consumption without affecting the performance of IT devices and meeting the service-level-agreement. How many servers or virtual machines need to be on for the next 24 h or a week considering expected workloads? What are the optimal schedules of servers and VMs for handling workloads, which are various from time to time? Where are the best operational schedules of cooling devices within the DC to have a maximum cooling effect? To answer these questions, we develop a simulation model that can consider IT devices (workloads) as well as cooling devices in one model based on a real data collected from one of the largest data centres in Turkey that run several commercial services on it. By utilising the real-time data from the data centre, we propose an accurate simulation model that can be utilised by practitioners to optimise their daily changing DC configuration.

This paper aims at finding answers to those questions for DC managers via a multi-disciplinary study. It takes a more holistic view by considering the system including servers, cooling system, backup power and electrical distribution system. Notably, a decision support system (DSS) that integrates functionalities, including workload and energy forecasting, generation of optimal operation scheduling of cooling and IT devices and simulation for impact analysis of DC operation strategies. Since the configuration of data centres is continuously changing over time, it is necessary for managers to provide forecasting (or simulation) tool for a new configuration. There are some suggestions and trials to develop such decision support systems [3, 4] though there are no or few tools available for practitioners yet.

2   Literature Reviews

Studies on energy consumption are primarily focused on understanding the engineering perspective of DC components (e.g., [5]). For example, Bhopte et al. [6] analyse effects of underfloor blockages on data centre performance using computational flow dynamics (CFD) simulator and report that some blockages under floor impact larger on cooling performance. Iyengar et al. [7] design server liquid cooling systems without a chiller. They report that they can reduce 90% of cooling energy on a relatively hot New York summer day. There are similar works that introduce new technologies to reduce cooling energy on DCs (e.g., [8, 9]).

Zhang, Wei, and Zhang [10] investigate the impact of several free cooling technologies (economiser) that are proper for a newly built data centres. They evaluate four free cooling methods that are currently available. Ham, Park, and Jeong [11] offer optimum supply air temperature ranges for each economiser set-up and climate condition. The other approaches for the economiser studies are to increase energy efficiency by reusing the waste heat from data centres (e.g., [12]) rather than reducing the waste heat itself. Cho et al. [13] analyse economic benefits for the seven options of data cooling strategies that include several kinds of the economiser. Song et al. [14] also calculate economic and operational benefits using chillers and economiser operating hours of the worldwide selected data centres. Cho and Kim [15] provide conceptual models that comprise the major cooling technologies and show the simulated results for each cooling technologies including economisers and several energy sources such as renewable energy considering climate zone and energy-saving levels.

The other stream of data centre research focuses on optimisation studies to minimise power consumption without impact on service level agreement. In the early stage of workload optimisation, Bash and Foreman (2007) can increase cooling efficiency by reallocating heavy-loaded servers on the cold area in a server room. They use computational fluid dynamics (CFD) simulation tool to sense the cold spots and hot spots in server rooms; they migrate high workloads into servers on the cold spots. More recent works using virtual machine reallocation strategies for the server room optimisation. Liu et al. [16] implement a framework that can monitor the energy consumption of a DC and migrate virtual machines to minimise energy consumption into idle servers. They report that new architecture can save up to 20% of energy consumption. Chen et al. [17] extend the prior research: their new algorithm can optimise virtual machines over the multiple data centres over the world considering daily/seasonal effects on each location. Chen and his colleagues assert that this approach reduces up to 40% energy consumption in comparison with other scheduling policies. Unlike previous studies, Parolini et al. [18] proposed an algorithm that controls both cooling management and workload reallocation using the constrained Markov decision process (CMDP) simultaneously. The authors report that the proposed control strategy is better than the traditional schemes that control computational and cooling subsystems separately. Banerjee et al. [19] propose a similar approach to Parolini et al.'s [18] and can achieve up to 15% energy saving.

Other groups of scholars focus on optimising network traffic in data centres. Gao et al. [20] introduce a flow optimisation based framework for request-routing and traffic engineering. By adopting this framework, they can reduce 10% of carbon footprint without increasing traffic latency or electric bills. Another team adopts a similar approach to optimise network traffic and reports that they can reduce up to 50% of network energy [21].

Even though the guideline of ASHRAE is broadened to higher inlet air temperature [refer the table 1 on 11], most practitioners try to keep their cooling environment conservative as before. But, recent studies show that increasing temperature does not harm IT devices in data centres as well as decrease energy consumption on cooling data centre (e.g., [22]). For example, El-Sayed et al. [23] check failure rates of most of the server components when cooling air temperature in data centres is increased. The authors report that increased inlet air temperature does not influence the server and its component reliability until 40 °C. They also find that increased inlet air temperature does not decrease the performance of the server and its components as well as there is no CPU or hard drives' throttling occurred up to 40 °C inlet air temperature. Breen et al. [24] also show that to increase the 1 °C inlet air temperature makes 4–5% of data centre energy costs without increasing equipment failure

To show the impact of the increasing inlet temperature, we need a simulator that can calculate the difference between the inlet temperature changes. Until now, thermodynamic fluid models are the mainstream of the cooling simulation that is used to calculate cooling energy consumption, visualise air flows within the data centre, and illustrate hot and cold spots in the server room. This approach is generally called computational fluid dynamics (CFD) models [25–28]. CFD models can generate accurate results for given parameters. However, CFD models need high computational power (and computing time), professional knowledge to model the target and commercial tools in general.

Other groups of scholars generate black-box models for cooling devices to estimate the power consumption of cooling devices in a data centre [11, 29–33]. This black-box modelling approach has some advantages compared to computational fluid dynamics models. Firstly, the black-box model is generally more straightforward than the CFD model. This feature is a significant advantage when we need to calculate many objects in a simulation model. The simplicity also helps us to use the black-box model in the everyday working environment. Secondly, it is essential to have professional knowledge of thermodynamics as well as data collection for CFD modelling. On the other hand, the black-box models can be described by basic mathematics. It helps us to adopt widely in a general data centre working environment.

3 Simulation Model

We design a simulation model with a straightforward black-box model from prior studies.

3.1 An Example of a Server Room in a Data Centre

Figure 1 depicts an example of a server room. There are two types of devices in a server room. One is IT devices that include server racks, servers, and network devices.

The other type is non-IT devices, including computer room air conditioners (CRACs), chillers, power distribution units (PDUs) and UPS. The primary power consumption of a server room comes from servers and cooling devices (air conditioners and chillers). Air conditioners supply cold air at the constant air volume [13]. So, the cold air is supplied more in the middle of the server room compared to the other locations, as described in Fig. 1.

Recently, data centre owners resell some space of a server room to other companies that can install their servers. It is called as 'collocation.' The collocation servers are maintained by the data centre owner, but there is no right for the data centre to access the data on it. It is a very general situation for data centre owners to reduce operating costs by utilising unused resources (server racks). But, because of the collocation service, it is impossible to measure all data from a server room as well as reallocate workloads or virtual machines in a server room. To overcome this limitation of data measurement, we propose a simple conceptual model of a server room in the next section. After the basic conceptual model development finished, we extend our conceptual model that can consider the collocation issue in a DC.

3.2 A Simple Conceptual Model of a Server Room in a Data Centre

In this section, firstly, we define a conceptual model, including IT devices (servers) and non-IT devices (air conditioners) like Fig. 2. For simplicity, we assume that there is only an air conditioner (CRAC) in a server room on the basic model. Second, we describe how the conceptual model can be generalised and how we define a server room using the simple conceptual model.

From the many black-box models for cooling devices [11, 29–33], we choose the simplest power model for CRAC (Dayarathna et al. 2016, p. 770) and modify it slightly. As we know the maximum power consumption of the CRAC from the manufacturer's technical specification, we replace the summation of power consumption of servers. The modified power model for CRAC is

$$c_k = \frac{p_{max}}{\eta}$$
$$\eta = 0.0068t^2 + 0.0008t + 0.458,$$

where c_k is the power consumption of the kth CRAC unit. p_{max} is the maximum power consumption of the CRAC. η is the coefficient of performance (CoP). The second equation is given for the water chilled commercial CRAC. t is the supply (inlet or target) air temperature of the CRAC unit. Our power model is only related to the target air temperature. Before we describe the model, we assume the simplest case of a data centre: there are only one server rack and one air conditioner in a server room of a data centre. In the server rack, there are several servers installed. Each server also contains several virtual machines (VMs). Each VM handles the given workload from the simulator.

In the inside of the server rack, each server uses fans to flow the cold air into the inside of the server. The cold air that enters the server through fans of each server takes heat from the CPU, memory, and hard disk and flows out of the server. The heated air expelled from servers goes up to the ceiling. Under 35 °C, a server consumes electricity

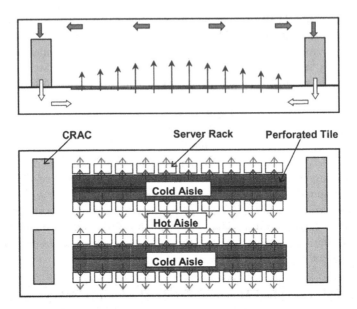

Fig. 1. An example of a server room in a data centre [1]

according to CPU utilisation. Over 35 °C, fans within the server start to blow air faster than the condition under 35 °C and the server consumes more electricity (El-Sayed et al. 2012). The air conditioner expels heat out of the server room until the temperature of the heated air that is returned to the air conditioner is the same as the target temperature. During the operation, the air conditioner expels the collected heat out of the building by exchanging the heat with the chiller. Even if there is no heat removal, CRAC consumes the minimum electricity to run fans to flow air. The total power consumption of the data centre is the summation of the power consumption of servers and the power consumption of CRAC.

3.3   Integrate the Workload Simulation Model

CloudSim is a toolkit for modelling and simulation of cloud computing environments (Son et al. 2015; Goyal, Singh, and Agrawal 2012). Based on the authors, it was used by several researchers from organisations such as HP to investigate cloud resource provisioning and energy-efficient management of data centre resources (Calheiros et al. 2011). This toolkit is widely adopted and used until now when scholars investigate date centre with given workloads for virtual machines and physical servers. For example, Srivastana et al. (2017) use the CloudSim as a basis to develop, implement, and experiment the optimization algorithm for a cloud computing environment. It is well-designed and widely used toolkit for data centre research. However, CloudSim does not implement cooling devices for the data centre, which consume the electronic energy of the data centre up to 40–50% [34]. This lack of implementation makes scholars hard to simulating the total power consumption of the target data centre using CloudSim. We implement this gap - the cooling devices with a simplified model of the datacentre.

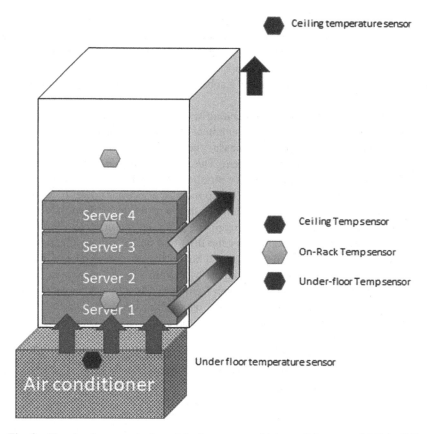

Fig. 2. The simple conceptual model of a server rack/air conditioner model for a DC

One of the main shortcomings of CFD simulation is that CFD simulations assume the given workload as constant over time. However, the workload for each server fluctuate over time, and it affects cooling loads change in a DC. To consider the fluctuated workload, we adopt the CloudSim as a basis for the simulation and extend it to include the cooling devices on it.

4   Data Collection and Expected Results Simulation Model

There are two primary sources of data from the data centre in Turkey. One is IT device (server) data from the Zabbix system. The other source is non-IT device measurement data from various sensors and metres installed. We chose one server room that is isolated to other server rooms. There are eight CRAC units, two external chillers connected to four CRACs respectively, two UPS, five rows of server racks. We chose two target server racks, of which location is different from each other to collect a different set of data for each server rack.

There are more than ten target servers in each target server rack. Each server is connected to the Zabbix system. Zabbix system creates logs of the physical and virtual machines' activities in real-time. For example, the logged data contains usage data of CPU, memory, hard drive, and network interfaces, number of processes in running states, and each server's specification. Zabbix system saves the information from the servers for every five minutes.

We installed energy metres, temperature sensors, smart PDU (Power Distribution Unit) to collect non-IT devices measurement data from various sources. We also connect non-IT devices that contain measurement functions for itself to a data centre infrastructure monitoring (DCIM) system. The installed devices are also connected to the DCIM system to collect the data. We install energy metres and temperature sensors on CRAC units. We install two SmartPDU to monitor a server's power consumption in the target racks. We also install three temperature sensors on the front and rear doors each to monitor inlet and outlet air temperature from the server racks. There are four temperature and humidity sensors under the floor and on the ceiling for each that can capture the supplied cold air temperature and hot air before consumed by CRAC units. The UPS and chillers provide their functions by themselves so that we can receive the total power consumption in the target room from the UPS, and we can get the ambient air temperature and humidity outside of the data centre building. The DCIM system also records the data every minute. Data centre programmers provide RESTful API to receive both datasets at once.

Since the target data centre provides highly demanded public and commercial services, the implementation of a data collection system is in progress. It is expected to be done within the second quarter of 2019.

5   Conclusions

In this study, we develop a decision support system to support data centre operations. Specifically, we develop a simulation model that can count for the server workloads and cooling performance simultaneously to provide a simulation-based optimisation approach for the data centre. For example, the simulation results can show the optimal target temperature for the target periods by calculating the forecasting server workloads and the expected cooling capacities that can be defined by the server workloads and the outside temperature for the target periods. Practitioners also use the simulation model to determine their future server demands. In the future, we will extend our basic cooling model with more constraints that are given for the DC operations.

References

1. Ni, J., Bai, X.: A review of air conditioning energy performance in data centers. Renew. Sustain. Energy Rev. **67**, 625–640 (2017)
2. Rong, H., Zhang, H., Xiao, S., Li, C., Hu, C.: Optimizing energy consumption for data centers. Renew. Sustain. Energy Rev. **58**, 674–691 (2016)

3. Sankar, S., Kansal, A., Liu, J.: Towards a holistic data center simulator. Microsoft Res. **3** (2013)
4. Gupta, S.K.S., et al.: GDCSim: a simulator for green data center design and analysis. ACM Trans. Model. Comput. Simul. **24**, 1–27 (2014)
5. Fulpagare, Y., Bhargav, A.: Advances in data center thermal management. Renew. Sustain. Energy Rev. **43**, 981–996 (2015)
6. Bhopte, S., Sammakia, B., Schmidt, R., Iyengar, M.K., Agonafer, D.: Effect of under floor blockages on data center performance. In: ITHERM, pp. 426–433. IEEE (2006)
7. Iyengar, M., et al.: Server liquid cooling with chiller-less data center design to enable significant energy savings. In: Annual IEEE Semiconductor Thermal Measurement and Management Symposium, vol. 1, pp. 212–223 (2012)
8. Habibi Khalaj, A., Halgamuge, S.K.: A Review on efficient thermal management of air- and liquid-cooled data centers: From chip to the cooling system. Appl. Energy **205**, 1165–1188 (2017)
9. Zimmermann, S., Meijer, I., Tiwari, M.K., Paredes, S., Michel, B., Poulikakos, D.: Aquasar: a hot water cooled data center with direct energy reuse. Energy **43**, 237–245 (2012)
10. Zhang, Y., Wei, Z., Zhang, M.: Free cooling technologies for data centers: energy saving mechanism and applications. Energy Procedia **143**, 410–415 (2017)
11. Ham, S.W., Park, J.S., Jeong, J.W.: Optimum supply air temperature ranges of various air-side economizers in a modular data center. Appl. Therm. Eng. **77**, 163–179 (2015)
12. Ebrahimi, K., Jones, G.F., Fleischer, A.S.: A review of data center cooling technology, operating conditions and the corresponding low-grade waste heat recovery opportunities. Renew. Sustain. Energy Rev. **31**, 622–638 (2014)
13. Cho, K., Chang, H., Jung, Y., Yoon, Y.: Economic analysis of data center cooling strategies. Sustain. Cities Soc. **31**, 234–243 (2017)
14. Song, Z., Zhang, X., Eriksson, C.: Data center energy and cost saving evaluation. Energy Procedia **75**, 1255–1260 (2015)
15. Cho, J., Kim, Y.: Improving energy efficiency of dedicated cooling system and its contribution towards meeting an energy-optimized data center. Appl. Energy **165**, 967–982 (2016)
16. Liu, L., et al.: GreenCloud: a new architecture for green data center. In: Proceedings of the 6th International Conference Industry Session on Autonomic Computing and Communications Industry Session, pp. 29–38 (2009)
17. Chen, C., He, B., Tang, X.: Green-aware workload scheduling in geographically distributed data centers. In: IEEE 4th International Conference on Cloud Computing Technology and Science Proceedings, pp. 82–89. IEEE (2012)
18. Parolini, L., Sinopoli, B., Krogh, B.H.: Reducing data center energy consumption via coordinated cooling and load management. In: Proceedings of the 2008 Conference on Power Aware Computing and Systems, p. 14 (2008)
19. Banerjee, A., Mukherjee, T., Varsamopoulos, G., Gupta, S.K.S.: Cooling-aware and thermal-aware workload placement for green HPC data centers. In: International Conference on Green Computing, pp. 245–256. IEEE (2010)
20. Gao, P.X., Curtis, A.R., Wong, B., Keshav, S.: It's not easy being green. In: Proceedings of the ACM SIGCOMM 2012, p. 211. ACM Press, New York (2012)
21. Heller, B., et al.: ElasticTree : saving energy in data center networks. In: Proceedings of 7th USENIX Conference on Networked Systems Design and Implementation, p. 17 (2010)
22. Mone, G.: Redesigning the data center. Commun. ACM **55**, 14 (2012)

23. El-Sayed, N., Stefanovici, I.A., Amvrosiadis, G., Hwang, A.A., Schroeder, B.: Temperature management in data centers: Why some (might) like it hot. In: Proceedings of the 12th ACM SIGMETRICS/PERFORMANCE Joint International Conference on Measurement and Modeling of Computer Systems (SIGMETRICS 2012), pp. 163–174 (2012)

24. Breen, T.J., Walsh, E.J., Punch, J., Shah, A.J., Bash, C.E.: From chip to cooling tower data center modeling: Part I Influence of server inlet temperature and temperature rise across cabinet. In: ITHERM, pp. 1–10. IEEE (2010)

25. Ni, J., Jin, B., Zhang, B., Wang, X.: Simulation of thermal distribution and airflow for efficient energy consumption in a small data centers. Sustainability **9**, 664 (2017)

26. Choi, J., Kim, Y., Sivasubramaniam, A., Srebric, J., Wang, Q., Lee, J.: A CFD-based tool for studying temperature in rack-mounted servers. IEEE Trans. Comput. **57**, 1129–1142 (2008)

27. Rambo, J., Joshi, Y.: Modeling of data center airflow and heat transfer: state of the art and future trends. Distrib. Parallel Databases **21**, 193–225 (2007)

28. Alkharabsheh, S., et al.: A brief overview of recent developments in thermal management in data centers. J. Electron. Packag. **137**, 040801 (2015)

29. Pakbaznia, E., Pedram, M.: Minimizing data center cooling and server power costs. In: Proceedings of the 14th ACM/IEEE International Symposium on Low Power Electronics and Design - ISLPED 2009, p. 145 (2009)

30. Patterson, M.K.: The effect of data center temperature on energy efficiency. In: 2008 11th Intersociety Conference on Thermal and Thermomechanical Phenomena in Electronic Systems, I-THERM, pp. 1167–1174 (2008)

31. Dayarathna, M., Wen, Y., Fan, R.: Data center energy consumption modeling: a survey. IEEE Commun. Surv. Tutorials. **18**, 732–794 (2016)

32. Liu, Z., et al.: Renewable and cooling aware workload management for sustainable data centers. In: Proceedings of the 12th ACM SIGMETRICS, pp. 175–186. ACM Press, New York (2012)

33. Mousavi, A., Vyatkin, V., Berezovskaya, Y., Zhang, X.: Cyber-physical design of data centers cooling systems automation. In: Proceedings of the 14th IEEE International Conference on Trust, Security and Privacy in Computing and Communications, vol. 3, pp. 254–260 (2015)

34. Ohadi, M.M., Dessiatoun, S.V., Choo, K., Pecht, M., Lawler, J.V.: A comparison analysis of air, liquid, and two-phase cooling of data centers. In: Annual IEEE Semiconductor Thermal Measurement and Management Symposium, pp. 58–63 (2012)

Investigating the Social, Political, Economic and Cultural Implications of Data Trading

Shefali Virkar[1]([✉]), Gabriela Viale Pereira[1], and Michela Vignoli[2]

[1] Danube University Krems, 3500 Krems, Austria
{shefali.virkar,
gabriela.viale-pereira}@donau-uni.ac.at
[2] AIT - Austrian Institute of Technology GmbH, Vienna, Austria
michela.vignoli@ait.ac.at

Abstract. Data market initiatives have, by assigning monetary value to data, and connecting the various actors responsible for its efficient production and consumption, far reaching consequences for national economies. The Data Market Austria (DMA) project represents a unique opportunity for Austria to leverage the enormous potential socio-economic benefits accruing from increased trade of data. At the same time, however, a number of key challenges to the successful uptake of the project needs to be considered, and new problems emerging from this new form of digital commercial infrastructure need to be anticipated and addressed. This study aims to examine how the benefits accruing to increased participation in a data-driven ecosystem can be applied to tackle the long-standing socio-cultural challenges and the possible societal and cultural impediments to the successful unfolding out of a data market. Theoretical discussions framed from arguments obtained through a systematic review of academic and scholarly literature are juxtaposed with empirical data obtained from data science experts and DMA project personnel to test whether they stand up to real-world practicalities and to narrow the focus onto the Austria-specific context. Our findings reveal that data is a dual-purpose commodity that has both commercial value and social application. To amplify the benefits accruing from increased data trading, it is vital that a country establishes a sound open data strategy and a balanced regulatory framework for data trading.

Keywords: Data market · Data trading · Social and cultural aspects

1 Introduction

A flood of structured information or data [1] is created every day through the interactions of people using computers, mobile phones, GPS, and other Internet-enabled devices. This all-pervasive data has become the life-blood of the modern global economy [2], and it is widely accepted that, if harnessed appropriately, such open data – obtained from both public and private sources – can add a new dimension to existing business analytics and give rise to novel, data-focused innovations [3]. Data is often also placed at the heart of strategic decision-making; be it in business firms or within government organisations [4]. The buying and selling of data generally occurs in what is commonly known as a data marketplace [5], a specific ecosystem created for the

© IFIP International Federation for Information Processing 2019
Published by Springer Nature Switzerland AG 2019
I. Lindgren et al. (Eds.): EGOV 2019, LNCS 11685, pp. 215–229, 2019.
https://doi.org/10.1007/978-3-030-27325-5_17

purpose by either vendors or consumers of large quantities of information or by third party organisations. A succinct definition of the concept is provided by [6], who define a data marketplace as *"...a platform on which anybody (or at least a great number of potentially registered clients) can upload and maintain data sets. Access to and use of the data is regulated through varying licensing models."* Further, a 'data marketplace' or a 'data market' may be considered as the virtual space where high quality digital data is offered by data producers as "products" or "services" to potential consumers for payment or for free [7]. Strategically using insights from big data to address many of the challenges that face societies has become an integral part of European Union policy in recent years [8]. The approach developed by the European Commission emphasizes the importance of addressing relevant socio-economic implications of big data processing and analytics, such as respect of ethical principles and related legislation during the implementation of flagship policies (cf. personal data protection and privacy, ensuring informed consent, dual use and potential misuse of the research results, fair benefit sharing when developing countries are involved, and environment protection) [9]. It is vital, therefore, that the benefits and challenges associated with the trade of big data and the degree to which the concept has meaning for the general public are better understood. Key questions to pose in this context are: What impact will the trade of big data have on society, the polity, the economy, and on culture? And who are the winners and losers of the modern knowledge economy?

This study aims to critically examine, within the context of the Data Market Austria (DMA) project, how the benefits accruing to increased participation in a data-driven ecosystem can be applied to tackle the long-standing socio-cultural challenges and the possible societal and cultural impediments to the successful unfolding out of a data market. The research paper is structured sequentially in five parts. The first chapter introduces the relevant fundamentals of data trading. Section 2 describes the findings of a systematic literature review. Section 3 then presents and discusses empirical data obtained from two qualitative research tools, a research workshop and a semi-structured research questionnaire. The results are subsequently synthesised and analysed in Sect. 4. The final section brings together the key observations, lessons learned, and recommendations arising from these and earlier discussions.

2   Research Design

In order to identify and better understand the benefits resulting from the trade of digital data and the potential challenges that could hinder the successful development of a data market, with a focus on the Austrian context, this study adopted a three-part research design to collect research data: a systematic literature review, followed by a pre-conference workshop, and finally a questionnaire.

Context of the Project. The Data Market Austria (DMA) project seeks to establish a data services ecosystem in Austria through the creation of a significantly improved technology base for secure data markets and cloud interoperability, and through the development of a data innovation environment [10]. The DMA does not host data, but instead is a facilitator platform that provides a catalogue for registered data sources.

Developers currently work with open data sets from Kaggle and the European Data Portal. Use of industry data is currently minimal for - besides those obtained from the pilots – these are not currently publicly available. Main DMA stakeholder groups can be classified as data providers; service providers; infrastructure providers; brokers; data market customers; research, education and development; and end-users [11]. The target groups of DMA comprise several different categories of data driven organisations and individuals, each with differing requirements for data. These have been broadly identified through initial research as Government, Industry, Research, Academia, the Public, the Media, and the Community [11]. The DMA research project is funded by the Austrian Ministry for Transport, Innovation and Technology via the Austria Research Promotion Agency (FFG). A Beta working version is expected to be ready at the end of the project, in September 2019.

Systematic Literature Review. A systematic literature review [12] was conducted to identify and discuss the benefits accruing and challenges posed to successful data trading. The Scopus database was selected as the primary source of research material, as it was noticed that this database encompasses many relevant papers in the fields Business, Economics, Political Science, and Information Science. Based on the research questions and after discussing about the keywords, it was decided to use <data market> OR <data-driven> OR <open data> OR <digital data> AND <social impact> OR <societal impact> OR <social implications>OR <societal implications> OR <society> to conduct the search in the title, abstract, keywords and full-text of publications. Specific keywords for each topic were also combined with the aforementioned ones to find related and relevant sources. It was decided to mainly focus on publications of the past ten years.

Workshop. An interim report on the socio-economic, political and cultural implications of data trading showed the need for a deeper, evidenced-based study of how the impacts of a data market are perceived from a variety of perspectives worldwide. In order to determine the prevailing global attitude towards the data market concept, and to deepen our evidence-based investigation of the socio-economic, political and cultural implications of data trading, a workshop was organised under the auspices of a major international conference [13]. Guided by a semi-structured protocol, three moderators from the project under study conducted and reported the discussion. In recognising that a workshop is a form of focus group, the design of proceedings was based on [14], as a research technique that uses group interaction for collecting data on a specific topic. The design can be considered as a mixed structured and unstructured approach as two overarching questions were discussed over the course of one hour, which allowed the participants to get deeper into each discussion.

Questionnaire. To obtain deeper insight into the central research problem, and to validate the findings of the pre-conference workshop, primary data in the form of attitudes, opinions, and perspectives was gathered from individual members of the Austrian Data Market Austria (DMA) project partners. The questionnaire method was selected for data collection as it facilitates the thorough exploration of existing patterns and trends required to effectively describe the social, economic, and political impacts of the DMA project. A self-administered [15] and semi-structured questionnaire [16] consisting of a mix of closed questions and open questions ordered in a structured sequence and with a pre-determined focus was used. In order to maximize coverage within the shortest period of time, we chose to administer the questionnaire online [17]. The questionnaire was developed by this research team following conventional best practices [17], and the finished survey was hosted on Google Forms. An invitation containing a link to the questionnaire was e-mailed to potential participants, and the number of responses tracked through the in-built counter.

3   Systematic Literature Review

This chapter summarises the key results of the systematic literature review, outlining the potential socio-economic, political and cultural of implications of data markets and data trading. From available scholarly and practitioner literature, six key domains have been derived: *economic growth, employment and job creation, ageing populations, migration, climate change*, and *small- and medium-sized enterprises (SMEs)*. From further examination of the literature, four critical societal and cultural impediments to the successful unfolding out of the DMA were identified: *privacy and trust, public decision making structures, social exclusion*, and *gender inequality*.

3.1   Benefits of Data Trading to Society

Economic Growth. A wide range of positive economic impacts result from the free flow of digital data across borders. A report by the Strategic Policy Forum on Digital Entrepreneurship [18] predicts that big data and digital platforms will bring enormous benefits to the European economy, as firms across many industries experiment with data-driven business models and use these as tools to drive product innovation. Further literature suggests that a unified digital market platform that facilitates the trade of data may revolutionize the way in which different forms of digital data are accessed by a wide range of stakeholders from across different sectors of the national and global economies; thus fostering increased business activity [19, 20], supporting streamlined business operations [21, 22], spurring data-driven innovation [23, 24], enhancing the competitiveness of individual entrepreneurs and SMEs [25, 26] and by connecting market participants otherwise separated by physical distance [27, 28].

Employment and Job Creation. The participation of businesses in a data-rich environment wherein knowledge and information are easily obtained can affect a labour market in several ways. Data analytics and related capabilities can improve business competitiveness and become an engine of labour productivity and job creation [29]; either by facilitating strategic business decision-making that improves firm performance in increasingly competitive national and global markets [30], or directly improving labour productivity by making available a variety of relevant information and knowledge accessible to employees at all levels via a dedicated portal [31]. Increased focus on labour productivity through data-driven value creation – a direct result of the commodification of data via regular trading across the data market – could also result in a direct reduction of the number of blue-collar or manual jobs needed within a particular industry [32]. As more economic actors choose to operate in the data marketplace, the demand for so-called high-income 'knowledge workers' capable of taking advantage of the available resources would outstrip that for manual labour. Similarly, highly-skilled workers capable of manipulating data using 'smart' machines and artificial intelligence systems would, in the future, be in demand, while those lacking the necessary skills would be left behind [33].

Ageing Populations. Nowadays, people over the age of 60 constitute the fastest growing population group with their numbers set to increase from 164 m to 222 m by 2030 [34]. In rich countries like Austria, older consumers are also amongst the most affluent in society, are more educated than previous generations, and are expected to become one of the few engines of growth driving an otherwise sluggish global economy [35]. This reflects a significant business opportunity for those companies willing to address the needs of people in later life. Further, ageing people require sustained access to a wide variety of highly specialised goods and services [36]. The growth in the number and proportion of older people is likely, therefore, to strongly impact and change the focus of business activity [37]. Finally, as younger employees become required to care for their ageing relatives, companies need to both understand how to compensate for employee absenteeism and target this emerging segment of specialised consumers [38]. Better product insight as a direct consequence of increases in the collection of data on what the elderly and their caregivers need, want, and are using by way of goods and services would also result in greater returns to scope [32], as the data market platform would begin to facilitate data linkages between various suppliers of information and knowledge. The elderly and those who care for them would therefore benefit from network effects [32] generated by the frequent trading of information and knowledge: as the providers of goods and services to the elderly connect with the data market network, they by default connect their client base of users to the data market community.

Migration. Migration is a complex global phenomenon with important policy ramifications for both Europe and for Austria. General consensus in policy and academic circles is that robust and accurate data is key to effective migration governance, and can positively impact both governments and individual migrants [39]. On the one hand, reliable migration data can support decision-making by informing policy makers on the impact that migration has on society and the economy [40]. For the individual migrant, on the other hand, timely access to relevant data, coupled with appropriate policy interventions based on such information, can mitigate the vulnerabilities and risks associated with emigration and integration [39]. Despite the great potential of reliable migration data to deliver insights into complex societal and economic problems, its current availability is still recognized as being very limited [41]. Therefore, a centralised data platform can help interested stakeholders to manage existing data, and to make better use of it [39].

Climate Change. Global warming has a range of potential ecological, societal and health impacts. Big climate data is, therefore, an essential resource for climate change estimates, which are a valuable input for policy makers, aid agencies, and industry representatives involved with building national resilience to climate change and developing adaptation strategies [42]. [43] identifies three ways in which climate-related big data can be used to fight climate change. The business case for climate-related data is made by [44], who argues that financial markets have the potential to help in the fight against climate change in situations where investors have access to accurate information on how companies are anticipating and responding (or not) to climate risks and opportunities. Climate change data, especially when mixed/overlaid with other data sets, is an important source for data-driven decision making [45, 46]. A number of data portals exist in the climate change domain – leading examples being the World Bank's Climate Change Knowledge Portal [47] and NASA's Climate Change Portal [48].

Small- and Medium-scale Enterprises (SMEs). The importance of big data for economic growth is already widely recognised within the European Union [49]. According to [50], however, SMEs often fail to successfully implement big data technology and analysis frameworks. Small- and medium sized enterprises are often slow adopters of big data analytics technologies, and it is essential to ease the adoption of such technologies by SMEs in order to support economic growth through big data. A data market infrastructure addressing the challenges to SME uptake of big data analytics has the potential to become an important instrument for fostering a sustainable, inclusive and growing data-driven economy [51]. [52] argues that big data for SMEs is all about identifying, joining up and consolidating the various available sources of data, and then facilitating the analysis of that information to extract business value. Next to this, it is important to create the right framework and conditions for realising inclusive growth of the digital economy [53]. Industry representatives have echoed these findings [54].

3.2   Potential Impediments to the Successful Uptake of a Data Market

Privacy and Trust. Privacy and security can be considered among the main challenges when dealing with the digital ecosystem. In particular, the sharing of data in a data marketplace, particularly personal data that is tied to individuals, raises legitimate concerns that must be addressed [55]. [56] affirm that, in the case of open data, only when private elements are added to the data sets does open data become private data. The management of data privacy thus is an important element, considering that private data are very often the case available in ecosystems such as the data market. There is also an identified risk of violating legislation (for instance the data protection law) by sharing and releasing data that could not be otherwise made available [57]. This scenario includes, for example, datasets which contain privacy identifying variables, sensitive variables; or have been created by multiple organizations that have different levels of security, policies, and comply with different laws [57]. According to [58], trustworthiness of vendors is an important dimension of the data market, which can be assessed based on the origin of the data and on how it is processed.

Public Decision-Making Structures and Social Exclusion. To create transparent public decision-making structures and enable active citizenship in a data market it is crucial to release information, data, and services that are usable for, and can be applied by all relevant stakeholders, including citizens (e.g. data related to social justice, public safety, and health). If the data market should be inclusive and not exclude any member of the society, going "beyond [the] rationales of increased efficiency, reduced costs, increased productivity, and economic growth" is essential [59]. In recognising the social aspects of the data economy, the European Commission aims to create a whole "digital society" founded on the training of citizens in digital skills, and the promotion of concrete actions to support projects related to jobs, employability, training, and social issues [60]. The NGO and charitable sectors are, thus, also important players in a data market wherein Big data offers many opportunities for social enterprises [61] (e.g. see the Nominet Trust 100 Social Tech Guide).

Gender Inequality. Usually, the choices of women are restricted by not only their educational pathways but also social factors, such as starting a family and the workplace environment [62], cultural barriers, gender stereotype, or misinformation [63]. Quantitative numbers show the underrepresentation of women in science, technology, engineering and mathematics (STEM) worldwide, and there is a need to identify the qualitative factors that shape women's decisions to pursue STEM careers. Sociocultural factors like societal beliefs and expectations of male/female differences in ability, and cultural pressures to pursue traditionally masculine or feminine interests, are shown to have a significant impact on career decisions [63]. The fact that sociocultural factors have such a strong influence over individual career decisions also means that we may intervene to alter these outcomes [63].

4   Discussion of Findings

This section presents a synthesis of the salient points of the research findings obtained with empirical research tools. The workshop took place in 2018, as part of a conference on Digital Government. Nine participants from eight countries and three moderators attended. The participants comprised of researchers, students, and practitioners from the e-government field, none of them specialists of data trading or related domains. The data was registered by the moderators and crosschecked for analysis, and the findings are presented in a narrative form [64]. The questionnaire was administered online over the period of March - July 2018. Potential respondents were initially invited to participate by e-mail, and contacted via the DMA project mailing list. To increase response rates, organization team leaders were contacted individually and were encouraged to circulate the questionnaire amongst members of their team. It is estimated that 80 people were invited to participate in the activity, out of which 21 responded.

4.1   Benefits of Data Trading to Society

Economic Growth. Empirical data indicates that research subjects not only endorsed this view, but also considered economic growth to be the primary benefit to Austria as a direct consequence of the DMA initiative. However, respondents did not believe that any industry or sector stood to gain advantage from increased data trading.

Questionnaire respondents argue instead that the benefits arising from business participation in the DMA would be distributed evenly across different sectors of the Austrian economy.

Employment and Job Creation. Although the responses of practitioner and experts underline the fact that increased data trading can boost employment and create new jobs, respondents indicate that only modest benefits will result from participation in the Austrian data market. A large number of research subjects were confident that the DMA would result in the creation of new types of jobs in Austria, and a rise in the number of people employed in data science and data protection-related fields, as businesses participating in the project become encouraged to adopt data-driven business models.

Ageing Populations. A large majority of project partners surveyed do not feel that the Austrian DMA project would substantially impact the lives of the elderly in Austria at all. This is because the current format of the DMA is not structured to target directly to the needs of this target population. Empirical research data further suggests that the DMA is not perceived as being as mechanism that affects the nature and supply of goods and services catering to an elderly population. This does not, however, foreclose for some respondents the potential for the platform to facilitate the provision of goods and services for senior citizens, provided that the current structure of the system is sufficiently altered.

Migration. Empirical research data indicates that research subjects do not believe that significant benefits will arise from the DMA project in the domain of migration. Responses suggest that migrant populations stand to receive almost no direct benefit from the platform in its current format. Most questionnaire respondents indicated that serving migrant communities did not fall within the current purview of the project. Some research subjects did signal, however, that this was a desirable objective in the long run, and that targeted relevant information in the form of aggregated data and visualisations on pertinent topics could be made available.

Climate Change. Evidence suggests that research subjects appear optimistic that the DMA project will result in a significant positive impact within the climate change domain. This sentiment was underlined by workshop and questionnaire participant responses, wherein individuals identified and deliberated upon how the current DMA structure and format could be improved to make climate change data more easily available. Research subjects also discussed in-depth the data analytics tools and methods that could be incorporated into the DMA portal to aid in better climate change governance. The role of the DMA as a data market in this context was also underlined.

Small and Medium-sized Enterprises (SMEs). Empirical data suggests that participation in a unified data market project like the DMA will greatly improve the competitiveness of SMEs and individual entrepreneurs. Research subjects see the platform as making available data previously held by larger firms, lowering cost barriers to data access, and connecting small players to other like-minded market participants. However, it was felt that the DMA needs to be restructured to be more "small company-friendly", and to be geared towards offering small businesses more comprehensive access to data products and services. The role of the Data Broker was highlighted as being central to the effective mapping of SME data requirements with appropriate data sources.

4.2 Challenges to Effective Data Trading

Privacy and Trust. Empirical research suggests that issues surrounding privacy and trust are considered by experts and practitioners to pose the most significant threat to the success of the DMA. Better internal regulation of market participants, and the provision of robust and stable basic system functionalities, emerged from responses as the key means by which the perceived trustworthiness of DMA data providers can be improved and incentives for increased participation can be created. System process transparency as a means of improving project trustworthiness was also highlighted.

Public Decision-Making Structures. While research subjects did not believe that a lack of citizen engagement in data trading initiatives posed a significant threat to the success of the DMA, they were categorical in their opinion that a lack of public sector involvement was a very serious problem. The role of government as a catalyst, pre-server, and vital link in the data trading infrastructure was repeatedly emphasised. The initiative, it was felt, would support the Austrian national open data strategy. However, questionnaire respondents were sceptical of whether the DMA would make a signifi-cant contribution to the opening of previously closed public sector data, as they felt the current format does not support the enforcement of public sector openness.

Social Exclusion. Empirical results suggest that social exclusion is not considered a serious risk to the success of the DMA project. Research subjects involved with the project argued that, as a business-to-business platform, the DMA was not structured to directly involve particular individuals or groups in society, and that firms and entre-preneurs would drive the platform's success by using its resources to fuel data-driven innovation. However, it was noted that that the third sector could and would benefit significantly if NGOs chose to participate as business actors over the platform.

Gender Inequality. Results from the empirical studies suggest that gender inequality is not considered a significant threat to the successful roll-out of the DMA in practice. But can the DMA be used as a mechanism to correct prevailing gender inequalities in Austria? Research subjects seem to think not – in its current format the DMA is not perceived to promote indiscriminate, gender-neutral access to data. Responses to the questionnaire indicate that the DMA format could be restructured to promote affir-mative gender-related action. From a technical standpoint, too, system design elements could be incorporated to analyse and rectify gender bias in traded datasets.

4.3 Emerging Themes and Issues

A fundamental idea emerging from our research is that data is no longer just an economic asset, it has also become a social good. When traded over a data market platform, being ascribed with a definite monetary value and possessing definite pecuniary advantages for those business entities that use it effectively, there is no doubt that data has substantial economic value. However, this same commodity often loses its free-market value when applied to tackle long-standing social problems and empower the vulnerable within a society. Conflict has already emerged between business priorities and the social imperative, and the success of a data market will hinge on whether or not data producers can look beyond monetary incentives and share their data for the benefit of society. Questions also arise about how value generated from the trade of data can be distributed within society. Evidence suggests that the nature and extent of economic and social value created through data trading is largely dependent on the actors within the ecosystem themselves, and the manner in which they interact. Co-creation, sharing, and collaboration are three mechanisms by which significant value can be extracted from data. Sectoral differences also determine the manner in which different businesses respond to, and generate value out of, traded datasets.

The role of Government within the context of a national data ecosystem, therefore, becomes critical on a number of levels. First, as government policy forms the backbone of any national open data strategy or digital innovation agenda, public agencies can be instrumental in encouraging market participants to open and share data. Second, the role of the public sector can be considered central to the diffusion within society of the benefits arising from data trading: this may occur largely through Government taking the lead in the regulation of data trading spaces; it may result from policies that promote the empowerment of marginalized or vulnerable groups of people – the elderly, migrants, or women; or, it can arise through taxation policy, where the economic value generated by businesses is channeled into priority development areas.

Value is also more easily extracted from data when the data ecosystem is mapped out, and the roles of the various actors within it – data providers, data consumers, data broker, etc. – are more clearly defined and legalised. This delineation makes it easier to know, and to understand, the different players that make up each data transaction; their particular characteristics, their specific interests, their relationship to other actors, and the value they ascribe to different types of data. Determining the ownership of data, and creating awareness about the latent monetary value of proprietary data, can also be considered important determinants of data market success. In order to correctly value traded data, it is important to ascertain the degree to which data owners have control over their data, as well as identify the economic incentives open to producers of data to share data products over a marketplace platform. Creating a sense of data ownership also contributes towards better data protection, and safeguards privacy, by encouraging more responsible data handling and data management practices.

Setting out the system- and national-level business case for data trading is central to creating a critical mass of data that can be used to drive innovation over the platform. In particular, it is important to clearly identify, amplify and promote those incentives that will encourage data producers to part with their resource holdings. Encouraging unfettered supply-driven innovation is also important in this context. To realise the benefits from increased data trading, and to mitigate the potential for conflict between free-market principles and notions of data as a public good, it is also vital for a country to establish a sound open data strategy and a balanced regulatory framework for data trading. These must take into account both national public priorities and free-market economic imperatives in order to help steer the development of a national data trading infrastructure in a direction that is at once socially desirable and profitable.

The final observation arising from this research is that, without the appropriate incentives and safeguards in place, the unfettered trading of data can result in the amplification of prevailing inequalities and biases. A data market project like the DMA needs to be carefully planned out, and its potential consequences – intended and unintended – thoroughly analysed from multiple perspectives, before it can be put into practice. It would be useful in this context, therefore, to compare social and cultural implications of a data market based on existing examples from around the world.

5 Conclusion

From a systematic review of relevant scholarly and practitioner literature, and a critical analysis of empirical research results obtained from workshop deliberations with data science experts and questionnaire responses from DMA project partners, a number of key themes, perspectives, lessons, and questions emerge and a number of conclusions arrived at. This research has identified benefits of a data-driven ecosystem especially related to long-standing socio-cultural challenges in the areas of economic growth, employment and job creation, ageing populations, migration, climate change, and small- and medium-sized enterprises (SMEs); and potential societal and cultural impediments to the success of a data market within the areas of privacy and trust, public decision making structures, social exclusion and gender inequality. Our findings reveal that data is a dual-purpose commodity that has both economic value and social application. Tension arises when its monetary value as a public good is not always the same as, indeed less than, its business or free-market value. In a commercial setting, data producers are less likely to share vital resources over a data market platform if they do not perceive significant economic returns. Further, without the appropriate incentives and safeguards in place, the unfettered trading of data can result in the amplification of prevailing societal inequalities and biases. Government, therefore, has a central role to play in reducing this friction. To realise the benefits from increased data trading, and to reduce the conflict between free-market principles and notions of data as a public good, it is vital for a country to establish a sound open data strategy and a balanced regulatory framework for data trading. Although presenting a comprehensive literature review and empirical analysis, the review is not exhaustive. Additional benefits and challenges of data-driven economy from areas beyond business, Economics, Political Science and Information Science could be identified with a different selection of database and keywords. Data collection in complementary data market initiatives could also bring light to contextual differences, adding value to the understanding of social, political, economic and cultural implications of data trading.

Acknowledgements. The Data Market Austria project is funded by the "ICT of the Future" program of the Austrian Research Promotion Agency (FFG) and the Federal Ministry of Transport, Innovation and Technology (BMVIT) under grant no. 855404.

References

1. Organisation for Economic Co-operation and Development (OECD): 'Data' - Glossary of Statistical Terms
2. Brown, B., Chui, M., Manyika, J.: Are you ready for the era of 'Big Data'? McKinsey Q. **4**, 24–35 (2011)
3. Manyika, J., Chui, M., Groves, P., Farrell, D., Van Kuiken, S., Doshi, E.A.: Open Data: unlocking innovation and performance with liquid information. Report by the McKinsey Global Institute, the McKinsey Centre for Government, and the McKinsey Business Technology Office, October 2013
4. Marr, B.: Big Data in Practice: How 45 Successful Companies Used Big Data Analytics to Deliver Extraordinary Results. Wiley, Chichester (2016)
5. Deichmann, J., Heineke, K., Reinbacher, T., Wee, D.: Creating a Successful Internet of Things Data Marketplace. Digital McKinsey, McKinsey and Company. http://www.mckinsey.com/business-functions/digital-mckinsey/our-insights/creating-a-successful-internet-of-things-data-marketplace. Accessed 22 May 2018
6. Schomm et al.
7. Li, C., Miklau, G.: Pricing aggregate queries in a data marketplace. In: Ives, Z.G., Velegrakis Y (eds.) Proceedings of the 15th International Workshop on the Web and Databases 2012, WebDB 2012, Scottsdale, AZ, USA, 20 May 2012, pp. 1–6 (2012)
8. European Commission: Building a European Data Economy. Communication from the Commission to the European Parliament, the Council, the European Economic and Social Committee, and the Committee of the Regions, Brussels 10.1.2017, COM (2017) 9 Final. https://eurlex.europa.eu/legalcontent/EN/TXT/PDF/?uri=CELEX:52017DC0009&from=EN. Accessed 24 May 2018
9. European Commission: Horizon 2020, Work Programme 2016 (2017). http://ec.europa.eu/research/participants/data/ref/h2020/wp/2016_2017/main/h2020-wp1617-societies_en.pdf. Accessed 22 May 2018
10. Ivanschitz, B-P., Lampoltshammer, T.J., Mireles, V., Revenko, A., Schlarb, S., Thurnay, L.: A data market with decentralized repositories. In: Verborgh, R., Kuhn, T., Berners-Lee, T. (eds.) Proceedings of the 2nd Workshop on Decentralizing the Semantic Web co-located with the 17th International Semantic Web Conference (ISWC 2018), vol. 2165, pp. 1–7, CEUR (2018)
11. Thurner, T., Kaltenböck, M.: Data Market Austria Deliverable - D2.1 Community Building Coordination, Dissemination & Exploitation Plan. Delivery date 07 September 2017 (2017). https://datamarket.at/wp-content/uploads/2017/10/D2.1-DMA-Community-Building-Coordination-Dissemination-Exploitation-Plan.pdf. Accessed 16 May 2019
12. Kitchenham, B.: Procedures for Performing Systematic Reviews. Joint Technical Report – Keele University Technical Report TR/SE-0401& NICTA Technical Report 0400011T.1, June 2004 (2004)
13. Viale Pereira, G., Virkar, S., Vignoli, M.: Exploring the political, social and cultural challenges and possibilities associated with trading data: the case of Data Market Austria (DMA). Article 128. In: Proceedings of the 19th Annual International Conference on Digital Government Research: Governance in the Data Age (Dg.o 2018), 2 pages. ACM Press, New York (2018)
14. Morgan, D.L.: Focus groups. Annu. Rev. Sociol. **22**(1), 129–152 (1996)
15. Wilson, M., Sapsford, R.: Asking questions. In: Sapsford, R., Jupp, V. (eds.) Data Collection and Analysis, 2nd edn. SAGE Publications, London (2006)

16. Adejimi, A., Oyediran, O.S., Ogunsanmi, E.B.: Employing qualitatively enriched semi structured questionnaire in evaluating ICT impact on Nigerian 'construction chain integration'. Built Hum. Environ. Rev. **3**(1), 49–62 (2010)
17. Kumar, R.: Research Methodology. A Step-by-Step Guide for Beginners, 4th edn. SAGE Publications, London (2014)
18. Strategic Policy Forum on Digital Entrepreneurship: Big Data and B2B Digital Platforms: The Next Frontier for Europe's Industry and Enterprises. Recommendations of the Strategic Policy Forum on Digital Entrepreneurship (2016)
19. Bhimani, A.: Exploring big data's strategic consequences. J. Inf. Tech. **30**(1), 66–69 (2016)
20. EYGM. Big Data. Changing the Way Businesses Compete and Operate. Insights on Governance, Risk and Compliance (2014)
21. Arellano, P.: Making decisions with data: how to put different data sources together. BIRST, 4 August 2015. Blog (2015). https://www.birst.com/blog/making-decisions-with-data-how-to-put-different-data-sources-together/. Accessed 06 June 2018
22. Business Roundtable: Putting Data to Work: Maximizing the Value of Information in an Interconnected World. Business Roundtable (2015)
23. Zillner, S., et al.: Big data-driven innovation in industrial sectors. In: Cavanillas, J., Curry, E., Wahlster, W. (eds.) New Horizons for a Data-Driven Economy: A Roadmap for Usage and Exploitation of Big Data in Europe, pp. 169–178. Springer, Cham (2016). https://doi.org/10.1007/978-3-319-21569-3_9
24. Parmar, R., Mackenzie, I., Cohn, D., Gann, D.: The New Patterns of Innovation: How to Use Data to Drive Growth. Harvard Business Review (2014)
25. Manyika, J., Lund, S., Bughin, J., Woetzel, J., Stamenov, K., Dhingra, D.: Digital globalization: the new era of global flows. McKinsey Global Institute Report (2016)
26. Oxera: Benefits of Online Platforms. Oxera Consulting LLP, Oxford (2015)
27. Duch-Brown, N.: The competitive landscape of online platforms. JRC Digital Economy Working Paper 2017-04. Joint Research Centre, European Commission, Seville (2017)
28. Libert, B., Beck, M., Wind, Y.(J.): 3 Ways to Get Your Own Digital Platform. Harvard Business Review, 22 July 2016, sec. Business Models (2016). https://hbr.org/2016/07/3-ways-to-get-your-own-digital-platform. Accessed 22 May 2018
29. Software & Information Industry Association (SIIA): Data-driven innovation – a guide for policymakers: understanding and enabling the economic and social value of data. SIIA White Paper Series (2013). [full citation unavailable]
30. Wamba, S.F., Akter, S., Edwards, A., Chopin, G., Gnanzou, D.: How 'big data' can make big impact: findings from a systematic review and a longitudinal case study. Int. J. Prod. Econ. **165**, 234–246 (2015)
31. Koegler, S.: The Empowered Employee: How 6 Companies Are Arming Their Teams with Data. IBM Blog - Cognitive Enterprise, 24 March 2017. https://www.ibm.com/blogs/watson/2017/03/empowered-employee-6-companies-arming-teams-data/. Accessed 07 Aug 2018
32. OECD: Data-Driven Innovation: Big Data for Growth and Well-Being. OECD Publishing, Paris (2015)
33. Brynjolfsson, E., McAfee, A.: Race Against the Machine: How the Digital Revolution Is Accelerating Innovation, Driving Productivity, and Irreversibly Transforming Employment and the Economy. Brynjolfsson and McAfee (2012)
34. Dobbs, R., et al.: Urban World: The Global Consumers to Watch, April 2016. McKinsey Global Institute (2016)
35. The Economist: The Grey Market. The Economist, 7 April 2016, sec. Schumpeter – Business (2016). https://www.economist.com/business/2016/04/07/the-grey-market. Accessed 07 Aug 2018

36. Kuenen, J.W., et al.: Global Aging: How Companies Can Adapt to the New Reality. The Boston Consulting Group, Amsterdam (2011)
37. Economist Intelligence Unit (EIU): A Silver Opportunity? Rising Longevity and Its Implications for Business. The Economist Intelligence Unit (2011)
38. Mochis, G.P., Lee, E., Mathur, A.: Targeting the mature market: opportunities and challenges. J. Consum. Mark. **14**(4), 282–293 (1997)
39. International Organization for Migration, and McKinsey & Company: More than Numbers. How Migration Data Can Deliver Real-Life Benefits for Migrants and Governments. Final version for World Economic Forum in Davos, 24 January 2018 (2018)
40. Laczko, F.: Improving data on international migration and development: towards a global action plan? Discussion Paper, German Federal Foreign Office (2016)
41. United Nations Organisation: In safety and dignity: addressing large movements of refugees and migrants. Report of the Secretary-General. United Nations General Assembly (2016)
42. Ford, J.D., et al.: Big data has big potential for applications to climate change adaptation. PNAS **113**(39), 10729–10732 (2016)
43. Augur, H.: Big data plays surprising role in fight against climate change. Dataconomy, 2 June 2016. http://dataconomy.com/2016/06/big-data-plays-surprising-role-fight-climate-change/. Accessed 08 July 2018
44. Carney, M.: Better Market Information Can Help Combat Climate Change. Financial Times, 28 June 2017, sec. Opinion (2017). https://www.ft.com/content/51e60772-5bf5-11e7-b553-e2df1b0c3220. Accessed 06 July 2018
45. Faghmous, J.H., Kumar, V.: A big data guide to understanding climate change: the case for theory-guided data science. Big Data **2**(3), 155–163 (2014)
46. Burke, M., Hsiang, S.M., Miguel, E.: Global non-linear effect of temperature on economic production. Nature **527**, 235–239 (2015)
47. World Bank Group, Climate Change Knowledge Portal. http://sdwebx.worldbank.org/climateportal/. Accessed 22 July 2018
48. NASA Jet Propulsion Laboratory. https://climate.nasa.gov. Accessed 22 July 2018
49. Sen, D., Ozturk, M., Vayvay, O.: An overview of big data for growth in SMEs. Procedia Soc. Behav. Sci **235**, 159–167 (2016)
50. Ogbuokiri, B.O., Udanor, C.N., Agu, M.N.: Implementing bigdata Analytics for Small and Medium Enterprise (SME) regional growth. IOSR-JCE **17**(6), 35–43 (2015). Version IV
51. Coleman, S., Göb, R., Manco, G., Pievatolo, A., Tort-Martorell, X., Seabra Reis, M.: How can SMEs benefit from big data? Challenges and a path forward. Qual. Reliab. Eng. Intl. **32** (6), 2151–2164 (2016)
52. Rossi, B.: How to Make Big Data Work for SMEs. Information Age, 6 July 2016. Blog (2016). https://www.information-age.com/how-make-big-data-work-smes-123461680/. Accessed 22 July 2018
53. Morovan, L.: Data the fuel of the digital economy and SME growth. Accenture Report, 2016. Accenture (2016)
54. Burns, E.: Why Haven't SMEs Cashed in on Big Data Benefits Yet? TechTarget SearchBusiness Analytics (2015). http://searchbusinessanalytics.techtarget.com/feature/Why-havent-SMEs-cashed-in-on-big-data-benefits-yet. Accessed 22 Aug 2018
55. Mundial, F.E.: Big Data, Big Impact: New Possibilities for International Development. Foro Económico Mundial. Cologny, Suiza. (2012). www3.weforum.org/docs/WEF_TC_MFS_BigDataBigImpact_Briefing_2012.pdf. Accessed 01 Oct 2017
56. Immonen, A., Palviainen, M., Ovaska, E.: Requirements of an open data based business ecosystem. IEEE Access **2**, 88–103 (2014)

57. Zuiderwijk, A., Janssen, M.: The negative effects of open government data-investigating the dark side of Open Data. In: Proceedings of the 15th Annual International Conference on Digital Government Research, pp. 147–152. ACM Press, New York (2014)
58. Schomm, F., Stahl, F., Vossen, G.: Marketplaces for data: an initial survey. ACM SIGMOD Rec. **42**(1), 15–26 (2013)
59. Howard, A: More than Economics: The Social Impact of Open Data. TechRepublic, 31 July 2014,   https://www.techrepublic.com/article/more-than-economics-the-social-impact-of-open-data/. Accessed 19 July 2018
60. European Commission: New Skills Agenda for Europe (2017). http://ec.europa.eu/social/main.jsp?catId=1223. Accessed 07 June 2018
61. Small, A., Anderton, E.: Believe the Hype: Big Data Can Have a Big Social Impact. The Guardian, 06 May 2014, sec. Guardian Sustainable Business - Social Enterprise Blog (2014). https://www.theguardian.com/social-enterprise-network/2014/may/06/data-open-social-impact-tips-tools. Accessed 07 July 2018
62. UNESCO: Women in Science (2014). http://uis.unesco.org/en/topic/women-science. Accessed 21 June 2018
63. Wang, M.T., Degol, J.L.: Gender gap in Science, Technology, Engineering, and Mathematics (STEM): current knowledge, implications for practice, policy, and future directions. Educ. Psychol. Rev. **29**(1), 119–140 (2017)
64. Bertrand, J.T., Brown, J.E., Ward, V.M.: Techniques for analyzing focus group data. Eval. Rev. **16**(2), 198–209 (1992)

AI, Data Analytics and Automated Decision Making

How to Streamline AI Application in Government? A Case Study on Citizen Participation in Germany

Dian Balta[1]([⊠]), Peter Kuhn[1] (ID), Mahdi Sellami[1], Daniel Kulus[2],
Claudius Lieven[2], and Helmut Krcmar[3]

[1] Fortiss GmbH, Guerickestr. 25, 80805 Munich, Germany
`balta@fortiss.org`
[2] Behörde für Stadtentwicklung und Wohnen, Neuenfelder Str 19,
21109 Hamburg, Germany
[3] Informatics 17 - Chair for Information Systems,
Technical University of Munich, Boltzmannstr. 3, 85748 Garching, Germany

Abstract. Artificial intelligence (AI) technologies are on the rise in almost every aspect of society, business and government. Especially in government, it is of interest how the application of AI can be streamlined: at least, in a controlled environment, in order to be able to evaluate potential (positive and negative) impact. Unfortunately, reuse in development of AI applications and their evaluation results lack interoperability and transferability. One potential remedy to this challenge would be to apply standardized artefacts: not only on a technical level, but also on an organization or semantic level. This paper presents findings from a qualitative explorative case study on online citizen participation in Germany that reveal insights on the current standardization level of AI applications. In order to provide an in-depth analysis, the research involves evaluation of two particular AI approaches to natural language processing. Our findings suggest that standardization artefacts for streamlining AI application exist predominantly on a technical level and are still limited.

Keywords: Natural language processing · Standardization · Government

1 Introduction

AI represents a concept that incorporates various characteristics of intelligent systems that follow particular goals, including a formal representation of (incomplete) knowledge and an automated logical interference based on that knowledge [1]. Application domains have been discussed as far as the 1960s (e.g. [2]), followed by principles for design and application in the 1980s (e.g. [3]). Currently, if designed in an ethical and a trustworthy manner, AI is expected to represent a huge leap from data analysis to high quality and efficiency predictions, and increases the value of informed judgements decisions by humans [4].

Still, being in the trends spotlight for more than 10 years (e.g. [5]), AI applications prove challenging in government practice (cf. e.g. [6]). While application examples continuously provided indications of AI's potential (cf. e.g. [7, 8]), they have yet to

I. Lindgren et al. (Eds.): EGOV 2019, LNCS 11685, pp. 233–247, 2019.
https://doi.org/10.1007/978-3-030-27325-5_18

deliver sustainable and reproducible results in the government domain. In particular, online citizen participation has been in the focus of research and practice in the last decades regarding natural language processing (e.g. text mining), that would provide a more efficient and effective service to citizens and government (cf. e.g. [9–11]).

This paper states the argument that standardized artefacts (e.g. business processes, models, shared terminologies, software tools etc.) are required in order to streamline AI application in government. To support this argument, we present findings from a case study in Germany and discuss their implications.

The rest of the paper is structured as follows. First, we introduce the required theoretical background. Next, we present details and background information on the case study and describe our research approach. After this, we present our findings and discuss implication for AI application in government.

2 Theoretical Background

2.1 Standardization

We apply the definition of a standard as "a uniform set of measures, agreements, conditions, or specifications between parties" [27], and standardization represents the process of reaching a standard encompasses stabilizing and solidifying its definition and boundaries [12, 28]. Hence, standardization can be described in detail as "the activity of establishing and recording a limited set of solutions to actual or potential matching problems directed at benefits for the party or parties involved balancing their needs and intending and expecting that these solutions will be repeatedly or continuously used during a certain period by a substantial number of the parties for whom they are meant" [29].

In order to analyze IT standardization artefacts in government, the following framework that consist of two dimension can be applied [12, 13]. The first dimension includes three levels of interoperability and the second dimension includes five functional views (cf. Table 1, with exemplary artefacts). The interoperability dimension is structured along three layers. First, the interoperability of business processes applied in delivering public service is found on the organizational layer. Second, interoperability regarding exchange of information and data as well as to their meaning between parties involved is found on the semantic layer. Third, interoperability regarding data structure and format, sending and receiving data based on communication protocols, electronic mechanisms to store data as well as software and hardware is situated on the technical/syntactic layer.

The second dimension includes five functional views [12]. The administration view includes predominantly non-technical standards. They affect personnel and process aspects as well as communication within or between public administrations. For instance, a standardized business process definition or standardized shared terminology to describe public services or a standardized business reporting standard represent particular artefacts in this view. Second, the modeling view includes reference models and architectures, as well as modelling languages for each corresponding interoperability level. For instance, an ontology can be applied to model a semantic standard towards the creation of a shared terminology and its sustainable use. Third, standards that focus the computation of data are included in the processing view. Exemplary artefacts in this view include a specific software application such as an information search service or a tax accounting software application. Fourth, corresponding standards for data and information exchange between different public administrations is handled in the communication and interaction view. For instance, a common metadata definition (i.e. data describing other data) is applied in a shared methodology in order to allow for an effective information search service. Fifth, the security and privacy view contains standards that aim at addressing issues such as definition of access management policies, application of cryptography methods or requesting a minimum of personal data and respecting privacy.

Table 1. Analysis framework and exemplary standardization artefacts in e-government

	Administration	Modeling	Processing	Communication & Interaction	Security & Privacy
Organizational	Business Process	Reference Process	Business Process Modeling Tool	Process Model Exchange Format	Information Access Policy
Semantic	Shared Terminology	Ontology	Information Search Service	Common Metadata Definition	
Technical / Syntactic	Business Reporting	Application Architecture	Tax Accounting Software Application	Data Format	Encryption Algorithm

An analysis of standards for e-government based on the described framework would include assigning them to one or several cells along the two dimensions. An assignment to multiple cells is possible, since a standardized solution might address different interoperability layers and functional views at the same time. Consequently, we apply the framework to analyze challenges (e.g. organizational and managerial, data as well as technological challenges [6]) of AI application in government and, in particular, in online citizen participation.

2.2 Online Citizen Participation

Online citizen participation can be described as a form of participation that is based on the usage of information and communication technology in societal democratic and consultative processes focused on citizens [14, 15]. Given the fact that different levels of online citizen participation and models to describe them exist [16], the participation referred to in our research can be described as collaboration between citizens and government. In particular, government employees and/or politician are still the ultimate decision makes, but a two-way communication between government and citizens takes place and the latter play an active role in proposing and shaping policy and decisions [17].

Implementation of online citizen participation is a challenging task [18] that includes the application of various techniques and technologies [19, 20]. With regard to existing models and frameworks of online citizen participation [21–23], the online citizen participation that lays the ground for our analysis can be described as follows. First, the participation process is steered top-down and is government led [23], where a public administration invites users to provide feedback by providing a set of topics and applies a set of participation techniques over a particular platform [19].

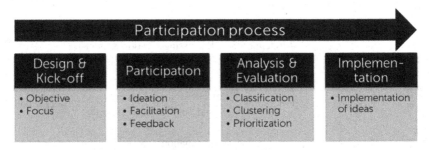

Fig. 1. Four generic steps of a citizen participation process

Second, the participation process can be described based on four generic steps from a government's perspective (cf. Fig. 1). In the first step, public administration representatives design and kick-off citizen participation by setting objectives and by adjusting the focus to the participation goals. In a second step, citizens are invited to participate and provide feedback. In this step, ideation techniques are applied, and public administration employees aim at facilitating the process. In the third step, public administration employees or instructed service providers analyse and evaluate the generated citizens' feedback. This includes classifying ideas based on a predefined set of topics and objectives as well as clustering all ideas into new feasible subsets in order to develop a summary report that includes a prioritization of citizens' ideas. This step can require substantial effort from the involved employees, given the potentially large amount of citizen input to be analysed and evaluated. Finally, based on predefined policy processes, the implementation of the ideas is triggered (e.g. by providing the summarized report to action-taking parties such as architects' offices).

2.3 Applied AI

According to the Association for Computing Machinery (ACM) Computing Classification System (CCS), AI is a broad research field with various application areas. In particular, AI employs machine learning methods that are based on algorithms that can learn from data without relying on rules-based programming. These methods emerged in the 1990s, making use of steady advances in digitization and cheap computing power, and enabling to efficiently train computers to develop models for analysis and prediction. Recent developments in machine learning include novel models for knowledge representation based on neural networks, and logical interference is based on deep learning [24]. Neural networks represent a biologically-inspired programming paradigm which enables a computer to learn from observational data, while deep learning represents a powerful set of techniques for learning in neural networks [24].

An application of AI with a particular relevance for online citizen participation is a methodology named natural language processing (NLP). With NLP, tasks such as information extraction and summarization or discourse and dialogue or even machine translation can be automated to a certain degree. Consequently, goals of applying NLP in online citizen participation include designing a more efficient participation process through supporting the ideation (e.g. suggesting keywords or related contributions during ideation) as well as the analysis and evaluation (e.g. clustering and classifying user contributions). NLP has been already applied in government practice (e.g. [7, 8]) as well as in online citizen participation (e.g. [9–11]). While various tools and automated programmable interfaces (APIs) exist (cf. e.g. [25] for an overview), recent analysis shows that open source tools, that allow for a better control of data privacy and on premise operation of NLP, perform well in comparison with established API providers over closed source logical interference software and knowledge models [26].

Given the great number of applications, methodologies and tools, there are also numerous challenges to be addressed [6]. Hence, it would be of interest to analyse standardized artefacts potentially suitable for application in the government and, in particular, in the online citizen participation domain in order to effectively manage and streamline AI.

3 Online Citizen Participation in the Free and Hanseatic City of Hamburg and the Project Civitas Digitalis

Hamburg is a vivid city in northern Germany, with over 1.8 million citizens that has a strong economic development and a steady growth in terms of urban development and infrastructure projects. Since this growth affects a large number of citizens, citizen participation obtains an important role. In order to intensify information and participation in urban development projects and environmental protection issues and to develop a new planning culture in Hamburg, the 'Stadtwerkstatt' (city workshop) was set up as an organizational entity in the state-ministry of urban development and housing in 2012. Consequently, the Hamburg follows the concepts of top-down participation [23] by providing an own platform for participation and thus steering the democratic participation process (cf. Sect. 2.2).

Since 2016, the city workshop unit offers a tool for online participation as part of its participation platform. The open source tool was developed in cooperation with the city's Agency for Geoinformation and Surveying (LGV) and since then has been used in more than 30 participation processes, with a total of over 10,000 contributions created by users. This geodata-based web application allows citizens to gather information about urban development projects and to submit contributions, including ideas, questions and criticism (cf. Fig. 2, accessible online https://geoportal-hamburg. de/beteiligung_grasbrook/mapview-beitraege).

Fig. 2. An exemplary application of the online participation tool

The online participation tool is a basic online service that allows citizens to participate at any time and from any location. For the city administration and those officials responsible for project planning, the focus is particularly on greater reach and inclusion of social groups that are not able to participate at in-person meetings and workshops. For citizens who would like to participate, the tool provides an overview over the discussed topics, a thematic filter function and a city map visualization.

Since 2016, the city workshop offers a tool for digital participation as part of its participation platform. The open source online participation tool was developed in cooperation with the city's Agency Geoinformation and Surveying (LGV) and since then has been used in more than 30 participation processes, with a total of over 10,000 contributions created by users. This geodata-based web application allows citizens to gather information about urban development projects submit contributions, including ideas, questions and criticism (cf. Fig. 2, accessible online https://geoportal-hamburg. de/beteiligung_grasbrook/mapview-beitraege).

The online participation is a basic online service that allows citizens to participate at any time and from any location. For the city administration and those responsible for project planning, the focus is particularly on greater reach and inclusion of social groups not able to participate at in-person meetings and workshops. For citizens who would like to participate, the tool provides an overview of which topics are discussed, a thematic filter function and a city map visualization.

A greater reach provides a higher number of citizens' ideas and, in consequence, a significantly bigger effort for the evaluation and analysis of the ideas by the public administration employees is required. Currently, contributions from digital and analog participation need to be merged in one digital file and are evaluated manually. The entire process is quite time-consuming. In several work steps, the contribution data are viewed, checked with regard to content and topic and, if necessary, differentiated into further categories or subcategories. At the end, the results are summarized, and potential courses of action are formulated.

In this context, the research project Civitas Digitalis (https://civitas-digitalis. informatik.uni-hamburg.de/en/about-the-project/) was initiated with Stadtwerkstatt as partner from practice. A project goal is to develop and evaluate a toolset for supporting a more efficient and effective online citizen participation.

4   Research Approach

We follow a qualitative analysis approach to explorative research. We aim at developing descriptive artefacts that can be categorized as a theory for analyzing [27]. Our research approach is rooted in the paradigm of pragmatism [28]. We studied the findings through an argumentative-deductive analysis [29].

4.1   Data Collection

For the analysis of this paper multiple types of data have been collected from three different sources. The first source of data are online citizen participation projects realized by the city of Hamburg in the last couple of years. We collected the ideas in German language from citizens in nine participation projects, cleaned the data by removing double entries or insufficient details entries. The total number of ideas was 3,859. The number of ideas per project vary from 95 to 1,689 ideas. The ideas, in turn, differ significantly in length, with the longest counting 1,079 words and the shortest 1 word. The median of words per idea is 15. Furthermore, the ideas have different properties. While most ideas consist of both the title and the description, some have only one of them. For instance, 1,018 ideas have no title. For every project, the ideas have been assigned by the citizen to a given category and after an idea has been submitted, the assignment has been analyzed, evaluated and potentially corrected by public administration employees. For the nine projects there is a total of 50 used categories–from now on called subcategories–that for the purpose of the analysis have been combined into eight groups –from now on called categories.

The second source of data are interviews conducted in the course of this research that lasted between 35 and 60 min. One interview was undertaken with a citizen participation expert from a service provider that operates participation processes for municipalities. The second interview partner was an expert from the Stadtwerkstatt Hamburg which supports offices of the city with participation processes. Both interviews were conducted via telephone and based on a semi-structured questionnaires. The third interview has been conducted with an AI expert in order to evaluate the feasibility of the planned applications.

A workshop with 11 officials from the city of Hamburg and experts from service providers was the third source of data. In this workshop, the participants were asked to categorize 25 ideas from a recent citizen participation process (which is not part of the previously mentioned nine processes) into five predefined categories. The exercise was concluded by three groups of 3–5 experts in parallel, resulting in three classifications. Participatory observations as well as the allocation of ideas by the participants have been documented in writing.

4.2   Data Analysis

The analysis of the collected data included manually conducted reviews of the summarized interview reports, workshop results and reports as well as an automated NLP. The manual analysis was conducted by one researcher in our research group and was reviewed by a second researcher to assure consistency and to correct potential errors.

With respect to methodological development and practical tool availability of NLP (cf. e.g., [10, 11, 30–33]), we decided to analyze data based on a traditional machine learning approach as well as on a neural network and deep learning approach (cf. our open source implementation https://civitasdigitalis.fortiss.org/ with data sets available upon request). Prior to applying each NLP approach, stratified sampling has been applied to the collected data set, splitting it into a training (80% - 3,087 ideas) and an evaluation (20% - 772 ideas) set, i.e. the resulting training and evaluation sets have the same distribution over the classes of ideas.

The first approach was based on the tool LingPipe [34] given its suitability for the analysis tasks (cf. e.g. [35, 36]). We implemented a character-level language-model based classifier. The classifier trains a model based on the occurrence count of characters and their combinations as well as the probability of both. The classifier predicts the assignment to a class based on the multivariate distribution of characters and their combinations to that class.

With regard to recent developments in neuronal network and deep learning approaches to NLP (cf. e.g. [37–39]), the second approach applied in our data analysis is a classifier based on BERT [40]. BERT implements a model architecture that includes a multi-layer bidirectional transformer encoder that can be configured to apply up to 1,024 hidden layers as well as 340 million parameters. Consequently, we decided to use the largest available BERT transformer that is pre-trained in a multilingual text setup and recommended for German language. We experimented with different characters sequence length, batch sizes, learning rates and number of epochs during the customization of the model, in order to evaluate accuracy.

5   Findings

5.1   Level of Standardization of AI Application in Online Citizen Participation

Based on the analysis of documents, interviews and workshop results, we apply the framework for standardization analysis as follows (cf. Table 2) and note "NA" in each table cell, if the analyzed data did not allow to present a finding. On the organizational level, there have been only general standardization artefacts regarding security and privacy. In particular, the EU General Data Protection Regulation (GDPR) has been considered as a guide for conducting any type of data analysis. For instance, there have been concerns regarding any application using an API or 3rd party software that was not hosted on computers in Germany or in our research group. These concerns have also been linked to still missing standards for communication and interaction, since vendor or tool lock-in could result. In terms of particular business processes or models, there have been only initial considerations such as at which step of the participation process AI would be suitable and of use.

Table 2. Analysis of standardization level of AI application in the case study

		Administration	Modeling	Processing	Communication & Interaction	Security & Privacy
Organizational		initial considerations	initial considerations	NA	vendor or tool lock-in concerns	GDPR
Semantic		shared terminology in similar participation projects	initial considerations	NA	NA	
Technical / Syntactic		initial considerations	NA	tools based on machine learning	model or technique specific	NA

At the semantic level, there has been a shared terminology regarding the classification of citizen ideas (e.g. "transportation" or "public space"). Still, this terminology has emerged and has not been a product of particular coordination effort. From a modeling functional perspective, there have been some implicit initial considerations (e.g. particular sentiment in an idea), but these have not been further detailed.

The technical and syntactic level included some initial considerations on how to integrate NLP techniques in existing tools (e.g. host an own analysis services, integration with front-end of the participation tool). Since the initial task of the researchers involved in the project was to apply NLP techniques, we were able to analyze a set of tools that can be applied and reused as standardized artefacts (e.g. LingPipe and BERT). Further, we were able to analyze standardization of communication and interaction between different tools. Based on the particular technology and technique applied, there are particular data exchange formats (e.g. a vector based representation of text for feature extraction). Still, there is no standard available and interoperability between tools and techniques have to be fitted to context.

5.2   AI Based Analysis

In order to compare both NLP approaches and their practical applicability, we conducted a number of tests with the data available (cf. Table 3). Consequently, we applied a statistical confusion matrix that summarizes true positives (TP), false negatives (FN), false positives (FP), and true negatives (TN) as well as the F1 score to measure the accuracy of the prediction. For each category (listed in German), we had a different number of ideas split into training data and prediction test data.

Table 3. Comparison of the applied NLP approaches

Category	LingPipe tool							BERT tool							Test Data	Training Data
	TP	FN	FP	TN	Recall	Precision	F1	TP	FN	FP	TN	Recall	Precision	F1		
Verkehr & Mobilität	326	12	120	314	96,45%	73,09%	**83,16%**	302	36	66	368	89,35%	82,07%	**85,55%**	185	1504
Wohnen & Arbeiten	24	24	21	703	50,00%	53,33%	**51,61%**	24	24	19	705	50,00%	55,81%	**52,75%**	15	225
Grün & Erholung	20	38	8	706	34,48%	71,43%	**46,51%**	32	26	28	686	55,17%	53,33%	**54,24%**	24	265
Sport & Freizeit	74	21	30	647	77,89%	71,15%	**74,37%**	76	19	32	645	80,00%	70,37%	**74,88%**	50	426
Klima & Umweltschutz	1	18	1	752	5,26%	50,00%	**9,52%**	7	12	8	745	36,84%	46,67%	**41,18%**	10	85
Städtebau & Stadtraum	20	50	10	692	28,57%	66,67%	**40,00%**	23	47	36	666	32,86%	38,98%	**35,66%**	33	317
Soziales & Kultur	25	28	11	708	47,17%	69,44%	**56,18%**	34	19	20	699	64,15%	62,96%	**63,55%**	25	239
Sonstiges	26	65	55	626	28,57%	32,10%	**30,23%**	27	64	38	643	29,67%	41,54%	**34,62%**	44	412

For the NLP approach implemented with LingPipe, an average of 66.84% accuracy was observed. The accuracy varied significantly between categories. Although no correlation was analyzed in detail, our initial findings suggest that categories with higher numbers of ideas have better accuracy results.

The NLP approach implemented with BERT achieved an improvement of 1.56% and resulted in a total of 68.4% accuracy. In summary, both approaches showed promising results, the data available is of reasonable quality and there is a large enough data set. For instance, the best results were generated for the category "Verkehr

& Mobilität" (transportation & mobility). This category contains 1.689 ideas in the data set and, arguably, the data quality is consistent among all ideas. On the contrary, the category "Sonstiges" (miscellaneous) contains 456 ideas in the data set that appear to be of varying quality, i.e. ideas were put in this category only if not matching any other. Apparently, there were no further semantic or any other classification rules applied.

5.3   Comparing AI and Human Based Analysis

The collected human-based classification obtained in the workshop and the above described analysis allow for a comparison of human-based and AI-based categorization of participation ideas. The baseline for this comparison is the original category assignment of the contributor which we will consider as the correct category.

The groups of experts in the workshop categorized 14, 15 and 16 out of 25 categories correctly. This corresponds with a success rate of 60% in average. While some categories seemed to be easier to categorize for the experts, others appear to be less so – potentially, due to semantic heterogeneity. This was also reflected in the discussions among the workshop participants.

For the AI-based categorization, we applied both NLP approaches and selected the results with highest accuracy. Moreover, we developed an analysis improvement that delivered not only the first best fitting category, but also the second best fitting category. Considering, with the first best guesses considered, 8 out of 25 categories have been classified correctly which corresponds with a 32% success rate. Including also the second-best guesses, 13 out 25 ideas have been assigned to their correct category, resulting in a success rate of 52%. As for the human-based results, the success rate by category varied also for the AI-based assignment.

Table 4. Human and AI based analysis

	Human based				AI based	
	Group 1	Group 2	Group 3	average	first-best guess	first and second-best guess
Correctly assigned ideas	14	16	15	**15**	8	**13**
Success Rate	56%	64%	60%	**60%**	32%	**52%**

In comparison, the AI-based categorization is not as effective as the human-based one (cf. Table 4). Considering the average of the workshop groups and the more favorable AI-based counting (including the second-best guess), there still remains a difference of two ideas less assigned correctly.

6 Discussion and Conclusion

The objective of this paper was to address the question of how to streamline AI application in government and, in particular, in the online citizen participation. We presented theoretical background on standardization, online citizen participation processes and application of AI and developed and argument that a standardization of AI artefacts at different levels and from different functional perspectives is required towards streamlining AI application. Based case study in Germany, we presented findings on levels of standardization, results from applying two different AI techniques for natural language processing as well as a comparison between human and AI performance.

Our findings show the following implications regarding AI application in government and, in particular, in online citizen participation. First, there are already NLP tools and pre-trained models available that can provide efficient support along the steps of the participation process. Quality, amount and availability of data seem to be of high importance for sufficient prediction, though. Second, human based analysis still has a number of advantages. As the results of our workshop show, humans are capable–in the course of intensive discussion and collaboration–to outperform AI and NLP. Additionally, the arguments provided by the workshop participant explained why a particular idea was assigned to a particular category. In the case with the implemented NLP techniques and tools, we were not capable of providing these insights.

Table 5. Future research on streamlining AI application in online citizen participation

	Administra-tion	Modeling	Processing	Communi-cation & Inter-action	Security & Privacy
Organizational	How does an online participation process with AI look like?	What is a reference model or an architecture, based on e.g. [22, 41]	How to integrate AI in existing tools for the design of online participation?	How to assure a technology shift?	How can GDPR conformity be evaluated and assured?
Semantic	What are shared context-specific concepts that can be integrated using AI?	What is a suitable ontology, e.g. based on [17, 23]	What are available AI services that fit requirements of online citizen participation?	How to share language specific AI results?	
Technical / Syntactic	How to monitor and manage AI applications?	How to integrate AI applications in existing IT infrastructures?	How to improve data quality and customize models?	Which competencies are required for the application of AI?	Are the any certified tools available?

Third, our findings suggest that a standardization of AI application in government and, in particular, in online citizen participation is still in its infancy. There were only a few standardized artefacts available, predominantly on the technical/syntactic level. Due to this current status, available data in suitable quality for efficient and effective AI application is even more challenging.

This research presents a first glimpse of the potential of and barriers to standardized artefacts for streamlining AI application in government. Given the contextual limitations–a case study on online citizen participation in Germany, data set size and quality, available tools and techniques etc.–we would like to encourage researchers to dig deeper in the sketched challenges and derive potential remedies. Therefore, we have summarized a number of questions that emerged during our research and could be addressed in future (cf. Table 5). Additionally, future research could focus on interactions between the different standardization levels and their implications to adoption of AI in government. Given the number of human languages available and the expected potential of AI in government, we hope that future research would allow for a more efficient development and sustainability of AI application.

Acknowledgements. This research was partially funded by the German Federal Ministry of Education and Research (BMBF) with the project lead partner PTKA (Projektträger Karlsruhe am Karlsruher Institut für Technologie/KIT) in the context of the project Civitas Digitalis (funding code '02K15A050').

We thank our reviewers for their careful reading and their constructive remarks.

References

1. Russell, S.J., Norvig, P.: Artificial Intelligence: A Modern Approach. Pearson Education Limited, Malaysia (2016)
2. Minsky, M.: Steps toward artificial intelligence. Proc. IRE **49**, 8–30 (1961)
3. Nilsson, N.J.: Principles of Artificial Intelligence. Springer, Heidelberg (1982)
4. Agrawal, A., Gans, J., Goldfarb, A.: Prediction Machines: The Simple Economics of Artificial Intelligence. Harvard Business Press, Boston (2018)
5. Chen, H.: AI, e-government, and politics 2.0. IEEE Intell. Syst. **24**, 64–86 (2009)
6. Sun, T.Q., Medaglia, R.: Mapping the challenges of Artificial Intelligence in the public sector: evidence from public healthcare. Gov. Inf. Q. **36**, 368–383 (2018)
7. Androutsopoulou, A., Karacapilidis, N., Loukis, E., Charalabidis, Y.: Transforming the communication between citizens and government through AI-guided chatbots. Gov. Inf. Q. **36**, 358–367 (2018)
8. Tambouris, E.: Using Chatbots and Semantics to Exploit Public Sector Information. EGOV-CeDEM-ePart 2018. 125 (2018)
9. Teufl, P., Payer, U., Parycek, P.: Automated analysis of e-participation data by utilizing associative networks, spreading activation and unsupervised learning. In: Macintosh, A., Tambouris, E. (eds.) ePart 2009. LNCS, vol. 5694, pp. 139–150. Springer, Heidelberg (2009). https://doi.org/10.1007/978-3-642-03781-8_13
10. Maragoudakis, M., Loukis, E., Charalabidis, Y.: A review of opinion mining methods for analyzing citizens' contributions in public policy debate. In: Tambouris, E., Macintosh, A., de Bruijn, H. (eds.) ePart 2011. LNCS, vol. 6847, pp. 298–313. Springer, Heidelberg (2011). https://doi.org/10.1007/978-3-642-23333-3_26

11. Rao, G.K., Dey, S.: Decision support for e-governance: a text mining approach. arXiv preprint arXiv:1108.6198 (2011)
12. Balta, D.: Effective management of standardizing in E-government. In: Corporate Standardization Management and Innovation, pp. 149–175 (2019). https://doi.org/10.4018/978-1-5225-9008-8.ch008
13. Balta, D., Krcmar, H.: Managing standardization in eGovernment: a coordination theory based analysis framework. In: Parycek, P., Glassey, O., Janssen, M., Scholl, H.J., Tambouris, E., Kalampokis, E., Virkar, S. (eds.) EGOV 2018. LNCS, vol. 11020, pp. 60–72. Springer, Cham (2018). https://doi.org/10.1007/978-3-319-98690-6_6
14. Sæbø, Ø., Rose, J., Flak, L.S.: The shape of eParticipation: characterizing an emerging research area. Gov. Inf. Q. **25**, 400–428 (2008)
15. Susha, I., Grönlund, Å.: eParticipation research: systematizing the field. Gov. Inf. Q. **29**, 373–382 (2012)
16. Al-Dalou, R., Abu-Shanab, E.: E-participation levels and technologies. In: The 6th International Conference on Information Technology, ICIT 2013, pp. 8–10 (2013)
17. Wimmer, M.A.: Ontology for an e-participation virtual resource centre. In: Proceedings of the 1st International Conference on Theory and Practice of Electronic Governance, pp. 89–98. ACM (2007)
18. Islam, M.S.: Towards a sustainable e-Participation implementation model. Eur. J. ePractice **5**, 1–12 (2008)
19. Tambouris, E., Liotas, N., Kaliviotis, D., Tarabanis, K.: A framework for scoping eParticipation. In: Proceedings of the 8th Annual International Conference on Digital Government Research: Bridging Disciplines & Domains, pp. 288–289. Digital Government Society of North America (2007)
20. Tambouris, E., Liotas, N., Tarabanis, K.: A framework for assessing eParticipation projects and tools. In: 2007 40th Annual Hawaii International Conference on System Sciences, HICSS 2007, p. 90. IEEE (2007)
21. Youthpolicy: Participation Models: Citizens, Youth, Online. A chase through the maze (2012). http://www.youthpolicy.org/wp-content/uploads/library/Participation_Models_2012 1118.pdf
22. Scherer, S., Wimmer, M.A.: E-participation and enterprise architecture frameworks: an analysis. Inf. Polity **17**, 147–161 (2012)
23. Porwol, L., Ojo, A., Breslin, J.G.: An ontology for next generation e-Participation initiatives. Gov. Inf. Q. **33**, 583–594 (2016)
24. Nielsen, M.A.: Neural Networks and Deep Learning. Determination Press, USA (2015)
25. Hagen, L., Harrison, T.M., Uzuner, Ö., Fake, T., Lamanna, D., Kotfila, C.: Introducing textual analysis tools for policy informatics: a case study of e-petitions. In: Proceedings of the 16th Annual International Conference on Digital Government Research, pp. 10–19. ACM (2015)
26. Braun, D., Hernandez-Mendez, A., Matthes, F., Langen, M.: Evaluating natural language understanding services for conversational question answering systems. In: Proceedings of the 18th Annual SIGdial Meeting on Discourse and Dialogue, pp. 174–185 (2017)
27. Gregor, S.: The nature of theory in information systems. MIS Q. **30**, 611–642 (2006)
28. Goldkuhl, G.: Pragmatism vs interpretivism in qualitative information systems research. Eur. J. Inf. Syst. **21**, 135–146 (2012)
29. Wilde, T., Hess, T.: Forschungsmethoden der Wirtschaftsinformatik. Wirtsch. Inform. **49**, 280–287 (2007). https://doi.org/10.1007/s11576-007-0064-z
30. Stumme, G., Hotho, A., Berendt, B.: Semantic web mining: state of the art and future directions. Web Semant. Sci. Serv. Agents World Wide Web **4**, 124–143 (2006)
31. Berry, M.W., Castellanos, M.: Survey of text mining. Comput. Rev. **45**, 548 (2004)

32. Tan, A.-H.: Text mining: the state of the art and the challenges. In: Proceedings of the PAKDD 1999 Workshop on Knowledge Discovery from Advanced Databases, pp. 65–70. sn (1999)

33. Mirończuk, M.M., Protasiewicz, J.: A recent overview of the state-of-the-art elements of text classification. Expert Syst. Appl. **106**, 36–54 (2018)

34. Carpenter, B., Baldwin, B.: Text Analysis with LingPipe 4. LingPipe Inc., New York (2011)

35. Carpenter, B.: LingPipe for 99.99% recall of gene mentions. In: Proceedings of the Second BioCreative Challenge Evaluation Workshop, pp. 307–309. BioCreative (2007)

36. Carpenter, B.: Phrasal queries with LingPipe and Lucene: ad hoc genomics text retrieval. In: TREC, pp. 1–10 (2004)

37. Alberti, C., Lee, K., Collins, M.: A BERT Baseline for the Natural Questions. arXiv preprint arXiv:1901.08634 (2019)

38. Gao, J., Galley, M., Li, L.: Neural approaches to conversational AI. Found. Trends® Inf. Retr. **13**, 127–298 (2019)

39. Hu, D.: An Introductory Survey on Attention Mechanisms in NLP Problems. arXiv preprint arXiv:1811.05544 (2018)

40. Devlin, J., Chang, M.-W., Lee, K., Toutanova, K.: Bert: pre-training of deep bidirectional transformers for language understanding. arXiv preprint arXiv:1810.04805 (2018)

41. Santana, E.F.Z., Chaves, A.P., Gerosa, M.A., Kon, F., Milojicic, D.S.: Software platforms for smart cities: concepts, requirements, challenges, and a unified reference architecture. ACM Comput. Surv. (CSUR) **50**, 78 (2018)

Artificial Intelligence in Public Administration

A Possible Framework for Partial and Full Automation

Jan Etscheid[(✉)]

Zeppelin University, Am Seemooser Horn 20, 88045 Friedrichshafen, Germany
jan.etscheid@zu.de

Abstract. The constant increase of technical possibilities makes the automation of processes more and more attractive for the public administration. Due to the advances in Artificial intelligence, processes can be automated today which only a few years ago had to be carried out by humans. But not all administrative processes can be automated from a technical point of view. From the multitude of several thousand administrative procedures, decision-makers must select those processes which are deemed appropriate for partial or full automation. This paper seeks to present a possible framework to evaluate opportunities for automation through the decomposition of administrative procedures.

Keywords: Artificial intelligence · Process automation · Smart government

1 Introduction

After the successful implementation of automation processes in the private sector, the idea of the automation of processes is now taken up by the public administration. Although decision-supporting systems have been used in the German administration for some time, the full automation of processes has become the centre of attention only recently. The reason is a new legal regulation which came into force at the beginning of 2017. The Federal Administrative Procedure Law basically permits the full automation of all administrative procedures if there is no necessity for assessment or discretion and if a specific legal regulation has been made for the individual process [1]. Additionally, limits in terms of technical transformation persisted for quite some time. Nowadays, however, numerous activities can be automated, which just a few years ago had to be carried out by humans. To pursue an implementation, it must be known which procedures are suitable for automation in the first place. In view of the large number of administrative procedures, a categorizing scheme is required. Said scheme can be used to assess the automatability on the basis of overarching criteria.

The present article demonstrates a framework for analysis to assess the automatability of administrative procedures. Conclusively, the research question is: "Which criteria can be used to assess the automatability of individual decision phases in administrative procedures?". In a first step, the approaches of artificial intelligence, process automation, as well as the course of an administrative procedure, will be presented based on previous literature and research in relation to the application case.

© IFIP International Federation for Information Processing 2019
Published by Springer Nature Switzerland AG 2019
I. Lindgren et al. (Eds.): EGOV 2019, LNCS 11685, pp. 248–261, 2019.
https://doi.org/10.1007/978-3-030-27325-5_19

In a second step, the administrative procedure is broken down into its sub-processes, which are examined individually. Finally, results as well as recommendations for action are presented.

2 Terminologies

2.1 Artificial Intelligence

How to define artificial intelligence is a difficult question. At present, there is no generally accepted definition. If anything, it is a term which is collectively used to describe different technologies and approaches in different degrees of maturity for the simulation of intelligent behaviour by technical systems. A fortiori, conceptual clarity is of utmost importance in any research involving the idea of artificial intelligence.

The term artificial intelligence differs from natural intelligence, which is attributed to humans. In colloquial language, people who are able to think quickly and who manage to solve complex problems are referred to as intelligent. The debate continues of whether intelligence is a relatively simple or highly complex information-processing practice [2]. Scientifically controversial intelligence tests measure primarily mental abilities such as the knowledge of words and their context-dependent meaning, speed and precession in arithmetic tasks, or deductive reasoning using a sequence of numbers or symbols [3].

In the scientific realm, the definition of intelligence diverges as well. William Stern, author of the intelligence quotient IQ, defined intelligence as "[…] the general ability of an individual to consciously adjust his thinking to new demands, a general mental adaptability to new tasks and conditions of life" [4]. A different approach is conducted by a group of world-leading intelligence researchers who defines intelligence as "[…] a very general mental ability that includes, among other things, the ability to reason, plan, solve problems, think abstractly, understand complex ideas, grasp quickly and learn from experience" [5]. Howard Gardner's theory of multiple intelligences, published in 1998, goes far beyond this classical concept of intelligence by defining naturalistic, musical, spatial, physical, intrapersonal and interpersonal intelligence in addition to linguistic and logical-mathematical intelligence [6].

Based on this broad variation of concepts concerning intelligence, the question arises of how *artificial intelligence* (AI) can be defined. The term "artificial intelligence" has been used in science since the 1950s. In 1966 Marvin Minsky defined AI as "[…] the science of making machines do things that would require intelligence if done by men" [7]. The Turing Test, developed by Alan Turing at the beginning of the 1950s, deals with the differentiability of interpersonal communication from communication with a technical system, whereby he optimistically assumed that by the year 2000 it would no longer be possible to distinguish between humans and computers [8]. Steven Finlay describes AI as the "replication human analytical and/or decision making capabilities" [9]. A broad working definition by Klaus Mainzer describes systems as intelligent if they "can solve problems efficiently on their own" [10].

Whereas practical approaches toward artificial intelligence usually involve the processing of very large amounts of data, artificial neural networks or self-learning algorithms. Scientists differentiate between weak AI, strong AI and sometimes even super intelligence. Weak AIs are usually developed and used for a specific type of applications, including expert systems, speech recognition, navigation systems and translation services [10]. Applications based on weak AI are already widely used today; they even gained entry in the everyday life in the form of intelligent search suggestions or optimized route calculations. Within the theory of multiple intelligences, weak AIs are primarily the replication of linguistic and logical-mathematical intelligence. This understanding is strongly reflected, for example, in the definition of Finlay.

By contrast, strong AIs describe systems that are able to independently think, plan, learn and make logical decisions under uncertainty [10]. The concept of super intelligence is based on a system that is intellectually superior to any human being. Such a system should therefore be able to map all dimensions of multiple intelligences better than any human being [10]. So far, and probably also in the upcoming decades, strong artificial intelligence and superintelligence are reserved for science fiction. However, such representations still strongly shape the ideas and expectations of artificial intelligence. The current developments are all at the level of the weak AI. Nevertheless, systems in certain areas have already succeeded in surpassing human performance. Programs like Deep Blue or Alpha Go could beat the world's best players in Chess or Go; but they were developed especially for this task. They do not succeed in acquiring the knowledge of other games to the same extent as humans do. In this respect, these cases remain in the category of weak AI, even though the human performance was partially exceeded and some elements assigned to the category of strong AI already exist.

Early AI systems from the middle of the 20th century, often referred to as expert systems, were basically comprehensible for the developer and user because they operated according to defined rules. These expert systems were primarily intended to present relationships transparently in order to explain multi-causal phenomena. While this traceability can be regarded as a strength, early AI systems could only inadequately depict the real world with its uncertainties. Newer AI technologies take exactly this circumstance into account: rule-based algorithms are not able to map a reality which is characteristically complex and uncertain. Self-learning technologies, which deliver a better result but whose solution cannot be understood, are often called black boxes. The research area "Explainable AI" tries to present the functionality of algorithms of artificial intelligence in a comprehensible way, not only to create transparency and trust in systems, but also to generate additional knowledge by recognizing logics and contexts. Especially in public administration, which must be democratically controlled, the transparency and verifiability of decisions is an elementary prerequisite [22].

The term artificial intelligence thus describes a broad concept in different stages of development. While weak AIs aim at the partial simulation of human intelligence, focusing on logical-mathematical and linguistic intelligence, strong AIs and super intelligence try to emulate and surpass humans in every aspect of intelligence. However, since there is a great deal of uncertainty at this stage as to whether a truly strong AI can ever be realized, this work is based on the understanding of weak AI. From this point onward, if we talk about artificial intelligence, we mean systems that simulate the logical-rational and linguistic elements of human intelligence.

2.2   Process Automation

The term automation originates from the industrial context. Automated systems are systems that have the technical ability to work independently. On a simple level, these can be everyday things such as vending machines for drinks or tickets. According to the definition, automation is the transfer of functions from humans to artificial systems [11]. Process automation in turn represents a specification of the broad concept of automation. In public administration, the majority of processes are decision-making processes [12]. Deciding in this context means choosing between two or more alternatives. Although it is the outcome of decisions which finds most attention, the decision itself must be seen as a process with several phases. The psychological decision theory is based on six stages: problem definition, determination of alternatives, evaluation of alternatives, selection, implementation and evaluation [13].

Process automation can itself be divided into several stages. Overall, processes can usually be subdivided into several sub-process steps, such as the phases of the decision-making process mentioned above. Sub-process automation refers to the transfer of individual sub-process steps to technical systems. One or more sub-steps are executed by a system and then inserted into the overall process by a human operator. The human being is responsible for the non-automated sub-steps and the coordination of the overall process. Full automation, on the other hand, includes the transfer of all sub-steps as well as the coordination of the entire process to a technical system. Ergo, the entire process runs without human intervention [14].

The possibility of a partial automation of administrative procedures has been anchored in administrative procedural law for many years and is also widely used in many areas. At the beginning of 2017, however, the legislator also specified the possibility of full automation. This means that administrative files can be processed completely automatically as long as there is no necessity for assessment or discretion and a special legal basis has been created for the individual administrative procedure [1]. This illustrates the increasing relevance of process automation in public administration.

2.3   Administrative Procedures

As almost every administrative action is based on decisions previously made, Administrative Science can be placed within the field of Decision Science [15]. Conclusively, this article considers the administrative process as a decision-making process. To identify automation potentials within an administrative procedure, it is necessary to divide the process into individual sub-steps.

Administrative decisions are primarily legal decisions. If the general psychological model of decision-making is adapted to a legal case, the administrative procedure can be divided into seven main phases (whereby said phases can be subdivided into several partial decisions) [16]:

- Recognition of the problem
- Fact-finding
- Norms finding and norms concretisation
- Application of law and subsumption

- Legal consequence analysis
- Realization
- Evaluation

The level of problem recognition corresponds to the orientation phase in the classic model of decision-making. The first step is the awareness by the administration of the necessity for a decision. On the one hand, the administration itself can decide whether to open an administrative procedure in accordance with the official principle. It will receive the necessary information from various sources such as the media, other government agencies, citizens, interest groups or, increasingly, smart objects. On the other hand, there are administrative procedures which are only initiated upon request. In such cases, the administration must first check the identity and eligibility of the applicant [17].

The search phase of the decision-making model corresponds to the fact-finding phase of administrative decisions. The fact-finding intends to collect a basis of correct and complete information on which the decision can be made. Here, too, the administration relies on various sources of information. The authority has partial discretion as to which information is relevant in the specific case and at which point a sufficient amount of information was collected. In doing so, the authority must weigh different factors such as the need for additional information and time constraints. The scope of the decision and the complexity of the matter must also be taken into account [17].

The norm finding and concretisation describes the phase of finding and assigning the relevant legal norms. The facts of the case are analysed to determine which legal norms are to be applied in the individual case at hand. Indeterminate legal terms which are frequently used in administrative law sometimes offer a certain leeway for interpretation and assessment which call for an application suited to the individual case. There is a fluent transition to the phase of legal consequence assessment [17].

If the relevant legal norms are determined, possible legal consequences must be determined. During the step of subsumption a rough distinction can be made between bound and discretionary decisions. In the case of a bound decision, the legal consequences are already given by the law. In many cases, however, the legal consequence does either not result directly from the norm or must be specified beforehand. In this case, the administration has a leeway which is referred to as discretion. A distinction can be made between development fairs, on which the administration acts, and selection fairs, which select the measure. In the case of discretionary decisions, the administration must interpret the standard in such a way that the effect intended by the legislator is achieved in the individual case. At the end of the legal consequence investigation, the administration decides what action it will take [17].

After the decision-making process follows the implementation stage. However, for the question at hand the actual implementation is only of secondary importance. The presentation and justification of the administrative decision appear to be more relevant. In most cases, the administration is legally obliged to justify how it reached a certain decision. This serves not only the purposes of transparency and comprehensibility, but also rationality. As a rule, *rational* decisions are considered to be justifiable and not the result from personal impressions [18].

The decision-making process is concluded by the control and evaluation phase. The result of the decision is thoroughly assessed to see whether the actual result corresponds to the result initially intended. Therewith, future decisions could be adjusted on the basis of previous experience. This does not mean, however, that in the case of multiple decisions each one has to be controlled for individually. Basically, a distinction can be made between external and internal control. Since further specification is not necessary for the investigation of the automatability, the evaluation and control phase may be neglected at this point.

3   Identifying Entry Points for Automatization in Administrative Tasks

In order to assess the suitability of administrative procedures for partial or full automation, the phases of the decision-making process must be considered individually.

3.1   Problem Definition

As previously demonstrated. the level of problem recognition can be divided into the cases of initiation by proposal and initiation on the basis of the official principle. If administrative proceedings are initiated by an external proposal, the first phase is essentially limited to the identification of the applicant and the examination of eligibility. Identification and eligibility are often closely linked, since eligibility is based, for example, on citizenship, place of residence, or age. In this respect, the primary task is a doubtless identification. In Germany, the electronic identity card is mainly used for this purpose; internationally, other solutions such as PIN/TAN systems or mobile phone signatures exist as well. At this point, it is crucial to make the identification process as easy as possible for the citizen in order to increase the acceptance for its usage. As the usage of electronic ID cards is neither widely spread nor very popular in Germany, artificial intelligence could be used in conjunction with a PIN procedure. The lower level of security of the PIN procedure could be combined with the application of a webcam which is able to generate a biometric comparison of the applicant´s face with the photo stored in the passport. A similar system is already used for the automated border control "EasyPASS" [19].

The case of a problem identification initiated on the basis of the official principle proves to be more difficult. First of all, the administration must recognise whether it is necessary to initiate a procedure. Simply put, the administration must decide if the actual values deviate from the target values. An easy example is the usage of an algorithm which can detect whether and when the amount of particulate matter measured exceeds the permissible limits. The simplicity is rooted in the quantifiability of the circumstances. Then again, many problems evade such quantitative data. Rather, the administration is dependent on information from different sources which must be evaluated, classified and inserted into the overall context. Not only the ability to weigh and evaluate, but also the use of experience values is indispensable. This step cannot be performed by conventional algorithms. At this point the use of artificial intelligence is necessary [10]. The AI must "understand" the target goal, which cannot be defined directly on the basis of individual key figures. One example is the problematic of advertising installations which may contain disfiguring characteristics. In this case, neither clear colours nor sizes are sufficient reference points. The evaluation necessitates the understanding of the individual case. To be more precise, the AI must understand how individual components are connected and how their formation makes up the entire system. The same applies to the actual state. Finally, the AI-based system must be able to compare the complex states of the actual and targeted state in such a way that blatant deviations are detected. At least in complex constellations, this requires the ability to think logically independently which is attributed to the strong AI not yet available today. Instead, less complex cases can be automated even with weak AIs. The ability to automate thus strongly depends on the quantifiability of the information as well as the complexity of the case. In this phase, multi-agent systems could be used to record and process situations from different perspectives. Several intelligent assistants can be linked together to detect deviations from the desired outcome.

In the problem definition phase, the following guiding questions assist in the evaluation of possible automatability: Is there an external request or must the administration itself recognize the necessity of a procedure? In the case of official procedures, to what extent are criteria for initiation prescribed by law, in the sense of fixed limits or indefinite legal concepts? To what extent is the direct measurability of these criteria possible or does it require an individual interpretation?

3.2   Fact-Finding

In case of the initiation of the administrative procedure, the fact-finding state follows the first stage of problem definition. The fact-finding stage is an essential and significant part of the administrative procedure. In this phase, all information must be collected which are deemed necessary for the decision. Thus, the basis for the final judgement must be created.

In general, the degree of structuredness of the procedure is decisive for automation. In many administrative procedures, it is clearly defined which information must be used for the decision. A simple case would be the comparison of the information provided by the applicant to the data available to the administration, e.g. reporting data. If the necessary information is defined clearly, it must first be ensured that an automated system can collect and process this information. Should the decision-relevant information be clearly definable, an automated information collection is possible which enables the creation of a decision basis. There are many advantages to automation. Technical systems can process a multitude of information in almost real time. Especially in combination with smart objects and cyberphysical systems, it is possible to create decision bases which rely on actual and current facts instead of on models and calculations [21]. Information that is solely available in unstructured forms, such as oral statements or informal texts, however, poses a difficulty. In the context of fact-finding, unstructured information must already be brought into a structured form so that the information can be used in the upcoming steps of the process. Similar to the previous phase, multi-agent systems are a suitable option to collect and process information from different sources.

The automation of the fact-finding process is even more difficult in cases in which the required information is derived from the concrete facts of the case. Formulations such as "Information that is important for the individual case must be taken into account" leave some leeway as to which information is to be regarded as significant. In addition, most issues offer a multitude of information available for judgment which requires a preset point in the process at which sufficient information is available as a basis for decision-making. An example would be the proceedings involved in acquiring a building permit. As stakeholders have the right to submit information they perceive as relevant in the decision-making, the first step would encompass an evaluation as to which information is relevant for the present case and which aspects might be neglectable. The wording "relevant information" must be interpreted according to the individual case. Automation with the help of weak artificial intelligence only seems possible when a certain degree of structure is present. This does not necessarily have to be a matter of legal requirements; often, there are also regulations from administrative practice. It becomes difficult, however, if the necessary information only appears in the middle of the procedure. A high proportion of unstructured information also makes automation more difficult, since these must first be translated into a structured form in order to examine their relevance to the individual case. Thus, an AI would have to be able to understand context-based natural language. In order to determine the facts of the case, it can therefore be stated that clearly defined information and the existence of structured information facilitate automation in advance. With increasing openness regarding the relevant information, an increasing degree of unstructuredness and growing complexity, a more powerful AI is needed for automation.

In the phase of fact finding, the following questions can guide the analysis. Is the information that serves as a basis for decision-making clearly defined or must it be determined individually in each individual case? Is the information available from clearly defined sources or does it have to be collected on a case-by-case basis? Is the information available in machine-readable formats?

3.3   Finding and Concretising Legal Norms

If there is a sufficient basis of information for decision-making, the norms relevant to the decision must be determined. One possible approach is the distinction between proposed procedures and official procedures from the problem recognition phase. In the case of a proposed procedure, the relevant standards are usually firmly defined. Conclusively, the norms of the case are already determined by the relevant legal framework. The application for a passport, for example, is based on clearly defined rules of law which shall in any event apply to the application. The procedure becomes more difficult if there is no formal application and the relevant law must be derived from the individual case. For this purpose, the collected information must be understood in its entire breadth and complexity in order to be able to determine the relevant norms. If, for example, excessive noise emissions are found from a commercial enterprise, the administration must first examine the legal basis on which it can act in this case. Furthermore, individual criteria, such as the location in a residential area, must be taken into account. At this point, the effectiveness of the artificial intelligence would have to rise with the complexity of the situation. It is questionable whether the present state of a weak AI would be suited to fulfil this task [20]. Expert systems are able to technically represent the content and interpretation of legal standards and thus assign them to the appropriate circumstances.

Many difficulties arise in the phase of the application of the law as this is closely linked to finding the appropriate norm. Particularly in administrative procedural law, there are numerous indeterminate legal terms which cannot be applied to individual cases without further concretisation. While many indeterminate legal terms can be relatively easily operationalized due to their regular use in administrative practice, others have to be embedded in the individual case in a much more individualised way. In addition, there are complex procedures such as the interpretation of legal norms, the linkage of the literal law text with the lived administrative practice and the appropriate jurisdiction. At the present time, it still seems impossible to automate the phase of the application of law in the case of complex facts and norms in the context of indefinite legal terms. Feasible for automation processes would be those norms which can be applied on the basis of clear criteria and require only little interpretation in individual cases. A certain degree of interpretation based on previously clearly defined criteria can already be provided today by weak AIs.

Key questions in the phase of norm finding and concretisation resemble the guiding questions of the problem definition phase as the underlying legal norms are often clearly defined within the framework of application procedures. It is also relevant whether indefinite legal terms make the classification more difficult.

3.4   Determination of Legal Consequences

The core of the decision-making process is the determination of legal consequences based on the facts established and the norms relevant to the case. Here, the distinction between bound and discretionary decisions, which is also used by the German legislator in the context of full automation, can be used. It seems obvious that bound decisions are better suited for automation, since they result in legal consequences without further leeway from the law. Bound decisions therefore do not represent a major challenge for automation in the phase of legal consequence determination [20]. These cases can even be automated without AI by using if-then decisions. The situation is different if there is scope for discretion or assessment. Primarily, the leeway was granted to the administration to achieve the intended results in individual cases. In order to be able to automate such decisions, the system would have to be able to detect the leeway, understand the intended effect of the legislator and then make the necessary decision within the available scope. If said scope is not always directly apparent from the text of the law, and existing scopes are not available through practical experiences, an automated recognition of the leeway appears to be, at least at the present, out of the question. One best case scenario which seems feasible would be a margin with clearly stated criteria, previously defined by humans. However, since the scope for decision essentially serves to establish justice in individual cases and often also contains ethical components, automation should only be used extremely carefully and restrictively. Understandably, bound administrative decisions offer much greater potential at this point. The missing technical means for the automation of decisions with considerable leeway render the German legislator sceptical towards the full automation of administrative procedures [21]. The use of the rule management systems offers the possibility of applying rules (defined as norms through the application of specific framework conditions) and presenting them transparently.

The most important question at the legal consequence assessment stage is therefore whether the decision is of a tied or a discretionary nature. Furthermore, one must consider whether clear criteria for the exercise of discretion have been defined. Conclusively, are the objectives to be achieved by discretion measurable on the basis of clear criteria?

3.5 Implementation

In the present case, the implementation phase shall be reduced to the preparation of an official notification. As the implementation of numerous administrative decisions goes far beyond this scope, there is a great deal of potential for automation. However, since the present article refers to the process of administrative decisions in the narrower sense, the implementation beyond the preparation of an official notification may be neglected for now.

If the implementation is regarded solely as the creation of an official notification, this phase represents a relatively formalised process. Standardised elements such as instructions on legal remedies, for example, can only be adapted to the case and be inserted automatically as text modules. In the notice the result of the preceding process, in particular the standard finding and legal consequence determination, is represented in writing. For the purpose of comprehensibility most administrative decisions must be justified according to law. To automate the creation of notices, the system must be able to present and justify the administrative decision in natural language. While conventional algorithms can only process data in machine-readable form, artificial intelligence is already partially able to understand and speak natural language. Hence, in many cases the presentation of the result of the decision-making process is not a major difficulty anymore. Yet, the justification and transparency of the administrative decision appears to be more difficult, especially since AI is often referred to as black box technology. Explainable AI can make an important contribution in this respect in the future. Here it appears decisive to what extent the decision criteria are given to the system and to what extent the system itself classifies and weights factors.

In the context of the present consideration with the focus on the preparation of the official notification, the following questions must be clarified: to what extent can the results of the procedure be presented in natural language? And to what extent can the decision itself be presented transparently?

3.6 Evaluation

The final phase of control and evaluation is relatively similar to the problem identification phase. Here, too, the targeted and actual states are compared. As this has already been explained in previous passages and monitoring and evaluation are not at the core of the decision-making process, we will not go into further detail for now (Fig. 1).

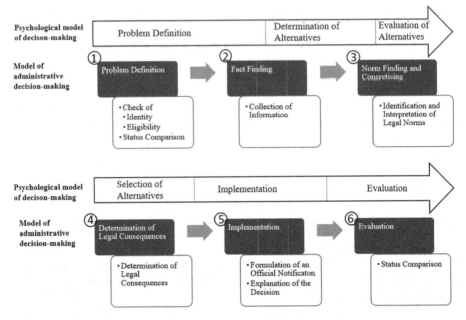

Fig. 1. Process sequence in the psychological and administrative model

4   Levels of Automation

If the administration wants to partially or completely automate procedures, it seems advisable first, to consider the individual steps of the administration procedure; second, to define concrete contents and requirements and third, to evaluate the possibility of automation. Overall, it can be concluded that a generally decreasing degree of pre-set structure and an increasing complexity intensify the difficulty for automation.

If the administrative procedure is broken down into the different phases, the possibility for automation can be individually evaluated for each step. Ergo, one does not consider the entire process, but only its sub-processes. For this, algorithms can be evaluated in respect to their suitability for automated stages in the administrative procedure. The result would be automatically handled phases whereby the output would be delivered to the human supervisor for further processing. It is also possible for a human processor to enter the input, required for an automated step, into a system so that the subsequent process can run automatically. In order to *fully* automate an administrative process, it would be necessary to perform all process steps and the coordination of the entire process automatically. In a nutshell: procedures, which do not contain automatable components, are not suitable for partial or full automation. Nevertheless, technical systems can also support the human decision-maker in such procedures, for example by automatically collecting information, graphically processing information or by giving suggestions for evaluation [14].

To translate all administrative procedures into automated systems appears to be an impossible task. Conclusively, the present paper suggests to deconstruct administrative processes into individual phases in order to evaluate which individual stages can be automated and which parts must be (at least at present) left to the human evaluation. With growing technical possibilities and experience, it is likely that more and more phases can be automated in the course of time.

5 Conclusion

Against the background of tight budgets, lack of skilled staff and pressure for more customer-friendly services, politicians and the general public are often pushing for the rationalisation and automation of administrative procedures. Especially in the light of new technical possibilities offered by artificial intelligence, new potentials seem to be realizable. The article has defined artificial intelligence and automation in an administrative context and demonstrated the different phases of administrative procedures which might offer possibilities for automation.

There are over 5000 different administrative procedures in Germany. In order to be able to assess their automatability, the procedures should be mapped as digitally as possible in order to be able to analyse the individual steps. It deems a good idea to use a scheme for simpler classification. The explanations in this paper have shown that the different phases of an administrative procedure entail different sub-processes which in turn offer different opportunities and challenges for automation. In the problem recognition phase, the ability to synchronize complex situations is particularly important. The fact-finding phase requires the collection of information as well as the subsequent structuring and classification. The norm finding process presupposes an understanding of legal texts, the actual wording, the everyday administrative practice as well as the jurisprudence. The phase of legal consequence determination used here within the context of decision-making in the narrower sense, contains the allocation of legal consequences partly under use of evaluation leeway. In the context of the paper, the phase of implementation was regarded as answer production; conclusively it focuses on the representation and reason for the decision. In the final phase of control and evaluation, the actual state is again compared with the targeted state. An autonomous system or an AI must be able to perform these tasks in order to automate the step. Some steps are obviously better suited for automation than others. In particular, the phases of norm finding and determination of legal consequences are currently difficult, since technical systems are not yet in a position to interpret legal texts beyond the wording. In general, it can be said that a high degree of structure and low complexity facilitate automation. The extent of the defined space of which information must be consulted and how these are weighted against each other should be provided by humans as far/much as possible. Furthermore, the quantifiability of information represents an important aspect towards the extent to which it can be converted into machine-readable formats. Following this paper, future research would focus on the in-depth analysis of the individual phases and the development of concrete indicators for the degree of automation. This would result in an instrument usable by the administration and political decision-makers to assess the automatability of specific phases or entire procedures.

Today's weak AI already offers a number of possibilities, especially if it was developed for a specific task. Nevertheless, there is also fear and scepticism about the use of AI in the current social debate. Despite all technical possibilities, the requirements of the rule of law and the demands of citizens must be taken seriously, especially in the context of public administration. Even automated administrative decisions must always be comprehensible for the citizens involved. In addition, international examples from Australia and Norway already show how quickly the public's trust in automated decisions can be lost. Particularly in sensitive areas such as social security, where administrative decisions have a direct influence on people's livelihoods, systems should only be used when the error rate is acceptable. Questions about the responsibility for automated decisions or the right of a person to control decisions are still not sufficiently clarified. These aspects demonstrate the vast range of the topic which is influencing societies, politics and economics and will do so even more in the future. Evidently, important questions remain which go way beyond the scope of this paper. These must be addressed, however, if the implementation of automated processes should be successful.

References

1. Braun Binder, N.: Weg frei für vollautomatisierte Verwaltungsverfahren. In: Jusletter IT, 22 September 2016
2. Franken, S.: Verhaltensorientierte Führung. Gabler Verlag, Wiesbaden (2010)
3. Katz, M.: IQ-Tests. Haufe-Verlag, Freiburg (2008)
4. Stern, W: Psychologische Begabung und Begabungsdiagnose. In: Petersen, P. (ed.) Der Aufstieg der Begabten. G. Teubner, Leipzig, Berlin (1916)
5. Zimbardo, P., Gerrig, R.: Psychologie. Pearson Studium, München (2004)
6. Gardner, H.: Frames of Mind: Theory of Multiple Intelligences. Harper Collins Publishers, New York (1993)
7. Minsky, M.: Computation: Finite and Infinite Machines. Prentice-Hall, Englewood Cliffs (1967)
8. Turing, A.: Computing machinery and intelligence. In: Mind, vol. LIX (236) (1950)
9. Finlay, S.: Artificial intelligence and machine learning for business. Relativistic (2017)
10. Mainzer, K.: Künstliche Intelligenz – Wann übernehmen die Maschinen?. Springer, Heidelberg (2016)
11. Lauber, R., Göhner, P.: Prozessautomatisierung 1. Springer, Heidelberg (1999)
12. Becker, B.: Öffentliche Verwaltung. RS Schulz, Starnberg (1989)
13. Drummond, H.: Effective decision making. Kogan Page, London (1996)
14. Etscheid, J.: Automatisierungspotenziale in der Verwaltung. In: Mohabbat, R., et al. (eds.) (Un)Berechenbar?. Kompetenzzentrum Öffentliche IT, Berlin (2018)
15. Brühl, R.: Die Verwaltungsentscheidung als Fixpunkt eines verwaltungs-wissenschaftlichen Studiums. In: Eilsberger, R., Schmahl, H. (eds.) Auf dem Weg zur Verwaltungswissenschaft. Schriftenreihe der Fachhochschule des Bundes für öffentliche Verwaltung (1989)
16. Erbguth, W., Guckelberger, A.: Allgemeines Verwaltungsrecht. Nomos Verlag, Baden-Baden (2017)
17. Nesseldreher, A.: Entscheiden im Informationszeitalter. Der Andere Verlag, Tönning (2006)
18. Garrn, H.: Zur Rationalität rechtlicher Entscheidungen. Franz Steiner Verlag, Stuttgart (1986)

19. Djeffal, C.: Künstliche Intelligenz in der öffentlichen Verwaltung. Berichte des NGEZ, Berlin (2018)
20. Luthe, E.: Der vollständig automatisierte Erlass eines Verwaltungsakts nach § 31a SGB X. In: SGb 2017, Erich Schmidt Verlag, Berlin (2017)
21. Hill, H.: Was bedeutet Künstliche Intelligenz (KI) für die Öffentliche Verwaltung? Verwaltung und Management **24**(6), 287–294 (2018)
22. Holzinger, A.: Explainable AI (ex-AI). Informatikspektrum **41**(2), 138–143 (2018)

Economic Crisis Policy Analytics Based on Artificial Intelligence

Euripidis Loukis[(✉)], Manolis Maragoudakis, and Niki Kyriakou

Department of Information and Communication Systems Engineering,
University of the Aegean, 83200 Samos, Greece
{eloukis,mmarag,nkyr}@aegean.gr

Abstract. An important trend in the area of digital government is its expansion beyond the support of internal processes and operations, as well as transactions and consultations with citizens and firms, which were the main objectives of its first generations, towards the support of higher-level functions of government agencies, with main emphasis on public policy making. This gives rise to the gradual development of policy analytics. Another important trend in the area of digital government is the increasing exploitation of artificial intelligence techniques by government agencies, mainly for the automation, support and enhancement of operational tasks and lower-level decision making, but only to a very limited extent for the support of higher-level functions, and especially policy making. Our paper contributes towards the advancement and the combination of these two important trends: it proposes a policy analytics methodology for the exploitation of existing public and private sector data, using a big data oriented artificial intelligence technique, feature selection, in order to support policy making concerning one of the most serious problems that governments face, the economic crises. In particular, we present a methodology for exploiting existing data of taxation authorities, statistical agencies, and also of private sector business information and consulting firms, in order to identify characteristics of a firm (e.g. with respect to strategic directions, resources, capabilities, practices, etc.) as well as its external environment (e.g. with respect to competition, dynamism, etc.) that affect (positively or negatively) its resilience to the crisis with respect to sales revenue; for this purpose an advanced artificial intelligence feature selection algorithm, the Boruta 'all-relevant' variables identification one, is used. Furthermore, an application of the proposed economic crisis policy analytics methodology is presented, which provides a first validation of the usefulness of our methodology.

Keywords: Policy analytics · Policy informatics · Artificial intelligence · Feature selection · Crisis

1 Introduction

An important trend in the area of digital government is the exploitation of ICT for supporting higher-level functions of government agencies, with main emphasis on public policy making, leading to the gradual development of 'policy analytics' (sometimes termed also 'policy informatics') [1–5]; it can be defined as the exploitation

© IFIP International Federation for Information Processing 2019
Published by Springer Nature Switzerland AG 2019
I. Lindgren et al. (Eds.): EGOV 2019, LNCS 11685, pp. 262–275, 2019.
https://doi.org/10.1007/978-3-030-27325-5_20

of existing data of government agencies, possibly in combination with data possessed by private sector firms (such as business information and consulting ones), using advanced quantitative analysis techniques, in order to support various stages of public policy making for the complex problems that modern societies face. Policy analytics represents a major and highly ambitious expansion of digital government, beyond the support of internal processes and operations, as well as transactions and consultations with citizens and firms, which were the main objectives of its first generations [6, 7], towards higher-level functions of government. Some first research has been conducted in this area of policy analytics, which has developed some useful knowledge concerning approaches and methodologies for exploiting various sources of public sector data, in order to support various stages of the policy making cycle in some domains of government intervention, such as the economy, the social insurance, the environment, the energy, the justice and the management of emergency crises [8–13]. However, this promising area of policy analytics is still in its infancy, and the potential of the large quantities of the data that government possesses for supporting and enhancing policy making has been exploited only to a limited extent. So it is necessary to conduct extensive research in order to exploit these data for supporting the highest-level government functions of policy making, focusing on the most important problems/challenges our societies face.

Another important trend in the area of digital government is the increasing exploitation of artificial intelligence (AI) techniques by government agencies. According to a recent relevant report of the EU [14] AI can be defined as a group of technologies that enable computers to become more intelligent, by learning from their environment, gaining knowledge from it, and using this knowledge for taking intelligent action or proposing decisions. There are several technologies in this group that provide such learning capabilities, with the most important of them being definitely the Machine Learning (ML). Though most of the AI technologies, and in particular the ML algorithms, exist for several decades, it is only recently that an increasing 'real life' exploitation of them has started, mainly by private sector firms, and to a lower extent by government agencies, due to: (a) the availability of large amounts of data enabling more effective training of AI algorithms (i.e. extraction of more reliable rules and models); (b) advances in computing power and cost reduction of it; (c) substantial improvements of the AI algorithms [14, 15]. The multiple success stories of the first experimentations of AI exploitation in the private sector have generated high levels of interest in exploiting and applying AI techniques in the public sector as well, in order to automate or support more sophisticated mental tasks than the simpler routine ones automated or supported by the traditional operational IS of government agencies [16–19]. However, the exploitation of AI in the public sector so far has been mainly for the automation, support and enhancement of daily operational tasks and lower-level decision making (e.g. [20–24]), but only to a limited extent for the support and enhancement of higher-level functions, and especially policy making. So it is necessary to conduct extensive research in order to exploit at AI for supporting this highest-level government function of policy making.

Our study contributes to the advancement and the combination of these two important and promising digital government trends, policy analytics and AI exploitation, towards filling the abovementioned research gaps, focusing on one of the most serious problems that governments face: the economic crises [25, 26]. In particular, it proposes a policy analytics methodology, which exploits existing data of taxation authorities, statistical agencies, and also of private sector business information and consulting firms, in order to support the design of policies for reducing the negative consequences of the economic crises, which repeatedly occur with varying intensities in market economies, leading to serious contractions of economic activity, with quite negative consequences for huge numbers of citizens (see Sect. 2.1). In particular, our methodology enables the identification of characteristics of a firm (e.g. with respect to strategic directions, resources, capabilities, practices, etc.) as well as its external environment (e.g. with respect to competition, dynamism, etc.) that affect (positively or negatively) its resilience to economic crisis with respect to sales revenue (i.e. the degree of sales revenue reduction due to economic crisis). For this purpose we are using a 'big data oriented' AI technique, feature selection (FS), which enables filtering from a large number of potential independent variables (contained in the available high-dimensionality big datasets) the ones that actually affect a dependent variable of interest; in particular, we are using the Boruta 'all-relevant' variables identification FS algorithm [27, 28] (see Sect. 2.2). The proposed policy analytics methodology can provide a substantial support for the design of public policies for reducing the negative impact of economic crises on firms, which can significantly impair both short-term and also medium- and long-term performance and competitiveness. This is highly beneficial as economic crises of various origins and intensities frequently occur in market economies, being an inevitable trait of them, have quite negative consequences for the economy and the society, so they are among the toughest challenges that governments face. Furthermore, an application of our methodology is presented, which is based on Greek firms' data concerning the economic crisis period 2009–2014, leading to interesting conclusions/insights, providing a first validation of the usefulness of our methodology.

In the following Sect. 2 the background of our economic crisis policy analytics methodology is outlined, while in Sect. 3 the methodology is described, and in Sect. 4 its abovementioned application is presented. The final Sect. 5 summarizes conclusions and proposes directions for future research.

2 Background

2.1 Economic Crises

One of the most serious problems of market-based economies are the fluctuations of economic activity that repeatedly appear, which cause many problems to the economy and the society in general, so they have to be addressed by government through appropriate policies, aiming on one hand at reducing their intensities and durations, and on the other hand at mitigating their negative consequences on firms and citizens [25, 26]. Economic crises can be defined as significant reductions of economic activity, which can be due to the 'business cycles' (i.e., the fluctuations that economic activity usually exhibits in market-based economies), or caused by various kinds of events in the society or economy (such as the oil crisis in the early 1970, or banking crises) [26]. The economic crises have negative short-term as well as medium- and long-term consequences for the economy and the society. The short-term consequences usually are reductions of the demand for many goods and services, which result in serious decrease of firms' sales, production and profits, as well as personnel employment (increasing unemployment) and materials' procurement (propagating the crisis towards the suppliers). Furthermore, during economic crises firms usually reduce capital investment in production equipment, ICT, buildings, etc., and also in product, service and process innovations, which reduce the degree of renewal and improvement of their equipment, products, services and operations, as well as exploitation of emerging new technologies, and this has serious medium- and long-term consequences on their efficiency and competitiveness [25, 26, 31]. Therefore it is imperative that government agencies, especially the ones having competences and responsibilities for the domains of economy and social welfare, design and implement public policies for reducing the above negative short-term as well as medium- and long-term consequences of the economic crises.

However, it should be noted that the above negative consequences of the economic crises are not the same for all firms: the more efficient and effective firms, which offer higher value-for-money products and services, and have higher capacity to make the required adaptations, are more resilient to the crisis, and have less negative consequences on their sales revenue, and therefore on their employment, procurement, as well as their capital investment and innovation, than the less efficient and effective ones. Therefore, it is important and highly useful to develop policy analytics methodologies for identifying characteristics of the firm, as well as its external environment, that affect positively or negatively its resilience to economic crisis. Our study makes a contribution in this direction, based on the Boruta 'all-relevant' FS algorithm, which is outlined in the following section.

2.2   Artificial Intelligence Feature Selection – The Boruta Algorithm

The FS algorithms are an important class of 'big data oriented' AI algorithms, which aim at determining from a large number of features - potential independent variables - the ones that actually affect a dependent variable of interest [30]. They can be divided into two main categories: (i) the 'minimal – optimal' ones, which determine a small - minimal set of features affecting the dependent variable, which can provide optimal prediction accuracy for it (most traditional FS algorithms belong to this category); (ii) the 'all-relevant' ones, which determine all the features that affect the dependent variable, not only the non-redundant ones, as it happens in 'minimal – optimal' FS algorithms (there is a smaller number of novell algorithms belonging to this category) [27–30]. Therefore if there are a number of features that affect the dependent variable, which are to some extent redundant (i.e. there is some degree of association among them), the 'minimal-optimal' FS algorithms will select only some of them (a minimal subset), which have low levels of redundancy (association) among them; however, they will not select some other features, which affect the dependent variable, but have high levels of association with the selected ones, as the latter features do not increase further the prediction accuracy of the dependent variable, beyond the accuracy achieved based on the former features. On the contrary the 'all-relevant' FS algorithms will select all the features affecting the dependent variable, regardless of possible associations among them.

Since the objective of this study is the to extract from available datasets as much knowledge and insight as possible concerning characteristics of a firm as well as its external environment that affect the degree of sales revenue reduction due to economic crisis we are using an 'all-relevant' FS algorithm. In particular, we are using the Boruta 'all-relevant' variables identification algorithm [28, 29], which is a FS approach, particularly useful when one is interested in understanding the mechanisms related to a dependent variable of interest, rather than just building a 'black box' predictive model of it with good prediction accuracy. The basic idea of the Boruta algorithm is that based on the original feature set, another artificial set of features is created, which consists of shuffled copies of all features (which are called 'shadow features'). This shadow set is then merged with the original one, a Random Forest classifier is constructed based on the merged data set, and for each feature an importance measure is calculated (the default one is the 'Mean Decrease Impurity' (MDI) of the feature), in order to evaluate the importance of each feature. At each iteration, Boruta FS algorithm evaluates one real feature, by assessing whether it has a higher importance than the best of the shadow features, and if this does not happens the feature is removed as unimportant for the dependent variable. Finally, the algorithm stops when either all features gets confirmed or removed, or it reaches a specified limit of runs.

The Boruta FS algorithm offers three crucial advantages:

(I)   It can handle large numbers of features without performance and reliability deterioration, so it is appropriate for exploiting really 'big data'; this does not happen in other techniques that might be used for the same purpose, such as regression analysis, in which when the number of independent variables increases, the confidence intervals of the estimated bi coefficient increase as well, so some statistically significant ones may incorrectly be found non-significant.

(II)   If there are associated – correlated features that all affect the dependent variable the Boruta FS algorithm will not omit some of them due to their association – correlation with other selected features; again this does not happen in other techniques that might be used for the same purpose: for instance in regression analysis, if some independent variables that actually affect the dependent variable have high levels of correlation, then for some of them their bi coefficients might be incorrectly found statistically non-significant (multi-collinearity problem).

(III)   Also, the Boruta FS algorithm can identify not only the features that have linear effects on the dependent variable, but also the ones having non-linear effects.

3   The Proposed Methodology

The proposed economic crisis policy analytics methodology aims to identify characteristics of the firm and its external environment that affect its resilience to economic crisis, with respect to the most important negative aspect/consequence of economic crisis: the reduction of firms' sales revenue. Therefore the dependent variable of our methodology is the degree of firm's sales revenue reduction due to the crisis. The capabilities and advantages offered by abovementioned advanced Boruta AI FS algorithm (outlined in Sect. 2.2) allow us to examine a large number and a wide thematic range of potential independent variables, in order to identify all the relevant and influential ones. The above can provide a substantial support for the design of policies for reducing this negative impact of economic crisis on firms, which can significantly impair their short-term and also their medium- and long-term performance and competitiveness.

Our methodology exploits existing data from two main sources:

(I)   from taxation authorities: data about firms' sales revenue before and during the economic crisis, from which sales revenue reduction due to crisis can be calculated;

(II) from statistical agencies, and also from private sector business information and consulting firms: data concerning various characteristics of firms (concerning strategic directions, resources, capabilities, practices, etc.) and their external environment (concerning the intensity of competition, the degree of dynamism, etc.).

These data undergo two stages of processing:

(a)   An initial selection of potential independent variables (characteristics of firm as well as its external environment) from the numerous variables that might be available in the large government and private sector datasets we are using, based on theoretical foundations from previous management science research. One of them is definitely the classical 'Leavitt's Diamond' framework [32], which defines four main elements of a firm, which should be strongly interconnected: (a) task (=the strategies as well as the administrative and production processes of the firm); (b) people (=the skills of firm's human resources of the firm); (c) technology (=the technologies used for implementing the above processes); and (d) structure (=the organization of the firm in departments, and the communication and coordination patterns them). Also, highly useful can be theoretical foundations developed in previous research concerning firm's resources as well as capabilities [33, 34], both ordinary and dynamic ones [35, 36]. With respect to the selection of external environment characteristics useful can be foundations from previous research concerning 'generalised competition' (such as Porter's Five Forces Framework [33]) and environmental dynamism [37].

(b)   Processing of the selected variables through the abovementioned Boruta AI FS algorithm in order to identify 'all-relevant' ones (i.e. all the variables that actually affect the degree of sales revenue reduction due to the crisis).

In particular, we can select potential independent variables of the following eight categories:

- Strategic Orientations: this category can include variables concerning the degree of adopting the main strategies described in relevant strategic management literature [33], such as cost leadership, differentiation, focus, innovation, export, etc.
- Processes: it can include various characteristics of firm's processes, such as complexity, efficiency, formality, flexibility, etc.
- Human Resources: it can include variables concerning the general education/skills level of firm's human resources (e.g. shares of firm's personnel having tertiary education, vocational/technical education, etc.), as well as the possession of specific skills concerning various ICT, the provision of relevant training, etc.
- Technology: variables concerning the use of various important ICTs (such as Enterprise Resource Planning (ERP) systems, Customer Relationships Management (CRM) systems, Supply Chain Management (SCM) systems, Business Intelligence/ Business Analytics (BI/BA) systems, Collaboration Support (CS) systems, e-sales, social media, cloud computing, etc., or the use of various production technologies).
- Structure: variables concerning various aspects of the structure of the firm, such as main structural design (functional, product/service based, geographic, matrix), degree of differentiation, specialization, centralization/decentralization, use of organic structural forms (such as teamwork, job rotation), etc. [38].
- Ordinary Capabilities: variables concerning the levels of firms capabilities to perform efficiently and effectively the main firm's functions, such as the ones proposed by Porter's Value Chain Model (Inbound Logistics, Operations, Outbound Logistics, Marketing and Sales, Service (primary ones), and Human Resource Management, Technology Development, Procurement, Infrastructure) [33]; and also the levels of various ICT capabilities of the firm [34].
- Dynamic Capabilities: variables concerning various aspects of firm's ACAP (such recognition and acquisition or relevant external knowledge, assimilation of it, integration/combination of it, and exploitation for innovations in its processes, products and services) [39, 40], agility (e.g. with respect to emergence of new technologies, new suppliers, new products and services as well change of prices by competitors) [37, 41].
- External Environment: variables concerning the intensity of the five aspects of the 'generalized competition' proposed by Porter's Five Forces Framework [33]: price and non-price competition, bargaining power of buyers, bargaining power of suppliers, threat of new entrants and threat of substitutes; and also variables concerning various aspects of dynamism of firm's [35–37].

4   Application

An application of the economic crisis policy analytics methodology described in the previous section has been made for the identification of characteristics of Greek firms as well as their external environment that affect the degree of their sales revenue reduction due to the long and intensive economic crisis that Greece experiences since

2009. For this purpose, we have used existing Greek firm's data for the period 2009–2014 from three sources: (i) the Ministry of Finance – Taxation Authorities; (ii) the Hellenic Statistical Authority; and (iii) the ICAP S.A., a well-known business information and consulting firm. In particular, we have used data from these sources for 363 Greek firms; 40.2% of them were manufacturing ones, 9.4% constructions, and 50.4% services ones; 52.6% of them were small, 36.1% medium and 11.3% large ones.

Our dependent variable was the percentage of sales revenue reduction due to the economic crisis in the period 2009–2014, which was discretized by the Ministry of Finance (in order to avoid providing too detailed data about this critical topic) into a variable with 13 possible discrete values (SALREV_RED): increase by more than 100%; increase by 80–100%; increase by 60–80%; increase by 40–60%; increase by 20–40%; increase by 1–20%; unchanged sales; decrease by 1–20%; decrease by 20–40%; decrease by 40–60%; decrease by 60–80%; decrease by 80–100%; decrease by more than 100%. We selected the following 64 independent variables, from 7 out of the 8 categories described in the previous section (with the only exception of the 'Processes' category, for which we did not find any variable in the available datasets):

- Strategic Orientations: degree of adopting a cost leadership strategy (STRAT_CL), a differentiation strategy (STRAT_DIF), a product/service innovation strategy (STRAT_INNOV) (five levels ordinary variables); introduction of product/service innovations in the last three years (INNOV_PRS), introduction of process innovations in the last three years (INNOV_PROC) (binary variables); percentage of sales revenue coming from new products/services introduced in the last three years (NEW_PRS_P), percentage of sales revenue coming from products/services significantly improved in the last three years (IMPR_PRS_P) (continuous variables); introduction of innovations in the production processes or in the services delivery processes (INN_PRSD), introduction of innovations in the sales, shipment or warehouse management processes (INN_SSWM), introduction of innovations in support processes (such as equipment maintenance) (INN_SUPP); conduct of R&D (R&D) (binary variables); exports as percentage of firm's sales revenue (EXP_P) (continuous variable).
- Human Resources: number of employees (EMPL); percentage of firm's employees having tertiary education (EMPL_TERT), vocational/technical education (EMPL_VOT), high school education (EMPL_HIGH), elementary school education (EMPL_ELEM); percentage of firm's employees using for their work computer (EMPL_COM), firm's Intranet (EMPL_INTRA), Internet (EMPL_INTER); ICT personnel as a percentage of firm's total workforce (EMPL_ICT) (continuous variables).
- Technology: degree of ERP systems use (D_ERP), CRM systems use (D_CRM), SCM use (D_SCM), BI/BA use (D_BI_BA), CS systems use (D_CS) (five levels ordinary variables); conduct of e-sales (E-SAL) (binary variable); use of social media for sales' promotion (SM_SALPRO) for collecting customers' opinions and complaints about firm's products and services (SM_OPCOM), for collecting ideas for improving products and services (SM_IMPR), for finding personnel (SM_PERS), for internal co-operation within the firm (SM_INT), for information

exchange with other partner firms (SM_PART) (three levels ordinary variables); use of cloud computing (CLOUD) (binary); degree of using cloud computing IAAS (CL_IAAS), cloud computing PAAS (CL_PAAS), cloud computing SAAS (CL_SAAS) (five levels ordinary variables).

- Structure: use of organic structural forms (teamwork, job rotation) (ORG) (binary variable).
- Ordinary Capabilities: six variables concerning the main ICT capabilities [34] for: ICT strategic planning (ICT_PLAN), cooperation between ICT and business units (ICT_BUS), cooperation with ICT vendors (ICT_VEND), development of ICT applications (ICT_DEV), modification of ICT applications (ICT_MOD), integration of ICT applications (ICT_INT) (five levels ordinary variables).
- Dynamic Capabilities: four variables concerning the main aspects of ACAP [39, 40]: external relevant knowledge recognition and acquisition (ACAP_ACQ), dissemination and analysis (ACAP_DIS), assimilation and integration in firm's knowledge base (ACAP_INT) and exploitation for process, products and services innovations (ACAP_EXP); and six variables concerning the main aspects of organizational agility [37, 41] with respect to introduction of new products and services by competitors (AG_PRS), new pricing policies of them (AG_PRI), changes of the demand for its products and services (AG_DEM), customization of products and services to customers' special needs (AG_CUST), expansion to new markets (AG_EXP) and change of suppliers (AG_SUP) (five levels ordinary variables).
- External Environment: number of competitors (N_COMP) (continuous variable); intensity of price competition (INT_PCOM), non-price competition (INT_NPCOM); and also four environmental dynamism variables concerning changes in products and services (DYN_PRS), technologies (DYN_TECH), competitors' movements (DYN_COMP) and demand for our products/services (DYN_PRS) (five levels ordinary variables) [35–37].
- General: sector (SECT) (binary variable: manufacturing/services).

The results from processing these variables using the Boruta FS AI algorithm are shown in Table 1, in which we can see 'all-relevant' identified variables affecting the degree of sales revenue reduction due to the crisis in order of importance. In particular, ten variables have been identified that actually affect the degree of sales revenue reduction due to the crisis (SALREV_RED). For each of them we examined whether it has a positive or negative effect: for the binary and ordinary variables this was done by calculating and comparing the averages of SALREV_RED for all their discrete values; for the continuous variables we first discretized them (initially we recoded them into corresponding binary variables based on their median values; and then we recoded them into corresponding four levels variables based on their quartile values) and followed the same procedure. The results are shown in the second column of Table 1.

Table 1. Relevant variables affecting the degree of sales revenue reduction due to the crisis.

Variable	Effect
Use of organic structural forms (teamwork, job rotation) (ORG)	Negative
Percentage of sales revenue coming from new products/services introduced in the last three years (NEW_PRS_P)	Negative
Introduction of innovations in support processes (such as equipment maintenance) (INN_SUPP)	Negative
Introduction of innovations in the sales, shipment or warehouse management processes (INN_SSWM)	Negative
Number of employees (EMPL)	Negative
Degree of ERP systems use (D_ERP)	Negative
Percentage of personnel having vocational/technical education (EMPL_VOT)	Positive
Exports as percentage of firm's sales revenue (EXP_P)	Negative
Percentage of personnel having tertiary education (EMPL_TERT)	Negative
Capability for integration of ICT applications (ICT_INT)	Negative

We remark that the most important of the examined variables for the degree of sales revenue reduction due to the crisis is the use of organic structural forms (such as teamwork, job rotation), which belongs to the structural characteristics category; it has negative impact on SALREV_RED, so it reduces the negative consequences of the crisis on firm's sales revenue. The economic crises give rise to big changes in firms' external environment (e.g. decrease of the demand for their products and services, changes in customers' needs and preferences, new products and service offerings by competitors, etc.) and increase its complexity; the adoption of organic structures (mainly horizontal teams) allows a more intensive exchange and synthesis of information and knowledge among employees from different functions, departments and geographic locations, so they enable a better and understanding of these changes/complexities, and a more effective design and implementation of actions for responding to them (such as new pricing policies, new products/services with higher value-for-money, expansions to new markets, both domestic and foreign ones, etc.).

Also, we remark that four out of the ten identified relevant variables belong to the strategic orientations' category, and all of them have negative impact on SALREV_RED, so they represent strategies that increase firms' resilience to economic crisis. Three of them concern innovation strategies: percentage of sales revenue coming from new products and services, and process innovations concerning sales, shipment, warehouse management and support activities (such as equipment maintenance). Therefore, the introduction of new products and services creates new markets and sales opportunities, so it reduces the negative impact of crisis on sales revenue; also the above process innovations increase efficiency, which increases resilience to the difficult conditions of economic crisis. The fourth one concerns export strategies: it indicates that exports generate sales revenue from foreign markets, and reduce the reliance on firm's domestic market, so they decrease negative consequences of crises in the latter.

Furthermore, there are two of the identified relevant variables that belong to the technology category, and concern ICTs, both of them having negative impact on

SALREV_RED: the use of ERP systems and the capabilities for integration of existing ICT applications. This reveals two important firm's technological characteristics that increase its resilience to economic crisis is. The use of ERP systems provides comprehensive and integrated electronic support of all firm's functions, so it enhances their efficiency, which is quite useful for coping with the crisis. Also, high level of capability for integrating existing ICT applications enables isolated 'islands of automation' (belonging to the same or different departments) to be interconnected and evolve towards an integrated ICT infrastructure, enabling data and functionality of one ICT application to be exploited by others as well; this improves cooperation and coordination between firm's departments, and enhances firm's efficiency, which increases its resilience to crisis. Finally, there are two of the identified relevant variables that concern belong to the human resources category: the employment of personnel with tertiary education increases firm's ability to cope with the crisis, however the employment of personnel having lower vocational/technical level education (though less costly) has the opposite effects. The number of firm's employees has a also negative impact on SALREV_RED, indicating that larger firms have lower reductions of sales revenue due to the crisis.

The above findings indicate that the Greek government agencies in order to reduce the negative consequences of the economic crisis on firms should design and implement effective public policies (such as legislation, financial support, provision of training and consulting, etc.) for promoting firms' innovation and export activities. Furthermore, it is necessary to design and implement effective public policies for promoting the adoption of ERP systems, organic structural forms (complementing their hierarchical structures with horizontal teamwork), and for employing personnel of higher educational level. These public policies should be focused mainly on the small and medium firms.

5 Conclusions

In the previous sections has been presented a policy analytics methodology, which exploits existing public and private sector data, based on an advanced big data oriented AI FS algorithm, in order to support policy making concerning one of the most serious problems that governments repeatedly face: the economic crises. It allows identifying firms' characteristics that affect their resilience to economic crisis. Furthermore, a first application of it has been presented, which provides a first validation of the usefulness of this methodology, and leads to interesting conclusions and insights.

Our research has interesting implications for research and practice. With respect to research, it creates new knowledge in two emerging, highly important for the society, but minimally researched, digital government research domains: policy analytics and government AI exploitation. With respect to practice, it provides support to government agencies for designing policies for reducing the negative impact on firms of one of the most important problems of our market economies: the economic crises. In general, it provides an approach for combining and exploiting multiple sources of public and private sector data in order to understand the characteristics of firms exhibiting various positive behaviours/evolutions (e.g. export, expansion to other countries, adoption of new technologies, etc.) or negative ones (e.g. reduction of personnel employment, disinvestment, etc.), which will be useful for the design of relevant public policies. However, further application of our methodology is required in various national contexts, at both national and sectoral level, using a wider range of potential independent variables, and based on the experience gained improvements of the methodology.

References

1. Janssen, M., Wimmer, M.: Introduction to policy-making in the digital age. In: Janssen, M., Wimmer, M., Deljoo, A. (eds.) Policy Practice and Digital Science – Integrating Complex Systems, Social Simulation and Public Administration in Policy Research. Public Administration and Information Technology, pp. 1–14. Springer, Cham (2015). https://doi.org/10.1007/978-3-319-12784-2_1
2. Tsoukias, A., Montibeller, G., Lucertini, G., Belton, V.: Policy analytics: an agenda for research and practice. EURO J. Decis. Process. **1**(1–2), 115–134 (2013)
3. Daniell, K.A., Morton, A., Rios Insua, D.: Policy analysis and policy analytics. Ann. Oper. Res. **236**(1), 1–13 (2016)
4. De Marchi, G., Lucertini, G., Tsoukias, A.: From evidence-based policy making to policy analytics. Ann. Oper. Res. **236**(1), 15–38 (2016)
5. Gil-Garcia, J.R., Pardo, T.A., Luna-Reyes, L.F.: Policy analytics: definitions, components, methods, and illustrative examples. In: Gil-Garcia, J.R., Pardo, T.A., Luna-Reyes, L.F. (eds.) Policy Analytics, Modelling, and Informatics. Public Administration and Information Technology, pp. 1–16. Springer, Cham (2018). https://doi.org/10.1007/978-3-319-61762-6_1
6. Janowski, T.: Digital government evolution: from transformation to contextualization. Gov. Inf. Q. **32**(3), 221–236 (2015)
7. Lachana, Z., Alexopoulos, C., Loukis, E., Charalabidis, Y.: Identifying the different generations of e-Government – an analysis framework. In: Proceedings of 12th Mediterranean Conference on Information Systems (MCIS 2018), Corfu, Greece (2018)
8. Hiltz, S.R., Diaz, P., Mark, G.: Introduction: social media and collaborative systems for crisis management. ACM Trans. Comput. Hum. Interact. **18**(4), 1–6 (2011)
9. Baer, D., Wimmer, M., Glova, J., Papazafeiropoulou, A., Brooks, L.: Analysis of policy cases in the field of energy policy. In: Janssen, M., Wimmer, N., Deljoo, A. (eds.) Policy Practice and Digital Science – Integrating Complex Systems, Social Simulation and Public Administration in Policy Research'. Public Administration and Information Technology, pp. 355–378. Springer, Cham (2015). https://doi.org/10.1007/978-3-319-12784-2_16
10. Ekstrom, J.A., Lau, G.T., Law, K.H.: Policy analytics tools to identify gaps in environmental governance. In: Gil-Garcia, J.R., Pardo, T., Luna-Reyes, L.F. (eds.) Policy Analytics, Modeling, and Informatics – Innovative Tools for Solving Complex Social Problems. Public Administration and Information Technology, pp. 289–314. Springer, Cham (2018). https://doi.org/10.1007/978-3-319-61762-6_13
11. Park, C.H., Johnston, E.W.: An event-driven lens for bridging formal organizations and informal online participation: how policy informatics enables just-in-time responses to crises. In: Gil-Garcia, J.R., Pardo, T., Luna-Reyes, L.F. (eds.) Policy Analytics, Modeling, and Informatics – Innovative Tools for Solving Complex Social Problems. Public Administration and Information Technology, pp. 343–361. Springer, Cham (2018). https://doi.org/10.1007/978-3-319-61762-6_15

274   E. Loukis et al.

12. Van den Braak, S., Choenni, S.: Development and use of data-centric information systems to support policymakers: applied to criminal justice systems. In: Gil-Garcia, J.R., Pardo, T., Luna-Reyes, L.F. (eds.) Policy Analytics, Modeling, and Informatics – Innovative Tools for Solving Complex Social Problems. Public Administration and Information Technology, pp. 343–361. Springer, Cham (2018). https://doi.org/10.1007/978-3-319-61762-6_5
13. Van Dijk, V., Kalidien, S., Choenni, S.: Smart monitoring of the criminal justice system. Gov. Inf. Q. **35**(4), 24–32 (2018)
14. Craglia M., et al. (eds.): Artificial Intelligence - A European Perspective, EUR 29425 EN. EU Publications Office, Luxembourg (2018)
15. Makridakis, S.: The forthcoming Artificial Intelligence (AI) revolution: Its impact on society and firms. Future **90**, 46–60 (2017)
16. Eggers, W.D., Schatsky, D., Viechnicki, P.: AI-Augmented Government. Using Cognitive Technologies to Redesign Public Sector Work. Deloitte University Press, New York (2017)
17. Desouza, K.C., Krishnamurthy, R., Dawson, G.S.: Learning from Public Sector Experimentation with Artificial Intelligence. Brookings, Washington D.C. (2017)
18. Desouza, K.C.: Delivering Artificial Intelligence in Government: Challenges and Opportunities. IBM Center for The Business of Government, Washington D.C. (2018)
19. Sun, T.Q., Medaglia, R.: Mapping the challenges of Artificial Intelligence in the public sector: evidence from public healthcare. Gov. Inf. Q. **36**(2), 368–383 (2019)
20. Rockoff, J.E., Jacob, B.A., Kane, T.J., Staiger, D.O.: Can you recognize an Effective teacher when you recruit one? Educ. Financ. Policy **6**(1), 43–74 (2010)
21. Chandler, D., Levitt, S.D., List, J.A.: Predicting and preventing shootings among at-risk youth. Am. Econ. Rev. **101**(3), 288–292 (2011)
22. Kang, J.S., Kuznetsova, P., Luca, M., Choi, Y.: Where not to eat? Improving public policy by predicting hygiene inspections using online reviews. In: Proceedings of Empirical Methods in Natural Language Processing Conference 2013, pp. 1443–1448 (2013)
23. Camacho-Collados, M., Liberatore, F.: A Decision Support System for predictive police patrolling. Decis. Support Syst. **75**, 25–37 (2015)
24. Ku, C.H., Leroy, G.: A decision support system: Automated crime report analysis and classification for e-government. Gov. Inf. Q. **31**(4), 534–544 (2014)
25. Keeley, B., Love, P.: From Crisis to Recovery - The Causes, Course and Consequences of the Great Recession. OECD Publishing, Paris (2010)
26. Knoop, T.A.: Recessions and Depressions: Understanding Business Cycles, 2nd edn. Praeger, Santa Barbara (2015)
27. Kursa, M.B., Jankowski, A., Rudnicki, W.R.: Boruta – a system for feature selection. Fundamenta Informaticae **101**, 271–285 (2010)
28. Kursa, M.B., Rudnicki, W.R.: Feature selection with the Boruta package. J. Stat. Softw. **36**(11), 1–13 (2010)
29. Alelyani, S., Wang, L., Liu, H.: The effect of the characteristics of the dataset on the selection stability. In: Proceedings of the 23rd IEEE International Conference on Tools with Artificial Intelligence (2011)
30. Tang, J., Alelyani, S., Liu, H.: Feature selection for classification: a review. Data Classif. Algorithms Appl. 37–64 (2014)
31. Izsak, K., Markianidou, P., Lukach, R., Wastyn, A.: The impact of the crisis on research and innovation policies. European Commission, DG Research, Brussels (2013)
32. Leavitt, H.J.: Applied organization change in industry: structural, technical, and human approaches. In: Cooper, S., Leavitt, H.J., Shelly, K. (eds.) New Perspectives in Organizational Research, pp. 55–71. Wiley, Chichester (1964)
33. Johnson, G., Whittington, R., Scholes, K.: Exploring Corporate Strategy, 9th edn. Financial Times/Prentice Hall, Harlow (2010)

34. Chen, Y., Wang, Y., Nevo, S., Jin, J., Wang, L., Chow, W.S.: IT capability and organizational performance: the roles of business process agility and environmental factors. Eur. J. Inf. Syst. **23**(3), 326–342 (2014)
35. Teece, D.: Explicating dynamic capabilities: the nature and microfoundations of (sustainable) enterprise performance. Strateg. Manag. J. **28**(13), 1319–1350 (2007)
36. Drnevich, P.L., Kriauciunas, A.P.: Clarifying the conditions and limits of the contributions of ordinary and dynamic capabilties to relative firm performance. Strateg. Manag. J. **32**(3), 254–279 (2011)
37. Sherehiy, B., Karwowski, W., Layer, J.K.: A review of enterprise agility: concepts, frameworks, and attributes. Int. J. Ind. Ergon. **37**(5), 445–460 (2007)
38. Jones, G.R.: Organizational Theory, Design, and Change, 7th edn. Pearson Education Limited, London (2013)
39. Cohen, W.M., Levinthal, D.A.: Absorptive capacity: a new perspective on learning and innovation. Adm. Sci. Q. **35**(1), 128–152 (1990)
40. Camisón, C., Forés, B.: Absorptive capacity: new insights for its conceptualization and measurement. J. Bus. Res. **63**(7), 707–715 (2010)
41. Lu, Y., Ramamurthy, K.R.: Understanding the link between information technology capability and organizational agility: an empirical examination. MIS Q. **35**(4), 931–954 (2011)

Using Disruptive Technologies in Government: Identification of Research and Training Needs

Alexander Ronzhyn[1(✉)] ⓘ, Maria A. Wimmer[1], Vera Spitzer[1],
Gabriela Viale Pereira[2], and Charalampos Alexopoulos[3] ⓘ

[1] Institute for IS Research, University of Koblenz-Landau, Koblenz, Germany
{ronzhyn,wimmer,vesp91}@uni-koblenz.de
[2] Department for E-Governance and Administration, Danube University Krems,
Krems, Austria
gabriela.viale-pereira@donau-uni.ac.at
[3] Dept. Information and Communication Systems Engineering,
University of the Aegean, Samos, Greece
alexop@aegean.gr

Abstract. Over the past years, a number of new technologies have emerged with a potential to disrupt many spheres of the society. While public sector traditionally lacks behind business in innovation, significant changes are anticipated with the use of disruptive technologies. The implementation of the new technologies for the government service provision, along with possible benefits, need to be well thought through and challenges need to be carefully discussed, analysed and evaluated. This paper uses scenario-technique to identify research and training needs for the implementation of disruptive technologies in government services. Using the input of 58 experts from three workshops, research and training needs for the internet of things, artificial intelligence, virtual and augmented reality, as well as big data technologies have been identified. The identified needs can serve as a starting point for a broader and more informed discussion about the knowledge and skills that the researchers and practitioners of digital government need to obtain for the broad use of such new (disruptive) technologies.

Keywords: Digital government · Disruptive technologies · Research needs · Training needs · Scenario-technique

1 Introduction

Digital government refers to the use of information and communication technologies (ICT) for the provision of public services with the aim of increased efficiency, effectiveness and improved quality of services for the citizens [1, 2]. Over time, along with the changes in the expectations and needs of citizens and the increasing ubiquity of technology in societies, digital government services have also been changing.

The changes in the way the public services are provided can be used as an evidence for identifying distinct stages of digital government evolution [3, 4]. The increase in participatory services and social media use by the public bodies parallel to the

© IFIP International Federation for Information Processing 2019
Published by Springer Nature Switzerland AG 2019
I. Lindgren et al. (Eds.): EGOV 2019, LNCS 11685, pp. 276–287, 2019.
https://doi.org/10.1007/978-3-030-27325-5_21

emergence of Web 2.0, allowed speaking of Government 2.0 or participatory government [5, 6]. In a different classification of phases, Janowski [7] suggested that digital government evolution can be delimited into four stages based on how government is transformed by the ICT. Broadly speaking, Janowski's third stage "Engagement or Electronic Governance" corresponds to the Government 2.0, characterized by increased participation and engagement, trust building and focus on transparency and accountability [7].

Lachana et al. argue that the recent changes in the technologies used and the focus of the use of these technologies allow identifying a new stage in digital government – Government 3.0 [8]. This new stage is characterized by the extensive use of disruptive technologies for provision of customized services and data-driven evidence-based decision making [9]. The term "disruptive technology" refers to the technologies, whose application has potential to drastically alter the processes and operations in a particular field of the public sector [10]. Artificial intelligence (AI), Internet of things (IoT), natural language processing (NLP), Virtual and Augmented reality (VR, AR), big data and block chain are such examples of technologies [9].

Government 3.0, as defined above, largely corresponds to the fourth stage of Janowski's [7] classification: "Contextualization or Policy-Driven Electronic Governance", which emphasizes the contextualization of the digital government efforts. This technological and thematic shift poses ethical and research challenges [11] and creates new research and training needs. The current research is a part of the Gov 3.0 project [12] that is concerned with establishing Government 3.0 as a research domain and creating a Master curriculum addressing the needs of this new stage. The current paper describes the first steps of identification of these needs using the future scenario research technique [13]. The identified needs will serve as a basis for the Government 3.0 roadmap and later the Master-level education curriculum, developed during the subsequent work packages within the project.

In the context of the paper, a "research need" is a gap identified by relevant stakeholders as important and if addressed will help to resolve a specific real-world problem [14]. A "training need" is a gap in the existing training curricula (either formal or vocational), which when addressed allows the recipients of training to manage effectively a specific real-world problem. A "problem" in both of the definitions refers to the implementation of the disruptive technology in public service as illustrated in the scenarios.

The remainder of the paper is structured as follows. Section 2 details the methodology used for collecting input from the experts in the workshop setting. Section 3 provides an example of a scenario used (Sect. 3.1) and details the findings related to the research (Sect. 3.2) and training (Sect. 3.3) needs. Section 4 synthesises the findings and details the conclusions, suggesting directions for the future research.

2   Methodology

The use of future scenarios is an established method for research of possible futures in various fields, both public and private [15, 16]. Scenarios typically describe possible future developments in a specific area [17], detailing the involvement of various stakeholders and interplay between these stakeholders [18]. The aim of the scenario use is to look at the problem from different viewpoints and better understand possible future evolution directions [19], thus improving decision making [20]. In contrast to forecasts and prognoses, the goal of the scenarios is to suggest several possible developments with varying degree of probability, rather than identifying the most probable future [21, 22].

The research is guided by the following two questions:

1. What are the research needs regarding the implementation of disruptive technologies in digital government?
2. What are the training needs connected to the implementation of disruptive technologies in digital government?

In this research, we use scenario methodology as described in Ronzhyn et al. [13]. First, future scenarios describing the use of the disruptive technologies were developed by the research team. These scenarios were consequently presented to the experts at the workshops to elicit input about possible research and training needs for the implementation of the scenario. The workshops were organized within one or two conference sessions and include: (a) introduction to the overall task, (b) scenario introduction, (c) group discussion of the individual scenarios led by group moderators (addressing both, research and training needs, and prioritising these needs), and (d) summary of the workshop with brief discussion of the scenarios by all the participants. As a result of the discussion, experts provide a list of research and training needs along with the assessment of how important or pressing a particular need is. The assessment is a result of the expert consensus within a group. For prioritisation a three-level system is used: green – low importance, yellow – medium importance, and red – high importance.

Three workshops were organized to collect input from the experts in the field of digital government: the Roadmapping workshop at Samos Summit (Samos, Greece) in July 2018, the Roadmapping workshop at the EGOV-CeDEM-ePart 2018 conference (Krems a.d. Donau, Austria) in September 2018 and the Workshop at the NEGZ: Herbsttagung Conference (Berlin, Germany) in November 2018. In total seven different scenarios were discussed (some of them at more than one workshop). Scenarios included possible future implementations of AI, ML, NLP, IoT, AR, VR and Blockchain technologies as well as implementations of the broader concepts of smart city, gamification and co-creation of public services. Most of the scenarios involved more than one technology. For example, one of the scenarios described the use of crowdsourced sensors to monitor air quality in cities (IoT, smart city) and automated decision making to make sense of the collected data (ML, AI). A different scenario described an example of implementation of gamification of social services based on the AR technology. A total of 58 experts participated in workshops, among them academics, public officials, government representatives and private sector representatives. Experts involved were also rather varied geographically: the majority of participants came from European organizations; several participants came also from the Americas, Asia and Australia. The diversity among experts allowed gathering diverse and original input based on experts' individual backgrounds and experiences.

62 distinct research needs, and 54 trainings needs were collected, and additional notes by workshop moderators were taken along the discussions and used in the

analysis to better understand the suggested needs. The prioritisation of the needs was done by the experts in the workshop, however, if a specific need was prioritized differently by different groups in distinct workshops, then an average prioritisation was given to the need. The needs have been classified into categories based on the area of concern (6 research and 5 training need categories, see Sects. 3.2 and 3.3). The classification was done by four researchers of the project employing an inductive method (described e.g. in [35]).

3 Findings

Below, one of the scenarios is introduced along with a poster as an example of how the use of a disruptive technology in public service was presented during the workshop. Subsequently, in Sects. 3.2 and 3.3 the results of the workshops are described together with the categories that emerged during analysis.

3.1 Scenario Example

The example scenario "Intelligent citizen portals connected across Europe using chatbot interface for easy interaction with citizens" details a possible use of AI and machine learning coupled with natural language processing technology, realizing a chatbot interface for better cross-border public services. Figure 1 provides a brief textual description of the scenario – a more detailed version was presented to the workshop participants.

Relocating to another country or similar action involving two or more different countries often carry high administrative burden. Citizens not only have to organize many documents over a short period of time, but also have to consider the different regulations of their home vs. destination country. In the future, the use of intelligent citizen portals with chatbot interface simplifies the organisation of complicated procedures involving authorities in multiple countries.

A citizen uses a smartphone to contact the government chatbot and requests help with the process. The citizen can send messages written in natural language without the need to use specific commands. A chatbot then processes the text using Natural Language Processing and AI to understand the meaning of the request and provides relevant answer. In a further future, a chatbot can even process the voice commands and provide answers.

The chatbot acts as an interface connecting a citizen to the intelligent portal. The portal is designed in a way to interoperate with other portals and databases across Europe. If eID is used by the citizen, the portal application can then use it to access the relevant information across borders (according to the Once-Only Principle[1]). The application can also identify the missing information required for the relocation of the citizen and ask necessary questions to gather this information. Furthermore, the intelligent portal can automatically complete foreign forms and help with understanding the specific terms, providing assistance through the conversation with a chatbot.

Based on the Once-only principle, AI, NLP and the intelligent citizen portal, relocating abroad (and other similar cross-border formalities) is no longer a complicated matter for the citizen and for public authorities.

Fig. 1. Short description of the "Intelligent Portals" scenario

As described in the methodology, the scenario provides an example of possible future implementations of disruptive technologies in public service provision. While most of the relevant technologies can be implemented practically even today, some parts depicted in the scenario are still not quite ready (for example OOP has not been fully implemented across European borders and interoperability between different public organization is still a challenge; even more so between public and private organizations).

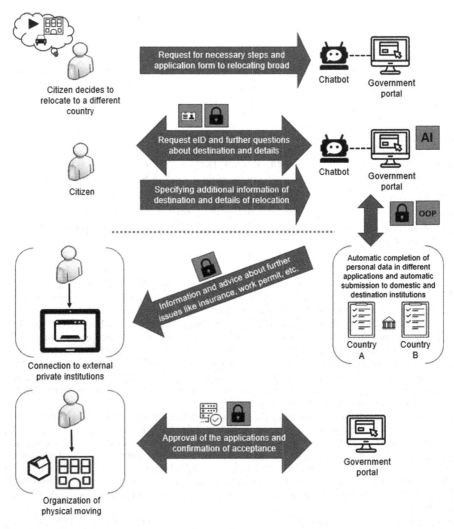

Fig. 2. Scenario poster – "Intelligent citizen portals connected across Europe using chatbot interface for easy interaction with citizens"

The poster used along with this scenario is shown on Fig. 2. On the poster, the arrows represent the exchange of information between the actors, while the boxes show technological enablers that are involved at each of the steps for information processing (e.g., AI system) and for information exchange (e.g., encryption). Both artefacts were used to deliberate research and training needs with the experts in the different workshops. The subsequent descriptions outline the main research and training needs identified during the workshops.

3.2   Research Needs

3.2.1   Standardisation and Interoperability of Disruptive Technologies

Standardisation includes the needs for further research of possible standards for the disruptive technology implementation: standards for the use of AI for automated decision making, standardisation of collected data by IoT and the standardisation of the IoT devices. Common standards are especially important in IoT as different models of sensors can be used as a network to provide valuable results, so the data collected by these sensors needs to be compatible and interoperable.

Linked to standardisation, interoperability research needs deal with ensuring that different implementations of the same technology are able to effectively "talk to each other". These needs are of high priority both in IoT (especially technical interoperability of different sensors [23]) and in AI/ML research (in the intelligent portals scenario, where cross-border interoperability is a necessity).

3.2.2   Analysis of Stakeholders

This category describes the engagement of stakeholders in the implementation of modern technologies as a fundamental requirement for successful implementation and use of these technologies. Stakeholders are those who affect or are affected by decisions or actions [24]. In the implementation of disruptive technologies, it is necessary to understand who the stakeholders are, how to engage various stakeholders effectively and identify the needs of target groups to involve them adequately in the implementation process. Technologies like Blockchain, AI and Machine Learning have been the biggest research needs in stakeholder (citizen) engagement, co-creation and improvement of already existing solutions both in public and private sectors. Further research needs include the user studies comparing the use of traditional web search functions and modern solutions such as Chatbots. How far can a Chatbot based on AI and ML take over the functions of traditional web and how can the digital divide between different user groups be overcome in the future, with the use of AI-driven technologies? Another research need arises as to whether citizen engagement/co-creation and outsourcing to the private sector could increase the acceptance of and trust towards IoT, AI and ML systems. Similarly, it is necessary to examine existing architectures of technologies for their suitability in the public sector.

3.2.3   Evaluation and Policy Making

The category refers to the necessity of assessment of impact and costs of the disruptive technologies' implementation. The research needs of the present category were raised when discussing AI (adapting legislation to the use of cross-border data) and IoT (automated policy making based on IoT data). Further research is necessary to identify the ways to adapt legislation for effective implementation of some technologies in public sector (like video monitoring regulation for AI/ML) and the implications of using AI for the creation of regulations and policy (e.g., exploring the dangers of bias in ML [25, 26]).

The proper way of using simulation and data modelling for e-government services is another research need. Simulation can be used for policy modelling in different settings and in the design of predictive models. In both cases it may be used as a basis for data-driven decision making. The issues of accuracy of data and accountability need to be addressed when using simulation and data modelling for making decisions.

Research needs of this category are often transdisciplinary and also very much dependent on the field where the technology is to be used. For different scenarios involving IoT, research needs may include research of urban environment (when IoT are implemented as a part of a Smart City imitative) or "earth/water evaluation" (when IoT sensors are used in agriculture).

3.2.4   Data Security and Data Privacy

Data security and data privacy are two important topics for research of the use of disruptive technologies in public sector. The willingness to allow collection, sharing and the use of sensitive citizen data is contingent on high trust in these technologies and administrations deploying them. In particular, the security and privacy of the Block-chain technology need to be addressed in the context of public service. While implemented private-sector solutions (e.g. in finance) are being used and further developed, the potential for the use of Blockchain in the public sector needs to be researched and evaluated further in the context of e-government [27] while most of the papers tend to focus on benefits of the technology rather than possible challenges of its implementation [28]. Privacy and security issues need to be researched in the context of storing sensitive personal data and allowing specific actors the access to these data [29].

Data privacy is a significant issue in IoT as well, especially in urban setting. In case studies [30], data privacy and security were found to be the main impediments on the strategic level for the introduction of IoT for e-government. Data accuracy is another issue critical for the implementation of IoT in smart cities. Research needs in data quality are connected to the standardization issues described in Sect. 3.2.1.

3.2.5   Automated Decision-Making

Due to the digitization of the public sector processes, the use of modern technologies and automation mechanisms is indispensable. Thus, the possibilities of using disruptive technologies and their possible effects must be investigated. The big data collected by sensors can be automatically processed and analyzed using the AI and ML technologies to provide real-time decisions. Such system may offer significant advantages over "manual" regulation and improve the quality of life in cities [31], yet it poses a number of challenges concerning transparency and accountability. There are also concerns related to adaptability of such systems: as different environments offer different challenges, there might be no one standard way of organizing automated decision-making based on the collected environment data. Further case-study research is necessary to see how AI and ML may be adapted on the local level [32].

The use of autonomous agents also poses a concern related to the inclusivity and trust. Further research on the integration of autonomous systems in public services is necessary: addressing both the technological issues (design of such agents) and behavioral issues (public perception of the agents).

The challenges of implementation of VR and AR in the public sector reveal further research needs. In particular, the possibilities and benefits of VR and AR in connection with smart buildings must be examined in more detail. Also in regard to the training needs, further research is needed on the benefits of gamification methodology in the VR and AR contexts.

3.2.6   Ethical Issues

A common research need in the discussion of the disruptive technologies is ethics and moral issues. By far, AI is the most ethically controversial technology. Research directions regarding AI include privacy research (surveillance, profiling), ethics of automated decision making (especially concerning sensitive decisions, e.g., in law enforcement, health), issues of responsible research. The discrepancies between the real world and the data used for AI-based decision making was identified as a high-priority research issue as decisions based on incomplete (or even biased) information may be unfair and problematic. One of the ethical issues raised in regard to the implementation of IoT is the sustainability of sensors infrastructure; if IoT sensors are used in rural environments, they are much more difficult to control and recycle properly. Possible pollution is an ethical concern that needs to be researched. An earlier study [11] showed that there is significant number of ethical issues connected to implementation of disruptive technologies in public service.

3.3   Training Needs

3.3.1   Technology

AI and Machine Learning, Blockchain and IoT are the technologies with most technical requirements for using and implementing them in public sector. When using AI/ML, field experts in multidisciplinary domains are required to have expertise in modelling and tools, which requires professional training. Public officials must be able to deal with non-standard situations in requests through digital agents and addressing multiple identities in the system. For the implementation of these technologies, skills on app development, security encryption and access rights are fundamental. For implementing blockchain technical training of identity providers, employers, public sector and social workers is necessary, as well as the understanding the impact of decentralized distributed system on current administrative processes. Public officials training on the use of specific devices are important for the use of VR/AR equipment and IoT sensors. Implementing IoT also requires skills on decision system modelling, monitoring systems and fog computing/infrastructure.

3.3.2   Management

Management training is found to be relevant for applying AI/ML, Blockchain and IoT in public sector. Considering AI/ML applications, relevant aspects include the ability to involve citizens in the process, as well as knowledge management and business models of social work (social innovation). Training on process/change management is important for using VR/AR in government. Similarly, IoT applications require courses for public employees on project management, entrepreneurship, doing business and cost-benefit analysis.

3.3.3   New Technologies in Public Management and E-Government

Training on public management and e-government is important for applying most of the discussed disruptive technologies such as AI/ML, Blockchain and IoT. For government employees using AI/ML, skills on new technical components (IT systems) and new legal basis are required, as well as the ability to establish a framework for cooperation with private companies. For blockchain, including a basic training for public sector specialists on the technology use in government is required. When using IoT in government applications, training needs refer to introductory topics of e-government such as enterprise architecture, public administration and public sector innovation, as well as the emergent digital transformation domain, which refers to complete redesigning of the government services to fulfil changing user needs [33].

In addition to the major training needs of this category, our research indicates the lack of soft skills mainly for the public officials and citizens regarding acceptance of disruptive technologies such as AI and blockchain. A "train the trainers" approach seems to be the most efficient one for covering this need.

3.3.4   Data Science and Data Security

Most of the training needs concerning data science and security are connected to the implementation and use of the AI, ML and IoT technologies. It is worth mentioning that these 3 technologies have been used in different tested scenarios (except 3 and 6). Our results reveal lack of knowledge on data analysis and artificial intelligence tools, the ways of achieving data trust and security including accuracy of the IoT devices and user input for the target groups of civil servants, professionals and citizens. Legal issues training is identified as a very important training need for all target groups including researchers, especially concerning the blockchain and AI technologies.

3.3.5   Responsibility and Sustainability

The last category of the identified training needs has to do with responsible research and sustainability of the applied solutions. Again, in regard to AI, a need to train the researchers in ethics was identified, specifically concerning the ethical solutions to the problems of automated decision-making. For public servants, the focus is on the managerial training needs: sustainability assessment of the applied solutions (IoT) in the public sector understanding what technology should be applied and if this technology is covering the current needs.

4   Discussion and Conclusions

The number and diversity of identified research needs is rather high, reflecting the novelty of application of the disruptive technologies for public service provisioning. First, researchers need to carefully examine the necessity for the implementation of services based on these technologies: evaluate the advantages (or disadvantages), which the new technology will bring in the specific cases. Then, there are research needs regarding the effective and ethical use of the data collected and its use for decision making. The critical issues of privacy and security have to be addressed to ensure the responsible implementation of such services and their acceptance by the public. Finally, as many public services are not limited to one country, research and development of standards is important to ensure interoperability of services.

Many of the research needs discussed in this paper have already been mentioned by the researchers of the specific technologies: for IoT in public services, interoperability and standardisation are seen as a major issues [34], in the AI research, ethics has been a steady concern [35] and privacy is a huge pressing issue in ICT generally [36] and with the implementation of the once-only principle. The research needs highlighted in the context of disruptive technologies in public service shall stimulate the discussion and help to further advance the digital government research and practice.

The analysis of training needs reveals two types of training that are needed. For the academics and professionals who are going to implement the new services, training in the technology is necessary: both general training regarding data security, privacy and sustainability, and specific training on particular technologies. At the same time, for public officials, soft and managerial skills training is particularly important for ensuring citizen trust towards the disruptive technologies. Services based on these technologies are significantly different from the ones of the current generation and acceptance of the new services by the public is a critical issue. In this regard, training the trainers (public officials, administrators) is the critical need so that stakeholders are able to use the new technologies and explain the benefits and functionality to the public.

Involving experts in the discussion of the new technologies in public services is very important. The chosen scenario-based technique has shown good results in stimulating the discussion and gathering diverse insights on disruptive technologies in digital government. Still, the workshop-based scenario approach has some limitations that need to be acknowledged: First, the competence area of an expert has an effect on the type of suggested needs. Experts from public service tend to view problems from the perspective of a government employee, while people with background in informatics are more interested in issues connected to the technical realisation and data. This means that if a particular discussion group at the workshop lacked experts from the scenario's field, the importance of some of the research and training needs was conceivably underestimated. Policy makers (largely absent from the workshops) could provide a unique vantage point and new useful needs. The second limitation of the approach is that it does not produce 'ready' research and training needs, and the experts need to be involved after the workshops, at the stage of analysis, to refine the participants' contributions and draw useful conclusions.

As stated in the Introduction, this paper does not aim to provide an exhaustive list of research and trainings needs. Instead, the goal is to specify a starting point for a broader discussion of the necessity to address some issues that arise as the result of implementation of disruptive technologies in digital government. An example of such an issue to be addressed is the negative consequences of the disruptive technologies, which can be the topic of the future research.

The research within the project will continue to further develop the findings described in this paper and to produce useful recommendations regarding the implementation of disruptive technologies in public service. The insight gained through the scenario-based workshops and described in this paper will be used further within the Gov 3.0 project [12]. First, in the elaboration of the Government 3.0 research roadmap and, secondly, for the development of the joint Master curriculum, addressing the identified training needs.

References

1. Yildiz, M.: E-government research: reviewing the literature, limitations, and ways forward. Gov. Inf. Q. **24**, 646–665 (2007)
2. Brown, M., Brudney, J.: Achieving advanced electronic government services: an examination of obstacles and implications from an international perspective. In: Proceedings of the Sixth National Public Management Research Conference (2001)
3. Mukabeta Maumbe, B., Owei, V., Alexander, H.: Questioning the pace and pathway of e-government development in Africa: a case study of South Africa's Cape Gateway project. Gov. Inf. Q. **25**, 757–777 (2008)
4. Baumgarten, J., Chui, M.: E-government 2.0. McKinsey Q. **4**(2), 26–31 (2009)
5. Bonsón, E., Torres, L., Royo, S., Flores, F.: Local e-government 2.0: social media and corporate transparency in municipalities. Gov. Inf. Q. **29**, 123–132 (2012)
6. Baumgarten, J., Chui, M.: E-government 2.0. McKinsey Q. **4**, 26–31 (2009)
7. Janowski, T.: Digital government evolution: from transformation to contextualization. Gov. Inf. Q. **32**, 221–236 (2015)
8. Lachana, Z., Alexopoulos, C., Loukis, E., Charalabidis, Y.: Identifying the different generations of Egovernment: an analysis framework. In: The 12th Mediterranean Conference on Information Systems (MCIS), Corfu, Greece, pp. 1–13 (2018)
9. Pereira, G.V., et al.: Scientific foundations training and entrepreneurship activities in the domain of ICT-enabled governance. In: Proceedings of the 19th Annual International Conference on Digital Government Research Governance in the Data Age - dgo 2018, pp. 1–2. ACM Press, New York (2018)
10. Kostoff, R.N., Boylan, R., Simons, G.R.: Disruptive technology roadmaps. Technol. Forecast. Soc. Change **71**, 141–159 (2004)
11. Ronzhyn, A., Wimmer, M.A.: Literature review of ethical concerns in the use of disruptive technologies in government 3.0. In: The Thirteenth International Conference on Digital Society and eGovernments, ICDS 2019, pp. 85–92. IARIA, Athens (2019)
12. Gov 3.0: Gov 3.0 – Scientific foundations training and entrepreneurship activities in the domain of ICT – enabled Governance. https://www.gov30.eu/
13. Ronzhyn, A., Spitzer, V., Wimmer, M.A.: Scenario technique to elicit research and training needs in digital government employing disruptive technologies. In: Proceedings of dg.o 2019: 20th Annual International Conference on Digital Government Research (dg.o 2019), Dubai, United Arab Emirates, 18 June 2019. ACM, New York (2019)
14. Chang, S.M., Carey, T.S., Kato, E.U., Guise, J.M., Sanders, G.D.: Identifying research needs for improving health care. Ann. Int. Med. **157**, 439–445 (2012)
15. Ratcliffe, J.: Scenario building: a suitable method for strategic property planning? Prop. Manag. **18**, 127–144 (2000)
16. Schwartz, P.: The Art of the Long View: Planning for the Future in an Uncertain World. Wiley, New York (1996)

17. Johnson, K.A., et al.: Using participatory scenarios to stimulate social learning for collaborative sustainable development. Ecol. Soc. **17**, 9 (2012)
18. Carroll, J.M.: Five reasons for scenario-based design. In: Proceedings of the 32nd Hawaii International Conference on System Sciences, pp. 1–11 (1999)
19. Janssen, M., et al.: Scenario building for E-Government in 2020: consolidating the results from regional workshops. In: 40th Annual Hawaii International Conference on System Sciences, pp. 296–297 (2007)
20. Ringland, G.G.: Scenarios in Public Policy. Wiley, Chichester (2002)
21. Peterson, G.D., Cumming, G.S., Carpenter, S.R.: Scenario planning: a tool for conservation in an uncertain world. Conserv. Biol. **17**, 358–366 (2003)
22. Bohensky, E.L., Reyers, B., Van Jaarsveld, A.S.: Conservation in practice: future ecosystem services in a southern african river basin: a scenario planning approach to uncertainty. Conserv. Biol. **20**, 1051–1061 (2006)
23. Khan, Z., Kiani, S.L.: A cloud-based architecture for citizen services in smart cities. In: 2012 IEEE Fifth International Conference on Utility and Cloud Computing, pp. 315–320. IEEE (2012)
24. Freeman, E.R.: Strategic Management: A Stakeholder Approach. Pitman, New York (1984)
25. Baeza-Yates, R.: Data and algorithmic bias in the web. In: Proceedings of the 8th ACM Conference on Web Science - WebSci 2016, p. 1. ACM Press, New York (2016)
26. Yapo, A., Weiss, J.: Ethical implications of bias in machine learning. In: Proceedings of the 51st Hawaii International Conference on System Sciences, pp. 5365–5372 (2018)
27. Ølnes, S.: Beyond bitcoin enabling smart government using blockchain technology. In: Scholl, H.J., et al. (eds.) EGOVIS 2016. LNCS, vol. 9820, pp. 253–264. Springer, Cham (2016). https://doi.org/10.1007/978-3-319-44421-5_20
28. Ølnes, S., Ubacht, J., Janssen, M.: Blockchain in government: benefits and implications of distributed ledger technology for information sharing. Gov. Inf. Q. **34**, 355–364 (2017)
29. Jun, M.: Blockchain government - a next form of infrastructure for the twenty-first century. J. Open Innov. Technol. Mark. Complex. **4**, 7 (2018)
30. Brous, P., Janssen, M.: A systematic review of impediments blocking internet of things adoption by governments. In: Janssen, M., et al. (eds.) I3E 2015. LNCS, vol. 9373, pp. 81–94. Springer, Cham (2015). https://doi.org/10.1007/978-3-319-25013-7_7
31. Song, T., Cai, J., Chahine, T., Li, L.: Towards smart cities by Internet of Things (IoT)—a silent revolution in China. J. Knowl. Econ. 1–17 (2017)
32. Zanella, A., Bui, N., Castellani, A., Vangelista, L., Zorzi, M.: Internet of things for smart cities. IEEE Internet Things J. **1**, 22–32 (2014)
33. Mergel, I., Kattel, R., Lember, V., McBride, K.: Citizen-oriented digital transformation in the public sector. In: Proceedings of the 19th Annual International Conference on Digital Government Research Governance in the Data Age - dgo 2018, pp. 1–3. ACM Press, New York (2018)
34. Ahlgren, B., Hidell, M., Ngai, E.C.H.: Internet of things for smart cities: interoperability and open data. IEEE Internet Comput. **20**, 52–56 (2016)
35. Dameski, A.: A comprehensive ethical framework for AI entities: foundations. In: Iklé, M., Franz, A., Rzepka, R., Goertzel, B. (eds.) AGI 2018. LNCS (LNAI), vol. 10999, pp. 42–51. Springer, Cham (2018). https://doi.org/10.1007/978-3-319-97676-1_5
36. Smith, H.J., Dinev, T., Xu, H.: Information privacy research: an interdisciplinary review. MIS Q. **35**, 989–1015 (2011)

Value of Big Data Analytics for Customs Supervision in e-Commerce

Boriana Rukanova[1]([✉]), Yao-Hua Tan[1], Micha Slegt[2],
Marcel Molenhuis[3], Ben van Rijnsoever[4], Krunoslav Plecko[5],
Bora Caglayan[5], and Gavin Shorten[5]

[1] Delft University of Technology, Jaffalaan 5, 2628 BX Delft, The Netherlands
{b.d.rukanova,y.tan}@tudelft.nl
[2] Customs Administration of the Netherlands, Amsterdam, The Netherlands
[3] Customs Administration of the Netherlands, Rotterdam, The Netherlands
[4] IBM Nederland B.V., Amsterdam, The Netherlands
[5] IBM Ireland, Dublin, Ireland

Abstract. Big data and analytics have received a lot of attention in e-government research over the last decade and practitioners and researchers are looking into the transformative power of this technology to create for example competitive advantage, and increase transparency. Recent research points out that while parties are aware of the transformative power of this technology, understanding the value that this technology can bring for their specific organizations still remains a challenge. Data analytics is in particular interesting to support supervision tasks of governments. Here we take the customs supervision as a typical example where data analytics is used to support government in its supervision role. The main question addressed in this paper is: *How to understand the value of big data analytics for government supervision?* To address this question this research builds upon a case study where big data analytics solutions are developed and piloted as part of the PROFILE EU-funded research project. We adapt and utilize a recently published integrated model of big data value realization of Günther et al. [5] as a conceptual lens to structure the case findings. As a result we develop a more detailed model for analyzing value of big data specifically in the context of customs as an example of a specific domain of government supervision. This research contributes to the eGovernment literature on articulating value from big data analytics, particularly focusing on the role of government supervision.

Keywords: Data analytics · Big data · Value · Customs ·
Government supervision · Web data retrieval · e-Commerce

1 Introduction

Big data and data analytics have received a lot of attention over the last decade and practitioners and researchers are looking into the transformative power of this technology to create for example competitive advantage or increase transparency. Big data has been considered to be a breakthrough technological development which brings opportunities, as well as challenges (e.g. [2, 3, 5, 12]). Big data is seen as "massive

Published by Springer Nature Switzerland AG 2019
I. Lindgren et al. (Eds.): EGOV 2019, LNCS 11685, pp. 288–300, 2019.
https://doi.org/10.1007/978-3-030-27325-5_22

amount of digital data being collected from all sorts of sources, is too large, raw, or unstructured for analysis through conventional database techniques" [8, p. 78] and analytics can help to generate new insights.

Although the business sector has been leading in using big data governments are also actively exploring the opportunity to use big data to address public sector challenges [2, 8]. A growing body of eGovernment research on big data focuses on Big Open and Linked Government Data [1, 6, 7, 9]. Often in these studies the focus is on government providing public access to their data to allow for applying further analytics; for example to increase transparency, or to extract further value from government data. In this context the government is more in a role of a data provider, opening up their data for wider use. In other cases, government can be seen as a user of information from business and non-government organization in order to create public value [4, 13]. Prior research [10] distinguishes three roles that a government can play which call for different use of big data and analytics in government. These roles are (a) *public supervision*, which deals with identification of irregularities (e.g. legal incompliance) and the respective responsive action; (b) *public regulation*, which focuses on regulating social activities and relations by using e.g. permits, prohibitions or orders; (c) *public service delivery* which focusses on providing services or products. In this study we focus on examining the use of big data and analytics by government in its supervision role where government is a user of big data to improve the supervision process.

As argued by some researchers [8] parties recognize that being able to create value from big data "represents a new form of competitive advantage" [8, p. 85]. However in a recent study [5] it is concluded that although big data has been considered to be a breakthrough technological development there is still limited understanding of how organizations translate its potential into actual social and economic value. The main question that we explore in this paper is related to understanding value of big data analytics for government in its supervision role or in other words: *How to understand the value of big data analytics for government supervision?*

To address this question we use the domain of customs, which is one example of a domain where government acts in its supervision role[1]. This research builds upon a case study in the customs domain where big data analytics solutions are developed and piloted as part of the PROFILE[2] EU-funded research project. The case studied in this paper concerns e-Commerce goods imported to The Netherlands. One of the issues with these streams is undervaluation, i.e. the declared value of the goods is lower than the actual value for which the goods are bought. Undervaluation is one of the examples of fiscal fraud. The effect of this undervaluation is loss of revenue from duties and taxes levied when goods are imported in the EU, translating in loss of revenue for the national and EU budgets. The pilot aims to investigate how contextual information could be collected, for example from e-Commerce websites in China and the US, and how this information can be used in the customs process to support targeting officers in their risk assessment on undervaluation. In our analysis we adapt the model of big data

---

[1] Other domains where governments act in their supervision role include areas such as tax, and food safety.

[2] https://www.profile-project.eu/.

value realization of Günther et al. [5] and use it as a conceptual lens to structure the case findings. Although the actual case in this paper is undervaluation, the societal value of this data analytics innovation is much broader. The same customs data analytics solutions that work for identifying undervaluation can also be used to identify unsafe and dangerous goods, such as counterfeited medicines that do not cure. Hence, the acute need for customs to develop data analytics solutions are a significant contribution to making our society a safer and more secure world.

The remaining part of this paper is structured as follows. In Sect. 2 we present our conceptual framework, followed by our interpretative case methodology in Sect. 3. Section 4 presents our case findings and we end the paper with discussion and conclusions.

2 Conceptual Framework

As argued in literature [8] parties recognize that being able to create value from big data "represents a new form of competitive advantage" [8, p. 85]. However in a recent study, based on a thorough literature review investigating the issue of value realization from big data, Günther et al. [5] conclude that although big data has been considered to be a breakthrough technological development there is still limited understanding of how organizations translate its potential into actual social and economic value. To address this issue, Günther et al. [5, p. 202] propose that it is imperative for organizations to "continuously realign work practices, organizational models, and external stakeholders interest to realize value from big data". The authors [5] formulated a number of propositions and propose an *Integrated model of big data value realization*. In their model Günther et al. [5] position *social and economic value of big data* in the middle and they propose that in order to address the value of big data, parties need to look at the interrelationships among three levels as follows: (a) *work practice level;* i.e. working with big data analytics in practice; (b) *organizational level;* i.e. developing organizational models; (c) *supra-organizational level*; i.e. dealing with stakeholders' interests. As directions for further research Günther et al. [5] call for further empirical research to examine the cross-level interactions and alignments, and that is what we do in this paper.

Before continuing further it is worth elaborating on the concept of value. Günther et al. [5] support the argument that the perception of value of big data for organizations depends on the strategic goals of the organizations for using big data. Günther et al. [5] give various examples of areas of social and economic value that organizations may pursue. Examples of social value include enhanced transparency, prevention of fraud, improved security, improved wellbeing through better healthcare and education. Examples of economic value include increase in profit, business growth, competitive advantage. In the case that we analyze later in this paper the focus is on improvements in fiscal fraud detection due to under valuation of the value of the imported goods from e-Commerce transactions. In the wider societal sense reduced fiscal fraud also means that more duties are collected to finance the EU and the national budgets which can then be distributed for services to citizens.

We consider the model of Günther et al. [5] as a useful conceptual model that could be instrumental also for understanding of value of data analytics in the context of government supervision as it positions value at the center and it brings a broader perspective on examining value by looking at the interactions among *work practice*, *organizational*, and *supra-organizational levels*. For the purpose of our analysis we adapted a simplified version of the model of Günther et al. [5] in order to keep the analysis manageable when applying it to the empirical case[3].

Fig. 1. Adapted model form Günther et al. [5]

In our adaptation (see Fig. 1) we chose to stick to the main elements of the Günther et al. [5] model, namely positioning the concept of *value* at the center and looking at the inter-relationships among *work practice, organizational* and *supra-organizational levels*. In our case we use the term *value* to refer both to *social* and *economic value* and we chose to use the terminology *Value of Big Data Analytics* as big data on its own is of little value and becomes valuable when analyzed or combined and analyzed to produce some new insights.

3 Method

To address our main question we used an interpretative case study method [14]. Data collection took place in the period June 2018–January 2019. The data collection took part in the context of the PROFILE EU-funded research project, where the goal is through the use of four real-life demonstration projects (called Living Labs) conducted in different EU countries to explore the potential of data analytics for customs. The Living Labs research approach "takes a development view of innovation and studies novel technologies in complex real-world setting" [15, p.32][4]. This study focusses on

---

[3] In order to keep the model manageable we also did not include explicitly portability and interconnectivity which are part of the original Günther et al. [5] model but they are implicitly taken into considerations.

[4] For earlier application of the Living Lab approach in the context of IT innovation in international trade and customs see e.g. [11]. See also http://tiny.cc/8s564y for other examples of applications of Living Lab approach.

the Dutch Living Lab, where Dutch Customs, IBM and the university partners are working together to develop and test data analytic innovations for the import of e-Commerce goods to The Netherlands. The aim of the Dutch Living Lab is to explore whether data analytics solutions can help customs to detect fiscal risks related to undervaluation. The data analytics solution that is used in the Dutch Living Lab is developed by IBM and is a web retrieval tool using a contextualization engine, a piece of software that can search on e-commerce websites in China and the US, and analyze for example price information of a product. The purpose of this web retrieval tool is to provide Customs officers with additional online publicly available information to cross validate the price that is declared on the import declaration.

While our empirical insights were predominantly gained form our interactions with the Dutch Living Lab they were further informed by our broader involvement in the PROFILE project, where more data analytics pilots are conducted. As a result of these iterations we identified an initial list of issues and considerations related to the value of data analytics in the customs process. As a next step we used the adapted model (see Fig. 1) based on Günther et al. [5] as a lens to structure our findings. In this process we arrived at a number of observations as follows:

1. We needed a further detailing of the *work practice level* (the customs process), as the value of data analytics can vary depending on where in the process data analytics is used and in what part of the process performance improvement is desired.
2. We needed further detailing on the organizational level to better capture issues related to value of data analytics that we identified. In this further detailing we added (a) outsourcing to other data analytics (DA) providers, (b) existing IT systems, (c) priorities, policies, capacity and other legal constrains.
3. We needed further detailing of the supra-organizational level by looking at (a) external data providers, (b) other customs; and supra-national (such as the EU).

Based on these findings we extended the adapted model (Fig. 1) and we arrived at our more detailed model for analyzing value of big data analytics in the customs process (see Fig. 2 below).

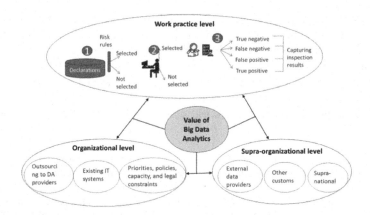

Fig. 2. A model for analyzing value of big data analytics in the customs supervision process

4   Case Findings

In this section we start by discussing the *Work practice level* by describing the e-Commerce customs process in The Netherlands and by explaining the big data analytics use in the Dutch Living Lab. We then demonstrate how our models (i.e. Fig. 2) is applied by using examples from the case.

4.1   Work Practice Level: The e-Commerce Customs Process in the Netherlands

Figure 3 below captures on a high level the e-Commerce customs process in The Netherlands. The bottom part of the figure illustrates an e-Commerce process, where a customer buys a product on the Internet. This could be via an e-Commerce platform (e.g. Alibaba) or directly via a e-Commerce website. The buyer pays for the goods via the e-Commerce platform or directly to the e-Commerce website. The seller on its turns sends the products to the customer.

Before the goods are sent to the final customer an e-Commerce declaration needs to be submitted to the declaration system of Dutch Customs. The submission of the e-Customs declarations is normally not done by the seller or the buyer but by a logistics service provider or a trader that handles the declaration procedures when the goods enter The Netherlands.

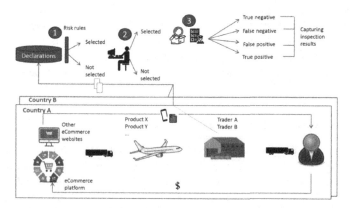

Fig. 3. High-level overview of the e-Commerce context and the customs inspection process for e-Commerce declarations in The Netherlands

Once the declarations are available in the declaration system an automated risk analysis is performed based on pre-defined risk rules software (marked as step 1 in Fig. 3). As a result a list is generated which marks declarations that are suggested to be risky, and hence selected for inspection. As a next step (marked as step 2 in Fig. 3) a targeting officer further analyses the declarations and the list of declarations that were automatically selected for inspection from the system and makes a final list of packages to be inspected. One important aspect in this process is that in making the final selection decision the targeting officer is limited in the number of declarations that can be selected for inspection. This maximum number is defined by customs policy. This maximum number is determined by the capacity limitations of the inspection team to carry out inspections. After the targeting officer makes the final choice the refined list of declarations that are selected is provided to the inspection team. Subsequently the inspection team inspects (marked as step 3 in Fig. 3) the packages and documents the inspection results. The goods that are inspected were either selected as they were suspicious or they were randomly selected. For the suspicious goods the outcome of the inspection can be either that something wrong was indeed found (hit), resulting in a true positive (TP) selection. In case nothing suspicious was found in goods that were considered suspicious we have a case of false positive (FP). One of the goals that would indicate improved targeting with use of data analytics is to find ways to reduce the false positive inspections or the cases where customs invests resources to inspect a package but at the end nothing was found. Reduction of false positive is important as it leads to unnecessary use of customs resources and delays the trade flows.

Inspections also take place based on random selection in order to check whether in the flow of goods that were not identified as suspicious by the risk rules there are also cases where something is wrong with the goods. The results of the inspections performed on the goods that are randomly selected can either be true negative (TN), meaning that the goods were not selected as suspicious and indeed they were not suspicious. The result however could be also false negative (FN), meaning that the goods were considered as not suspicious in the selection process but in reality something wrong was found during the inspection. The availability of false negatives means that goods which were suspicious were not identified in the selection process. Apart from reducing false positives selections, data analytics can be used to better reduce false negative cases which are not detected by the current system. In fact, an improved balance between false positive and false negative cases generated by the system may be achieved.

4.2 Data Analytics in the Customs Process

IBM developed a prototype that allows the user to input a description of any item from a customs declaration and the user is then presented with other potentially useful contextual information about this particular item. For example, in the first instance this could be information sourced from e-Commerce websites via API's but it is envisaged that this can be extended to include insights gained form previous declarations and inspections.

After inputting a search string, the user is presented with an analysis of other similar product descriptions related to the search query and a statistical analysis of attributes associated with that item (e.g. price) is performed on the data set that is retrieved from the e-commerce website via the API. The high-level architecture is presented in Fig. 4. The user interface allows the customs officer to be informed via a Customs Portal. The main components of the system highlighted in Fig. 4 are:

- Server-side (back-end) component which is retrieving item data (e.g., price, weight) from e-Commerce websites, performing analytical part and providing API (application programming interface).
- Client-side (front-end) component designed for user interaction and data visualization.

The proof-of-concept tool has a page with search bar functionality. Results are generated based on search term, visualized as box plot to display range of values together with some statistical metrics like min, max and median. Using the initial box plot results display, a user can choose to change the view to the tabular data format. Table view contains product description, price in currency retrieved from web data extraction component and additional column with price converted to Euro currency to show both values. In the pilot initial functionality was added where every row with product description is a hyperlink to the sources of information. The targeting officer can choose this option to get complete information about the product.

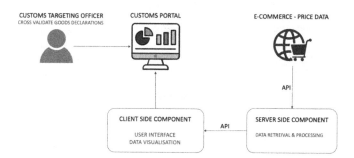

Fig. 4. High-level architecture of Customs Portal (dashboard)

4.3 Illustration of How the Model for Analyzing Value of Big Data Analytics in the Customs Supervision Process Can Be Applied

Figure 5 below uses a number of examples identified in our case to demonstrate how the model for analyzing value of big data analytics in the customs supervision process (Fig. 2) can be applied.

One of the decisions with which Dutch Customs was confronted was where in the customs process to place data analytics (see Fig. 5a). There are different possibilities where to include data analytics in the customs process, namely: (1) at the beginning of the customs process on the full set of customs declarations; (2) in the middle of the customs process, where pre-selection of declarations has already been made via running automated risk rules software and a sub-set of the declarations is presented to a targeting officer for further risk analysis. In this case data analytics can be used as a support tool for the targeting officer; (3) at the end of the customs process where data analytics (e.g. on scans) can be used to support the inspection process. In the Dutch Living Lab a decision was made to deploy data analytics in the second step, i.e. to provide decision support to the targeting officer. As such the immediate value of the data analytics solutions would be (on a work practice level) for the targeting officer.

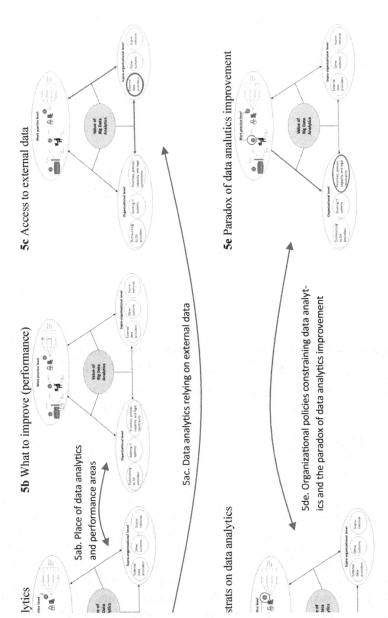

Fig. 5. Examples of application of the model and dependencies between decision aspects

To that extent the tool can be considered as a decision support tool which has big data analytics as an important element. In this case big data analytics is required because large number of web pages on The Internet with unstructured data need to be searched and analyzed on price information.

Taking a process improvement perspective however Dutch Customs also needed to decide how to measure the performance improvement brought by the data analytics on the customs process (See Fig. 5b). In the discussions with Dutch Customs three areas for measuring performance improvements were identified, i.e.: (a) to reduce the number of *false positive* inspections (i.e. reduce the number of boxes which are selected and there is nothing wrong); (b) to reduce the number of *false negatives*, meaning catching more illicit trade; (c) to handle *large increase in volumes* of declarations. In the Dutch Living Lab we found out that there is an inter-dependence between the decision on where to place data analytics in customs process and the decision on what aspects to focus when measuring performance improvement (see arrow 5ab in Fig. 5). Namely the choice that was made in the Dutch Case (i.e. to use data analytics in the second step of the customs process as a decision support tool for the targeting officer) allows to measure performance effects on the reduction on false positives and possibly also effects on handling large volumes. In discussions with performance measurements experts from Dutch Customs however it became clear that placing the data analytics later in the process (in our case at step 2, as a support tool for the targeting officer) makes it difficult to realize data analytics improvements related to the reduction of false negatives (i.e. catching more illicit trade), as a large number of the declarations are already pre-filtered earlier in the process, before data analytics is applied.

When deciding where in the process to deploy data analytics (in our case in step 2 of the process) a next question was: What kind of data to use for data analytics? In the Dutch case it was decided to use price data obtained from e-Commerce websites to cross-validate the price on customs declarations. The choice of this type of data and possible value that it can bring on a work practice level however triggered issues related to data access (see Fig. 5c, and arrow 5ac) at the *supra-organizational* and *organizational level*. On a supra-organizational level in the case we found out that in many cases e-Commerce platforms would not allow robots to crawl their websites. An alternative way to access the price information from e-Commerce platforms was identified, namely via APIs and there are defined terms and conditions of these e-Commerce platforms of how organizations can access this information via APIs. This triggers issues at *organizational level*, as Customs needs to decide whether to accept the terms and conditions and under what circumstances. This shows that even if using data analytics and external data could bring value at a work practice level, for making this possible issues at *supra-organizational* and *organizational level* need to be solved. If these are not solved, even if potentially the data analytic solution could bring value to the work practice level, due to the dependencies with the other two levels this value may not be possible to realize in this specific customs situation.

Another issue that emerged from the discussions was that data analytics improvements are constrained by the existing organizational models and policies (see Fig. 5d). In the Dutch case the available resources in customs put an upper limit to the maximum packages that can be selected for inspection per day, as there are limited resources of customs officers who could actually inspect the packages.

This maximum number of inspections is therefore an upper bound and even if data analytics can make the targeting officers very effective in selecting only packages that lead to true positive and they may be able to identify a large number of packages where things are wrong, the effects that data analytics will have on the whole customs process are limited by the inspection capacity that is set as policy from the customs organization. This shows how policies on an *organizational level* put an upper bound of what is possible to achieve (and the value that this data analytics solution can bring) at *work practice level* in this specific organization.

Another interesting issue that we identified in the case (see also Fig. 5e) is related to what we call here the paradox of data analytics improvement. To take a simple example. Customs may be able to inspect 100 packages per day. With the current methods some of these packages will be false positive, others will be true positive. For the false positive packages the inspection officer spends limited time, as it is mostly opening the package and identifying that nothing is wrong. In case of true positives there is much more processing time per package, as the customs officer needs to start procedures and follow-up activities. If with data analytics the customs inspection process is improved, and the false positives are reduced, with the available resources customs will be able to carry out less inspections (i.e. less than 100), as it takes more time to process packages where there is something wrong. Thus increased efficiency due to data analytics can overload inspection capacities. The arrow 5de in Fig. 5 shows this complex interdependency, where the value of the data analytics can be bounded by the available organizational capacity but also vice versa, that improvements with data analytics could influence the organizational model and available capacity.

5   Discussion and Conclusions

The main question that this paper set to explore was: *How to understand the value of big data analytics for government supervision?* As Günther et al. [5] argue it is "imperative for organizations to continuously realign work practices, organizational models, and external stakeholders interest to realize value from big data" [5, p. 202]. Building on Günther et al. [5] and on a case study of using data analytics in the customs domain we developed a model for analyzing value of big data analytics in the customs supervision process and demonstrate how it can be applied. As our analysis demonstrates there is no simple answer on what is the value that data analytics can bring in a specific customs supervision process and benefits at one level have effects on other levels. It is the understanding of these complex interdependencies from multiple level perspective that allows us to reveal the multiple considerations and effects which give a more complete picture for decision makers and policy makers about what value of data analytics is for their specific organization. This study is limited to the customs domain and one case study. Further research looking at the use of data analytics in other cases from the customs domain as well as from other domains where government acts in its supervision role could help to determine the applicability of the model in other contexts and refine the model. This will allow for a more complete view on how to analyse value of data analytics in the context of government supervision. Further research can specifically focus also on elaborating the *organizational* and *supra-organizational level* in more detail. Follow-up research can focus on elaborating elements from our model which we only highlighted here but which we were not able to go in detail (e.g. *outsourcing to other data analytics providers*). Another issue is that while many businesses companies do have highly skilled personnel to perform data analytics, many customs organizations do not have such in-house capabilities. Further research can examine what are successful organizational models where customs have successfully been able to incorporate such capabilities in their organizations. Next to that the supra-organizational level also deserves further attention, especially in the customs domain the links to other customs administration, as well as the link to the EU as a supra-national body would bring additional insights.

Acknowledgement. This research was partially funded by the PROFILE Project (nr. 786748), which is funded by the European Union's Horizon 2020 research and innovation program. Ideas and opinions expressed by the authors do not necessarily represent those of all partners. The authors would like to thank also the PROFILE consortium partners for the fruitful collaboration and discussions on the topic in the broader project context.

References

1. Bertot, J.C., Gorham, U., Jaeger, P.T., Sarin, L.C., Choi, H.: Big data, open government and e-government: issues, policies and recommendations. Inf. Policy **19**, 5–16 (2014)
2. Chen, H., Chiang, R.H.L., Storey, V.C.: Business intelligence and analytics: from big data to big impact. MIS Q. **36**(4), 1165–1188 (2012)
3. Fichman, R.G., Dos Santos, B.L., Zheng, Z.: Digital innovation as a fundamental and powerful concept in the information systems curriculum. MIS Q. **38**(2), 329–353 (2014)
4. Gil-Garcia, J.R.: Towards a smart State? Inter-agency collaboration, information integration, and beyond. Inf. Policy **17**(3, 4), 269–280 (2012)
5. Günther, W.A., Mehrizi, M.H.R., Huysman, M., Feldberg, F.: Debating big data: a literature review on realizing value from big data. J. Strat. Inf. Syst. **26**(3), 191–209 (2017). https://doi.org/10.1016/j.jsis.2017.07.003
6. Janssen, M., Konopnicki, D., Snowdon, J.L., Ojo, A.: Driving public sector innovation using big and open linked data (BOLD). Inf. Syst. Front. **19**, 189–195 (2017)
7. Janssen, M., van der Hoven, J.: Big and open linked data (BOLD) in government: a challenge to transparency and privacy. Gov. Inf. Q. **32**, 363–368 (2015)
8. Kim, G., Trimi, S., Chung, J.: Big-data applications in the government sector. Commun. ACM **57**(3), 78–85 (2014)
9. Lnenicka, M., Komarkova, J.: Developing a government enterprise architecture framework to support the requirements of big and open linked data with the use of cloud computing. Int. J. Inf. Manag. **46**, 124–141 (2019)
10. Maciejewski, M.: To do more, better, faster and more cheaply: using big data in public administration. Int. Rev. Adm. Sci. **83**(1S), 120–135 (2017)
11. Rukanova, B., et al.: Beer living lab – intelligent data sharing. In: Tan, Y.H., Björn-Andersen, N., Klein, S., Rukanova, B. (eds.) Accelerating Global Supply Chains with IT-Innovation, pp. 37–54. Springer, Heidelberg (2011). https://doi.org/10.1007/978-3-642-15669-4_3
12. Sivarajah, U., Kamal, M.M., Irani, Z., Weerakkody, V.: Critical analysis of Big Data challenges and analytical methods. J. Bus. Res. **17**, 263–286 (2017)

13. Susha, I., Jannsen, M., Verhulst, S.: Data collaboratives as a new frontier of cross-sector partnerships in the age of open data: taxonomy development. In: Proceedings of the 50th Hawaii International Conference on System Science, Big Island, HI, January 4th–7th, 2017a, pp. 2691–2700. IEEE Computer Society (2017)
14. Walsham, G.: Interpreting Information Systems in Organizations. Wiley, New York (1993)
15. Higgins, A., Klein, S.: Introduction to the Living Lab Approach. In: Tan, Y.H., Björn-Andersen, N., Klein, S., Rukanova, B. (eds.) Accelerating Global Supply Chains with IT-Innovation, pp. 31–36. Springer, Heidelberg (2011). https://doi.org/10.1007/978-3-642-15669-4_2

Artificial Intelligence in Swedish Policies: Values, Benefits, Considerations and Risks

Daniel Toll[1]([⊠]), Ida Lindgren[1], Ulf Melin[1],
and Christian Østergaard Madsen[2]

[1] Department of Management and Engineering, Information Systems,
Linköping University, 581 83 Linköping, Sweden
{daniel.toll,ida.lindgren,ulf.melin}@liu.se
[2] The IT University of Copenhagen, Copenhagen, Denmark
chrm@itu.dk

Abstract. Artificial intelligence (AI) is said to be the next big phase in digitalization. There is a global ongoing race to develop, implement and make use of AI in both the private and public sector. The many responsibilities of governments in this race are complicated and cut across a number of areas. Therefore, it is important that the use of AI supports these diverse aspects of governmental commitments and values. The aim of this paper is to analyze how AI is portrayed in Swedish policy documents and what values are attributed to the use of AI. We analyze Swedish policy documents and map benefits, considerations and risks with AI into different value ideals, based on an established e-government value framework. We conclude that there is a discrepancy in the policy level discourse on the use of AI between different value ideals. Our findings show that AI is strongly associated with improving efficiency and service quality in line with previous e-government policy studies. Interestingly, few benefits are highlighted concerning engagement of citizens in policy making. A more nuanced view on AI is needed for creating realistic expectations on how this technology can benefit society.

Keywords: Artificial intelligence · e-Government values · Public sector · Benefits · Risks

1 Introduction

Artificial Intelligence (AI) is currently discussed as an enabler for transforming the public sector; in fact, AI is described as a solution to most types of administrative challenges, regardless of industry or sector [1]. In recent years, AI has changed from being 'science fiction' to being developed and applied on a large scale and is quickly becoming ubiquitous. AI is also portrayed as the next big area of digitalization; some even call it a revolution [2]. AI is portrayed as a solution to many of the problems related to poor efficiency, lack of resources and competence experienced in the public sector. This echoes the praise of previous technological solutions in different waves of e-government [3–6]. Consequently, there are great expectations on what AI can do for public sector organizations, citizens and the society at large, in terms of e.g. improving service quality, reducing lead time and making unbiased decisions in case handling [7].

© IFIP International Federation for Information Processing 2019
Published by Springer Nature Switzerland AG 2019
I. Lindgren et al. (Eds.): EGOV 2019, LNCS 11685, pp. 301–310, 2019.
https://doi.org/10.1007/978-3-030-27325-5_23

AI is often discussed as something 'new', and in terms of its application areas this is correct. However, since its birth in the 1950s, AI as a phenomenon has had an unstable trajectory consisting of AI winters and AI springs [8]. During AI winters, funding, efforts and interest in AI have diminished dramatically. Such periods occur when the technology fails to meet the high expectations set by scholars and others. It appears that we now find ourselves in the midst of an AI spring. Currently, everyone is aboard; the tech industry, consultancy firms, media, and government. With the history of unmet expectations, it begs to question if AI will finally deliver values as promised, or if we will soon experience another AI winter. We currently see both utopian and dystopian accounts of AI; e.g., [9] portray AI as the humankinds' best hope to prevent extinction, whereas others fear an Armageddon caused by AI [10]. As AI enters into the e-Government domain, it is likely to affect public sector organizations and the lives of citizens. The conflicting portraits of AI call for further research in the area. It is imperative that we scrutinize how AI comes into play in the government domain, whether the expected transformative potential is realized, and what the implications for policy making are [7].

This paper aims to investigate how AI is portrayed in a set of policy documents for public sector organizations, and what value ideals are attributed to the use of AI. We depart from a case where the Swedish government asked a number of organizations to map the usefulness of AI for Swedish industry and society. The resulting documentation from this initiative sets the frame for the discourse on AI in the Swedish public sector. We contribute to e-government research and practice by identifying what values are attributed to the use of AI for public sector organizations, and relating these to previous discussions on technology in the e-government research field.

The paper is organized as follows; first, we present the policy documents in our analysis and their origin. Next, we explain our method and analytical strategy. Then, we present our findings of the analysis and discuss our findings in relation to the analytical framework by Rose et al. [11] and previous analyses of e-government policy and technology. We contribute to e-government research and practice by illustrating how AI is portrayed in Swedish policies, illustrating a need for a more nuanced understanding of the potentials of this technology for public sector organizations.

2   Theoretical Framing

e-Government research shows that IT-development and implementation in government organizations is difficult to plan and organize for and that IT often results in unexpected outcomes [12]. Why should the implementation of AI technologies be any different? One possible reason for the difficulties of managing e-Government initiatives is the multitude of public values that government organizations are designed to uphold [13]. Bannister and Connolly discuss how the use of new types of information and communication technology (ICT) may transform such public values [14]. Several scholars have created value typologies as analytical lenses for studies of ICT's transforming power [15, 16]. Rose et al. [11] have synthesized four value positions in e-Government management: professionalism, efficiency, service, and engagement (see Table 1). The professionalism ideal concerns legality, durability and infrastructure. The efficiency ideal concerns value for money, efficiency, productivity and automation. The service ideal concerns utility of the government for the citizen, accessibility and service quality. The engagement ideal concerns engaging with the citizen, democracy and participation. Much of the research on public values in e-Government is purely theoretical, therefore scholars have called for empirical research that puts these models to use [17].

Table 1. Four value ideals for e-Government management (adopted from [11], p. 542).

Value ideal type	Definition and representative values
Efficiency	Providing lean and efficient administration, which minimizes waste of public resources gathered from taxpayers. Representative values: Value for money, cost reduction, productivity and performance
Service	Maximizing the utility of government to civil society by providing services directed towards the public good. Representative values: Public service, citizen centricity, service level and quality
Professionalism	Providing an independent, robust and consistent administration, governed by a rule system based on law, resulting in the public record, which is the basis for accountability. Representative values: Durability, equity, legality and accountability
Engagement	Engaging with civil society to facilitate policy development in accordance with liberal democratic principles; articulating the public good. Representative values: Democracy, deliberation and participation

3 Methodology

We seek to analyze how AI is portrayed in Swedish policy documents, and the values attributed to the use of AI. We have chosen 10 documents for our analysis, which are presented in Table 1. The policy documents chosen for analysis are all a result of the initiative by the Swedish government to map and investigate the role of AI in Sweden, led by VINNOVA. They form a generative and representative sample of the discourse on AI for the Swedish public sector and are published by the following organizations;

- *VINNOVA* – Sweden's innovation agency, under the Ministry of Enterprise and Innovation, acts as the government's expert authority regarding innovation policy.
- *Governo* – a Swedish management consultancy firm, known for their close collaborations with public sector organizations e.g., VINNOVA.
- *the Swedish Association of Local Authorities and Regions (SALAR)* – a interest organization working for municipalities and regions in Sweden.
- *Inera* – an organization under SALAR focusing on healthcare.
- *WASP* – Wallenberg Artificial Intelligence, Autonomous Systems and Software Program. A research initiative initiated and financed by the Wallenberg foundation.
- The Swedish Government.

We treat the documents as *policy documents* in the sense that their content is likely to trickle down through the governmental structures in Sweden and constitute the foundation of policies in this area for both public sector and private sector organizations. There are similar reports that mention AI in the Swedish public sector, focusing more on digitalization and automation in general. We excluded these documents from our analysis, and focused instead on reports in which AI has a dominant role. We have a broad and inclusive treatment of AI in this paper and have not defined AI in a technical sense as to make limitations to a subset of specific AI technologies. The analysis instead focuses on the discourse regarding AI and as such encompasses a broad variety of AI technologies and definitions associated with the term 'artificial intelligence' (Table 2).

Table 2. The policy documents in the analysis.

Document (title, translated if originally in Swedish)	Year	Author organization	Doc. ID	#Pages
Mapping and analysis of artificial intelligence and machine learning's capabilities and application in Swedish industry and society	2017	Sweden's Government Offices	#1	3
Artificial intelligence – possibilities for welfare	2017	SALAR	#2	17
AI and automation of first line care	2017	Inera	#3	51
Artificial intelligence in Swedish business and society	2018	VINNOVA	#4	188
Artificial intelligence in the public sector	2018	Governo	#5	50
Correct payments with the help of AI	2018	Governo	#6	33
Automation of work	2018	SALAR	#7	36
Decisions within 24 h	2018	SALAR	#8	4
Collecting ideas and identifying challenges for future AI research in Sweden	2018	WASP	#9	28
National alignment for artificial intelligence	2018	Sweden's Government Offices	#10	12

We have performed a qualitative content analysis [18]. The research presented in this paper is hence qualitative and interpretive [19], although we quantify the results as a part of exploring patterns and interpretations. As an analytical lens, we used the four value ideals presented by Rose et al. [11]. We combined these value ideals with an inductive and iterative approach for analyzing the documents. We find the model by Rose et al. fitting for several reasons. First, it synthesizes previous literature on public sector values. Second, the Scandinavian origin of the model corresponds well with the Swedish culture and welfare system. Third, the model itself reflects the expectations and responsibilities of Scandinavian government organizations. In this paper, we have no ambition to further develop this model, but instead apply it as-is.

The analysis was performed in the following steps. (1) Each document was read to identify statements describing the nature and use of AI for public sector organizations. In total 522 statements were identified. (2) Each statement was condensed by high-lighting its main message, e.g., the statement *"AI can contribute to shortening lead times for case handling"* (Doc.#10, p. 4) was condensed to "Shortened lead times". (3) Each condensed statement was then coded in relation to the Rose et al.'s value set [11]. This coding was performed in an interpretive manner, seeking to find a match between the statements and the value ideals in the analytical framework. The condensed statement "Shortened lead times" was categorized as belonging to the "Efficiency" value ideal. (4) As the analysis progressed, it became evident from the empirical material that the statements could also be characterized along a different dimension, highlighting negative and positive outcomes of AI for the public sector. Thus, additional categories were formed inductively, including *benefits, considerations* and *risks* associated with use of AI (further described in findings). (5) We returned to the original statements and categorized each statement in relation to the inductively generated categories. For example, the statement *"AI can contribute to shortening lead times for case handling"* was categorized as a "Benefit" of AI. (6) Finally, we combined the two sets of categorizations for each statement, thereby integrating the theoretical and empirical dimensions.

4 Findings

In our analysis of how AI is portrayed in Swedish policy documents, we identified three categories in the empirical material. These inductively generated categories are *benefits, considerations* and *risks* associated with use of AI, as described in Table 3.

Figure 1 presents the distribution of the 522 statements across the two dimensions. First, most statements concern benefits associated with AI (281 statements) or considerations for public organizations when using AI (190 statements). Notably, only 50 statements concern risks associated with AI. Related to the four value ideals, most statements fall into professionalism (228 statements) and efficiency (157 statements). The service ideal appears less frequently (98 statements), and the engagement ideal is the least frequent one (39 statements). Professionalism is therefore the most frequent value ideal, and occurs almost six times as frequently as the least frequent ideal (engagement).

Figure 1 represents the distribution of statements across the categories and value ideals. In order to further display the content of the discourse on AI in the Swedish public sector, we have extracted condensed statements that exemplify the topics according to categories and value ideals (Table 4). These topics are discussed in the next section.

Table 3. The inductively generated categories, with examples.

Category	Definition	Representative quotes
Benefits	Desirable, positive effects or statements of how AI solutions will affect society in a positive way	*"The [AI] system makes the process more effective and saves time for personnel."* (Doc.#7, p. 10) *"High risk work environments do not need to be populated by people and strenuous jobs can be performed by automatons."* (Doc. #4, p. 56)
Considerations	Things that public sector actors must carefully think about and keep in mind when using AI	*"This is an area that needs to be investigated and where it can become necessary to change laws and regulations"* (Doc.#7, p. 15) *"Naturally, it has to be performed in a safe and transparent way"* (Doc. #5, p. 33)
Risks	Undesirable, negative effects or statements of how AI solutions will affect society in a negative way	*"AI can involve new types of intelligent cyberattacks or manipulated data which can have serious consequences"* (Doc.#10, p. 12) *"An example of such a risk could be decision support systems in the area of jurisdiction falling into the hands of criminals, enabling them to find ways to avoid prosecution."* (Doc. #7, p. 12)

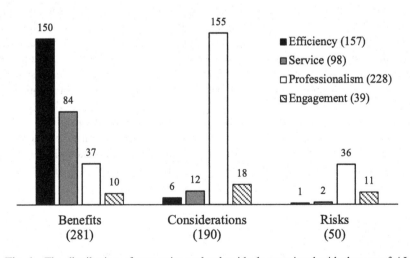

Fig. 1. The distribution of categories and value ideals associated with the use of AI.

Table 4. Typical statements for each category and value ideal.

Value ideal	Category		
	Benefits	Considerations	Risks
Efficiency	Efficiency Competitiveness Profits/Savings Automating processes	Costs Resources	Economic damage
Service	Service quality Personalization Accessibility	Loss of jobs Service quality	Data quality Loss of jobs
Professionalism	Security Sustainability	Competence Infrastructure Data availability Legality	Security Integrity Misinformation
Engagement	Citizen interaction	Transparency Trust Co-operation	Transparency Trust Democracy

5 Analysis and Discussion

This paper aims to investigate how AI is portrayed in a set of Swedish policy documents, and what value ideals are attributed to the use of AI. We depart from a Swedish case in which the Swedish government asked a number of organizations to map the usefulness of AI for Swedish industry and society. In the research discourse on AI, we see a strong polarization, where some scholars describe AI as a necessity for creating and maintaining a functioning society [9], and others see AI as a threat to the world we live in [10]. In the documents analyzed in this paper, we see a strong tendency towards the former (positive) view on AI; AI is presented as a way to maintaining and improving the well-functioning Swedish welfare system.

The main finding from our analysis is that the benefits of AI are highlighted extensively, whereas the potential risks of AI are few. Relating these statements on AI in the Swedish public sector to the value ideals presented by [11], we see that most benefits relate to increased efficiency of public sector processes. It is interesting, that the discourse does not regard risks to efficiency as a result of AI; using AI to increase efficiency is solely seen as creating desirable and positive effects. The second most frequent type of benefits concern service quality; hence, AI is described as both a way to increase competitiveness, make profit and savings, but also to increase quality and effectiveness of public sector processes. The focus on benefits may be explained by the purpose and nature of the documents included in the analysis; they are a result of an initiative to map the usefulness of AI for Swedish industry and public sector organizations. Hence, the purpose of the document is to inspire organizations to adopt and implement AI technologies. Overall, the discourse on AI is in line with the general discourse on digitalization in the public sector, highlighting the positive impact of the technology. In particular, technologies are promoted as means for increased efficiency and effectiveness, e.g., [3–6]. Consequently, our analysis confirms that the discourse on

AI for the public sector is characterized by an optimistic outlook on AI, and that there are great expectations on what AI can do for public sector organizations, citizens and the society at large.

In spite of the purpose of inspire AI use in the public sector, some considerations and risks are mentioned in the policy documents. The considerations typically fall under the professionalism value ideal [11]. We believe this as a result of the particular context highlighted in the professionalism ideal; the functioning bureaucracy. AI challenges the focus on the internal stability of government (status quo), e.g. in terms of how AI may lead to job redundancy in the public sector and a need for new competences. AI also requires new and different digital infrastructures, and poses questions on how the legality of public administration can be upheld. For these reasons, it is perhaps not surprising that the risks with AI highlighted in the policy documents were related to the values related to the professionalism ideal, e.g., security, integrity, and misinformation. Concerning the risks of AI, there are only a few risks mentioned that concern engagement. The engagement ideal is about engaging with society, about citizen participation and democracy; the communication between the citizen and the government [11]. Engagement is relatively underrepresented in the AI discourse; AI is not presented as an enabler of engagement and democratic discussions. This is interesting, because the Swedish Digital Agenda explicitly mentions citizen engagement as a benefit of digitalization [20]. However, in the discourse on AI we have analyzed, the values related to engagement of citizens in policy making are notably absent. This finding corresponds to previous policy studies in the e-government field, which have found that the democratic ideals often are sidelined in favor of New Public Management ideals of increased efficiency and effectiveness [6, 21, 22].

Based on the findings from our analysis, we see a likelihood that the discourse on AI is overly optimistic and resemble previous hypes on various uses of technologies in the public sector (cf. [3, 8]). Returning to the metaphor of AI winters and springs, it appears that we are indeed in the midst of an AI spring [8]. A core issue for future research will be to investigate whether we will soon find ourselves in a new AI winter, or if the AI spring will turn into an AI summer; where the AI-technologies are widespread and meet the high expectations attributed to them. An interesting difference that we see, compared to previous AI springs, is that the interest for AI is now widely spread, and not just seen in academia. It also appears that AI technology is likely to become more generally applied. As AI becomes more mainstream the expectations on this particular technology is likely to evolve and become more nuanced; therefore, it is vital that the e-government research community continue to follow this development.

6   Conclusions, Limitations and Future Research

In this paper, we performed a content analysis on 10 policy documents describing the usefulness of AI for public sector organizations and industry in Sweden. We applied the value ideals model presented by Rose et al. [11], combined with three inductively generated categories for coding value statements in the documents. We found that;

- AI is described as an enabler for increased efficiency and effectiveness in the public sector. This reflects an optimistic view on AI, highlighting the benefits of AI for public sector organizations.
- AI challenges the values related to professionalism, reflected in an emphasis on considerations and risks concerned with legality, security and integrity.
- AI is not described as an enabler for citizen engagement in government. This is an interesting contrast to general national policies stating that digitalization should be used to increase citizen engagement.
- The AI-discourse analyzed in this paper is in line with previous e-government research.
- A more nuanced view on AI is needed for creating realistic expectations on what this technology can do for society.

This paper has several limitations. First, the analytical model gives a simplified overview of the values guiding e-Government management. In the future, the findings presented here could be complemented with additional value conceptualizations or a modified version of the current analytical lens [11] with improved suitability for analyzing AI. A second limitation concerns that the particular discourse analyzed is taken from one national context at one point in time. Furthermore, the documents we have analyzed dealt with both industry and public sector organizations combined. Future research could add additional national contexts to the analysis and focus on the public sector context alone (but from multiple perspectives, e.g., from the viewpoint of trade-unions, citizens, and businesses). We also see potential for investigating the discourse on AI in a longitudinal manner and see if and how the policy documents come into practice. A third limitation concerns our interpretation of AI. AI encapsulates a variety of different technologies and we have not unpacked the meaning of AI here. Instead, we have treated AI in the same overarching manner as is found in the policy documents that we analyzed. As AI evolves, the meanings attributed to this concept are likely to become increasingly differentiated and hence more important to state explicitly.

References

1. Cave, S., Seán, D., Óhéigeartaigh, S.: An AI race for strategic advantage: rhetoric and risks. In: Proceedings of the AAAI/ACM Conference on Artificial Intelligence Ethics, and Society (2018)
2. Makridakis, S.: The forthcoming Artificial Intelligence (AI) revolution: its impact on society and firms. Futures **90**, 46–60 (2017). https://doi.org/10.1016/j.futures.2017.03.006
3. Rowe, C., Thompson, J.: People and Chips. The Human Implications of Information Technology. McGraw-Hill, London (1996)
4. Heeks, R., Bailur, S.: Analyzing e-government research: perspectives, philosophies, theories, methods, and practice. Gov. Inf. Q. **24**, 243–265 (2007). https://doi.org/10.1016/j.giq.2006.06.005

5. Madsen, C.Ø., Berger, J.B., Phythian, M.: The development in leading e-Government articles 2001–2010: definitions, perspectives, scope, research philosophies, methods and recommendations: an update of Heeks and Bailur. In: Janssen, M., Scholl, H.J., Wimmer, M.A., Bannister, F. (eds.) EGOV 2014. LNCS, vol. 8653, pp. 17–34. Springer, Heidelberg (2014). https://doi.org/10.1007/978-3-662-44426-9_2

6. Chadwick, A., May, C.: Interaction between states and citizens in the age of the Internet: "e-Government" in the United States, Britain, and the European Union. Gov. Int. J. Policy Adm. Inst. **16**, 271–300 (2003). https://doi.org/10.1111/1468-0491.00216

7. Lindgren, I., Madsen, C.Ø., Hofmann, S., Melin, U.: Close encounters of the digital kind: a research agenda for the digitalization of public services. Gov. Inf. Q. (2019). https://doi.org/10.1016/j.giq.2019.03.002

8. Natale, S., Ballatore, A.: Imagining the thinking machine. Converg. Int. J. Res. New Media Technol, 135485651771516 (2017). https://doi.org/10.1177/1354856517715164

9. Gurkaynak, G., Yilmaz, I., Haksever, G.: Stifling artificial intelligence: Human perils. Comput. Law Secur. Rev. **32**, 749–758 (2016). https://doi.org/10.1016/j.clsr.2016.05.003

10. McCauley, L.: AI armageddon and the three laws of robotics. Ethics Inf. Technol. **9**, 153–164 (2007). https://doi.org/10.1007/s10676-007-9138-2

11. Rose, J., Persson, J.S., Heeager, L.T., Irani, Z.: Managing e-Government: value positions and relationships. Inf. Syst. J. **25**, 531–571 (2015). https://doi.org/10.1111/isj.12052

12. Hood, C., Dixon, R.: A Government that Worked Better and Cost Less?: Evaluating Three Decades of Reform and Change in UK Central Government. Oxford University Press, Oxford (2015)

13. Almarabeh, T., Abuali, A.: A general framework for research proposals. Eur. J. Sci. Res. **39**, 29–42 (2010). https://doi.org/10.4018/978-1-61692-012-8.ch010

14. Bannister, F., Connolly, R.: ICT, public values and transformative government: a framework and programme for research. Gov. Inf. Q. **31**, 119–128 (2014). https://doi.org/10.1016/j.giq.2013.06.002

15. Rutgers, M.R.: Sorting out public values? On the contingency of value classification in public administration. Adm. Theory Prax. **30**, 92–113 (2018). https://doi.org/10.1080/10841806.2008.11029617

16. Jørgensen, T.B., Bozeman, B.: Public values inventory. Adm. Soc. **39**, 354–381 (2007)

17. Twizeyimana, J.D., Andersson, A.: The public value of E-Government – a literature review. Gov. Inf. Q. 1–12 (2019). https://doi.org/10.1016/J.GIQ.2019.01.001

18. Krippendorff, K.: Content Analysis: An Introduction to Its Methodology. SAGE, Thousand Oaks (2004)

19. Walsham, G.: Interpretive case studies in IS research: nature and method. Eur. J. Inf. Syst. **4**, 74–81 (1995). https://doi.org/10.1057/ejis.1995.9

20. Näringsdepartementet: För ett hållbart digitaliserat Sverige: en digitaliseringsstrategi (2017)

21. Jæger, B., Löfgren, K.: The history of the future: changes in Danish e-government strategies 1994–2010. Inf. Polity Int. J. Gov. Democr. Inf. Age. **15**, 253–269 (2010). https://doi.org/10.3233/ip20100217

22. Persson, J., Reinwald, A., Skorve, E., Nielsen, P.: Value positions in E-government strategies: something is (not) changing in the state of Denmark. In: 25th European Conference on Information Systems (ECIS 2017), 904–917 (2017)

Smart Cities

Demographic Profile of Citizens' Interest, Evaluation and Opinions of Local Government Apps in Smart Cities

Laura Alcaide Muñoz(ID) and Manuel Pedro Rodríguez Bolívar[(✉)](ID)

University of Granada, Campus La Cartuja s/n, 18071 Granada, Spain
{Lauraam, manuelp}@ugr.es

Abstract. Smart cities are fostering the interaction, collaboration and involvement of citizens in the city management models. To achieve this aim, technological tools like city mobile apps are being used for redefining the way citizens interact with smart cities. This paper seeks to analyse the demographic profile of citizens regarding the use of local government Apps for participation in public affairs and the digital divide through the evaluation, opinions and interest of citizens in these Apps in European smart cities. To achieve this aim, this paper focuses on an empirical research on Apps created by European smart cities included in the IESE Business School project. Findings indicate that the education level, gender and ages of the citizens can be factors to download, evaluate and opine about local government Apps, although its influence depend on the smart dimension in which the Apps are running.

Keywords: Smart city · E-participation · Citizen engagement · Apps

1 Introduction

The implementation of information and communications technologies (ICTs) in smart cities (SCs) is proposed as a solution to urban challenges. Indeed, the availability of ubiquitous ICTs in SCs stimulates the development of new services and applications by various types of users (Khodabakhsh et al. 2016) and have caused a revolutionary transformation in urban service delivery, creating more efficient and easily accessible environments to promote collaboration in problem-solving issues and innovation (Rodríguez Bolívar 2017a).

The apps provide one of the building blocks of today's smart city infrastructure (Solomon et al. 2016) because they are thought as a tool for crowdsourcing collaboration with the local governments to improve service efficiency and effectiveness, increasing the transparency and accountability of public services (Pak et al. 2017). Also, they can facilitate real-time interaction with the local government and enhance community-based public service (Tang et al. 2019).

In any case, the SCs are not focused only on technical aspects, but also recent scientific publications increasingly more emphasize the inclusion of "people aspects" in the conceptualization and governance models of SCs (Rodríguez Bolívar 2018a and 2018b). In this regard, citizens' acceptance of ICTs for SC apps is very important

© IFIP International Federation for Information Processing 2019
Published by Springer Nature Switzerland AG 2019
I. Lindgren et al. (Eds.): EGOV 2019, LNCS 11685, pp. 313–325, 2019.
https://doi.org/10.1007/978-3-030-27325-5_24

nowadays in the SCs environment since citizens are one of the main stakeholders of the resulting urban apps ecosystem within a city (Aguilera et al. 2016). Nonetheless, there is a lack of research regarding techniques of the use of demographic profile of citizens for designing and creating urban apps. In this regard, it could be interesting to analyse whether the demographic profile of citizens is influencing on the downloads (interest), score (useful) and opinions (collaboration) of the urban apps.

Therefore, to gain a better understanding of the reality outside the academic literature regarding the application of apps in SCs, and particularly, the demographic profile of citizens that use these technological tools in SCs, this paper seeks to test whether the gender, education level and the age of citizens could influence on the downloads, score and opinions about the use of local government Apps in European SCs.

To achieve this aim, we focus our analyses in European SCs included in the project "Cities in motion version 2018" headed by the IESE Business School University of Navarra, that ranks all SCs according to some indicators in different areas. The remainder of the paper is, therefore, as follows. The next section describes the hypothesis formulation, the sample selection and the methodology of the research. Then, we present the results of the study and finally, the conclusions section comes the paper to an end.

2   Empirical Research

The capability theory (Heres et al. 2005) explains the need to analyse the fitness between the personal profile (person's technological, economic and social situation) and the technology offered by governments, with the aim at understanding the acceptance and use of technological advances by citizens. In fact, this theory supports that the whole process of adoption of new technologies is influence by the demographic, educational and cultural factors in society.

Therefore, this paper formulates some hypothesis to be tested using an OLS regression analysis regarding the demographic profile of citizens in their use of local government Apps. Concretely, we consider demographic factors such as gender, age, and level of education of the citizens and the analysis of their influence on Smart City Apps.

To achieve this aim, this research is focused on European smart cities and the local government Apps created by these governments. The next subsections try to specifically explain and support all these issues of the research.

2.1   Hypothesis Formulation

2.1.1   Gender

Previous studies highlighted that gender plays an important role in the technology acceptance model, offering different evidences (Wang and Shih 2009; Venkatesh et al. 2012), given that men and women use different socially constructed cognitive structure in the making decisions process. Previous research (Wang and Shih 2009; Ahmad and Khalid 2017) highlighted that women trust more on the opinions of the others because they are more empathetic and aware of the other's feeling compared to men. However, other studies concluded that the intention to use Internet technologies is not different in men and women (Wang et al. 2009).

On the other hand, previous studies (Alotaibi and Roussinov 2016; Hoque 2016) found that gender influences on the adoption of M-Government and the user intention to adoption this M-Government. While others (Lian 2015) showed that gender did not moderate in the relationship between trust and adoption of e-invoice. Otherwise, there are studies that highlighted that male web users show higher open government platform activity that women, although the findings achieved also show that the gender had not effects on the intensity of the use of mobile phone and apps (Schmidthuber et al. 2017; Thomas and Streib 2003). Therefore, taking into account these previous different evidences, we think that could be appropriate and add value to the field of knowledge to analysis the influence of gender on behaviour with Smart Cities' apps, thus we propose the following hypothesis:

H1.1. Gender influences on the Smart City apps downloads.
H1.2. Gender influences on the Smart City apps score.
H1.3. Gender influences on the Smart City apps opinions.

2.1.2 Age

Another of the variables widely analysed in the previous literature is the age of use and its influence on the use of technology, mobile systems, apps and so on (Phang et al. 2006; Chung et al. 2010; Liébana-Cabanillas et al. 2014; Schmidthuber et al. 2017). According to Ahmad and Khalid (2017) and Liébana-Cabanillas et al. (2014), user's age is particularly useful for explaining variation their behaviour in the use of new technologies, systems and tools.

Previous studies highlighted that age is a moderator of the relationship between factors influenced the adoption of M-Government and the intention to adopt M-Government (Alotaibi and Roussinov 2016; Ohme 2015). However, other studies evidenced age does not moderate the relationship between social influenced and the adoption M-Government and the relationship between trust and the adoption of M-Government (Chopar and Rajan 2016; Lian 2015). In this sense, Dimitrova et al. (2006) and Nam (2012) found that younger age people use Internet more frequently for using e-Government, but Schmidthuber et al. (2017) found significative evidences that old people use Open Government Web and apps more frequently that younger people.

Given that, the findings on age are different in the previous studies we think that could be interesting to analysis the influence of age on behaviour with Smart Cities' apps, thus we propose the following hypothesis:

H2.1. Age influences on the Smart City apps downloads.
H2.2. Age influences on the Smart City apps score.
H2.3. Age influences on the Smart City apps opinions.

2.1.3 Level of Education

Finally, level of education is considered as the most important drivers in the analysis of the acceptance and usage of technology (Choudrie and Papazafeiropoulou 2006), because the users that have educational qualification are more likely to attain better jobs and are more likely to adopt new innovations (Dwivedi and Lal 2007).

In this sense, Al-Shafi and Weerakkody (2010) found significant evidences among adopters and non-adopters of e-Government depending on the users' level of education. Meanwhile, Dimitrova and Chen (2006) evidenced that the level of education has a positive significant relation with media use for public affairs, but a negative significant relation with frequency of use of e-Government services. In this way, Schmidthuber et al. (2017) showed that high-educated users use the platform les actively via app that low educated ones.

Taking into account, these previous studies showed conflicted results when they analysed the influence of education for the use of Internet and e-Government, we think that could be interesting to analysis the influence of education on behaviour with Smart Cities' apps, thus we propose the following hypothesis:

H3.1. Level of education influences on the Smart City apps downloads.
H3.2. Level of education influences on the Smart City apps score.
H3.3. Level of education influences on the Smart City apps opinions.

2.2   Sample Selection and Data Collection Method

In this study, we focused on local governments because in recent years, the local governments around the world are undergoing numerous reforms that have transformed these organizations to enhance the effectiveness, efficiency, and legitimacy of their public value creation processes. The implementation of new technology and organizational changes are complex processes that have developed into difficult problems that are often too difficult to be solved by local governments (Sørensen and Torfing 2011).

Together with the aforementioned, the local governments are considered the closest level of the government with the citizens, managing the largest number of services provided (Rodríguez Bolívar 2017b; Saiz 2011). Given that, they are the governments that most influence the daily life of citizens, the citizenship demands more public information to know how to manage the public resources, implement the public policies and adopt the decision-making.

In this sense, the local governments have made different communication channels (social media, platforms and mobile web services) available to citizens to interact with them and favour their participation in public affairs (Bonsón et al. 2015; Hung et al. 2000). The smart-phones and tablets offer greater data storage capacity, activities, systems, software and greater connectivity in real time, favouring e-democracy (Höffken and Streich 2013). Also, the governments have designed service platforms and mobile applications that enable citizens to report incidents and interact with them while on the move (Reuver et al. 2013).

This process of technological innovation has been accelerated in the context of the Smart Cities (Gil-García et al. 2016), which has posed continuous challenges for governments. The local governments have adapted their traditional structures and processes to the technological and innovative advances to create public value (Wirtz et al. 2019). But the smart context offers the necessary conditions to achieve of improved information, service provision, citizen engagement, and legitimacy (Yeh 2017), which create more affordable, participatory and transparent public sector management models.

Taking into account everything previously described, our study is focused on cities labelled as "Smart" in the project undertaken by the IESE Business School University of Navarra (see http://www.iese.edu/research/pdfs/ST-0396.pdf). In this paper, a SC is defined based on the European Union definition, as "a place where traditional networks and services are made more efficient with the use of digital and telecommunication technologies, for the benefit of its inhabitants and businesses" (Eurostat 2016). And the data collection method of this paper was based on an examination of the official websites of local governments in European Smart Cities during February 2019 with the specific purpose of collecting data about mobile applications offered by the city government. Thereafter, we accessed from the mobile phone via Apple Store (IOS software) or Google Play Store (Android software) to know the information about downloads volume, score obtained and number of users' opinions. In these platforms, each mobile application offers the information to satisfy the citizens' needs depending on the type of application concerned. For example, a Smart Mobility application provides information about where the nearest bike is, which is the faster route, which is the nearest free parking, and so on. In short, useful information to make the daily life of the citizens more comfortable and efficient management of the city's resources.

2.3   Research Methodology

Based on Sect. 2.1, and considering the factor that could influence on downloads of mobile applications, assigned score and number of users' opinions, we have selected three variables as factors that may influence on downloads, score and opinions in the sample local governments, which have been linked with hypotheses defined in Sect. 2.1 (see Table 1).

Table 1. Descriptive statistics.

Variables	Acronym	Description	Calculation
Downloads	DOWN	Apps' downloads	Total of apps' downloads
Score	SCORE	Score assigned by users	Apps' Score
Opinions	OPIN	Total of opinions	Total of opinions
Gender	FEM/MAL	[a]Population residing in the municipality	Percentages of females and males
Age	AGE_15/64	[a]Population residing with age from 15 until 64 years	Percentages of population with age from 15 until 64 years
Fiscal pressure	Edu_UPP/ Edu_HIGH	[a]Population residing with upper education and high school education	Percentage of population with these levels of education

Source: Own Elaboration
[a] EUROSTAT (https://ec.europa.eu/eurostat)

The first one is gender (FEM and MAL) (H.1) which can be defined as the population residing in a municipality and are measured using the percentages of females and males who reside in the municipality. The second one is age (AGE_15/64) (H.2) which is the population residing in the local government with age from 15 until 64. The last one is the level of education (Edu_UPP and Edu_HIGH) (H.3) which is the population residing in the city with upper education and high school education and are measured using the percentages of population with these levels of education who reside in the city.

Taking into account the structure presented by the dependent variables (DOWN, SCORE and OPIN), the association between the dependent and independent variables were tested using OLS regression analysis (STATA version 15), which produced the following equations:

Model 1 – Downloads = ß0 + ß1 FEM or MALi + ß2 AGE_15/64i + ß3 Edu_UPPi

Model 2 – Score = ß0 + ß1 FEM or MALi + ß2 AGE_15/64i + ß3 Edu_HIGHi

Model 3 – Opinions = ß0 + ß1 FEM or MALi + ß2 AGE_15/64i + ß3 Edu_UPPi

3 Analysis of Results

Having explained the data collection and research methods, this section shows the descriptive analysis about the Apps created by European Smart Cities. Firstly, we show an overview of the current state of the art (countries with more Apps as well as the type of mobile applications most offered by the Smart European municipalities) and we perform the hypotheses testing analysis to obtain interesting findings and insights regarding the citizens' demographic profile in the use of the Apps.

3.1 Descriptive Analysis

Taking into account the previous data collection criteria, our sample is composed of 26 European countries with 51 Smart Cities. Spain (13.72%), Germany (9.80%), France (7.84%), Italy (7.84%) and United Kingdom (7.84%) are the countries that host more Smart Cities. In this Also, these cities are those the more mobile applications offer (see Fig. 1): Spain (25.28%), Italy (11.80%), Germany (9.55%), France (7.87%), and United Kingdom (6.74%).

In this sense, Spain offer all application categories: Smart Living (37.78%), Smart Mobility (31.11%), Smart Environmental (11.11%), Smart Governance (11.11%), Smart People (6.67%) and Smart Economy (2.22%). In this case, the main Smart Cities are Barcelona (40.00%), Malaga (22.22%) and Valencia (13.33%). However, the rest of main Smart Cities offer mostly Smart Living applications, except Norway that offer Smart Mobility applications, highlighting Firenze (38.09%), Berlin (58.82%), Paris (62.50%), Oslo (100%) and London (58.33%). All these cities are characterized by being very tourist cities.

In general terms, the European Smart Cities bet on Smart Living (48.31%) and Smart Mobility (28.65%) apps (see Table 2). In the case of Smart Living apps, Spain (19.77%), Italy (17.44), France (9.30%) and United Kingdom (6.98%) are the cities that lead the ranking, highlighting Barcelona (58.82%), Firenze (40.00%), Marseille

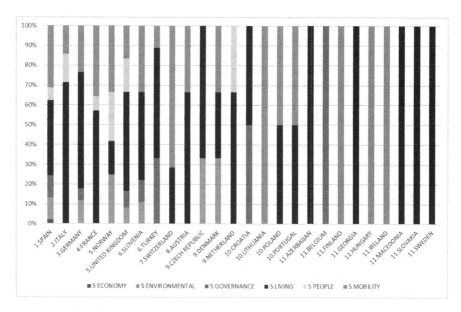

Fig. 1. Ranking of countries with Apps. Source: Own Elaboration

(50.00%) and London (66.67%). On other hand, Spain (27.45%), France (9.80%), Switzerland (9.80%), Germany (7.84%) and Norway (7.84%) are the main cities that offer Smart Living apps, where Barcelona (28.57%), Malaga (28.57%), Paris (80.00%), Zurich (80.00%), Berlin (75.00%) and Oslo (100%) are the cities that stand out from the rest.

Table 2. Apps categories.

Apps Categories						
Smart Living	48.31%	Smart Environmental	7.87%	Smart People	7.30%
Smart Mobility	28.65%	Smart Governance	7.30%	Smart Economy	0.57%
Smart Living Apps				**Smart Mobility Apps**		
Spain	19.77%	Italy	17.44%	Spain	27.45%	France	9.08%
France	9.30%	United Kingdom	6.98%	Switzerland	9.80%	Germany	7.84%
Austria	4.65%	Slovenia	4.65%	Norway	7.84%	Italy	5.88%
Turkey	5.81%	Others	31.40%	Slovenia	5.88%	Others	25.49%

Source: Own Elaboration

3.2 Statistical Tests of the Models

In the case of all mobile applications, we can observe (see Table 3) that the education level has a negative and significant relation ($\beta = -0.164$ and $\beta = -0.029$; $\rho < 0.050$)

with the number of downloads' mobile applications, when we analysed women and men, but the coefficient is stronger in the case of women. So, we cannot reject the H.3.1, because the citizens with upper education level are less likely to download mobile apps. In this case, the women have a positive and significant relation ($\beta = 0.113$; $\rho < 0.15$) with the number of downloads' mobile applications. So, we cannot reject the H1.1, because the gender influences on the downloads of the applications. The age show a negative and not significant relation with the downloads (we reject H2.1).

When we analysed the mobile applications' score and the number of opinions, we can observe that none of the variables analysed has a significant relation, so we reject H1.2, H1.3, H2.2, H2.3, H3.2 and H3.3. The gender, age and education do not influence on the mobile applications' score and the number of opinions.

Table 3. Statistical results of the models for all Apps.

Variables	Dependent Var: DOWNLOADS				Dependent Var: SCORE			
	Coef.	t	Coef.	t	Coef.	t	Coef.	t
Gender	0.11	1.50	-	-	0.05	0.63	-	-
Gender	-	-	-0.12	-0.67	-	-	-0.06	-0.79
Age	-0.02	-0.30	-0.01	-0.30	-0.02	-1.18	-0.10	-1.27
Level of Education	-0.16	-2.18**	-0.03	-2.25**	-	-	-	-
Level of Education	-	-	-	-	-0.02	-1.03	-0.08	-1.03
R^2	0.044**		0.033*		0.015		0.016	

Variables	Dependent Var: OPINIONS			
	Coef.	t	Coef.	t
Gender	-30.45	-0.14	-	
Gender	-	-	183.70	0.70
Age	20.33	0.49	25.33	0.60
Level of Education	-17.59	-0.97	-18.66	-1.03
Level of Education	-	-	-	-
R^2	0.006		0.009	

Source: Own elaboration
Significant at the 0.001^+; Significant at the 0.01^{***}; Significant at the 0.05^{**}; Significant at the 0.1^*

In the case of Smart Living applications, we can observe (see Table 4) that the education level has a negative and significant relation ($\beta = -0.027$ and $\beta = -0.029$; $\rho < 0.10$) with the number of downloads' mobile applications, when we analysed women and men, but the coefficient is a little stronger in the case of men. So, we cannot reject the H.3.1, because the citizens with upper education level are less likely to downloads mobile apps. However, we did not find a significant relation between gender and age with downloads, so we reject H1.1 and H2.1.

Also, we found a positive and significant relation between women and score's apps ($\beta = 0.215$; $\rho < 0.10$). However, there is not significant relation when we analysed men. So we cannot reject H1.2, because the women are more likely to value mobile applications. In addition, there is a negative and significant relation between high education level with score. So we cannot eject H3.2, because the citizens with High School education are less likely to value apps. This way, we did not find significant relation between age and score's apps (we reject H.2.2).

Table 4. Statistical results of the models for Smart Living Apps

Variables	Dependent Var: DOWNLOADS				Dependent Var: SCORE			
	Coef.	t	Coef.	t	Coef.	t	Coef.	t
Gender	0.09	0.50	-	-	0.22	1.94*	-	-
Gender	-	-	0.13	0.52	-	-	-0.13	-0.92
Age	-0.01	-0.10	-0.01	-0.07	-0.07	-0.67	-0.02	-0.88
Level of Education	-0.03	-1.62*	-0.03	-1.73*	-	-	-	-
Level of Education	-	-	-	-	-0.21	-1.88*	-0.04	-1.67*
R^2		0.036		0.035		0.069*		0.050*

Variables	Dependent Var: OPINIONS			
	Coef.	t	Coef.	t
Gender	-163.86	-0.42	-	-
Gender	-	-	551.30	1.04
Age	26.24	0.28	36.20	0.39
Level of Education	-36.87	-0.42	-39.76	-1.09
Level of Education	-	-	-	-
R^2		0.014		0.025

Source: Own elaboration
Significant at the 0.001^+; Significant at the 0.01^{***}; Significant at the 0.05^{**}; Significant at the 0.1^*

Finally, when we analysed the number of opinions, we can observe that age, gender and education has not a significant relationship, so we reject H1.3, H2.3 and H3.3.

4   Conclusions

The research of this paper is a first approach to identify factors that could explain the downloads, utility and use of urban apps. In this paper, we focus our efforts in the demographic profile of citizens' interest, score and opinions of local government apps in leading SCs, according to the IESE Business School project named "Cities in Motion", because In addition, demographical aspects can influence on the apps use (Gebresselassie and Sanchez 2018).

Findings indicate that SCs in Spain, Italy and Germany provide more than the 46% of the urban apps in the SCs included into the sample selection of this research. It is also worthy of note that, except for SCs in Spain and Norway, the rest of sample SCs are usually focused on smart living apps. This finding seems to confirm recent research that indicates that smart living is the most significant dimension for influencing the citizen's perception of quality of life (Rodríguez Bolívar 2019).

Besides, a recent research in Spain has indicated that the greatest interest of public administrations has been focused on the development of applications on tourism, perhaps due to the tourist aspect of SCs (Ugarte et al. 2017) or to the fact that younger tourists and tourists with higher incomes tend to use e-services more intensively (Neuts et al. 2013). Indeed, most of sample SCs are highly visited cities by foreign young and highly income tourists (see Eurostat dataset).

Also, road congestion has reached extreme levels in the major cities in the world and it seriously affects the quality of life of the citizens (Pacheco et al. 2018). Indeed, the mobility problems into the cities is a relevant issue and are forcing local governments in SCs to adopt strategies to address city mobility problems (Chow 2018), using smart mobility apps for avoiding these problems and making mobility management more efficient. Thus, our findings point out that the creation of smart mobility apps are also very relevant in sample SCs.

As for the hypothesis testing, based on the capability theory (Heres et al. 2005), our findings show differences in the use of sample Apps by citizens. This way, only a negative and significant association has been found between the education level and app downloads (model 1) (see research methodology section). Therefore, even the most educated users, i.e., those arguably most aware of and equipped with skills to use apps effectively, express very serious concerns regarding the interest and utility of those apps, perhaps due to emerging security and privacy challenges, which are critical to gain the citizens' acceptance of smart city apps (Daneva and Lazarov 2018).

On another hand, in the case of smart living apps, our findings indicate, again, a negative and significant association between the education level and the app downloads (model 1) and scoring (model 2), as well as a positive and significant association between women and the scoring of apps (model 2). Nonetheless, we have not found a demographic profile of the citizens and the opinions in the sample urban apps.

These findings seem to indicate that people more interested in using apps are both those in younger ages (millennials) and those that are not highly educated, perhaps because they are more prone to use smartphones to connect to internet (see http://www.pewinternet.org/fact-sheet/mobile/). Therefore, this result confirms current data of the use of smartphones in countries like Spain or USA and it is contrary to prior research that found that, in Germany, people that participated in apps were mostly male, middle-aged, politically and technically interested and already actively participating in society (Schröder 2014). In this regard, the uncertainty of the owner of the data generated in the apps could be a reason for supporting our findings (Mainka et al. 2018).

In brief, a careful analysis of the citizens' profiles suggested that it is possible to divide the users of smart city apps into three groups: the advocates, the worried users and the apathetic users of smart city apps. The advocates are women linked to the use of smart living apps. The worried users are highly educated people for all smart dimensions apps. Finally, the apathetic users are those not included into the previous groups and include males of different ages. Future research should make a deeper analysis of these three groups and know the reasons why these urban apps have not got enough success.

In this regard, a recent research indicates that local governments should never assume that citizens will automatically use apps once they are launched. By contrast, continuing citizen marketing campaigns tailored to different age groups and communities are needed (Tang et al. 2019). Also, the involvement of users in the app development process to provide feedback in different app development stage could be also very important in this issue (Tang et al. 2019). Therefore, future research could deep into these analyses in order to build models that explain the interest, use and collaboration of citizens in urban apps into SCs. In addition, it could be interesting a qualitative analysis of the opinions and perceptions expressed by the users about the use and usefulness of Apps using a survey or a questionnaire.

References

Aguilera, U., López-de-Ipiña, D., Pérez, J.: Collaboration-centred cities through urban apps based on open and user-generated data. Sensors **16**(7), 1022 (2016)

Ahmad, S.Z., Khalid, K.: The adoption of M-government services from the user's perspectives: empirical evidence from the United Arab Emirates. Int. J. Inf. Manag. **37**, 367–379 (2017)

Alotaibi, S., Roussinov, D.: Developing and validating an instrument for measuring mobile government adoption in Saudi Arabia. Int. J. Soc. Behav. Educ. Econ. Bus. Ind. Eng. **10**(3), 727–733 (2016)

Al-Shafi, S., Weerakkody, V.: Factors affecting e-government adoption in the state of Qatar. In: Proceedings in European and Mediterranean Conference on Information Systems 2010, Abu Dhabi, 12–13 April 2010

Bonsón, E., Royo, S., Ratckai, M.: Citizens' engagement on local governments' Facebook sites an empirical analysis: the impact of different media and content types in Wester Europe. Gov. Inf. Q. **32**(1), 52–62 (2015)

Chopar, S., Rajan, P.: Modeling intermediary satisfaction with mandatory adoption of e-Government technologies for food distribution. Inf. Technol. Int. Dev. **12**(1), 15–34 (2016)

Choudrie, J., Papazafeiropoulou, A.: Lessons learnt from the broadband diffusion in South Korea and the UK: implications for future government intervention in technology diffusion (2006)

Chow, J.: Informed Urban Transport Systems: Classic and Emerging Mobility Methods Toward Smart Cities, 1st edn. Amsterdam, USA (2018)

Chung, J.E., Park, N., Wang, H., Fulk, J., McLaughlin, M.: Age differences in perceptions of online community participation among non-users: an extension of the technology acceptance model. Comput. Hum. Behav. **26**(6), 1674–1684 (2010)

Daneva, M., Lazarov, B.: Requirements for smart cities: results from a systematic review of literature. In: 12th International Conference on Research Challenges in Information Science (RCIS), pp. 1–6. IEEE press, Nantes (2018)

Dimitrova, D.V., Chen, Y.C.: Profiling the adopter of e-government information and services: the influence of psychological characteristics, civic mindedness, and information channels. Soc. Sci. Comput. Rev. **24**(2), 172–188 (2006)

Dwivedi, Y.K., Lal, B.: Socio-economic determinants of broadband adoption. Ind. Manag. Data Syst. **107**(5), 654–671 (2007)

Eurostat: Smart cities Cities using technological solutions to improve the management and efficiency of the urban environment (2016). https://ec.europa.eu/info/eu-regional-and-urban-development/topics/cities-and-urban-development/city-initiatives/smart-cities_en

Gebresselassie, M., Sanchez, T.: "Smart" tools for socially sustainable transport: a review of mobility apps. Urban Sci. **2**(2), 45 (2018)

Gil-García, J.R., Zhang, J., Puron-Cid, G.: Conceptualizing smartness in government: an integrative and multi-dimensional view. Gov. Inf. Q. **33**(3), 524–534 (2016)

Heres, J., Mante-Meijer, E., Turk, T., Pierson, J.: Adoption of ICTs: a proposed framework. In: Mante-Meijer, E., Klamer, L. (eds.) ICT Capabilities in Action: What People Do, pp. 19–48. Office for Official Publication of the European Comunities, Luxemburg (2005)

Höffken, S., Streich, B.: Mobile participation: citizen engagement in urban planning via smartphones. In: Nunes Silv, C. (ed.) Citizen e-Participation in Urban Governance: Crowdsourcing and Collaborative Creativity, pp. 199–225. IGI Global, USA (2013)

Hoque, M.R.: An empirical study of mHealth adoption in a developing country: the moderating effect of gender concern. BMC Med. Inform. Decis. Making **16**(1), 51 (2016)

Hung, S.Y., Chang, C.M., Yu, T.J.: Determinants of user acceptance of the e-Government services: the case of online tax filing and payment system. Gov. Inf. Q. **23**(1), 97–122 (2000)

Khodabakhsh, P., Fathi, H., Mashayekhi, S.: Planning for future urban services in the smart city era: integrating E-services in urban planning process. Armanshahr Archit. Urban Dev. 9(16), 153–168 (2016)

Lian, J.: Critical factors for cloud based e-invoice service adoption in Taiwan: an empirical study. Int. J. Inf. Manag. 35(1), 98–109 (2015)

Liébana-Cabanillas, F., Sánchez-Fernández, J., Muñoz-Leiva, F.: Antecedents of the adoption of the new mobile payment systems: the moderating effect of age. Comput. Hum. Behav. 35, 464–478 (2014)

Mainka, A., Siebenlist, T., Beutelspacher, L.: Citizen participation: case study on participatory apps in Germany. In: Companion of the Web Conference 2018 on the Web Conference 2018, pp. 915–918. International World Wide Web Conferences Steering Committee (2018)

Nam, T.: Suggesting frameworks of citizen-sourcing via Government 2.0. Gov. Inf. Q. 29(1), 12–20 (2012)

Neuts, B., Romão, J., Nijkamp, P., van Leeuwen, E.: Digital destinations in the tourist sector: a path model for the impact of e-services on tourist expenditures in Amsterdam. Lett. Spat. Resour. Sci. 6(2), 71–80 (2013)

Ohme, J.: The acceptance of mobile government form a citizens' perspective: identifying perceived risks and perceived benefits. Mob. Media Commun. 2(3), 298–317 (2015)

Pak, B., Chua, A., Vande Moere, A.: FixMyStreet Brussels: socio-demographic inequality in crowdsourced civic participation. J. Urban Technol. 24(2), 65–87 (2017)

Pacheco, R.R., Rochman, A.G., de la Vega, A.V., Ornelas, E.L., González, O.M., Serrano, F.V.: Design of a digital collaborative tool to improve mobility in the universities. In: Nathanail, E. G., Karakikes, I.D. (eds.) CSUM 2018. AISC, vol. 879, pp. 591–598. Springer, Cham (2018). https://doi.org/10.1007/978-3-030-02305-8_71

Phang, J., Sutanto, A., Kankanhalli, Y., Li, B., Tan, H.T.: Senior citizens' acceptance of information systems: a study in the context of e-Government services. IEEE Trans. Eng. Manag. 53(4), 555–569 (2006)

Reuver, M., Stein, S., Hampe, J.F.: From eParticipation to mobile participation: designing a service platform and business model for mobile participation. Inf. Polity 18(1), 57–73 (2013)

Rodríguez Bolívar, M.P.: Policy makers' perceptions on the transformational effect of Web 20 technologies on public services delivery. Electron. Commer. Res. 17(2), 227–254 (2017a)

Rodríguez Bolívar, M.P.: Governance model for the delivery of public services through the Web 20 technologies: a political view in large Spanish municipalities. Soc. Sci. Comput. Rev. 35 (2), 203–225 (2017b)

Rodríguez Bolívar, M.P.: Creative citizenship: the new wave for collaborative environments in smart cities. Academia Revista Latinoamericana de Administración 31(1), 277–302 (2018a)

Rodríguez Bolívar, M.P.: Governance models and outcomes to foster public value creation in smart cities. Sci. Reg. 17(1), 57–80 (2018b)

Rodríguez Bolívar, M.P.: In the search for the 'smart' source of the perception of quality of life in European smart cities. In: Proceedings of the 52nd Hawaii International Conference on System Sciences, pp. 3325–3334. HICSS, Maui, USA (2019)

Sáiz, M.P.: La Ley De Economía Sostenible: La Sostenibilidad Financiera Del Sector Público. Revista De Contabilidad y Dirección 13, 21–42 (2011)

Schmidthuber, L., Hilgers, D., Gegenhuber, T.: Shedding light on participation in open government arenas: determinants of platform activity of web and app users. In: Proceeding of the 50th Hawaii International Conference on System Sciences, pp. 2761–2770. HICSS, Hawaii, USA (2017)

Schröder, C.: A mobile app for citizen participation. In: Proceedings of the 2014 Conference on Electronic Governance and Open Society: Challenges in Eurasia, Russia, pp. 75–78. ACM (2014)

Sørensen, E., Torfing, J.: Enhancing collaborative innovation in the public sector. Adm. Soc. **43** (8), 842–868 (2011)

Solomon, M.G., Sunderam, V., Xiong, L., Li, M.: Enabling mutually private location proximity services in smart cities: a comparative assessment. In: 2016 IEEE International Smart Cities Conference (ISC2), Italy, pp. 1–8. IEEE press (2016)

Tang, T., Hou, J., Fay, D.L., Annis, C.: Revisit the drivers and barriers to e-governance in the mobile age: a case study on the adoption of city management mobile apps for smart urban governance. J. Urban Aff. 1–23 (2019). https://www.tandfonline.com/doi/abs/10.1080/07352166.2019.1572455?journalCode=ujua20

Thomas, J.C., Steib, G.: The new face of government: citizen-initiated contact in the era of e-Government. J. Public Adm. Res. Theory **13**(1), 83–102 (2003)

Ugarte, T.B., Lorenzo, F.C., Martínez, M.S.: Ciudades inteligentes y apps para la ciudadanía Análisis de casos pioneros en España. Disertaciones. Anuario electrónico de estudios en Comunicación Social **10**(2), 225–236 (2017)

Venkatesh, V., Thong, J., Xu, X.: Consumer acceptance and use of information technology: extending the unified theory of acceptance and use of technology. MIS Q. **36**(1), 157–178 (2012)

Wang, Y.S., Shih, Y.W.: Why do people use information kiosks? A validation of the unified theory of acceptance and use of technology. Gov. Inf. Q. **26**(1), 158–165 (2009)

Wirtz, B.W., Weyerer, J.C., Schichtel, T.: An integrative public IoT framework for smart government. Gov. Inf. Q. **36**(2), 333–345 (2019)

Yeh, H.: The effects of successful ICT-based smart city services: from citiens' perspective. Gov. Inf. Q. **34**(3), 556–565 (2017)

Digital by Default: The Use of Service Channels by Citizens

Javiera Fernanda Medina Macaya[ID], André Francisco Alves[(✉)][ID],
Fernando Meirelles[ID], and Maria Alexandra Cunha[ID]

Getulio Vargas Foundation, Sao Paulo, SP, Brazil
andalves@gmail.com

Abstract. The use of information and communication technologies by governments is increasing, in many cases to establish new channels of interaction with citizens; and digital by default has been presented as a guide for the development of electronic services. This article discusses the possibility of creating new exclusion forms and is based on the analysis of the profile of use of service channels SP156 of the São Paulo City. To do so, it uses databases of service requests, made available through the City's Open Data Portal, as well as sociodemographic data from the city's districts. It was verified that there is a statistically significant correlation between the average monthly income level of the districts and the type of channel used by the citizen to make the requests. It is concluded that it is important to provide multiple channels for citizens to interact with governments so as not to lead to further social exclusion.

Keywords: E-government · Service-channels · Digital-by-default · Brazil

1 Introduction

The ways in which governments interact with their citizens, as well as how citizens interact with their governments, have changed over time. In part, this change has been leveraged by the governmental use of information and communication technologies (ICT), known as e-government, which aims to improve government performance and processes [3] and, consequently, the government itself [18]. In addition, the use of ICT contributes to transparency, increased accountability, and changes the role of citizens, allowing them to stop being mere consumers of public services [2]. This article focuses on the usage profile of service channels, captured by different service channels of a mega city in the global south, discussing and demonstrating another possible form of exclusion in the case of digital orientation by default. The provision of services solely through electronic channels, as a self-service based on the idea of digital by default, creates the pre-requisite that citizens are capable, have digital skills, and have the socioeconomic conditions to benefit from online services [24].

This study was financed in part by the Coordenação de Aperfeiçoamento de Pessoal de Nível Superior - Brasil (CAPES) - Finance Code 001.

I. Lindgren et al. (Eds.): EGOV 2019, LNCS 11685, pp. 326–337, 2019.
https://doi.org/10.1007/978-3-030-27325-5_25

The literature on e-government is vast, especially since the 2000s [4]. However, as already pointed out [25], there is a tendency to depoliticize digitalization, as if it were restricted to technical discussions, minimizing its political content and consequences [8, 12, 25], disregarding the context of social exclusion [24]. As noted by Schou and Pors [25], few research projects have addressed the provision of e-services and digital exclusion, although there are studies on digital divides and social exclusion [15, 25].

In order to understand the SP156 multichannel usage profile of São Paulo City, as a basis for discussion of the digital by default concept, this article provides a quantitative data analysis from the City's Open Data Portal [19]. In December 2016, the City of São Paulo improved the availability of online citizen service channels: the Service Portal SP156 – reformulating the former Citizen Assistance Service (SAC) with regard to the presentation of services and the most simple and user-friendly language – and SP156 App, a new service channel. Using these new platforms, citizens can register their requests to the municipal government through the website or app.

In an effort to understand how citizens from the 96 districts of the City of São Paulo interact with the municipal government to register requests for public services, this paper brings a data analysis of requests registered in citizen service channels, called SP156, which can be on-site, online or via call center, and which are available on the Open Data Portal of São Paulo City [20]. The aim is to answer the question *what is the usage profile of SP156 channels of São Paulo City Hall?*

São Paulo City's population is estimated to be more than 12 million inhabitants [10], ranking it among the world's largest cities, and it has a high Municipal Human Development Index for the Brazilian standard (0.805) [11], but also has high inequality among its population, with a Gini index of 0.6453 [6]. This paper is relevant because the discussion of digital orientation by default using the city of São Paulo data may inspire public managers to reflect on the offer of channels to the citizen and on the need to provide mechanisms other than digital ones, especially in the large cities of the Global South. The data processing of requests showing territory is also a contribution to the administrators of big cities, so that they can design services considering the territorial and social differences, like the income of a specific territory.

2 Service Channels

The ways governments and citizens interact have changed over time, in part influenced by the governmental use of ICT. More and more governments are required to offer electronic services (e-services), delivering services that empower citizens and meet their needs [4, 13]. The use of ICT in the provision of services aims to improve public management, as well as increase the provision, quality and effectiveness of the services provided [1], efforts that only make sense when they create value for citizens [14]. In this paper, we understand e-services as the use of ICT tools as a channel for providing public services to citizens [4].

One of the lenses used by scholars to study e-government is considering levels of interaction between governments and citizens through the use of ICT [3]: the first level would be the provision of public information on websites; the second adds forms of contact and interaction that members and organizations of society can use to obtain detailed information; the third level considers the possibility for citizens and organizations to carry out online transactions; the fourth level is ultimately tied to shared governance, with greater collaboration in the decision-making process, and a flow of information sharing and generation by governments and citizens.

This fourth level of e-government is also described in the literature as Government 2.0, referring to Web 2.0, which brings more interactive technologies, and whose main benefit is to promote transparency and citizen participation [1, 23]. Government 2.0 can be understood as being more interactive, communicative, and that has the potential to change the way governments and citizens interact [14, 23], including the possibility for citizens to play an active role not only in consumption but also in content creation [2] and the co-production of public services [24].

The new forms of interaction, leveraged by ICT, influence the growing use of multi-channel for interaction, especially electronic channels [7]. However, to make these new forms of interaction possible, it is necessary to consider the existing digital gaps which, if not considered, can reinforce current socio-economic and territorial inequalities. Schou and Pors [24] emphasize that citizens have increasingly been understood as being "digital by default" by decision makers, placing those who do not use digital technologies as non-standard. The criticisms [25] regarding the understanding of the digital by default are that, by including self-service solutions, citizens are understood as being responsible for seeking services themselves, impacting people who do not use digital technologies who will thus face new forms of exclusion.

These new forms of exclusion are known as digital divide and can be distinguished by two groupings or levels [5, 22]: the access divide, that include people who don't have access to the technology and those who do, faced mainly in developing countries; and the skills usage divide, that include people who do not have not skills to use technology and those who do, faced mainly in developed countries – where the first gap has already been closed or reduced. The lack of skills impacts the use of online government services [27] and this must be considered when more and more governments are offering online services and presuming that citizens are able to fully use all those online services [26].

When implementing policies that presume digital devices (mobile phones or computers) usage for interaction, it is also necessary to consider that the request may contain biases [17]. Those policies should consider that, in order to interact through digital solutions, citizens should "have access to the device and app, and the context" [18]; if there is no other form of interaction and citizens do not have access to any of these three conditions, they cannot, for example, engage in interactions with governments, generating forms of digital exclusion. O'Leary [18] cites the case of Street Bump, a mobile app implemented in the city of Boston (USA) to capture the holes in the streets of the city; to use it, citizens had to have the app installed, an iPhone and a car, conditions tied to socioeconomic issues that could result in the improvement of some areas of the city and not others. Therefore, it is important to consider the territory – and all the socioeconomic issues inherent to it.

These issues should be considered even more in a context such as Brazil's, where 67% of the population are Internet users[1] [16] – 74% in the Southeast region of the country, where the city of São Paulo is located – and 71% of the population in Brazil [17] – 76% of the population in that region – said that they had used the Internet in the last three months. Specifically, 96% of higher social class[2] users are Internet users by mobile phone, contrasting with 48% of lower class, numbers that approximate the proportion of individuals who have used e-government in the 12 months prior to the date of the survey: 86% from higher and 44% from lower classes [17].

3   Methodology

In order to answer the research question what is the usage profile of SP156 channels of São Paulo City?, an exploratory-descriptive study was carried out, with a quantitative approach, through secondary data analysis, and whose methodological procedures can be grouped into four distinct stages: data collection, obtained from Service Center SP156 of São Paulo City request records [19]; sociodemographic data, obtained from the Brazilian Institute of Geography and Statistics (IBGE) Demographic Census 2010 (Census 2010) [10]; Service Center SP156 data cross-referencing with the IBGE data; and citizen profile analysis regarding the interaction with SP156.

Data referring to the services recorded by the Service Center SP156 were extracted from Open Data on the São Paulo City website [20] on 10/15/2018[3] and, for this research, the service request data in the second half of 2017 and the first half of 2018 were considered.

Initially, a total of 720,529 occurrences were obtained. However, due to the focus of this paper being to analyze the usage profile of SP156 service channels, the following records, and respective amounts, were disregarded: records without district, 21,320 occurrences; records without service channel classification, 484 occurrences; service channel type "Integration"[4], 30,929 occurrences. In this way, the final sample

---

[1] Internet users are considered individuals who have used the network at least once in the three months prior to the survey [11].

[2] This social classification is based on Brazilian Economic Classification Criteria (CCEB), as defined by Brazilian Association of Research Companies (ABEP). In order to make the classification, it is considered the possession of some durable items of domestic consumption, plus the instruction degree of the domicile head, thus establishing the classification in economic classes A1, A2, B1, B2, C, D and E.

[3] It is important to note that every three months the databases can be replaced by more up-to-date versions. For example, the service request status can be updated with the most current information. In addition, requests may be reclassified by public service providers with more accurate information, as well as may be forwarded from one agency to another.

[4] The "Integration" service channel contains requests registered through the Integrated Systems SP156 - Military Police and Traffic Engineering Company (CET). It should be noted that the records of requests through the SP156 Integrated Systems were discontinued in December 2017 for Military Police and in June 2018 for CET, so that the requests were only referring to registrations made by citizens. As the purpose of the paper is to analyze the attendance of the districts of the city of São Paulo to the records made by citizens, it was decided to exclude "Integration" data from the database analyzed.

was 667,796 service requests. For the purpose of comparison, São Paulo City's population, according to the 2010 Census, was just over 11.2 million people, that is, the number of service requests is equivalent to 5.96% of the population, and the district that presented, proportionally, fewer requests was "Cidade Tiradentes", with the equivalent of 2.21% district's population. In this way, it can be inferred that the average income of the people who requested the service tends towards the district's average income.

Data referring to São Paulo districts' income was obtained through download from IBGE's website [9] and the most recent available data corresponded to the 2010 Census. As IBGE data is detailed by Census enumeration area[5], it was necessary to group such data by city district, in order to allow the information to be cross-checked with the SP156 service center records. Thus, the mean values of the monthly average nominal income of the persons responsible for permanent households, with and without income, were calculated being grouped by district.

Quartile nominal income average grouping analysis considers: Quartile 1, districts whose citizens have an average income equal to or less than R$ 1,172.00[6]; Quartile 2, districts whose citizens have an average income between R$ 1,172.01 and R$ 1,676.80; Quartile 3, districts whose citizens have an average income between R$ 1,676.81 and R$ 3,293.50; and Quartile 4, districts whose citizens have an average income equal to or greater than R$ 3,293.51.

It is important to note that it was not possible to carry out personal requesting analyses, since the available data is related to the service request, and not to the person who requested it. This would be an interesting analysis, since the results from other research show differences in the use of e-government by men and women (69% and 59% respectively), by education level, ranging from 26% for illiterate people to 85% for university graduates, by age group and social class [17].

The cross-checked information from Central SP156 records and IBGE's socio-demographic data was carried out using the software Excel version 365, considering the "District" column in the records of Central 156 and column "Nome_do_distrito" in the IBGE database. Minitab version 18 was used as supporting software for statistical analysis, considering confidence intervals of 95% for the mean, and the individual standard deviations were used to calculate the intervals.

For data presentation and representation purposes, service channels will be referenced in figures and tables as follows: Application SP156 will be treated only by SP156 App; Central SP156 will be denominated Call Center; Portal of Service SP156 will be treated as Web Portal; and for Service Centers the nomenclature is maintained.

---

[5] Census sector is a territorial unit for census operations' collection, as defined by IBGE.

[6] R$ 1.00 is equivalent to US$ 0.26, according to the trading price of 3/15/2019.

4   The SP156

With the proposal of modernizing the services offered through the 156 phone number, citizen service center, the City of São Paulo launched, in December 2016, the reformulation of the Service Portal SP156[7], and the SP156 App as new service channels for citizens. Thus, the population of the city of São Paulo now has two online channels[8] for requesting services from City Hall, as well as the SP156 call center and on-site Service Centers.

In addition to the expansion with two new platforms for service requests, the reformulation of the citizen service center ensured that its design was intuitive, and that the language used was simpler. Through the new platforms available, citizens can attach images to their requests, as well as evaluate the platforms and the services performed by the public authority. However, not all services can be requested online.

The Citizen Service Centers' modernization was one objective of the 2013–2016 Goals Program[9],[10] [20]. The expansion of online services is one of the lines of action of the current management of the City of São Paulo; and one of its goals is to "reduce the average service time of the five main services requested from 90 to 70 days, in relation to the last four years," as one of the lines of action to expand the "number of online services available in the Service Portal SP156" [21].

4.1   Data Analysis and Discussion

When analyzing citizens' preference by channel type used to make the request (Fig. 1), it is verified that Central SP156 is the most used channel for requests, being responsible for 64.62% of total recorded occurrences, followed by Service Portal SP156, with 22.82%, by the SP156 App, with 6.15% and, finally, by Service Centers, with 6.41%.

The preference for Central SP156 can be explained by the fact that, for a long time, the only way for municipal services to be requested was exclusively by telephone and it

---

[7] The City of São Paulo provided online services through the Citizen Assistance Service (SAC), which was deactivated in November 2016, with the launch of the new Service Portal SP156. One of the modifications was in relation to the language used, to be simpler for the citizens, the inclusion of evaluation of both the service channels and the services, as well as the availability of the data referring to the requests, used in this research.

[8] Registration is not mandatory to use SP156 channels, that is, it is possible to request a service anonymously. The advantage that the platforms offer to the citizen signed up is the greater facility in request follow-up and in the City Hall contact that can be established with the citizen. Thus, while anonymous requests must be accompanied by the protocol number, those requested by a signed-up person will be concentrated in the Service Portal SP156 and/or the App SP156.

[9] According to the São Paulo Targets Program Law - Amendment no. 30 of the Organic Law of the Municipality of São Paulo - since 2008, the elected mayor is obliged to present the Management Targets Program within 90 days after possession.

[10] Amendment No. 30 changes the wording of Article 69 of the Organic Law of the Municipality of São Paulo, specifying that the Program of Targets "(...) will contain the priorities: strategic actions, indicators and quantitative targets for each of the sectors of the Municipal Public Administration, City Districts and Districts, observing, at a minimum, the guidelines of its electoral campaign and the objectives, guidelines, strategic actions and other norms of the Law of the Strategic Master Plan".

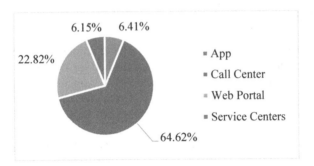

6.15%   6.41%

22.82%

■ App
■ Call Center
■ Web Portal
■ Service Centers

64.62%

Fig. 1. Channel usage by type (n = 667,796).

was also established that the contact number would be the same for all municipalities[11]. Thus, in people's minds, the action of contacting 156 is an activity restricted to the phone call.

However, this distribution does not happen uniformly, depending on the district. The districts that had the most requests registered by the SP156 App were Cursino (17.46%), Vila Leopoldina (13.98%) and Itaim Bibi (12.57%). On the other hand, the districts that had more registrations through the Service Portal SP156 were Tucuruvi (70.39%), Vila Sônia (40.01%) and Vila Mariana (36.69%). Considering Central SP156, Brás (88.89%), Sé (87.88%) and Belém (82.60%) were the districts that used this channel the most. Concerning the Service Centers, the districts with the highest number of requests for such a channel were Marsilac (34.07%), Parelheiros (28.94%) and Perus (19.97%).

The difference of the monthly average income of the districts by type of service channel used should be noted. The three districts that made the most applications for the SP156 App had an average income above R$ 2,500.00 (Cursino with R$ 2,566.82, Vila Leopoldina with R$ 5,130.97 and Itaim Bibi with R$ 6,384.04), and the districts that used the most Service Centers presented monthly average income under R$ 1,000.00 (Marsilac with R$ 665.74, Parelheiros with R$ 747.13 and Perus with R$ 966.26).

Nine types of services account for more than 50% of the services requested when analyzing the most demanded services by citizens (Table 1), with "Social Service for Homeless People" (12.49% of requests) and "Pot-Hole Repair" (10.74% of requests) respond to almost 1/4 of the requests registered by citizens.

The type of service requested also varies according to the service channel (Table 1). When considering SP156 App, the most requested services were "Pot-hole repair" (2.06%), "Noise pollution complaint" (0.71%) and "Removal of vehicle/carcasses abandoned on public roads" (0.54%), with these three services representing more than half of the requests made by the citizens who used the app.

---

[11] National Telecommunication Agency (Anatel) resolution no. 357 of March 15, 2004, standardized the codes for Public Utility and Support to the Switched Fixed Telephone Service (STFC), with the number "156" for municipal services.

Table 1. Most requested services

Service	App	WEB portal	Call center	Service centers	Sum
Social Approach to Homeless People	0.16%	0.12%	12.21%	0.01%	12.49%
Pot-hole repair	2.06%	3.13%	4.81%	0.74%	10.74%
Tree assessment and services in public areas	0.38%	1.20%	4.29%	1.04%	6.91%
Removal of vehicle/carcasses abandoned on public roads	0.54%	0.91%	2.36%	0.18%	3.99%
Removal of large objects on public roads	0.03%	0.44%	3.36%	0.09%	3.90%
Removal of debris on public roads	0.05%	0.72%	2.90%	0.12%	3.79%
Noise pollution complaint	0.71%	0.98%	1.56%	0.14%	3.40%
Trimming of squares, beds and stream banks	0.17%	0.65%	2.22%	0.27%	3.31%
Complaints	0.00%	0.57%	2.66%	0.21%	3.24%
Other services	2.32%	14.09%	28.26%	3.56%	48.23%

Regarding the other service channels, type of service requested is distributed in a more dispersed way, with the sum of the three most requested in the range of 30% or less of the proportion. The "Pot-hole repair" service (3.13%) was the most demanded by the citizens who used the Service Portal SP156, "Service of Social Approach to Homeless People" (12.21%) was the most demanded by citizens who used the Central SP156 and "Tree assessment and services in public areas" was the most requested by the citizens who used the Service Centers. It should be noted that this last service can be requested through the other three service channels.

The "Pot-hole repair" service was the only one that appeared among the three most requested on all channels, with 2.06% of the requests through the SP156 App, 3.13% of the requests through the SP156 Service Portal, 4.81% through Central SP156 and 0.74% through the Service Centers.

Figure 2 shows an interval plot of districts average income according to the service channel usage. It is noted that the service request for districts made through the SP156 App had an average income of R\$ 2,876.60, those who used the SP156 Service Portal had an average income of R\$ 2,658.70, those who used the SP156 Central had an average income of R\$ 2,360.50 and those who used the Service Centers had an average income of R\$ 1,911.50. The difference of means was statistically significant ($p < 0.001$) with a significance level of 0.05 according to the analysis of variance (ANOVA) conducted.

Furthermore, when analyzing the correlation between the percentage of use of the service channel by districts and the average income of the districts, it is verified that there is a statistically significant correlation ($p < 0.001$) for all channels, with a correlation coefficient (r): 0.55 for SP156 App; 0.42 for the Service Portal SP156; -0.30 for Central SP156; and -0.40 for Service Centers.

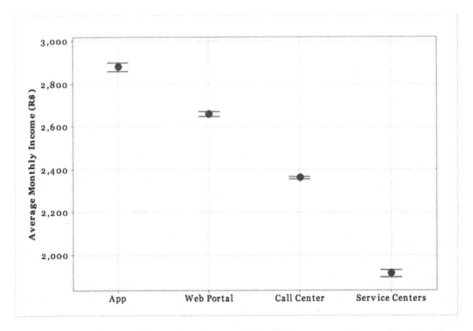

Fig. 2. Interval plot of the average income of the districts grouped by service channel

Correlation analysis, together with the variance analysis, indicates that citizens who live in districts with a higher average income tend to prefer to use the App or the Web Service Portal SP156, and citizens who live in districts with a lower average income tend to prefer to use Central SP156 or the Service Centers. Or, by making the inverse analysis, the lower the district's average income, the higher the Service Centers and Central SP156 usage tends to be, and the higher the district's average income, the lower the use of these service channels tends to be.

Table 2 presents the three most requested services by the citizens considering the quartiles grouping of middle income of the district; it is possible to notice the little variation in the services requested by the citizens of Quartiles 2, 3 and 4. In these quartiles, the presence of the "Service of Social Approach to Homeless People" was observed, a service that for Quartile 1 appears only as the sixth most requested, with 3.89% of requests.

The largest number of requests for "Service of Social Approach to Homeless People" could be explained by the tendency for more people to be living in street conditions in higher-income, more generally middle-income neighborhoods in more central areas of the city, or even that the presence of people in such a situation becomes more "noticeable" in districts with higher incomes. Still considering Table 2, for the citizens in Quartile 1 the presence of "Removal of large objects on public roads" among the three most requested services was verified.

Table 2. Most requested services grouped by income quartiles

Quartile	Service	Percentage
Quartile 1	Pot-hole repair	11.18%
	Tree assessment and services in public areas	6.19%
	Removal of large objects on public roads	5.48%
Quartile 2	Service of Social Approach to Homeless People	16.08%
	Pot-hole repair	11.21%
	Tree assessment and services in public areas	6.36%
Quartile 3	Service of Social Approach to Homeless People	14.97%
	Pot-hole repair	11.57%
	Tree assessment and services in public areas	6.60%
Quartile 4	Service of Social Approach to Homeless People	14.97%
	Pot-hole repair	9.08%
	Tree assessment and services in public areas	8.65%

5 Conclusion

The purpose of this paper was to analyze the usage profile of the SP156 service channels of the City of São Paulo. To do so, the databases of the public service requests, made available through the Open Data Portal of the City of São Paulo, and the sociodemographic data of the districts of the city, made available by the Brazilian Institute of Geography and Statistics were used.

Nine types of services requested by citizens (Table 1) correspond to more than 50% of the requests made. In addition to identifying the most requested services in the city, it was possible to identify the most requested services by type of service channel – the only service that is one of the main services for the four service channels is "Pot-hole repair".

The analyses also allowed us to identify that there is a statistically significant difference in how citizens of districts with different income brackets make their requests. People with higher incomes tend to prefer digital channels (App and Web Portal) for their service requests, whereas people with lower incomes tend to prefer more conventional service channels (Call Center and Service Centers). That is, it is not enough for the government to create digital channels for requesting services, based on the digital by default idea, since this may generate new exclusions of people who are already socially excluded. This finding corroborates studies that show the importance of considering the territory in decision making [17], and of offering different means to register requests, without presuming the digital by default characteristic [24]. Future studies could further analyze the data on the usage profile of individuals by district of the city considering devices used, Internet use, use of e-government, for example. This information could help with local government decision-making so that they could better understand what it takes, for example, for citizens from lower middle-income districts to opt for Central SP156 or Service Centers.

In addition, by analyzing the user profile of each service channel, it would be possible to make adaptations that would better serve a specific audience, such as alternative service schedules, understand the reasons that lead people to choose to use one platform instead of the other, or if there is, for example, a stage in the process that somehow causes people to prefer one platform over another. In this context, the opinion of those who use and those who do not use the channel(s) is of the utmost importance and their inclusion in stages of the process can mean more effective direction of efforts. Understanding the usage profile of each platform and the profile of those who use each platform may mean, for example, minimizing stories such as those reported at the beginning of this article.

A limitation of the analysis is the inference of people's average income who requested services as being equivalent to the district's average income. Additionally, it is important to acknowledge that the requests sample, despite being large enough, is non-parametric. In addition, it has been inferred.

Finally, it is recommended that, for public policy and future research purposes, the databases be made available with other sociodemographic breaks, such as the gender and age of the requesting person, respecting and following the privacy and data protection policies, ensuring data anonymity. Also, it would be valuable to analyze the data from other cities and citizens, in order to understand how this phenomenon occurs in other contexts.

References

1. Araujo, M.H., Reinhard, N., Cunha, M.A.: Serviços de governo eletrônico no Brasil: uma análise a partir das medidas de acesso e competências de uso da internet. Revista de Administração Pública 2(4), 676–694 (2018)
2. Bonsón, E., Torres, L., Royo, S., Flores, F.: Local e-government 2.0: social media and corporate transparency in municipalities. Gov. Inf. Q. 29(2), 123–132 (2012)
3. Chun, S.A., Shulman, S., Sandoval, R., Hovy, E.: Government 2.0: making connections between citizens, data and government. Inf. Polity 15(1–2), 1–9 (2010)
4. Cunha, M.A., Miranda, P.R.M.: O uso de TIC pelos governos: uma proposta de agenda de pesquisa a partir da produção acadêmica e da prática nacional. Organizações & Sociedade 20 (66), 543–566 (2013)
5. Ebbers, W.E., Jansen, M.G., van Deursen, A.J.: Impact of the digital divide on e-government: expanding from channel choice to channel usage. Gov. Inf. Q. 33(4), 685–692 (2016)
6. DATASUS. Índice de Gini da renda domiciliar per capita – Brasil. http://tabnet.datasus.gov.br/cgi/ibge/censo/cnv/ginisp.def. Accessed 15 Mar 2019
7. Giritli, N.K., Axelsson, K., Melin, U.: Multi-channel service management in public sector – three interpretative frames illustrating e-government and work practice in a Swedish state agency. Electron. J. e-Gov. 12(1), 115–128 (2014)
8. Hall, P.: Throwing discourses in the garbage Can: the case of Swedish ICT policy. Crit. Policy Stud. 2(1), 25–44 (2008)
9. IBGE: Censo Demográfico 2010. ftp://ftp.ibge.gov.br/Censos/Censo_Demografico_2010/Resultados_do_Universo/Agregados_por_Setores_Censitarios/. Accessed 30 Oct 2018
10. IBGE: Brasil em Síntese: São Paulo. https://www.ibge.gov.br/cidades-e-estados/sp/sao-paulo.html. Accessed 15 Mar 2019

11. ITU: Manual for measuring ICT access and use by households and individuals 2014. http://www.itu.int/dms_pub/itu-d/opb/ind/D-IND-ITCMEAS-2014-PDF-E.pdf. Accessed 15 Mar 2019

12. Löfgren, K., Sørensen, E.: Metagoverning policy networks in e-government. In: Weerakkody, V. (ed.) Applied Technology Integration in Governmental Organizations: New e-Government Research, pp. 298–312. IGI Global, Hershey (2011)

13. Lopes, K.M.G., Macadar, M.A., Luciano, E.M.: Public value: citizens at the center of public management. In: Barbosa, A. (ed.) Pesquisa Sobre o Uso das Tecnologias de Informação e Comunicação no Setor Público Brasileiro. CGI.br, São Paulo (2018)

14. Meijer, A.J., Koops, B.J., Pieterson, W., Overman, S., Tije, S.: Government 2.0: key challenges to its realization. Electron. J. e-Gov. 10(1), 59–69 (2012)

15. Mota, F.P.B.: Digital divide, internet access, and sociodemographic conditions. In: Barbosa, A. (ed.) Pesquisa Sobre o Uso das Tecnologias de Informação e Comunicação nos Domicílios Brasileiros. CGI.br, São Paulo (2017)

16. NIC.br: Pesquisa sobre o uso das tecnologias de informação e comunicação nos domicílios brasileiros: TIC Domicílios 2017. https://cetic.br/tics/domicilios/2017/individuos/. Accessed 15 Mar 2019

17. O'Leary, D.E.: Exploiting big data from mobile device sensor-based apps: challenges and benefits. MIS Q. Exec. 12(4), 179–187 (2013)

18. OECD: The e-government imperative: Main findings. OECD, Paris (2003)

19. Prefeitura Municipal de São Paulo: Portal de Dados Abertos da Prefeitura de São Paulo: Dados do SP156. http://dados.prefeitura.sp.gov.br/pt_PT/dataset/dados-do-sp156. Accessed 25 Oct 2018

20. Prefeitura Municipal de São Paulo. Programa de Metas 2013–2016. https://www.prefeitura.sp.gov.br/cidade/secretarias/upload/planejamento/arquivos/15308-004_AF_FolhetoProgrmadeMetas2Fase.pdf. Accessed 21 Oct 2018

21. Prefeitura Municipal de São Paulo. Programa de Metas 2017–2020. http://planejasampa.prefeitura.sp.gov.br/assets/Programa-de-Metas_2017-2020_Final.pdf. Accessed 13 Mar 2019

22. Reddick, C.G., Abdelsalam, H.M.E., Elkadi, H.A.: Channel choice and the digital divide in e-government: the case of Egypt. Inf. Technol. Dev. 18(3), 226–246 (2012)

23. Rodríguez Bolívar, M.P.: User centric services under the Web 2.0 era. Coproduction, execution and efficiency of public services. In: Saeed, S., Ramayah, T., Mahmood, Z. (eds.) User Centric E-Government. Integrated Series in Information Systems. Springer, Cham (2018). https://doi.org/10.1007/978-3-319-59442-2_8

24. Schou, J., Pors, A.S.: Digital by default? A qualitative study of exclusion in digitalised welfare. Soc. Policy Adm. 53, 464–477 (2018)

25. Senne, F.: Espaço e inclusão digital na cidade de São Paulo: uma análise desde a perspectiva da multidimensionalidade das desigualdades sociais e territoriais. In: 11th CPR Latam Conference, Varadero, Cuba, pp. 173–184 (2018)

26. Van Deursen, A.J., van Dijk, J.A.: Improving digital skills for the use of online public information and services. Gov. Inf. Q. 26(2), 333–340 (2009)

27. Deursen, A.: Where to go in the near future: diverging perspectives on online public service delivery. In: Wimmer, M.A., Scholl, J., Grönlund, Å. (eds.) EGOV 2007. LNCS, vol. 4656, pp. 143–154. Springer, Heidelberg (2007). https://doi.org/10.1007/978-3-540-74444-3_13

Behind the Scenes of Coproduction of Smart Mobility: Evidence from a Public Values' Perspective

A. Paula Rodriguez Müller$^{(\boxtimes)}$ ⓘ and Trui Steen ⓘ

Public Governance Institute, KU Leuven, Leuven, Belgium
anapaula.rodriguezmuller@kuleuven.be

Abstract. The advances in information and communication technology (ICT) have extended the applicability of citizen coproduction in government service delivery and have entailed transformative changes, especially at the city level. City governments around the globe increasingly rely on the private sector to set ICT-based urban innovations, like initiatives to involve citizens in the coproduction of smart mobility. Although there are many benefits of ICT-based coproduction, there is nevertheless the potential for tension between private companies and the government with whom they are cooperating. Those tensions are built on the differences in interests and values of private and public actors, and the way of realizing them, and they can compromise the vision and duty of the government. We, therefore, aim to understand the potential impact of private companies' involvement on the expectations and perceptions of coproducing actors towards social-oriented and service-oriented public values. We conducted an exploratory in-depth case study of the smart bike-sharing system in one of the major cities in Flanders, Belgium. Data were collected through official documents and 27 semi-structured interviews with key coproducing actors. These data were then qualitatively analyzed using Nvivo software. Our exploratory case study indicated that the private actor upholds the realization of values such as efficiency, reliability, and ease of access by bringing in resources and expertise to coproduce smart mobility. However, certain social-oriented values like citizen empowerment and engagement, and (digital) inclusiveness are not part of the private partner's vision. The study highlights the potential assets and risks for the realization of public values when dealing with conflicting interests between coproducing actors, and in this way considers a different angle on private companies' involvement in the coproduction of public services.

Keywords: Coproduction · ICT · Public values · Smart mobility ·
Private actors

1 Introduction

ICT-based coproduction of public services is alleged to improve the realization of public values in the city, as it allows citizens and non-state actors to be more actively engaged with the delivery of public services [1, 2]. As a result, this leads to a more collaborative and open government, e.g., users can have more control over the services

© IFIP International Federation for Information Processing 2019
Published by Springer Nature Switzerland AG 2019
I. Lindgren et al. (Eds.): EGOV 2019, LNCS 11685, pp. 338–352, 2019.
https://doi.org/10.1007/978-3-030-27325-5_26

and greater fulfillment of their needs [3]. Specifically, in the so-called 'smart city', governments need to involve private companies due to the technological and financial complexities behind smart services. This ideally encompasses a sustainable cooperation, sharing risk, and resources [4].

Nevertheless, the role of the government runs the risk of becoming ambiguous with the increasing involvement of private companies, who can act as intermediaries between the government and its citizens. Because of their technological and financial capacity, private companies could end up assuming government's tasks and functions. The end result could be the private sector obstructing the vision and duty of the government while prioritizing profitability over a wide range of public values [5–7].

In order to explore the challenges involved in the coproduction of smart mobility, we use the coproduction theory, digital government (smart cities), and public values perspective. We aim to step back from the normative perspective that highlights only the potential 'good outcomes' and promises of ICT-based collaborations and to look into the black-box [2, 3]. Our study is guided by the following research question: to what extent does the involvement of private companies in ICT-based coproduction affect the expectations and perceptions of the coproducing actors (i.e., governmental actors, private actors, citizen-users) towards public values being realized or obstructed? To address the research question, we conducted an exploratory in-depth case study on ICT-based coproduction of smart mobility.

The next section briefly deals with the definition and context of the coproduction of smart mobility. Section 3 outlines the potential and challenges of ICT-based coproduction's ability to realize public values. Section 4 summarizes our methodological approach towards the case study. Section 5 provides a discussion of the findings and limitations. Finally, Sect. 6 delivers our conclusions, implications, and avenues for future research.

2   Coproduction of Smart Mobility

The conception of coproduction fits in the New Public Governance paradigm that recognizes the provision of public services as a model based on networks and inter-organizational relationships. It is understood as the collaboration between 'regular producers' and 'citizen producers' in different phases of service management. The 'regular producers' are the professional coproducers working directly (e.g., government employees) or indirectly (e.g., private actors) with the government. The 'citizen producers' are lay actors who voluntarily coproduce (individually or collectively) as citizens and/or customers [8–10].

Technological advances have led to an increased ability to perform coproduction activities [3, 11–15], and have entailed transformative changes, especially on the city level [16, 17]. These initiatives came with new promises. ICT is claimed to empower service users, enhance the speed and reach of communications, and promote multilateral and rich information exchange without time and space constraints [12, 15]. Smart mobility is an example of adopting ICTs to coproduce, as the sharing aspect implies the involvement of multiple stakeholders and the 'crowd', while the 'smartness' entails a reconfiguration of the interactions between the actors involved and their surrounding environment [3, 5, 18]. The main premise behind these smart systems is to offer an accessible and inclusive alternative mobility solution. Specifically, when examining city bike sharing, this solution also involves the innovative movement from private ownership of vehicles to 'usership', and a redefinition of the citizen-users role, since they become both recipient and source of the services' information, and they bring in their resources to shared platforms [19].

In the context of the evolution of the public service provision, the public sector outsources most of the technological solutions to the private sector [20, 21]. This means that city governments collaborate with private companies to provide their citizens with smart solutions, like bike-sharing systems. As the digital government paradigm proposed, the role of non-state actors in the policy design and provision of public services has been spreading-out, leading to a more open and collaborative government. This collaboration between private and public actors can lead to each adopting new roles, engaging in different types of interaction, and navigating changing accountability dynamics. Based on the coproduction literature, it is assumed that the coordination of expertise, knowledge, resources, technology, and processes leads to better results than when working independently [1].

Nevertheless, it comes with further challenges in terms of private companies assuming tasks and responsibilities traditionally performed by the government [5–7]. There is a risk of 'disintermediating government', characterized by private companies providing public services directly to citizens and the government relegated as a supporter. For instance, private companies become responsible for not only the infrastructure of smart services, like bike-sharing systems, but also the operation and the interaction with citizens. Despite the dangers of unequal distribution of responsibility, information asymmetry can positively contribute to the collaboration process between the public and private sector when it exists in a complementary form. Data are one of the most valuable commodities behind smart mobility that allow governments to support the realization of public values. Yet the private sector is displacing the government as a principal source of data, becoming 'data landlords' instead of 'data tenants' [19, 22].

Although the private sector opens the door to innovation, "the social values inherent in public services may not be adequately addressed by the economic efficiency calculus of markets" [23]. The involvement of private companies in smart services brings in a market logic, a 'corporate storytelling', while it is necessary to prioritize the social and political aspect within a value system [24]. In this respect, the government not only needs to focus on the technological and managerial side of these innovative collaborations and economic growth, but also on the contributions of coproduction of smart services to realize other values, such as inclusion, equity and citizen engagement [22, 25].

3 Public Values

Public values theory is considered one of the most significant subjects in public administration and policy [26], and it has been gaining particular interest in the so-called 'smart cities' context [25, 27]. It refers to "the procedural ethics in [...] and outcomes made possible by producing public services" [28], and it is understood as a concept used to give direction to public action or legitimize it [29]. Bozeman [30] defines public values as:

(1) The *rights, benefits, and prerogatives* to which citizens should (and should not) be entitled; (2) the *obligations* of citizens to society, the state, and one another; and (3) the *principles* on which governments and policies should be based[1].

Bozeman's [30] definition focuses purely on the citizen-side, whereas society and 'the public interest' involves further actors, such as non-profits and private companies. This distinction is particularly relevant in the context of coproduction, where public values are expected to be upheld through collaboration among diverse stakeholders.

ICT-based coproduction initiatives are expected to enhance the realization of better and more democratic public services [1, 2] through collaboration with external stakeholders, including citizens. Bearing this in mind, we clustered the expected public values in the context of ICT-based coproduction into two categories [31, 32]. First, *social-oriented values* illustrate the democratic quality of the service delivered, for instance, the level of inclusiveness, equal treatment or citizen empowerment [31, 33, 34]. Digital democracy studies highlight that internet-based practices may improve democratic values by bringing dispersed populations closer, allowing for more citizen participation [35]. ICT-based coproduction could potentially increase inclusion [36] and equity [37] as it promises to provide the same opportunities to different actors [38], foster local activism, unleash social innovation and reinvigorate democracy [13, 39].

Second, *service-oriented values* refer to service quality, responsiveness, effectiveness, among others. Coproduction is expected to improve the quality as well as increase the quantity of public services [40–42] through expertise and information provided by citizens/users, not available otherwise [43]. The advances of ICT in coproduction provide unique means for real-time, community-wide coordination, "presenting tremendous opportunities for data-driven decision-making, improved performance management, and heightened accountability" [13]. These initiatives can improve the efficiency of processes, speed up response times, and make them more secure/reduce human errors [38].

In the context of New Public Management driven reforms, service-oriented or business-like values have been the primary drivers of ICT use in the public sector, while democratic values have been relegated [44, 45] or even trampled [46]. As Bannister and Connolly [30] claim, values such as citizens' information privacy, equal access, and social inclusion have a high potential of being negatively affected by ICT. ICT is not value-neutral but instead has the potential for positive or negative impact on public values. Whereas technology can "follow its own logic", ICT's users are also responsible for the value embedded on the technologies and its applications [46].

---

[1] Scholars such as Alford [53] and Osborne et al. [54] discuss the co-creation of 'public *value*' (singular), which Moore [55], representative of this line of thought, refers to as an appraisal "on behalf of the public" of the outcome of public service delivery. Nevertheless, this study will provide insights from the Bozeman [30] strand of thought, as "these public values can serve as reasons or reference points for valuing the 'public value' created" [56].

The involvement of external coproducers, such as private companies, can account for variations in public values expectations. Since ICT-based coproduction allows the government to combine non-state actors' resources with its own, it is seen as a way to enhance government cost savings and deliver better-personalized services [13, 39]. The involvement of private actors can also be considered a method to advance market values such as efficiency, innovation, and flexibility [47]. Reynaers [48] found that service's quality expectations increase with the involvement of the private sector. Although the private and public sector may hold common core organizational values (e.g., expertise, accountability, reliability), "the extent to which an organization belongs to the public or private sector strongly determines values preferences". For instance, profitability scored high for private sector expectations [49]. However, other public values such as citizen empowerment and innovation can be hampered by private companies when they hold the data and do not release it openly and make it accessible [50], restricting evidence-based decision making [18].

The potential impact on public values shows the relevance of disentangling the promises and assumptions behind ICT-based coproduction, and of identifying the actual possibilities and limitations behind the different expectations and interests of the coproducing actors.

4 Research Approach

4.1 The Case: Smart Bike-Sharing System

The presented research is based on a qualitative in-depth case study of a dock-based smart bike-sharing service coproduced in one of the major cities in Flanders, Belgium, hereafter referred to as *Smart-Bike*. A case study allows us to deeply understand a real-life phenomenon while considering the contextual conditions, even with a limited number of observation units. In this way, we can gain insights into complex social phenomena [51], such as smart mobility systems. These can be defined in the frame of technological transition as a "set of connected changes, which reinforce each other but take place in several different areas, such as technology, the economy, institutions, behavior, culture, ecology and belief systems" [52].

The Smart-Bike public service was launched in 2011, led by the city's Department of Urban Development. The primary provider is a private company which offers this service internationally, although Smart-Bike responds to both the city and the private partner. The service is part of the city's efforts to introduce smart solutions and innovations in different public services, specifically in mobility.

The smart bicycle system aims to offer an alternative mobility service that is available 24/7 and provides a solution to the 'first/last mile problem'. It is one of the most successful public smart bike-sharing systems in Belgium in terms of the growing number of active users, with 172% more active users than in 2012. It offers a mobile application which allows users to report service-related issues (e.g., bikes malfunctioning, empty stations, software problems), helping the provider to improve and optimize the service. Although the mobile application and the website are the means to do the reporting, citizens can also help by turning the saddle 180°, which is a signal for the technicians that something is wrong with that bike. The citizen-users have the right to choose how active they want to be, as the reporting-service is not specified in the rules.

4.2   Data Collection and Analysis

Our qualitative data collection included two sources: documents and semi-structured in-depth interviews [n = 27], which took place from October 2017 to February 2018. First, we conducted two face-to-face pilot interviews with two public servants involved in the project from its beginning, as well as with the Smart-Bike's operational manager. They provided us with official documents, including promotion materials, policy documents, the contract, and KPIs' and research reports. We also consulted relevant online texts like the official website, the city's open data platform, and news articles to acquire a complete overview of the project and its context. For our second step, following a snowball approach, the interviewees recommended other potential respondents from both the city and the private partner who are/were actively involved. We interviewed all the key actors, such as senior managers, operational managers, coordinators, and IT analysts/experts from the private company and the city Department of Urban Development. In this way, we were able to gather feedback from a wide range of perspectives. The contact with the citizen-users was made through a public call sent by Fietsersbond[2], which is an independent association with more than 23,000 members and 500 volunteers that advocates for all cyclists from Flanders and Brussels. The final selection resulted in 8 interviews with public servants and 5 with private actors [n = 13], followed by 14 interviews with citizen-users[3]. The interview questions were tailored to the roles of individuals. On the regular producers' interviews, the first questions were on the role of the respondents in their organization and the project. Then respondents were inquired about the project in general, relevance and their motivations and expected outcomes. Specific questions were asked about the collaboration with other stakeholders and the challenges and advantages; and finally, about the overall impact of technology on (coproducing) public services. Citizen-users were asked about their experience with the service and the reporting system, their expected and perceived outcomes and their motivations for using the service. The interview ended with questions about their experience with the service's technology (e.g., mobile application). The interviews lasted between 45 and 70 min and were recorded, transcribed, and kept confidential. The representatives of the city were identified by the letter "A", the representatives of the private partner by the letter "B", and the citizen-users by the letter "C", all followed by an identification number.

From the official documents, we were able to gather insights on the expected public values expressed in the mission, vision, and goals of Smart-Bike's project. We also identified the main stakeholders involved and their responsibilities. The information deployed in the open data platform allowed us to get data on the service, e.g., location of the stations. Users' information and details on the reporting system were provided by

---

[2] https://www.fietsersbond.be/.

[3] Detailed information on the respondents and interview protocol can be provided upon request.

344   A. P. Rodriguez Müller and T. Steen

the private partner. All these documents allowed us to gain a holistic understanding of the project and its context, as well as to delimit the interview protocol.

The resulting data from the interviews were analyzed with the support of qualitative analysis software NVivo 12. In the first round of coding, the interviews were divided into segments wherein different variables are discussed and labeled following the theoretical framework on coproduction, public values, and digital government. Next, sub-codes for every variable were added through open coding (e.g., public values sub-coded as 'realized' vs. 'obstructed'). Second, a round of axial coding was executed to identify relationships connecting the open codes. Detailed findings from our analysis of the smart bike-sharing system are presented below.

5 Findings

5.1 The Involvement of Private Actors

Public servants highlighted the importance of having an external partner to coproduce smart mobility because of their lack of technological and personnel capacity, and due to the high operational costs. The private partner provides the city with more flexibility to start new projects as they share the risks. The company's operations manager claimed that their risk-sharing partnership is strongly defined by the contract and its rules: "*you have a contract, and you have to follow the contract that they give you. So, it is a relationship based on the contract*" (B9). Still, public actors experienced issues relating to accountability. Although the private sector's actors claimed it is a relationship based on the contract, that contract did not always seem to be strictly followed.

The city is challenged not only by a lack of capacity to analyze data about users and service performance, but also by a lack of accessibility. Public servants point out that requesting data is an arduous process since it takes time to get it, and sometimes they need to move the request to higher levels (i.e., political level).

Even though the collaboration between the private and public parties is characterized by the contract-based dynamics, three other factors were identified as affecting the collaboration, and thereby the potential realization of public values. These factors are communication, trust, and shared understanding.

All respondents mentioned that communication is the key in Smart-Bike's partnership: it is essential to speak the same language as a way to achieve their goals. Despite sharing this belief, communication issues still arise. For instance, the public servants find it difficult to translate the issues to the private actors, whereas the private partner perceives the demands from the city as unrealistic. Although there is room for communication improvement, much has been accomplished based on mutual trust. Trust between the parties allows for a more flexible, open, and innovative interaction. This kind of open dynamic avoids the need to hold meetings every month. A respondent explained that "*if you do not have to discuss every little detail, every comma… that reflects we can trust each other, and that is very important*" (A3). The private actors perceive the city's trust as a benefit and advantage, "*if there is no trust between the municipality and the private partner, we would not be here anymore*" (B7). They pointed out that trustworthy cooperation was essential to overcome operational issues.

According to the public sector's professionals, they have to let go of control because there is no room for distrust as there are "no open books" (A5). Another challenge was to align the diverse expectations of politicians, administration, company, and citizen-users. Private actors accentuated the need of having a common vision, *"we need to be aware and informed about where the city is going so that we can adapt, prioritize correctly or adjust our operations and strategy so that we are aligned with theirs"* (B7, also B8).

5.2   Co-producers' Public Values Expectations and Perceptions

In order to pinpoint the challenges that might arise due to private actors' involvement, we discuss perceptions of public values realization or obstruction following the two sub-clusters outlined in Sect. 3: service-oriented values (i.e., service quality and business-like values) and socially oriented values (i.e., democratic quality of the service delivered).

Service-Oriented Values

Service Quality. The 'waiting list' refers to the periods when no additional citizens were allowed to subscribe to the service. The quality and effectiveness were put above the inclusiveness of the service. *"It's not so nice for the political level either to say we have a bike sharing system for everybody but 'oh, by the way, sorry, there is a waiting list and we don't know when this waiting list will be cleared.' We didn't have another choice"* (B7). Citizen-users expected to have better quality bikes. Users that have had a subscription from the beginning stated that, when the service started, the quality of the bikes was inferior, but by now it has improved. Nevertheless, they agreed that due to the low price of the service, they do not expect to get the best bikes.

Ease of Access. The company expects to deliver an accessible service: *"ease of access is vital for us. So, no need to fill out 10 forms and write 20 emails before you can use the system"* (B7). The dense network of stations and the 24/7 availability allow a high rate of accessibility to the service. Therefore, they monitor the service continuously. This also relates to the digital side of the service. The mobile application is the bridge between the location of the stations and the citizen-user, completing the experience of the user. As the city's coordinator states, *"everybody who has a smartphone wants to know everything right now and make it possible to order something right now"* (A3). However, challenges emerge when citizen-users do not have a smartphone or digital literacy, which are both necessary in order to use the mobile app or website. For them, the perceived value – accessibility – is the opposite as they are not able to look for that information in advance.

Responsiveness. The city has no direct interaction with the citizen-users. All communication happens via the private partner, who receives the data from the users and takes the information they believe to be pertinent to the meetings with the city. The private actor claimed that it is essential to consider user's feedback for decision-making, *"it has to do with raising awareness about what is bike-sharing so that the users know what is expected from them and what they can expect from us"* (B7).

The user-friendliness of the mobile app is important for the private actor so that users can reach them easily, to report broken bikes or technical issues. Yet the company's intentions are mainly about their image: *"If there is a complaint or suggestion, you have to do something with it. You cannot ignore it. If you ignore it, you will get bad publicity"* (B9). This is reflected in the users' perceptions; they agreed that the efforts of getting citizen-users feedback and use it are far from reality. As some users described: *"once I filled in a long question list with more than 100 questions, and for example, there were only one or two questions about the technical condition of the bikes"* (C24); *"they are always friendly, but they do nothing about the problem"* (C23).

Innovation. For the managerial level of the city's department, innovation is crucial: *"you must have an open mind, an eye for innovation in different aspects of society and be aware of innovations, having a broad network with people in the sector"* (A5). They have concerns about the innovative capacity of their private partner, and not about financial means: *"my perception is that [the private partner] is not a very market player, an innovative player. Our system is 7, 8 years old"*, states the director of the urban development department (A5). This clarifies the private actor's perceptions of innovation: *"one of the most difficult things is managing expectations of the city versus the budget you have to do things. Sometimes it is hard to find the funding to be able to innovate"* (B10). Priorities differ, as a respondent explained: *"better technology is the second step. It's like you are a person who needs to drink, who needs to eat, but if you already have all this, you will want something extra. From the moment that the basics needs are met, then we have to go for that little extra"* (B8). It is also related to the contract-based relationship. City actors believed that having a more open contract or work with more partners would allow more room for innovation. The company, on the contrary, believed that the city's expectations should be better managed: *"[h]ow can you innovate, how can you get budget to do new things when it is not part of the tender, and that really depends on where the request is coming from"* (B10).

Social-Oriented Values

Citizen Empowerment. Empowerment does not seem to be a relevant value for the project, based on the interviewees' responses. A private actor stated that *"the more you give them the ability to do things on their own, the more they can do things on their own. But of course, there are always people that might not be able to, and that's why we always have a front-office where you can go and get help if needed"* (B10). The citizens' voice is taken as a part of the service, but sometimes it is merely a formality, as the suggestions need to be "good and right" to get discussed (A2). The citizen-users of this sample believe that they do not have a genuine voice in the process, although they expect to have it. *"I made a suggestion to [Smart-Bike], and they accepted it: 'Oh, that's a nice thing, we will take it'. But they don't do anything with it"* (C1). In general, citizen-users claimed that individual efforts are worthless; rather, they need to act as a group or through non-profit organizations to get their voices heard.

Inclusiveness. For private actors, efficiency is more valued than inclusiveness. For example: *"you might say that there is no waiting list, but then you get under-capacity, and you risk failing completely, then the system is not adopted anymore by the users because it does not offer a solution anymore*" (B7). They are aware of the difficulties of aligning different visions, "*sometimes, the decisions are hard to take for the city; even more when different organizations have something to say in the story*" (B8). The low level of inclusiveness is reflected in the digitalization of the services. A citizen-user argued: "*they skip a group of people who are not digital. They can't use it because they can't get an account or they don't know how to use the app or the screen. We are a forgotten group, and they should take care of us*" (C1, also C2, 3, 5, 6, 10, 12). This is seen again in the numbers behind the mobile application's reports from 2016 to 2018. Whereas 47% of the users are younger than 35 years old, more than 70% of the reports via the mobile app came from this group. Moreover, both private and public actors accept that the 'offline' experience is not the same as the 'digital' one. As a user stated: "*you can use the system without a mobile phone, but for me, it feels like half a system*" (C6). The city claims to not have enough data to understand who is included and who might be left behind, digitally and in terms of language and cultural aspects. The company is aware of this problem, yet inclusiveness is not prioritized: "*you also have people who get angry because they can't give us a paper, but it's too expensive to have offices and people everywhere*" (B8).

Privacy and Security. Private actors showed more concern in terms of privacy and security policies and regulations than the city. With new regulations like GDPR, the company needs to change procedures: "*we had to change what we ask. We also had to implement a procedure if people want to delete their personal data*" (B8). It was striking that – despite the involvement of private companies – the users interviewed did not have any concern about privacy and security regarding their data since they understood that the city is behind the service and believed that their personal information would not be compromised. As some users claimed: "*Because the city is backing up the project, it feels more reliable*" (C3); "*if they are more commercial the risk that they will spread the data around is bigger. And if it's more government-oriented or social profit, I don't believe they misuse it*" (C6). On the other hand, a MaaS expert (Mobility as a Service) of the city (A6) pointed out that no privacy and security policy on smart services has yet been defined in their regulations. The expert highlighted that the interest of the city is now put on opening the data and creating projects interesting enough for MaaS providers, as a "political game".

6   Discussion

The private sector has been insourcing most of the technological solutions in the public sector, playing a pivotal role in initiatives such as ICT-based coproduction of smart – sharing – services. Still, private actors' expectations regarding the service tend to diverge from the public actors. Although this might not be striking, the significant aspect lies in the public nature of the coproduced service, and therefore, the importance of public values being realized through the coproduction process. This paper aimed to unveil the impact that the involvement of private actors has in the delivery and coproduction of smart mobility on the realization of service-oriented and social-oriented public values. The findings advance our understanding of the public values expected or aimed for, in how far these values are actually being realized, and which factors enhance the realization of public values.

In the context of Smart-Bike, the city's shortage of specific expertise, skills, staff, financial resources, and technology required to set up the smart mobility project made it necessary to involve a private company. This involvement is determined by a contract-based collaboration between the parties. All the actors, both public and private, agree that the project's primary motivation is its effectiveness as a real solution and an alternative for improving mobility in the city. However, from that point on, the actors tend to differ in what they value most.

The private actors prioritize the realization of public values such as efficiency, reliability, and ease of access, whereas social-oriented values like citizen engagement and (digital) inclusiveness are not part of their core vision. They do highlight values like responsiveness or empowerment but in a 'defensive way'; the main concern is to protect the company's image. As citizen-users manifest, there are no genuine opportunities to give feedback and be heard. Moreover, the company sustains that the service is inclusive, although the digital limitations of certain groups of the society are not taken into consideration. The users need digital skills and resources to fully enjoy the smart service fully, which might hamper not only equal access (a fundamental value of public service) but also the effectiveness of the service.

Concerning innovation, it is expected that the private partner fosters and facilitates venues to develop new smart solutions. Nevertheless, our case study reveals that the private partner points to the budget and contract-based dynamics as an obstruction to innovate, while the public actors believe that the issue is related to the company not being up to date on the market's innovations. In contrast, the private actors show a higher concern about values such as privacy and the security of citizen-users' data. However, while Smart-Bike is presented as a city's service, the users may hold mistaken perceptions of their privacy and security of the data they share.

In the case studied, four specific factors of the coproduction's collaborative process play a role in the realization (or obstruction) of public values: contract-based dynamics, communication between the stakeholders, building trust, and shared understanding of the interests, goals, and vision of the different involved parties. The evidence suggests that contract-based collaboration might foster efficiency, while innovation, citizen empowerment, and privacy and security aspects are hindered due to the restricted access of the city to the service's data and system. Communication has been a problem between the private and public actors, mainly because of the disparities in the perceptions of the role that each party has in the decision-making process and in their various ways of achieving goals. Furthermore, the private partner being solely responsible for the interaction with citizen-users entails barriers to advance social-oriented values. However, mutual trust helps to balance those issues by providing more flexibility and openness within the collaboration. At the same time, trust is fundamental in terms of efficiency (e.g., time and flexibility), and accountability. Although the city has no direct and open access to all the facts and data from the service, trust has been playing a crucial role in the sustainability of the project. Another influential factor is the shared understanding in working together that facilitates the alignment of different motivations and priorities, even if they do not share all their expectations. For instance, the private actors aim to line up their plans with the city's priorities (e.g., political level), while public professionals also include the citizens' visions as part of the bigger picture. Shared understanding also facilitates the pooling of key resources and common values. To sum up, the evidence suggests public actors need to correctly align the resources, expertise, legal frameworks, and goals to balance public values priorities when involving external partners in the coproduction of smart public services.

7   Concluding Remarks

This paper provides evidence consistent with existing research on ICT-based coproduction, smart services, and conflicting interests between private and public actors. Additionally, it highlights how important it is to understand private actors' involvement in coproduction through a public values' lens. This study offers a new angle on the conflicting interests among different coproducing actors and the long-standing tension between social-oriented and service-oriented values. It also pinpoints some factors of the coproduction process that may help to detect possible venues to handle the differences in public values' priorities. Overall, the identified factors reveal that the collaborative process may be more relevant than the actual coproducing actors' resources and expertise when it comes to upholding public values.

An early thinking on the potential downside and risks behind future ICT-based coproduction projects will broaden the possibilities of developing innovative and efficient solutions in the field of smart mobility while safeguarding the social aspect of public services. Our study offers some suggestions for such collaborative projects. First, attention should be given to the contract and the legal framework behind the initiative. The potential power asymmetry between the cities and private companies at the time of coproducing smart services underpins the relevance of a well-defined legal framework. In Smart-Bike, the lack of regulations in terms of data access has become an obstacle to improving the service, evaluating the level of inclusiveness, fostering innovation, and assessing the general performance of the private partner. In particular, our analysis points at the need for clear approaches in terms of data and information sharing that protect and uphold the realization of public values. It also stresses the importance of clearly defining the tasks and responsibilities between the parties to manage expectations. Second, transparency can be a significant factor in the collaborative process, mainly towards citizen-users who need to be aware of the parties involved in the service, e.g., who is handling their data and how. Finally, future research on ICT-enabled coproduction and realization of public values should incorporate insights from public-private partnership literature and public-private innovation networks. For example, it would be useful to look into power asymmetries between principal and agent, the government's ability to adequately prepare the contract, and the competencies needed for purchase and procurement. In contrast to the first factor (i.e., the contract), the other three identified factors (i.e., communication, trust, shared understanding) link more with insights from collaborative governance theory and the more 'soft' side of inter-organizational collaboration.

Our research is not without limitations. The reporting conclusions are based on a small-scale single case study of a smart mobility public service in one of the major cities in Flanders, Belgium. The resulting conclusions are case-specific and cannot be generalized to other cases. Yet the insights derived from our case study might be relevant to other cities coproducing smart services in related conditions or with similar characteristics. Future research could examine initiatives from different policy fields (e.g., health care, social care) which may shed light on other public values being upheld or obstructed due to collaboration with private actors. As the involvement of private actors will remain necessary for ICT-based coproduction initiatives, more research is needed to further reflect on the potential trade-offs between delivering a better service and fostering democratic quality. We also need studies to show how to successfully deal with the tensions that arise due to different public values being prioritized in a context of power asymmetry, where the private sector seems to orchestrate the changes behind the government ICT-based projects.

Acknowledgments. This project has received funding from the European Commission (H2020) under grant number: 726755, project CITADEL, and KU Leuven C1 research fund under the grant number: C14/15/011, project "For the public, by the public".

References

1. De Vries, H., Bekkers, V., Tummers, L.: Innovation in the public sector: a systematic review and future research agenda. Public Adm. **94**(1), 146–166 (2016)
2. Lember, V., Brandsen, T., Tonurist, P.: The potential impacts of digital technologies on co-production and co-creation. Public Manag. Rev. (2019, forthcoming)
3. William, C., Webster, R., Leleux, C.: Smart governance: opportunities for technologically-mediated citizen co-production. Inf. Polity. **23**(1), 95–110 (2018)
4. Liu, L., Ju, J., Feng, Y., Hu, Q.: Impact of governance structure characteristics of public-private partnerships on smart city project success: evidence from a multi-case study in China. In: 52nd Hawaii International Conference on System Services (HICSS), pp. 3285–3294. IEEE (2019)
5. Ma, Y., Lan, J., Thornton, T., Mangalagiu, D., Zhu, D.: Challenges of collaborative governance in the sharing economy: the case of free-floating bike sharing in Shanghai. J. Clean. Prod. **197**(1), 356–365 (2018)
6. Anthopoulos, L.G., Reddick, C.G.: Understanding electronic government research and smart city: a framework and empirical evidence. Inf. Polity **21**, 99–117 (2016)
7. Klievink, B., Janssen, M.: Challenges in developing public-private business models. Eur. J. ePractice **18**, 9–23 (2012)
8. Bovaird, T., Loeffler, E.: From engagement to co-production: the contribution of users and communities to outcomes and public value. Voluntas **23**(4), 1119–1138 (2012)
9. Nabatchi, T., Sancino, A., Sicilia, M.: Varieties of participation in public services: the who, when, and what of coproduction. Public Adm. Rev. **77**(5), 766–776 (2017)
10. Bracci, E., Fugini, M., Sicilia, M.: Co-production of public services: meaning and motivations. In: Fugini, M., Bracci, E., Sicilia, M. (eds.) Co-production in the Public Sector. SAST, pp. 1–11. Springer, Cham (2016). https://doi.org/10.1007/978-3-319-30558-5_1
11. Johnston, E.: Governance infrastructures in 2020. Public Adm. Rev. **70**, S122–S128 (2010)
12. Fugini, M., Teimourikia, M.: The role of ICT in co-production of e-Government public services. In: Fugini, M., Bracci, E., Sicilia, M. (eds.) Co-production in the Public Sector. SAST, pp. 119–139. Springer, Cham (2016). https://doi.org/10.1007/978-3-319-30558-5_8

13. Linders, D.: From e-government to we-government: defining a typology for citizen coproduction in the age of social media. Gov. Inf. Q. **29**(4), 446–454 (2012)
14. Lember, V.: The increasing role of digital technologies in co-production. In: Brandsen, T., Steen, T., Verschuere, B. (eds.) Co-Production and Co-Creation: Engaging Citizens in Public Services. Routledge, London (2017)
15. Meijer, A.J.: Coproduction as a structural transformation of the public sector. Int. J. Public Sect. Manag. **29**(6), 596–611 (2016)
16. Townsend, A.M.: Smart cities: big data, civic hackers, and the quest for a new utopia. WW Norton & Company, New York (2013)
17. Cardullo, P., Kitchin, R.: Smart urbanism and smart citizenship: the neoliberal logic of "citizen-focused" smart cities in Europe. Environ. Plan. C: Polit. Space. **0**, 1–18 (2018)
18. Gil-Garcia, J.R., Zhang, J., Puron-Cid, G.: Conceptualizing smartness in government: an integrative and multi-dimensional view. Gov. Inf. Q. **33**(3), 524–534 (2016)
19. Docherty, I., Marsden, G., Anable, J.: The governance of smart mobility. Transp. Res. Part A Policy Pract. **115**, 114–125 (2018)
20. Lember, V., Kattel, R., Tonurist, P.: Public administration, technology and administrative capacity. In: The Other Canon Foundation and Tallinn University of Technology Working Papers in Technology Governance and Economic Dynamics 71, TUT Ragnar Nurkse Department of Innovation and Governance (2016)
21. Alford, J., O'Flynn, J.: Rethinking Public Service Delivery. Managing with External Providers. Palgrave, Houndmills (2012)
22. Johnson, P.A.: Disintermediating government: the role of open data and smart infrastructure. In: 52nd Hawaii International Conference on System Services (HICSS), pp. 2864–2871. IEEE (2019)
23. Hefetz, A., Warner, M.: Privatization and its reverse: explaining the dynamics of the government contracting process. J. Public Adm. Res. Theory **14**(2), 171–190 (2004)
24. Söderström, O., Paasche, T., Klauser, F.: Smart cities as corporate storytelling. City **18**(3), 307–320 (2014)
25. Meijer, A., Rodríguez Bolívar, M.P.: Governing the smart city: a review of the literature on smart urban governance. Int. Rev. Adm. Sci. **82**(2), 392–408 (2016)
26. Jørgensen, T.B., Bozeman, B.: Public Values. Adm. Soc. **39**, 354–381 (2007)
27. Rodríguez Bolívar, M.P.: The relevance of public value into smart cities. In: Setting Foundations for the Creation of Public Value in Smart Cities (2019). https://doi.org/10.1007/978-3-319-98953-2_1
28. Bryson, J., Sancino, A., Benington, J., Sørensen, E.: Towards a multi-actor theory of public value co-creation. Public Manag. Rev. **19**(5), 640–654 (2017)
29. Witesman, E.: From public values to public value and back again. Working Paper Prepared for the Public Values Workshop Hosted by the Center for Organization Research and Design, pp. 1–35. Arizona State University (2016)
30. Bozeman, B.: Public Values and Public Interest: Counterbalancing Economic Individualism. Georgetown University Press, Washington (2007)
31. Jaspers, S., Steen, T.: Realizing public values: enhancement or obstruction? Public Manag. Rev. **21**(4), 606–627 (2019)
32. Bannister, F., Connolly, R.: ICT, public values and transformative government: a framework and programme for research. Gov. Inf. Q. **31**(1), 119–128 (2014)
33. Vanleene, D., Verschuere, B., Voets, J.: The professional's dynamic role in the democratic quality of co-productive community development. J. Rural Community Dev. **10**(1), 94–108 (2015)

34. Verschuere, B., Vanleene, D., Steen, T., Brandsen, T.: Democratic co-production: concepts and determinants. In: Brandsen, T., Steen, T., Verschuere, B. (eds.) Co-production and Co-creation: Engaging Citizens in Public Services, pp. 243–251. Routledge, London (2018)
35. Schwester, R.W.: Examining the barriers to e-Government adoption. Electron. J. e-Gov. 7 (1), 113–122 (2009)
36. Michels, A.: Innovations in democratic governance: how does citizen participation contribute to a better democracy? Int. Rev. Adm. Sci. 77(2), 275–293 (2011)
37. Jakobsen, M.: Can government initiatives increase citizen coproduction? Results of a randomized field experiment. J. Public Adm. Res. Theory. 23(1), 27–54 (2012)
38. Uppström, E., Lönn, C.-M.M.: Explaining value co-creation and co-destruction in e-government using boundary object theory. Gov. Inf. Q. 34(3), 406–420 (2017)
39. O'Reilly, T.: Government as a platform. In: Open Government: Collaboration, Transparency, and Participation in Practice, pp. 11–39. O'Reilly Media, Sebastopol (2010)
40. Calabro, A.: Coproduction: an alternative to the partial privatization processes in Italy and Norway. In: Pestoff, V., Brandsen, T., Verschuere, B. (eds.) New Public Governance, the Third Sector and Co-Production, pp. 317–336. Routledge, New York (2012)
41. Pestoff, V.: Citizens and co-production of welfare services. Public Manag. Rev. 8(4), 503–519 (2006)
42. Vamstad, J.: Coproduction and service quality: a new perspective for the Swedish welfare state. In: Pestoff, V., Brandsen, T., Verschuere, B. (eds.) New Public Governance, the Third Sector and Coproduction, pp. 297–316. Routledge, New York (2012)
43. Loeffler, E., Bovaird, T.: From participation to co-production: widening and deepening the contributions of citizens to public services and outcomes. In: The Palgrave Handbook of Public Administration and Management in Europe, pp. 403–423. Palgrave Macmillan, London (2018)
44. Chadwick, A., May, C.: Interaction between states and citizens in the age of the internet: "e-Government" in the United States, Britain, and the European Union. Governance 16(2), 271–300 (2003)
45. Chun, S.A., et al.: Government 2.0: making connections between citizens, data and government. Inf. Polity Int. J. Gov. Democr. Inf. Age. 15, 1–9 (2010)
46. Adams, M., Prins, C. (Corien): Digitalization through the lens of law and democracy. In: Prins, C. (Corien), Cuijpers, C., Lindseth, P.L., Rosina, M. (eds.) Digital Democracy in a Globalized World, pp. 3–26. Edward Elgar Publishing, Cheltenham (2017)
47. Nabatchi, T.: Public values frames in administration and governance. Perspect. Public Manag. Gov. 1(1), 59–72 (2018)
48. Reynaers, A.: Public values in public-private partnerships. Public Adm. 74(1), 41–50 (2013)
49. Van Der Wal, Z., Huberts, L.: Value solidity in government and business: results of an empirical study on public and private sector organizational values. Am. Rev. Public Adm. 38 (3), 264–285 (2008)
50. Jarman, H., Luna-Reyes, L.F., Zhang, J.: Public Value and Private Organizations. In: Jarman, H., Luna-Reyes, L.F. (eds.) Private Data and Public Value. PAIT, vol. 26, pp. 1–23. Springer, Cham (2016). https://doi.org/10.1007/978-3-319-27823-0_1
51. Yin, R.K.: Case Study Research: Design and Methods. Sage, Thousand Oaks (2009)
52. Rotmans, J., Kemp, R., van Asselt, M., Van Asselt, M.: More evolution than revolution: transition management in public policy article information. Foresight 3(1), 15–31 (2001)
53. Alford, J.: Co-production, interdependence and publicness: extending public service-dominant logic. Public Manag. Rev. 18(5), 673–691 (2016)
54. Osborne, S.P., Radnor, Z., Strokosch, K.: Co-production and the co-creation of value in public services: a suitable case for treatment? Public Manag. Rev. 18(5), 639–653 (2016)
55. Moore, M.H.: Creating Public Value: Strategic Management in Government. Harvard University Press, Cambridge (1995)
56. Vandenabeele, W., Leisink, P.L.M., Knies, E.: Public value creation and strategic human resource management: public service motivation as a linking mechanism. In: Managing Social Issues: A Public Values Perspective, pp. 37–54. Edward Elgar, Cheltenham (2013)

Factors Influencing Trust in Smart City Services

Dmitrii Trutnev$^{(\boxtimes)}$ (ID) and Lyudmila Vidiasova (ID)

ITMO University, 49 Kronverksky pr., Saint Petersburg 197101, Russia
trutnev@egov-center.ru,
bershadskaya.lyudmila@gmail.com

Abstract. The introduction of Smart City technologies is aimed at creating various types of public values, including operational, political and social values. One of the basic values created by the Smart City is the increase in trust by its stakeholders. Trust is often considered as one of the most important factors contributing to the success of Smart Cities. The level of trust affects the interactions between actors, which is the basis for the successful development of a Smart City. Interaction is needed the generation of the required public values. Therefore, it is important to know the sources of trust and the degree of their presence in the city turned into a smart one. This paper describes one of the recent studies of trust factors done within the framework of the "Smart St. Petersburg" development project. The findings show that the willingness to participate in the Smart City's strategy development discussion and its development plans co-creation highly depends on the willingness to trust municipal authorities and the familiarity with the Smart City's solutions from around the world.

Keywords: Trust · Smart City · E-services

1 Introduction

The active development of Smart Cities and the introduction of information technologies in all spheres of people's lives around the world have raised the question of which factors influences its success. Many researchers agree that mutual trust is one of the main enablers of smart cities benefits; it requires special attention and individual studies [1–4].

The desire of the government of the Russian Federation and the Administration of St. Petersburg to benefit from digital development has led to the emergence of a number of legislative initiatives. These initiates lay the foundation for further development of the Digital Economy of the Russian Federation [5], and include: The strategy of economic and social development of St. Petersburg for the period up to 2030 [6], the City priority program "Smart St. Petersburg" [7], and the Standard "Smart City" [8]. These and other documents define the goals, strategy and development plans of St. Petersburg as a Smart City. During the first years of implementing a number of factors were not adequately taken into account and managed. This led to the failure in achieving the most of goals [9]. Also, an incentive to search for new solutions was as a

I. Lindgren et al. (Eds.): EGOV 2019, LNCS 11685, pp. 353–365, 2019.
https://doi.org/10.1007/978-3-030-27325-5_27

result of the relatively low level of trust among citizens in the state institution. This is confirmed by recent international research showing that Russia is one of the countries with the lowest level of citizens' trust in government, which has even a tendency to further decrease [9].

The project office of Smart St. Petersburg was founded at ITMO University and headed by the governor of St. Petersburg in early 2018. Such a high status of the project office allowed initiating a series of research projects aimed at studying the problems of development towards becoming a Smart City. Among them were several ones dedicated to the study of the problem of trust. This increase in attention to the problems of trust and the expansion of its interpretation has been observed only recently. Gradually, it comes to the understanding that studying the trust of citizens solely on the safety aspects and technical reliability of the created IT systems, which has been practised in Russia so far, does not answer pressing questions. It also does not correspond to current trends and challenges.

The research questions of this study is "Which trust factors have the most significant impact on the citizens' and civil servants' intention to participate in smart city services" The study is conducted for Smart St. Petersburg services which limits its generalizability. The novels of the study described in this article are:

(a) A significant expansion of the conceptualization of the terms "Smart City" and "Trust" in comparison with that previously practiced in Russia and in St. Petersburg (described in the Literature Review section);
(b) Formulation of research hypotheses that have not been analysed in relation to the problems in the development of St. Petersburg and its solution which is not reflected in the regulatory documents so far (described in the Hypotheses Development section);
(c) The applied methodology based on various sources of information (polls of citizens and government officials, regulations, official statistics, websites of civil initiatives and analysis of publications in social networks) that complement and double-check each other (described in the Research Methodology section).

Some of the most important, in our opinion, research results with their interpretations and discussions are given in the sections: Findings and Reflections, conclusion.

2 Literature Background

2.1 Trust and Trust in Innovations

The history of the theory of trust development within sociology began with authors such as Fukuyama [10], Sztompka [11], Luhman [12], Barber [13], Coleman [14], and Hardin [15]. These authors viewed trust as a critical element of social relations in modern society, which is essential for harmony and economic prosperity.

While trying to answer the question of trust in innovations, some researchers relied on the theory of diffusion of innovations by Rogers [16]. In this theory, the development of any new technology was considered as the result of a comparative assessment by the user of five main factors: comparative advantages when using this technology, its compatibility with previous technologies of the same type, the complexity of learning new skills, the ability to independently test the new technology and its visibility.

A simpler theory named that "technology acceptance model" (TAM) was proposed by Davis [17]. TAM described the intention to use new technology as a result of a rational correlation of the expected benefits of the technology with the expected difficulties in its development.

However, both of these theories exclude the social context within which technological innovations are adapted. Content is considered often as essential. The introduction of new technologies, especially information technologies has created a lot of new problems associated with trust in them. Two of the first researchers in the field of assessing the role of trust based on the theory of social construction of technology were MacKenzie and Vedzhkman [18]. Carter and Belanger [19] extend TAM and include trust was identified as the main factor contributing to the adaptation of information and communication technologies, expected benefits and expected ease of development.

The introduction of information technology in the public sector is often associated with the creation of electronic services and research in this area we consider relevant to our tasks. Analysing the problem of adapting to public electronic services, Carter and Weerakkody [20] clarified the concept of "trust", dividing it into trust in information and communication technologies and trust in authorities, who offer to use their services in electronic form.

Later, this concept was further elaborated by M. Horst, M. Kutshreuter and J.M. Gutteling. In their work, trust in the authorities was interpreted as the need of users to trust the ability of the authorities to manage the new service delivery system ("information management capacity"). Trust in the authorities was also defined as confidence in the technical reliability of the relevant infrastructure and its services [21].

Empirical studies have shown a direct correlation between the level of trust in government and the willingness to use its electronic services. In the above mentioned study by M. Horst and his co-authors on Dutch material, it was demonstrated that the higher the level of trust in the ability of authorities to provide services in an electronic form and the less the worry in the technical reliability of the electronic services system, the stronger the respondents express their intention to use such services [21]. In other words, trust in the authorities is a strong positive incentive that contributes to the adaptation of government electronic services.

The same conclusions were made by J. Lee, H.Yu. Kim and M.J. Ahn, who investigated the attitude of small and medium-sized entrepreneurs to e-government in South Korea [22]. They showed that a high level of trust is based on the personal experience of citizens and implies satisfaction with the quality of existing public services. Also, the Korean authors made the assumption that there is not only a direct, but also an inverse correlation between the level of satisfaction with traditional services and the readiness to use their electronic equivalent. Therefore, a high level of trust in the authorities can act not as an incentive, but as a barrier to the transition. In this case, with a high level of satisfaction with traditional services, citizens may not feel the need and might not be willing to take risks, moving to a new type of service.

On the contrary, with a low level of satisfaction with the work of state institutions, citizens may have hope that interacting with the authorities in electronic form, they will be able to avoid the unavoidable personal interactions. In the course of research in Korea, this assumption was not true as entrepreneurs considered the high quality of public services as a pledge that the authorities will be able to provide the same quality of work in electronic form. Therefore, their satisfaction with the quality of services increased their willingness to switch to the electronic format of interaction with officials and dissatisfaction dramatically reduced the estimated utility of such services. However, one should not discard this assumption completely.

2.2   Smart City

Before answering questions about various aspects of trust in the Smart City, we need to understand what the Smart City term means. It should be recognised that in world practice, there are many ways for describing the term and concept of a Smart City [23, 24]. For the purposes of our study, we have found some useful approaches proposed by several authors.

A higher impact on the formation of a Smart City image had a techno-centric approach, offering such a definition as "The vision of smart cities is the urban centre of the future, made safe, secure, environmentally green and efficient because all structures whether for power, water or transportation are designed, constructed, and maintained making use of advanced, integrated materials, sensors, electronics and networks which are interfaced with computerized systems" [25, p. 5]. However, over time, more and more attention in the definition of smart cities is being paid to achieving the goals related to the well-being of the inhabitants and their leading role in shaping development policies: "The concept of Smart City (SC) as a means to enhance the life quality of citizen has been gaining increasing importance in the agendas of policymakers" [26, p. 35]; A city "connecting the physical infrastructure, the IT infrastructure, the social infrastructure, and the business infrastructure to leverage the collective intelligence of the city" [27, p. 361]; "A city well performing in a forward-looking way in economy, people, governance, mobility, environment, and living, built on the smart combination of endowments and activities of self-decisive, independent and aware citizens" [28, p. 11].

Thus, in spite of the fact that even the Wikipedia gives us a techno-centric definition "A smart city is an urban area that uses different types of electronic Internet of things (IoT) sensors to collect data and then use this data to manage assets and resources efficiently" [29]. The same article states that these technologies are used to engage effectively with local people in local governance and decision by use of open innovation processes and e-participation. Thus, improving the collective intelligence of the city's institutions through e-governance, with emphasis placed on citizen participation and co-design [29]. The same point of view about the mandatory involvement of citizens to achieve success in the Smart cities' development was supported by Glasmeier and Christopherson [30] and Robinson [31].

2.3 Trust in the Smart City' Context

A standard model conceptualizing a Smart City does not exist and each city must create its own original smart solutions depending on its unique requirements and for the best satisfaction of the interests of its citizens. Taking a citizen-centric approach implies the active participation of citizens in the construction of a Smart City that is possible only if there is trust between all interacting parties. Trust, in turn, is closely related to mutual understanding between the interacting parties regarding common goals and methods for achieving them. However, because smart cities are usually discussed as projects between technology providers, engineers, local authorities and universities, the ordinary people who vote for politicians, pay taxes, buy products, use public services and make businesses work are not even aware of the idea, let alone supportive of it [32]. Government leaders have an opportunity to build trust by communicating the strategic thinking and vision behind new programs that affect the long-term future of the community and which are often irreversible [33]. The success and sustainability of Smart City projects depend on the level of citizen trust in such initiatives and the ability of city governments and partners to ensure transparency and deliver valuable benefits and higher quality of life. As it said by BSI: "Transparency is important in order to build trust … this means that the leadership of a Smart City programme should aim to publish all key vision and strategy documents, make names and contact details of programme leaders openly available and publish regular updates of the performance and delivery against the Smart City roadmap" [33, p. 18].

In 2016, at the initiative of the IBM, a large-scale study of US government websites "Smart Trust Survey" was conducted and in the results, it was discovered that none of the city websites mentioned whether they have a Smart City strategy available (e.g., in the form of a strategy publication) to citizens and other stakeholders. This fact was regarded as a strong factor in reducing the level of trust [34]. In the same 2016, a study sponsored by the Institute of Engineering and Technology (IET) found a basic lack of awareness among the British public about what a Smart City does and its potential to improve citizens' quality of life. The danger is that smart cities may be developed without sufficient insight about what people actually want them to deliver [35]. Another study in the UK found the need to strengthen the activities of the government to enhance public engagement and user satisfaction towards smart services in order to realise the promises of such solutions [36]. Such citizen involvement can be implemented in many forms, but among the most promising is direct personal participation of a citizen in Smart City projects or taking part in the discussion of plans and strategies for its development [37, 38]. A trust-building framework for smart cities is multi-dimensional and should include the six major components [39]:

1. Clarifying Smart City commitment and strategy;
2. Delivering high quality of communication regarding planned projects, benefits and risks;
3. Ensuring civic engagement, participative democracy and co-creation;
4. Demonstrating the capability to innovate and deliver Smart City services;
5. Ensuring equitable solutions that offer value to all segments of society;
6. Providing guides and user-friendly apps to facilitate the adoption of new services.

3 Research Methodology

The desire of the Administration of St. Petersburg to improve the performance of projects comprising of the Smart St. Petersburg program has set the Project Office to the task of studying the level of trust between stakeholders and its impact on the overall program's performance. Specifically, the focus is on the implementation of the research of cyber social trust in the context of the use and refusal of information technology funded by the Russian foundation for basic research.

Our study aims to answer the following research question: Which trust factors have the most significant impact on the citizens' and civil servants' intention to participate in the development and use the Smart St. Petersburg services?

As a result of reviewing several models of theoretical studies proposed by different authors, we chose the model proposed by Alsaghier [39]. This model has been slightly adapted to the Smart St. Petersburg context (Fig. 1).

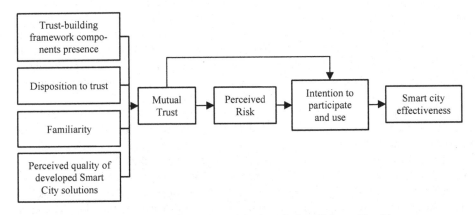

Fig. 1. Theoretical research model adapted after Hisham Alsaghier

Based on the chosen theoretical research, the study elaborated the following factors:

7. **Trust-building framework components presence** - are levels of presence of six major components of the trust-building framework described above.
8. **Disposition to trust** - this is a general state of citizens' and civil servants' trust in other people and society as a whole.
9. **Familiarity** is a personal attitude based on previous experience, studying and understanding who and why created it.
10. **Mutual trust** - the general level of trust between all interacting parties.
11. **Perceived Risk** – is the opinion of citizens and civil servants. Do they consider the benefits of using Smart City solutions to exceed the possible negative consequences of such use?
12. **Intention to participate and use** – is the opinion of citizens and civil servants. Do they wish to take an active part in the creation of Smart City solutions and use them?

13. **Smart City effectiveness** - What is the degree of achievement of the targeted benefits of Smart City?

Disclaimer: Since the target benefits of the Smart St. Petersburg program are still under discussion, the present study limited itself to studying the influence of trust factors on citizens' and civil servants' intention to participate in the development and use the Smart St. Petersburg services.

During the research, qualitative and quantitative methods were used.

Quantitative research consisted of two studies:

1. A street survey of city residents was used to explore the end users' perceptions. The end-user group consists of average e-service users or potential users. Extensive questionnaires were prepared by researchers and volunteers collected the required answers during personal interviews with random passers-by in various parts of the city in December 2018. The total number of respondents and fully completed questionnaires was 600. Various social strata, level of education, IT-competence, income, sex were represented in proportion to their presence in the city.
2. Combination of a street survey and a survey of civil servants of various committees of the Administration of St. Petersburg conducted in March 2019. The main focus was on the experience of use and readiness to participate in the creation of new services of a Smart City. The total number of respondents and fully completed questionnaires was 600. The ratio of residents and civil servants was 50/50. Different level of education, IT-competence, income, sex was represented in proportion to their presence in the city.

The qualitative research was organized in the form of collective discussion and attempted to interpret the evidence obtained from the surveys together with the discrepancies found between the planned and actual results of the projects during regular meetings of the project office members. The participating members of the Smart St. Petersburg project office had a direct influence on both the decision-making in the field of creating the Smart City's solutions and its implementation in the life of the city and utilization of expected benefits. The goal of the meetings was to understand which measures should be used by them to build citizens' trust in Smart City solutions.

The baseline data consists of respondents' answers in the form of a unified scale of 1 (disagree) – 5 (agree) with the proposed statements (A total of over 80 statements for evaluation in two surveys).

The list of variables used for the analysis is given in the Appendix.

4 Findings

The data was analysed using various statistical analysis. Figure 2 shows the averaged values of the data collected during the surveys for the selected variables.

There is a significant gap between the relatively high level of familiarity of the respondents with conventional information technologies and the low level of knowledge of the Smart City solutions.

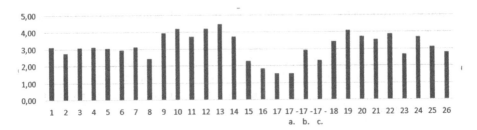

Fig. 2. Averaged values of the data collected during the surveys for the selected variables (variable numbers correspond to the list in the previous section).

Figure 3 allows us to see the differences in the observed trust-building framework components in different areas of city life. Observed significant differences will help us to make a subsequent correlation analysis to find the main dependencies between the variables under study.

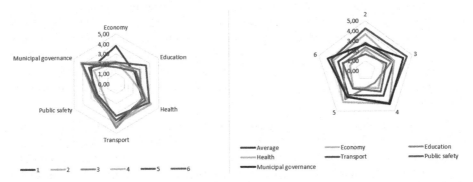

Fig. 3. Averaged values of the trust-building framework components by city life areas (variable numbers correspond to the list in the previous section).

Since the main focus of our study was on finding trust factors (variables 1–20) with the greatest impact on the citizens' desire to participate and use smart St. Petersburg's solutions (variables 21–26), in Table 1 we present only part of the correlation analysis illustrating the sought dependencies.

Table 1. The results of the evaluation of the impact of selected variables on the intention of residents to participate in the development and use the Smart St. Petersburg services (variable numbers correspond to the list in the previous section).

	1	2	3	4	5	6	7	8	9	10	11	12	13	14	15	16	17	17a	17b	17c	18	19	20
21	0,69	0,72	0,28	0,76	0,74	0,52	0,41	0,34	0,48	0,44	0,22	0,82	0,84	0,44	0,59	0,88	0,33	0,47	0,18	0,35	0,88	0,28	0,39
22	0,46	0,52	0,33	0,28	0,32	0,45	0,25	0,56	0,39	0,42	0,35	0,84	0,88	0,42	0,52	0,65	0,37	0,29	0,51	0,31	0,45	0,79	0,34
23	0,53	0,28	0,68	0,32	0,34	0,39	0,26	0,62	0,28	0,32	0,38	0,88	0,92	0,38	0,64	0,69	0,38	0,32	0,28	0,55	0,59	0,35	0,88
24	0,66	0,51	0,32	0,58	0,62	0,42	0,15	0,67	0,18	0,25	0,24	0,38	0,34	0,17	0,4	0,74	0,25	0,24	0,22	0,3	0,76	0,28	0,56
25	0,45	0,66	0,26	0,63	0,58	0,36	0,23	0,78	0,14	0,34	0,19	0,39	0,39	0,15	0,45	0,71	0,22	0,2	0,18	0,28	0,69	0,23	0,62
26	0,37	0,43	0,29	0,45	0,46	0,22	0,26	0,32	0,09	0,15	0,22	0,57	0,61	0,21	0,56	0,62	0,19	0,18	0,18	0,22	0,54	0,14	0,34

Table 1 shows clearly that the highest level of residents' desire to use the Smart City services depends on the following factors:

1. Availability and relevance of smart city development plans, expected risks and benefits;
2. Quality of the created Smart City solutions and services;
3. Benefits obtained by various beneficiaries;
4. Level of citizens' familiarity with the PC, Internet and the Smart City's solutions from around the world;

These main dependencies were explained during expert councils as follows:

1. The publication of various strategic plans that are not being implemented is quite familiar to our environment. A more detailed description of the detailed planned actions, associated risks and expected benefits is unusual, attracts interest and inspires confidence;
2. Personal experience of using well or poorly created Smart City's solutions has a direct impact on trust/distrust of future ones;
3. The knowledge that various beneficiaries expect benefits that are meaningful to them gives rise to the hope that they will do their best to get them, which will lead to a belief in positive outcomes for all;
4. Since Russia is not a world leader in e-government and smart cities, it's understandable that trust in solutions has already been tested and led to positive results in other countries. Those familiar with such solutions are willing to create and use them to a much greater degree than those whose level of awareness is low.

Also, it is noted that he willingness to use feedback and e-participation tools depends primarily on the quality of these tools. The willingness to participate in the Smart City's strategy development discussion and its development plans co-creation highly depends on the willingness to trust municipal authorities and the familiarity with the Smart City's solutions from around the world.

The relatively weak influence of factors that were originally considered significant turned out to be a surprise for members of the Smart St. Petersburg's project office:

- The intensity of Smart City solutions promotion - Residents formed in the conditions of state propaganda and the promotion of false values have developed a certain immunity to attempts of state promotion of anything;
- Willingness to trust other people – This level was high on average, but had very slight variations, which did not allow detecting its effect on potentially dependent variables. It may be necessary to improve the methodology for evaluating this variable in further studies;
- Willingness to trust the Internet and service providers - Traditionally, St. Petersburg has a high level of confidence in the Internet and service providers with small fluctuations, which, just as in the previous case, does not allow to evaluate its impact;
- Level of familiarity with existing local Smart City solutions - Citizens with a very different level of familiarity with local solutions were included in the research sample. The low correlation of this variable with the desire of citizens to participate and create smart city solutions is difficult to explain and needs further research.

5 Conclusions

In this study factors influencing trust in smart cities were investigated. The results of the study will help the city administration and the project office of the Smart St. Petersburg program to find the most optimal solutions to make the city more prosperous and comfortable for life. The study contributes to the understanding of trust factors in Smart City projects development. Four main factors were found, including Availability of published and current statements of commitment and strategy; Quality of the created Smart City solutions and services; benefits obtained by different beneficiaries, and level of citizens' familiarity with the PC, Internet and the Smart City's solutions from around the world.

The framework proposed could be of interest for GCIOs and IT- managers facing some issues of e-services and Smart City solutions effectiveness and expected benefits gaining. Among the main decisions developed based on the results of this study and which have already begun to be implemented are:

- Preparation of the order in the city's administration on the adaptation and publication of the strategy and work plans of the project of Smart St. Petersburg for their public discussion;
- Shifting the emphasis of creating Smart St. Petersburg from the digitization of the city to creating values for the main groups of its citizens based on the optimal choice of Smart City solutions from among the possible ones when drawing up plans for the next year.

Also, there is confidence in the city administration that the conducted research brings real benefits and such studies will continue.

Further planned research in this area will be focused on improving both the theoretical model used and on increasing the openness for citizens and the scientific community of discussion and interpretation of the results obtained. Also, the analysis of the obtained data will be more and more profound in further work.

Acknowledgements. The study was performed with financial support by the grant from the Russian Foundation for Basic Research (project №18-311-20001): "The research of cybersocial trust in the context of the use and refusal of information technology".

Appendix

Trust-Building Framework Components. (According to Glasco J., by the economy, education, health, transport, public safety, municipal governance):

1. Availability of published and current statements of commitment and strategy;
2. Availability and relevance of Smart City development plans, expected risks and benefits;
3. Availability, convenience, performance of e-participation tools;
4. Quality of the created Smart City solutions;

5. Benefits obtained by various beneficiaries;
6. The intensity of Smart City solutions promotion.

Disposition to trust

7. Willingness to trust other people;
8. Willingness to trust municipal authorities;
9. Willingness to trust Russian Internet and service providers;
10. Willingness to trust foreign Internet and service providers;
11. Willingness to trust social network administrators.

Familiarity

12. Level of familiarity with the PC;
13. Level of familiarity with the Internet;
14. Level of familiarity with traditional public services;
15. Level of familiarity with e-government services;
16. Level of familiarity with the solutions of Smart City from around the world;
17. The level of familiarity with the local Smart City solutions.
    a. Services;
    b. Feedback;
    c. Participation tools;

Perceived quality of developed Smart City solutions

18. Quality of the Smart City services;
19. Quality of feedback tools;
20. Quality of e-participation tools;

Intention to participate and use

21. Willingness to use Smart City services;
22. Willingness to use feedback tools;
23. Willingness to use e-participation tools;
24. Willingness to participate in the Smart City's strategy development discussion;
25. Willingness to participate in the Smart City development plans co-creation;
26. Willingness to participate in the Smart City specific solutions creation.

References

1. Baudouin, P.: Trust is key to the success of smart cities. IDATE DigiWorld (2016). https://en.idate.org/insight_smart_city_pb-2/. Accessed 16 May 2019
2. Calderoni, L.: Distributed smart city services for urban ecosystems. Doctoral thesis, Dottorato di Ricerca in Informatica, University of Bologna (2015). https://doi.org/10.6092/unibo/amsdottorato/6858
3. Belanche, G., Casalo, L., Flavián, C., Schepers, J.: Trust transfer in the continued usage of public e-services. Inf. Manage. **51**(6), 627–640 (2014). https://doi.org/10.1016/j.im.2014.05.016

4. Janssen, M., Nripendra, P., Slade, E.L., Yogesh, K.: Trustworthiness of digital government services: deriving a comprehensive theory through interpretive structural modelling. Public Manag. Rev. **20**(5), 647–671 (2018)
5. Order of the Government of the Russian Federation No. 1632-p of 28.07.2017 on the approval of the program "Digital Economy of the Russian Federation". Electronic document: Legal portal of the Russian Federation. http://pravo.gov.ru/proxy/ips/?docbody=&link_id=0&nd=102440918&intelsearch=&firstDoc=1. Accessed 16 May 2019
6. The strategy of economic and social development of St. Petersburg for the period up to 2030, 13 May 2014. http://spbstrategy2030.ru/?page_id=102. Accessed 16 May 2019
7. City priority program: Smart St. Petersburg, 15 February 2017. https://www.petersburgsmartcity.ru/. Accessed 16 May 2019
8. Basic and additional requirements for smart cities (Standard of "Smart Cities"), 04 March 2019. http://www.minstroyrf.ru/upload/iblock/74f/Standart.pdf. Accessed 16 May 2019
9. Vransky, K.: Hoping for a "Smart City". New Izvestia, 26 December 2008. https://newizv.ru/article/tilda/26-12-2018/v-nadezhde-na-umnyy-gorod-pochemu-peterburg-proigryvaet-moskve-i-sochi. Accessed 16 May 2019
10. Fukuyama, F.: Trust: Social Virtues and the Creation of Prosperity. Penguin Books, London (1996)
11. Sztompka, P.: Trust: a sociological theory. Soc. Forces **79**(3), 1187–1188 (2001). https://doi.org/10.1353/sof.2001.0022
12. Luhman, N.: Trust and Power. Wiley, New York (1979)
13. Barber, B.: The Logic and Limits of Trust, vol. 96. Rutgers University Press, New Brunswick (1983)
14. Coleman, J.: Foundations of Social Theory. The Belknap Press Harvard University Press, Cambridge (1990)
15. Hardin, R.: Trusting persons, trusting institutions. In: Zechauser, R.J. (ed.) Strategy and Choice. The MIT Press, Cambridge (1991)
16. Rogers, E.: Diffusion of Innovations, 5th edn, p. 512. The Free Press, New York (2003)
17. Davis, F.: Perceived usefulness, perceived ease of use, and user acceptance of information technology. MIS Q. **13**(3), 319–339 (1989)
18. McKenzie, D., Wajcman, J. (eds.): The Social Shaping of Technology, 1st edn, p. 462. Open University Press, Maidenhead (1985)
19. Carter, L.: The utilization of e-government services: citizen trust, innovation and acceptance factor. Inf. Syst. J. **15**(1), 5–25 (2015)
20. Carter, L.: E-government adoption: a cultural comparison. Inf. Syst. Front. **10**, 473–482 (2008)
21. Horst, M., Kuttschreuter, M., Gutteling, J.M.: Perceived usefulness, personal experience, risk perception and trust as determinants of adoption of e-government services in the Netherlands. Comput. Hum. Behav. **23**, 1838–1852 (2007)
22. Lee, J.: The willingness of e-government service adoption by business users: the role of offline service quality and trust in technology. Gov. Inf. Q. **28**, 177–186 (2011)
23. Albino, V., Berardi, U., Dangelico, R.: Smart cities: definitions, dimensions, performance, and initiatives. J. Urban Technol. **22**(1), 3–21 (2015). https://doi.org/10.1080/10630732.2014.942092
24. Smart cities definitions: Electronic document. https://www.centreforcities.org/reader/smart-cities/what-is-a-smart-city/1-smart-cities-definitions/. Accessed 17 Mar 2019
25. Hall, R.: The vision of a smart city. In: 2nd International Life Extension Workshop, Paris, France. Brookhaven National Laboratory. https://www.osti.gov/servlets/purl/773961/. Accessed 17 Mar 2019

26. Neirotti, P., De Marco, A., Cagliano, A., Mangano, G., Scorrano, F.: Current trends in smart city initiatives: stylised facts. Cities **38**, 25–36 (2014)
27. Harrison, C., et al.: Foundations for smarter cities. IBM J. Res. Dev. **54**(4), 350–365 (2010). https://doi.org/10.1147/JRD.2010.2048257
28. Giffinger, R., Fertner, C., Kramar, H., Kalasek, R., Pichler-Milanović, N., Meijers, E.: Smart cities: ranking of European medium-sized cities. Centre of Regional Science (SRF), Vienna University of Technology, Vienna, Austria (2007). http://www.smart-cities.eu/download/smart_cities_final_report.pdf. Accessed 17 Mar 2019
29. Wikipedia contributors: Smart City. Wikipedia, The Free Encyclopedia. https://en.wikipedia.org/wiki/Smart_city
30. Glasmeier, A., Christopherson, S.: Thinking about smart cities. Camb. J. Reg. Econ. Soc. **8**, 3–12 (2015). https://doi.org/10.1093/cjres/rsu034
31. Robinson, R.: Why smart cities still aren't working for us after 20 years. And how we can fix them (2016). https://theurbantechnologist.com/2016/02/01/why-smart-cities-still-arent-working-for-us-after-20-years-and-how-we-can-fix-them/. Accessed 17 Mar 2019
32. Glasco, J.: Breakthrough! Innovation Management in Practice. CreateSpace Independent Publishing Platform, Scotts Valley (2013). ISBN-10: 1-45283-080-0
33. British Standards Institution: Smart cities framework — Guide to establishing strategies for smart cities and communities. BSI Standards Publication, PAS 181:2014 (2014)
34. Ho, A., McCall, B.: Ten actions to implement big data initiatives: A study of 65 cities. IBM Center for the Business of Government (2016)
35. IET Future Cities: Smart cities - Time to involve the people? A report based on research commissioned by The Institution of Engineering and Technology (2016)
36. Peng, G., Nunes, M., Zheng, L.: Impacts of low citizen awareness and usage in smart city services: the case of London's smart parking system. IseB **15**, 845–876 (2016)
37. Mader, I.: The new social contract: from representative to participative democracy (4.0). Excellence Institute. http://www.excellence-institute.at/en/the-new-social-contract-from-representative-to-participative-democracy-4-0/. Accessed 14 Mar 2019
38. Glasco, J.: Building Trust in Smart Cities: The Importance of Clarity, Communications and Civic Engagement. https://www.researchgate.net/publication/317870057/. Accessed 14 Mar 2019
39. Alsaghier, H.: Conceptualising Citizen's Trust in e-Government: Application of Q Methodology. Electronic Journal of e-Government. http://www.ejeg.com/issue/download.html?idArticle=148. Accessed 14 May 2019

Author Index

Printed in the United States
By Bookmasters